PRESENTED

To The

JOHN K. TENER LIBRARY

IN MEMORY OF

by

NEWS FOR ALL

NEWS FOR ALL

America's Coming-of-Age
with the Press

THOMAS C. LEONARD

New York   Oxford

OXFORD UNIVERSITY PRESS

1995

OXFORD UNIVERSITY PRESS

Oxford   New York
Athens   Auckland   Bangkok   Bombay
Calcutta   Cape Town   Dar es Salaam   Delhi
Florence   Hong Kong   Istanbul   Karachi
Kuala Lumpur   Madras   Madrid   Melbourne
Mexico City   Nairobi   Paris   Singapore
Taipei   Tokyo   Toronto

and associated companies in
Berlin   Ibadan

Library of Congress Cataloging-in-Publication Data
Leonard, Thomas C., 1944–
News for all : America's coming-of-age with the press / Thomas C. Leonard.
p. cm.   Includes bibliographical references and index.
ISBN 0-19-506454-2
1. American newspapers—History.
I. Title.
PN4855.L46   1995   071'.3—dc20
94-42351

Portions of Chapters 1 and 3 of this work appeared in a different form in, respectively,
Proceedings of the American Antiquarian Society 102, part 2 (1993): 379–401 and Jeremy
D. Popkin, ed., *Media and Revolution: Comparative Perspectives* (Lexington, Ky., 1995),
pp. 115–35.

9 8 7 6 5 4 3 2 1

Printed in the United States of America
on acid-free paper

For Carol, Peter, and Anne

CONTENTS

INTRODUCTION:

A PROMISCUOUS . . .

NEWSPAPER?

Nearly three centuries ago, Americans began to read news in print. This book is about that part of national life. The content of the news will be in the background. It is the people who followed the news who most concern us. Here "news" means everything in a newspaper or magazine: fact and opinion, words and pictures, editorial and advertising matter. Of course news can be defined more narrowly. But this would be unwise in a search to find out what has connected people to print media. Every page Americans turn tells us something about journalism . . . and about Americans.

A hunger for print journalism has often seemed to set Americans apart from the lands they came from. This New World was frequently defined by its obsession with a page of news. The Reverend Samuel Miller in his *Brief Retrospect of the Eighteenth Century* (1803) noted "a spectacle never before displayed among men, and even yet without a parallel on earth. It is the spectacle, not of the learned and the wealthy only, but of the great body of people . . . having free and constant access to the public prints, receiving regular information of every occurrence, attending to the course of political affairs." Alexis de Tocqueville, on his tour of the United States in 1831–32, made the passion for news part of the archetype of this "nation of conquerors who . . . shut themselves in the American solitudes with an axe and some newspapers." The determination of Americans to bring the newspaper everywhere they went, and to use it for every social enjoyment, was noted by a congressman in high flight over the House floor:

> The only thing in the world, excepting the dews of heaven, its light and heat, that suits the tastes of all, is the promiscuous newspaper.

Superlatives were exhausted in the effort to explain an American's love of newsprint. The judicious Edward Dicey, a Victorian journalist and world traveler, said that "the American might be defined as a newspaper reading animal."[1]

Native Americans, too, saw that news reading preoccupied the newcomers. When the Council of the Seneca Nation had advice for the frontier community of Pittsburgh, these Seneca asked that "our talk may be put on the great paper." Omaha Indians, on visits to St. Louis, mimicked newspaper reading as a courtesy when they sat with white men. In 1811 some Omaha villagers politely welcomed a man they had seen in St. Louis by holding up buffalo robes and pretending to read them.[2]

Historians have treated the conspicuous consumption of news as a given, as if the reading had no more significance than the habit of sitting in chairs. We have been too busy with other matters: What was the news? What were journalists' motives? What did their stories accomplish? The result is that our picture of the past is filled with momentous headlines, grasping publishers, and dashing reporters, but few pictures of the people who got this news. Cold circulation figures are about all we have offered, and so we have created our own phantom public. A recent textbook presents more than two hundred illustrations of the rise of media in America, but hardly a trace of the audience for news. The cover of this text is a watercolor by one of the authors: a ghostly scene of men in top hats and bowlers, glancing at the papers.[3]

Before any more of us resort to the brush, the full historical record on readers would be a good thing to have. The reading public was not an abstraction in early America. Illustrators, writers, and plain busybodies reported the behavior of people getting news. Similarly, the reader has been probed and dissected by social scientists and marketing people in the twentieth century. Hollywood has put its brightest stars into films about journalists serving the public. This book puts this story together for the first time. *News for All* argues that the antique patterns of circulation in early America lead straight to the marketing dilemmas faced by publishers at the end of the twentieth century. The public today comes into better focus when we appreciate how Americans were won over to news in the first place.

Another payoff in taking readers seriously is a better understanding of what they read. We can study the same journalism read by the contemporaries of Jefferson, Lincoln, or Roosevelt. But unless we learn something of how they read these texts, we cannot understand what this news meant.

Reading, many scholars remind us, has many social complexities. Historians look for an interpretive community, those who may read the printed words to others and who certainly enlarge on the meaning of what is read. The plantation owners who read the Bible to slaves "in its original purity and simplicity" were attempting to make an interpretation stick. Black Americans who based spirituals on biblical verse offered a competing reading of this same text, often with a subversive meaning that the master did not grasp. Interpretive communities do more than determine which texts shall count and what words mean; they also create a setting that shapes the message. Slave spirituals had no strict canon; a song might be sung a half dozen ways at a single service, and groups of believers were expected to pick and choose through the biblical verse they knew to create new versions of songs. Spirituals were songs of freedom not simply because of symbolic references from the Bible, but also because African Americans shared in the work of creating their meaning.[4]

News, too, has had its interpretive communities and settings. It is time to bring them back to life. The parlors of America, and other comfortable spots for reading, were often arenas featuring winners and losers in the contest over who got the news first and what texts meant. Americans have been talking back to their press and editing it in their own ways since the days of Benjamin Franklin. This is the direction the public is headed into the twenty-first century, and this course will be clearer if we retrace the first steps.

"Market" is another name for the space in which a reader found news in print, and this notion, too, has been neglected in telling the story of the American press. There was little that was inevitable in the spread of news as a commodity. Giveaways, deep discounting, and a shrill sales pitch helped to create and to shape this consumer habit, and so it will not do to think of love for the "promiscuous" paper as a natural urge. Tricks of the trade to build reader loyalty have met reader resistance. This venerable conflict, another reality of Franklin's time, reveals much about what people really think about the press. The Rev. Miller, Tocqueville, and others dazzled by the power of the press thought that printers could not wait to produce papers and that the public could not wait to read them. This was a high-minded view but missed the element of humbug and resentment. *News for All* shows that in the making of a democratic reading public, there was no age of innocence. Deception and defiance have always helped to circulate the news, and today's problems will be clearer if they are not set, falsely, as a fall from grace.

The commerce of news helped to form an idea of citizenship and Americans' sense of their national community. News in print was the first consumer good to build these notions, and this journalism remains one of the few things for sale that can develop a sense of community. The making of a democratic public in the marketplace is at the center of *News for All*. The evidence here will not please those who wish simply to worship or to demonize market forces.

The character of the press often shows itself in the business ledgers, postal account books, and subscription lists of yesterday's news. But this is not, primarily, a quantitative study for the good reason that the historical record is too spotty to proceed this way. Very few publishers saved systematic evidence about their readers. The challenge is to use the statistics that survive with the more abundant testimony about news in people's lives.

What is the American commitment to an informed public? Through most of its history this nation has subsidized the press, granted it constitutional protection, and shaped laws so that it has been profitable and safe to provide news for all. Yet this book shows that many people have tried to shut readers off from the press. Press-hating mobs have tried to stop the spread of news. Through subtler social pressure, males have kept a tight grip on papers. Journalists themselves have played a role in excluding the public as they came to fear that the wrong kind of reader would displease advertisers. The instinct for news that once defined the American no longer seems so clear. At the end of the twentieth century, Americans buy less than half as many newspapers per capita than the Japanese, the Finns, and the Swedes; the British and the Germans also are better customers. *News for All* is the story of what happened in American's troubled love affair with their press.

The notion of a coming-of-age is a metaphor and an argument. The metaphor draws attention to a press and a people who have acquired a broader and a more varied interest in news. The argument is that with maturity came choices and doubts. Once the press learned how to circulate news for all, journalists had to decide what kinds of messengers they wished to be. Once the public had an abundance of news, they had choices about how to use the media. The idea of news for all has inspired impolite debate, fantasies about the power of journalists, rage at both the messenger and the public who will not listen.

Choice, choice of unprecedented variety, is the outcome of three centuries of news in print. This may seem an astonishing statement to people familiar with the critical literature on the American press. The twentieth century has seen a decline in the number of daily papers and the percentage of Americans who read them. Fewer owners control more traditional media outlets than ever before in the United States. People at the bottom of the economic order were more likely to be served by publications keyed to their political aspirations in the 1890s than in the 1990s. The spectrum of political views that gets into mass circulation is narrower than in many other countries. But while this was happening, the power of individuals to select news they wanted did grow. Readers have some of the power once held by editors. The Gutenberg era of printing, during which the page that came from the press was a standard product, has ended. Access to news of special interest has never been easier. The customization of the print medium raced ahead, especially as words have leaped from the old medium of paper to the new computer screens. There are, indeed, many forces in America that make for conformity and a timid exploration of issues. But the choices opened up by the new methods of publishing the news have created a new world for the citizen.

Part I of *News for All* shows how the news-reading habit took hold in the nineteenth century. Part II is a history of the negotiations carried on by active readers from these early days to our own: choosing what to read, fearing what others might read and see, telling journalists off. Part III explains how, in the twentieth century, the dream of universality has become technically more possible and socially more difficult.

The American engagement with news in print has many beginnings. A history of news in people's lives cannot be told in one narrative marching relentlessly forward. There has been a counterpoint in reading the news of social feeling and self-absorption, deference and independence, gratitude and resentment. Like the conflicting themes of individual maturity, these are best followed back to the experiences that first defined them. To arrive, finally, at the end of the twentieth century, we will have to return frequently to the curious readers familiar to the Rev. Miller, Tocqueville, and the Omaha villagers.

PART ONE

THE
CREATION
OF AN
AUDIENCE

I

HOW AMERICANS

LEARNED TO

READ THE NEWS

In 1776 the American diplomat Silas Deane told the French that one reason his people would win their independence was that they read and debated the political news "in a Circle of their Neighbors." During the terrible winter of that year, after patriot troops fled from the British across the Delaware, General George Washington made use of this reading habit. Shortly before Christmas he summoned his men from their tents and had them stand in the snow while officers read Tom Paine's "The Crisis." "These are the times that try men's souls," the reading began. The article had been published a few days earlier in the *Pennsylvania Journal*. This military exercise was a performance in which the citizen with a text in hand favored fellow citizens who were without. Though the setting was extraordinary, getting the news in this way contained those crucial elements of fellowship and deference that were common when people and print came together. Americans in the early republic took news in company, seldom alone. Newspapers and magazines were shared with a display of sights and sounds, social standing and beliefs. This full setting for news made people comfortable with texts and was one reason why print journalism seemed to be "half the life of an American" in the view of Europeans. In many circles of the new republic, not just in Washington's armed camp, reading the news ushered in American nationalism.[1]

Tom Paine reached Americans who did not have their own copy of his words, and this sharing and borrowing would long be the way news in print circulated. In a land famous for news readers, only one household in five subscribed to a paper when the federal government was born, and at the beginning of the nineteenth century two of every three households were still non-subscribers. Even in the largest printing centers of the new nation—Boston, New York, and Philadelphia—most readers went without their own copy. At the beginning of the nineteenth century, New York produced just one daily paper for every thirty-two residents.[2]

A hunger for the sight of a paper was common, especially during Northern winters. A woman in East Hampton complained in 1806 that "we get no paper, and know no more of the affairs of the world than if we were not in it." John Greenleaf Whittier, born the following year in Haverhill, Massachusetts, grew up, like many in New England, without a periodical in his home except for a small weekly paper. In "Snow-Bound" the poet memorialized the arrival of the newspaper ("And all the world was ours once more!") and touched a chord in a nation that could remember the deprivation when cut off from their newspaper.[3]

Southerners had more reason than Yankees to feel sorry for themselves about missing the news in the new nation. A newspaper was a rarer sight in the South than in the compact communities of New England. A Southerner with a newspaper was a citizen to be envied. During the Revolution, Thomas Jefferson at Monticello begged for his papers from Williamsburg. The printer of the *Virginia Gazette* sent what he could and explained that he could spare copies for only his most illustrious subscribers. Shortly after the federal government was set up in 1789 a Maryland printer noted the unmet need for papers on the Eastern Shore and flattered his subscribers as "gentlemen of information." In antebellum South Carolina, Caroline Gilman recalled, the first business of coming to church was news, and "he was the most sought who had seen the last newspaper."[4]

If *all* the newspapers published in 1790 had been evenly distributed, each American would have received just one issue that year. A half century later, American presses were still not capable of producing one newspaper a month for every citizen. Even in the largest cities, a newspaper for every reader was only a dream until the end of the nineteenth century. In the first decades of American life, only Bibles and almanacs were more commonly read than newspapers. But the pages of news passed through many more hands.[5] (See Chart 1.1.)

The meaning of the news was determined as people gathered around papers to watch and listen. Taking the news while nobody noticed and making up one's mind in silence must have been unusual. The broadcasting of newspapers by voice was so common that a bright slave boy who tended the public rooms of

Chart 1.1 Source: S. N. D. North, *History and Present Condition of the Newspaper Periodical Press in the United States* (Washington, D.C., 1884).

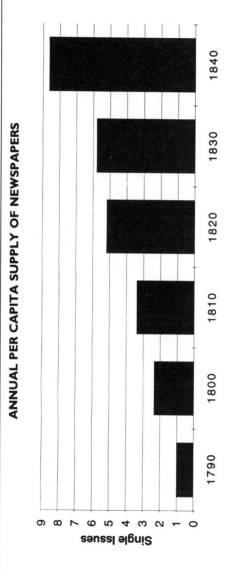

ANNUAL PER CAPITA SUPPLY OF NEWSPAPERS

a hotel in Columbus, Georgia, believed "that the readers were talking to the paper, rather than the paper talking to them." Printed news reached people as a theatrical display, the sounds and gestures so clear that they helped establish the meaning of texts. African Americans who could not read a word could point out the stories that they wanted literate blacks to read out to them. Open ears and a sharp eye at the hearth had revealed where to look. Listening to trusted readers completed the process of getting the news. As we shall see, face-to-face meetings, not simply printed pages, were the mass media of the early republic.[6]

Direct testimony about what passed through people's minds as they followed the news is rare in all eras. The historian's job is not to guess. In the eighteenth and nineteenth centuries, mind reading is not necessary for there is a wealth of observed behavior. The display of reading the news in taverns, post offices, and private homes drew wide attention. Artists and illustrators found these compelling scenes. The young republic drew students of society from all over the world, and the novelty of a self-governing people acquiring information was a spectacle that these visitors pondered.

The setting for the sharing of news was rarely so dramatic as that of Washington's camp in 1776. But we will make sense of getting the news only if we recognize it as a common performance. The newspaper was a prop in one of those transactions of daily life in which people managed the effects produced on others and defended their social status.

1. Tavern as News Room

The surest way to find newspapers in the New World was to enter that fixture of American life, the drinking establishment. Boston supported one tavern for every hundred inhabitants when its first newspapers took root, early in the eighteenth century. Taverns (with accommodations as a side or main business) were easy to find in all cities and along the post roads. There was one tavern on every mile of many turnpikes. In the early republic the average male left home to pass time with a small circle of neighbors in a tavern once a week.[7]

The printed page was, perhaps, not the first thing requested. Never have Americans spent more of their leisure raising glasses. Between 1790 and 1830, the per capita consumption of alcohol in the United States was nearly three times greater than at the end of the twentieth century. But newspapers were an important part of the fellowship of drinkers. Tavern keepers boasted of their subscriptions as well as their drink. George Burns opened the Horse and Cart in Manhattan with the announcement that "to gratify his Customers he takes in the Boston, Philadelphia and New York papers." On the edge of settlement in the new nation, the appeal was the same. A tavern keeper in Delaware, Ohio, assured customers that the latest newspapers and magazines "will always be furnished." An Englishman advised his countrymen in the early 1820s that travellers to the United States would find a public reading room in the inns of the smallest towns, with an iron bar down the middle of each newspaper file to prevent readers from taking issues away.[8]

The number of different papers in public rooms was a wonder to foreigners. At Hagerstown, Maryland, an Englishman found ten newspaper files from different states in one tavern. Another visitor asked casually if the young city of Cincinnati had a newspaper, and his hotel offered him a choice of sixteen local publications plus newspapers from other regions. A reading room in Eastport, Maine, offered guests some thirty American newspapers in 1826. The record may have been set in Lexington, Kentucky, in 1807 when an Englishman noted forty-two files of American newspapers along with the ample stock of bourbon. The public house truly anticipated the public library of a later day.[9]

Unlike today's libraries, the tavern in the early republic did not provide for privacy or quiet contemplation with the news. One was not alone with a text. The tavern-goer took company with the news. There was a trade-off: in exchange for diverse reading not available in private, customers revealed their taste and opinions to their neighbors.

The reading public, in the first place, talked the news. This was going on as early as 1744, when Dr. Alexander Hamilton fled the heat of his native Maryland for New Hampshire, only to find that a traveller could not get rest up north when the post arrived. Hamilton complained to his diary of a "numerous company" at his inn that kept him up three hours "reading the news." The tavern broadcast of newspapers, like many hazards of travel, was destined to become picturesque. John Lewis Krimmel painted his *Village Tavern* (1814) with all the customers excited as the newspapers were announced to the room. Washington Irving brought Rip Van Winkle to his village tavern to *listen* to newspapers (a scene John Quidor painted in 1839). This same year, Francis W. Edmonds painted a scene from a Tobias Smollett novel in which men shared a newspaper with their cups. Smollett's readers may have remembered the explosion of interest as the news was read out: "Avast! overhaul that article again."[10]

Philip Freneau, a celebrated poet of the Revolution, listed the main activities in the American tavern as drinking, smoking, spitting, and reading the news. But not all Americans were equals in these pastimes. Taking the news made one conspicuous, for to ask for a paper (or not to ask) allowed neighbors to draw certain conclusions. An impressive broadcast of the newspaper marked some citizens for distinction. The pretense of reading newspapers was a common scene in taverns as customers struggled with the printed word to keep up appearances. The self-reported literacy rate of white males approached 90 percent early in the nineteenth century (a level that white women matched by mid-century). But speed and fluency in reading was another matter. Self-improvement with the tavern sheet was irritating enough to require a posted warning: "Gentlemen learning to spell are requested to use last week's newsletter."[11]

Political beliefs could also embarrass the customers who took news with their drink. In cities and in the countryside, taverns became clubhouses for political factions. Especially during the Revolution, news could transform a drinking establishment into a political rally. In 1774 Nicholas Cresswell, a loyal Englishman, sat in a Virginia tavern and heard defiant statements from the Continental Congress read aloud and discussed. He noted in his diary, "I am obliged to act the hypocrite and extol these proceedings as the wisest productions of any assembly on Earth, but in my heart I despise them and look upon them with contempt." Loyalists, similarly, intimidated thirsty patriots. During the Revolutionary War, New York's King's-Head Tavern (a name that suggested its politics) set up 200 candles to illuminate transparencies which condemned the rebels. According to one report, "general indignation" was roused against the Continental Congress as well as the new President (who glowed beside a grinning devil).[12]

The conversion of the tavern into a shrine for party or faction was a hazard to many seeking the news in the formation of the republic. When the sign out front said THE RIGHTS OF MAN or WILKES AND LIBERTY, the boundary on the conversation inside was clear. A false face, like the one Cresswell put on, would continue to be the true price for information. Some proprietors sought to keep peace by banning political discussion, but censorship at the bar proved impossible. The public lounge of American inns was called the "news room." Hospitality and argument were bound together, putting travellers and neighbors on their guard. Frederick Marryat, a retired captain from the Royal Navy, visited St. Albans, Vermont, while British forces were putting down a rebellion across the border in Canada. Captain Marryat chose an inn that he thought would abide his political sympathies. This inn proved to be not tolerant enough for his comfort. The British officer sought to correct a newspaper's account of the Canadian rebellion, and word of his unorthodox views attracted more than a hundred townsfolk to the inn. "Thinks I to myself, I'm in for it now, and if I get away without a broken head, or something else, I am fortunate," Marryat noted in his diary. The Captain stalled with an hour's discourse on Canadian history before trying flattery and jokes. Eventually his criticism of the newspaper was forgotten as glasses were raised. A bleary consensus seems often to have been the result of taking news from drinking partners.[13]

Taverns sometimes exploded as guests read. One Englishman survived such a political discussion in western Pennsylvania, though he could only give a partial report. His memoir breaks off, "Here I—slipped out at the side door into the water-melon patch." Americans with newspapers were renowned for trying the patience of anyone willing to share a confined space for a little while. Europeans visiting the United States in the nineteenth century often noted the cocksureness of citizens in the taverns and travelling compartments as news-paper paragraphs were shared. It was a Kentuckian in 1820 who denounced the *Ventoso* of the taverns "who assumes the privilege of retailing the scraps gathered from newspapers, which he constantly reads and reverberates."[14]

Not everyone was welcome to get the news. Apprentices, servants, and seamen were sometimes barred from taverns, and often blacks and Indians were excluded. Certainly there were public rooms where a woman would be made to feel out of place. In Philadelphia, the largest city of the early republic, class lines seem to have divided drinkers by 1800, more so than at the beginning of the eighteenth century. But foreign visitors make clear in their travel writings that a very broad sample of Americans were at home in the taverns. Segregation by gender, for example, was an ideal rarely achieved in the New World. Women worked and boarded at public houses. Men had no monopoly on the supply of newspapers near the bar. A British naval officer complained that females who waited table at village inns would not hover around the diners to be of service. They sat down with their newspapers unless the diner made a request. "During my whole travels, I never knew a waiting-man take a similar liberty," he said.[15]

When Mrs. Frances Trollope began her American travels in 1828, she found these establishments distressingly democratic. At the time of her visit, Mrs. Trollope noted, the English worker did not visit a pub because of a thirst for knowledge, and she was not easily convinced that Americans were different. When she met a milkman in Cincinnati who said that he spent so much time with newspapers to meet his civic duty, she asked,

> "It is from a sense of duty, then, that you all go to the liquor store to read the papers?"
>
> "To be sure it is, and he'd be no true-born American as didn't. I don't say that the father of a family should always be after liquor, but I do say that I'd rather have my son drunk three times in a week, than not look after the affairs of his country."[16]

The tavern crowd was hard-drinking in the genre scenes of news reading painted by Krimmel, Quidor, and Edmonds. Reports on the news rooms of American inns show that there was a narrow line between dissipation and attention to public questions. American restlessness and heedlessness were on display. "The usual custom is to pace up and down the news-room in a manner similar to walking the deck at sea," an Englishman said on a visit to Louisville in 1817. He found "not a man who appears to have a single earthly object in view, except spitting and smoking segars." Baltimore's City Hotel, which boasted it was the largest in the country, posted its news room: "Five dollars reward for the discovery of *the villain who cuts or tears the newspapers!!*" A Louisville hotel put up a sign asking its guests to get toilet paper from the management and not to rip up its file of newspapers for this purpose.[17]

Even the sight of Americans *reading* a newspaper in a public place was unsettling. There are several paintings of the mid-nineteenth century similar to Nicolino Calyo's canvas which caught layabouts in New York's Astor House, gripping their newspapers in both hands as they rocked back in their chairs and put their feet on the table.[18] English visitors, in particular, could not get over this cantilever of the male legs, and in the travel literature there is a competition of high sightings. A travel book published in 1823, for example, claimed to have seen American gentlemen with their heels on the mantelpiece. Francis Lieber, the German academic, noted "two characteristics of the Americans, their lounging habit, and their eagerness to read." American posture was indeed a calculated assault on aristocratic manners, and these visitors were correct to claim its cultural and even political importance: "Imagine a man sitting in this manner with a segar in his mouth, and you have a complete picture of American independence!"[19]

It was not independence but rather mimicry that outraged a patriotic American, the Rev. Timothy Dwight, in the taverns he visited in the Hudson Valley. Dwight, the president of Yale College, censored those rustics who behaved as they thought men of great affairs behaved. "To exhibit this resemblance to each other, and to strangers, is always a favorite object of their attention," Dwight said. He despaired for his country as he noted the determination of these country folk "to haunt taverns; to drink; to swear; to read newspapers . . . ."[20]

This putting on of airs with the news was condemned because it was a

"How We Sit in Our Hotel Homes."
(Harper's Weekly, December 26, 1857)

Lefevre J. Cranstone, sketch done near Bridgeport, Ohio, June 1860.
Courtesy of the Lilly Library, Indiana University.

Nicolino Calyo, *Reading Room, Astor House,* c. 1840.
Museum of the City of New York. Gift of Mrs. Elon Huntington Hooker.

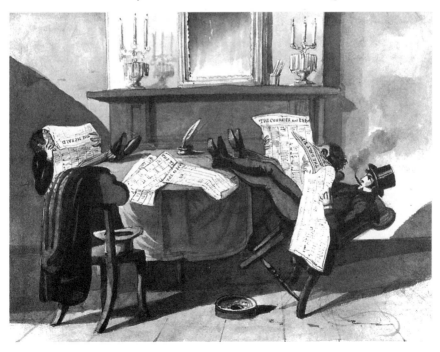

challenge to observers whose rank entitled them to deference. The vandal in the news room, the lounger, and the oaf, were cousin to the insolent readers who rocked, tilted, or refused to wait tables. Few of these had real power in the news room. The tavern keeper or the paying guests were in a position to command. But all of these Americans had taken dramatic control of the room to which the community came for its news. There was wide latitude for conduct in the early republic, especially when alcohol was served. Deportment in the taverns had to be extreme to gain attention, and it was. To be sure, Americans did not need the prop of a newspaper to display the manners that earned the censure of Europeans. But the play for attention in the news room had special significance. The loud talk that engulfed the news was, first of all, an assertion that the audience considered itself more important than the story. No matter what a printed text said — crises, misfortunes, crimes, or wonders — stories were put in their place when an American democrat gripped the page. Truly, all people could get their hands on this news. To visit a tavern was to see that the "gentlemen of information" had been taken down a peg. The newspaper was not a sacred text, worthy of respect and hushed attention. The stupefied lounger made the same point without speaking: news was no reason to wake up. Journalists were in no privileged position when they issued the news; they could be gainsaid just as anyone in the tavern could be treated to the sight of another citizen's feet in the air . . . reading the news.[21]

To pass through the tavern door is to see features of the press that are not clear in a visit to a modern library where the news of this era is carefully preserved. The columns of partisan news did indeed reach party loyalists in a tavern. But the setting for the strident, political press of the early republic continually tested parochial sentiment. With a variety of reading matter close at hand and with strangers passing through, political insularity was hard to maintain. Editors could preach, but, unlike in a church, heretics sat in the congregation and some were passing out their own versions of the truth. Stories in the press of the early republic should be read as gambits, provocative first moves in a game the reader would then play as other texts were read and arguments helped to pass the day.

2. Mail and Other People's Business

There was an arena for news where the government itself sought to enforce decorum: the mail. Through the early nineteenth century, the post office was the most tangible sign Americans had that the federal government was at work. Competing with a vigorous system of private "expresses," no branch of the government grew more vigorously. In 1820 there were sixty post offices for every one in service in 1789. Through the 1830s and 1840s, post offices multiplied faster than Americans. No European government had this reach into local communities. At mid-century there were four American post offices for every one in Great Britain, though the U.S. population was only about 75 percent of the English population. The American post office might be a humble corner of a hotel or tavern, but what went on when mail arrived was a reminder of power in the republic. In many communities this establishment was the only place of fellowship outside church on Sunday, and in some villages the mail coach was the only vehicle that could be driven on that day. The government's model post coach was vermillion below, green on top, with yellow lettering near the spread eagle insignia. This regal standard was not kept up, but the thunder of a four-horse stage and the burst of the coachman's horn were everyday flourishes to the arrival of mail.[22]

A great deal of the mail was newspapers. Nearly as many papers as letters passed through post offices during the first two decades of the United States, and in the next half century papers frequently outnumbered all hand-written messages. By one estimate, the news made up roughly 95 percent of the total weight of mail by the 1830s. At mid-century, a desperate heroine in a Catherine Sedgwick story searched for a letter from a loved one amidst newspapers "in multitudes like the plague of frogs" at the village post office.[23]

A variety of public servants knew which paper a citizen took through the post. In the early republic, Americans frequently sent subscription requests for newspapers to their representatives in Congress. This errand for constituents was one way that senators and representatives gauged the mood of voters. The executive branch, too, monitored reading habits. The post office kept an account book of the postage paid by subscribers (before the Civil War, it was the reader, not the publisher, who normally paid the cost of delivery). In Jacksonian America, these lists were shipped off four times a year to Washington, where they were studied by political appointees. Mrs. Trollope, fresh from her investigation of alcoholic readers, concluded that sober Washington bureaucrats used these records to "feel the pulse" of the democracy. This probably gave the young civil service in the capital too much credit for political espionage. But in small towns, the postmaster knew what everybody read and was likely to discuss this freely. Sedgwick called this official an "oracle." A Connecticut man complained in 1833 that his newspaper had become "sport." A clerk had taken the wrapper off, marked items, and made fun of him before the village. It was generally true that by the time a subscriber showed up to collect the paper, the postmaster had ample opportunity to read it. A regulation of 1825 set a fine for snooping through newspapers in the mail, but the rule did not set back this form of education. In one debate over postal reform a senator commended surreptitious news reading "as a sort of compensation" for the postmaster's trouble. When Abraham Lincoln was the postmaster at New Salem, Illinois, in the mid-1830s, he furthered his education by reading subscribers' newspapers.

Townsfolk who met Lincoln walking around New Salem often found that he carried their reading matter in his clothes.[24]

Lincoln apparently did not go as far as many postmasters who helped patrons choose their periodicals . . . or made the choice for townsfolk. Thomas Jefferson's Postmaster General told his deputies in the field to encourage patrons to take local papers rather than those from distant publishers. Thus the department would save the expense of long hauls, and rural Americans would be safe from the corruption of big cities. Favoritism in delivery appealed to Jefferson's opponents, the Federalists, and the evidence is strong that these conservatives stalled Jeffersonian papers. A generation later, it was the conservatives' turn to complain. In 1835 Whigs in Congress accused the Democrats who controlled the post office of censorship. Postmasters saw that Jacksonians got their newspapers, the Whigs said, but "throw obstacles in the way of the circulation of those of an opposite character." Postmasters commended the paper of the party that guaranteed their job and found the reading taste of their supervisors to be contagious. Joseph Medill, who had deployed his Chicago *Tribune* to elect Abraham Lincoln, knew this when he asked the administration to make a *Tribune* editor the postmaster in Chicago. With this grip on patronage, Medill explained, "the country postmasters of the Northwest would work to extend our circulation . . . and promote the legitimate influence of our paper."[25]

"I can't pass this," a clerk said as he tore up the *National Anti-Slavery Standard* before the eyes of a patron in a Baltimore post office in 1843. The postmaster apologized to the subscriber for this activity the next day, but the officer insisted on his duty as a monitor. The postmaster asked the reader if he was showing good citizenship by reading such matter. Postmasters were important agents of surveillance when antislavery papers spread across the land (a story that will be told more fully in chapter 3). President Andrew Jackson proposed that postal records be used to publicize the names of citizens subscribing to this subversive literature. Virginia had a state law to collect such lists.[26]

Postmasters also guided American reading when there was money or friendships to be made. A postal handbook of the mid-nineteenth century said that as a matter of course the postmaster previewed the upstart newspaper and "uses his exertions to procure subscribers for it." This is how Henry J. Raymond took his first step into the newspaper world during a dull winter in upstate New York. This fifteen-year-old store clerk asked his postmaster what he should read. That man handed him some specimen issues sent by publishers, and Raymond picked one edited by Horace Greeley. Raymond would later work for Greeley on a path to founding his own paper, the New York *Times*.[27]

In many rural communities, dozens of readers were identified as having a common interest and brought together by the postmaster. Clubs of readers were created by this patron of journalism, and the postmaster was enriched by the added postage he collected. Thomas Ritchie, editor of a powerful paper in the South, used postmasters as intelligence agents to check up on subscribers who did not pick up the Richmond *Enquirer*. No one gained if the postage went unpaid.[28]

The arrival of newspapers and magazines with the general mail at the post office sent neighbors pell-mell into each other's business. The letters, newspapers, and periodicals were often dumped into a pile, and the postmaster, with the help of interested citizens, extracted the local mail. The rest was sent on its way to be gone through again at the next stop. Town idlers helped themselves to other people's papers. In 1842 a travelling Englishman observed that the Yankee reached for another man's newspaper in the post office as readily as he would pick an apple from a neighbor's tree. Helpful neighbors were as fully informed about reading tastes as the sneaks. Many newspapers reached the countryside, especially in New England, through "companies" of neighbors who contracted with a post rider and also often took turns in carrying papers to homes. Periodicals were shared through a network of exchanges among neighbors. The *American Agriculturist*, for example, discovered that 506 persons in 107 families were regular readers of the twenty-two copies that reached a post office. Who read what was common knowledge in this republic. A citizen's politics and taste were as clear to townsfolk as if the postal system had required a sign to be displayed by everyone's front door.[29]

The disclosure of what others were reading through the post was a favorite theme of painters of the era. Thomas Prichard Rossiter's *Rural Post Office* (1857) and D. G. Blythe's *In the Pittsburgh Post Office* (1856–61) show newspapers held like trophies, and much of the reading goes on over other people's shoulders. In the more famous post office scenes painted by Richard Caton Woodville and William Sidney Mount, a single newspaper draws all the customers to the subscriber. In the illustrations of newspapers in the nineteenth-century post office, few patrons left the paper folded up. In an era in which almost all papers were affiliated with a political party or faction, citizens displayed their political affinities just as surely as if they wore a sign.[30]

As several genre artists saw it, the postal patrons were made to re-enact the hierarchy of American society. Richard Caton Woodville's *War News from Mexico* (1848) and William Sidney Mount's *California News* (1850) show citizens transfixed by the men who hold newspapers. Both paintings are set at post offices where a lucky man holds the latest paper. All business stops as citizens press forward to read or stay back with cocked ears. Young white men dominate the charmed circle around the newspaper. The aged, the very young, and the blacks fill the space. They are literally outsiders who are not in the bright light of news. (There is a woman in Mount's work, close to the newspaper but

William Sidney Mount, *California News*, 1850.
The Museums at Stony Brook. Gift of Mr. and Mrs. Ward Melville, 1955.

made dependent on a young man with his hand on her shoulder to get the news.)[31]

These genre scenes highlight the play of deference and fellowship that is clear in so many of the accounts of getting the news in this democracy. In taverns and post offices, along paths and roads, the nineteenth-century artist put news into the hands of people with authority, then showed the news being shared. News placed the reader in society and also suggested a place for everyone seeking information.[32]

One of the most common and significant transactions necessary to get the news was when the citizen met the person who carried the mail. The "appointed rounds" of carriers have become part of a legend of fortitude, modesty, and trust. But in early American history, the post rider enjoyed the reputation for both lassitude and a diverting entrepreneurship. The last inspection of the postal system by the British found riders working off the books and transporting goods for their own profit. While the colonists waited for their mail, the carrier might leave the route to earn money serving summonses or even herding oxen. Under republican institutions, performance remained a problem. In 1802 the Postmaster General told a senator that mail coaches were designed to take passengers as a check on the dishonesty of the driver. The job had psychic as well as monetary rewards. When the mail arrived in good time, the press was ready to salute the messenger as loudly as the message. Thus in 1788 the *Massachusetts Centinel* commended the stage driver Levi Pease before reporting his "glorious intelligence" that Virginia had ratified the Constitution. Post riders expected to be appreciated, and Americans hungry for news in the early republic often feared their imperial air. In the countryside, it was common practice not to transport newspapers into the scattered settlements but to throw the papers from the stage along the road without stopping. Farmers in the area were expected to cooperate in this hunt for the news. Some coachmen were bold enough to edit the reading of subscribers. One driver in New England, for example, concealed the Republican papers he carried and gave out the Federalist ones.[33]

The everyday practices of drivers were galling enough: these messengers helped themselves to the newspapers they carried. Fines and warnings dating from the earliest days of the republic seem to have done little to stop the carriers from getting other people's news. Again, access to information was a matter of community knowledge, and the consumer bowed to the messenger.

When a newspaper reached an American community with momentous news, all citizens might be placed in the hands of coercive neighbors. Thus when the conservative students and faculty of Dartmouth College learned of Napoleon's ruin in the summer of 1814 they made "suitable arrangements" for the arrival of newspapers with the official dispatches from Europe. The mail was read from a Revolutionary War field piece which was fired after each item of news. The student body gave nine cheers to every dispatch, and the entire college was illuminated in the evening to celebrate the defeat of radicalism. Bonapartists in New Hampshire were watched and silenced as the community read the news.[34]

The editing and broadcasting of news was accomplished through the post far in advance of the days of modern electronic media. In the Rev. William Baker's memoir of Austin, Texas, during the Civil War, news summaries provided by the stage driver sent the community into a frenzy before anyone saw the newspapers he delivered. The driver's news (based on a glance at the newspapers he carried) was like a torch that blazed brighter each time it had been passed to the next horseman through the hundred hours that stretched back to the front. In Austin, the stage driver savored his moment of glory and made the crowd wait, then he announced the bulletin that usually made fantastic claims for Southern arms:

> Great battle at Corinth! Glorious victory! Yankees whipped all to smash! Beauregard's taken prisoners all he hasn't killed, an' that's fifty thousand! Battalions, gun-boats, brigades, all keptured!

The news rallied the town, the Rev. Baker recalled: "Such a brightening of faces, such a shaking of hands, such a chorus of yells! People hurry off to tell it to their waiting families. Men who live in the country can not wait till the mail is opened, but mount their horses, tied hard by, and gallop off at the risk of their necks through the darkness to tell the news at home, then to gallop back again for their papers." The news was read at the post office, finally, with the town bells adding to the celebration. Clearly, the community had learned the news in ritual before any reading took place, and the meaning of the texts was pre-established. Baker recalled that it was only those citizens who held themselves apart and deceived their neighbors about their political sympathies who could read between the lines of these papers and get a realistic picture of the South's chances.[35]

Foreign visitors to the young republic saw that the social transactions necessary to get the news in public were, simultaneously, forces for social dependence as well as for the smashing of deference. Few people could read a newspaper without the cooperation of a neighbor: in face-to-face contact Americans asked for their paper or borrowed a neighbor's. This distribution system allowed discretion at every step, and access to a newspaper could easily be cut off. John Lambert, an English traveller during the Jefferson administration, saw the code of manners that spread the news. He noted that men, women, and children on farms "scampered" up to the road as they heard the coachman's horn, "begging for their favourite paper." In town, Americans "flocked to the post-office and the inn, and formed a variety of groups round those who were fortunate enough to possess themselves of a paper. There they stood, with open mouth, swallowing *'the lies of the day,'* which would be as readily contradicted on the morrow." Lambert did not find this an inspiring spectacle, but he was sure he was seeing a transformation of attitudes not to be found in Europe. "Honest ignorant rusticity" was being lost in this new republic as neighbors gathered to get the news. Lambert credited newspapers for the Yankee's reputation as "artful and impertinent" with "knowledge and confidence." "Whatever inconveniences . . . may be felt from the diffusion of knowledge among the lower classes, by those who have been accustomed to homage and submission from their inferiors, yet a nation whose peasantry is thus instructed and enlightened must, I should think, feel the benefit."[36]

Lambert, swallowing hard, was accepting a new public sphere in America that was later embraced across Europe in the nineteenth century. Public questions were no longer to be resolved within the safe confines of one rank or order; the press opened these matters to much wider debate. Liberal theory, supported by an ascending middle class, condemned private and secretive debate and celebrated the new public forums for political questions. At least in the United States, the tavern and the postal system were agents for the opening of argument that liberal theory prescribed.[37]

3. News at the Hearth

Public behavior with news is one thing. What went on in the home? Many Americans could most easily get their hands on a paper in their household. The reading audience formed by the family circle was more significant in the United States than in Europe. Alexander Mackay, a brilliant London journalist, saw this on his American tour in the late 1840s. "The chief circulation of English papers is in exchanges, newsrooms, reading rooms, hotels, taverns, coffee-houses. . . . In America the case is totally different. Not only are places of public resort well supplied with the journals of the day, but most families take in their paper, or papers." Americans of the early republic were a hiving people. Few lived alone, and the taking in of kin was more common than in colonial days, far more common than at the end of the twentieth century. The newspapers of this democracy were communal, even when they entered the private home.[38]

All members of the household were not created equal with American independence. Within each family the male was expected to govern, a mandate that included reading. The Cleveland *Plain Dealer* was stating a commonplace when it said that a newspaper subscription "is a *duty* which every married man owes to his family, to see them thus supplied with the means of general intelligence and the motives of morality and economy." Beyond kin, the extended household often looked to their employers for the news. In the early republic, it appears that most females in New England worked for pay and lived in other people's households at some point in their lives. Out of every ten males in the new nation, two were slaves, two were servants or tenant farmers. Newspapers in the home were passed from master to servant, husband to wife, parent to child. For many readers, the news was a gift chosen by a superior who had judged the publication to be suitable for the household. The wish of the news giver was to reinforce lines of authority, and this has been memorialized in most nineteenth-century presentations of reading at home. These pictures are illuminating, so long as they are not taken simply at face value.[39]

The newspaper was a moral authority around the hearth in Harriet Beecher

Stowe's *Oldtown Folks* (1869). The novelist-historian described how a Tory family used newspapers "'to instruct the servants and put them on their guard.'" The domestic helpers were called to hear newspaper accounts of the revolution in France, "the massacres, mobbings, and outrages." "Ordering one's self lowly and reverently to one's betters," Stowe said, was the catechism that grew out of newspaper files. Lilly Martin Spencer, the leading female painter of Stowe's generation, memorialized her own instructional reading of a newspaper to her maid and children during the Civil War. The servant, presumably Irish, showed the general attitude of this group: contempt for the celebration of the Union cause.[40]

Upsetting servants with newspapers could be a serious business. The slave South was haunted by fear that African Americans might use their position on the plantation to see the news and know too much. These house servants were envied by blacks, and by whites. Hinton Helper, a poor-white Carolinian who despised blacks so much that he would have freed the slaves in order to banish them, numbered among his resentments that black servants, "of all the poor people in the South, had access, at all times, in the families of the rich and refined, to books, magazines, and newspapers."[41]

Children were less worry around a newspaper than servants. Papers were used in some classrooms as reading exercises, and parents found it convenient to continue the lessons at home. Stephen Allen of New York was raised by his uncle, a schoolteacher, during the Revolution, and the journalism in his guardian's home made a strong impression on the boy. Allen, not yet ten, was frequently asked to read aloud the same essays by Tom Paine that Washington's troops heard in camp. Allen recalled that he could not take in the meaning of the words he read out to his uncle, but that this man's comments on the passages he read stayed with him all his life (a life that propelled him far from his artisan beginnings as a sail maker to become mayor of New York). A modern reader of Paine may be struck by his confession that the fight was tenuous because of the threat posed by "summer soldiers" and "sunshine patriots." Allen, like the Continental soldiers themselves, was helped to discount fears by a reading performance. The boy learned to revere the soldiers while he read the "Crisis" papers. In an age in which many political commitments were proudly traced back to instruction at the hearth, the reading of political news as a child must have been a determining influence in many lives.[42]

Political indoctrination was not the primary function of news read with children. Still less was entertainment the goal. The family itself was to be preserved by sharing news across generations. The *American Farmer* (1819–97) told parents to summon their children when the "long and tedious" articles on agriculture arrived and to read the paper aloud:

> Contemplate the picture of innocence and happiness, represented by the honest husbandman, sitting with his helpmate after the toils of the day round the cheerful fire, in the midst of a groupe [*sic*] of happy, healthful children, each of whom reads alternatively that which improves them.[43]

Here news reading appeared to be a medicine dispensed by loving parents, unpleasant at times but for everyone's good.

The notion that a strong grip on a newspaper put one person above another was the most common message about reading the news in illustrations of the American home. Almost always, it was the man of the house who had the newspaper. There seem to be no paintings of the American home before the end of the nineteenth century in which the female has news and the male does not. This is true for the mainstream of family portraiture, and also among naive painters who had not mastered (or did not care to follow) the conventions of representational art. Primitive painters, too, with their flat, angular figures put a newspaper out of woman's reach.[44]

These American families look out on life from their parlor, anchored by dining table or hearth. In the early republic these scenes spoke of a new concern for private living space. The home itself, as well as the room where the

Attributed to J. H. Davis, *The York Family*, 1837.
Abby Aldrich Rockefeller Folk Art Collection.

family gathered together, was seen as a refuge. Far more often than in the colonial era, the ideal home was isolated from other families, decorated to uplift its inhabitants, and cut off from the workplace. The architecture and decor marked a new turning inward among American families. Paintings documented features of material culture that say much about the demeanor of families reading the news. Handwork and reading went on together, usually near the hearth. This conventional view of the home owed something to sentiment, but just as much to the state of lighting and heating. Families had no choice but to gather around readers, for warmth and good light were in short supply. Only toward the end of the nineteenth century could family members be separate and comfortable in their homes at night. At mid-century, furniture design itself began to distinguish the news reader from the non-reader. There was no strict determinism to this, but in the full range of illustration in the Victorian era women often sit in chairs without arms. This left more room for knitting and for the petticoats and skirts of the day. Thus some women could not easily settle back; they were propelled forward to the handwork that filled so many of their hours in the home. As they looked out at the room, they looked up. Men's chairs were symbolically thrones. They were higher off the ground with taller backs than the chairs for women. Armrests forced men back in the chair and positioned them to look down on people they addressed.[45]

In paintings of domestic scenes, newspapers received the attention and respect one might expect for guests. The paper established the pecking order and was sufficient reason for the dominant to ignore their inferiors. Usually the paper helped a man, but not always. Eastman Johnson gave patriarchs newspapers to hold like shields as they sat in family portraits. These are formidable readers of the parlor. In *The Brown Family* (1869) the gentleman near the hearth is planted like an oak and only tips his paper slightly to acknowledge the child who has reached out to interrupt reading. The father in *The Hatch Family* (1871) sinks behind his newspaper and is oblivious to his fourteen relatives in the drawing room. Evidently the men who commissioned these paintings were pleased to be walled off by the news. Condescension had been a virtue in aristocratic societies, and some of these patriarchs fairly glow with benevolence as they lower themselves to other members of the family. In a Currier & Ives lithograph, *The Four Seasons of Life: Old Age* (1868), the gentleman by the hearth takes his newspaper out of the child's face and looks down benignly at the young questioner. Still, most artists recognized that the newspaper had its own imperative. Cherishing the press was taken to dangerous extremes in Lilly Martin Spencer's *The War Spirit at Home* (1866) for here a young mother allows a squirming infant to teeter on her lap while she reaches up to display news of a Union victory in the New York *Times*. A female servant glowers at this daring reader. However, the children in the picture are

Eastman Johnson, *The Brown Family*, 1869.
The Fine Arts Museums of San Francisco. Gift of Mr. and Mrs. John D. Rockefeller 3rd.

marching to the news of victory, and there is no question that the woman with the newspaper is in control.

These sumptuous and mannered parlor scenes had an influence on Americans who lacked both affluence and leisure. Lithographs and magazine illustrations spread the picture of the heads of households taking charge of the news. In the magazines designed for homemakers, these were scenes for emulation,

Lilly Martin Spencer, *War Spirit at Home* (*Celebrating the Victory at Vicksburg*), 1866.
Collection of The Newark Museum. Purchase 1944. Wallace M. Scudder Bequest Fund.

not merely wonder. What one historian has called "parlor consciousness" cut across class lines. By the middle of the nineteenth century, many rooms for ordinary citizens were modeled after the upper-class parlor. Railway cars, steamboats, hotel lobbies, even working-class clubs, took on the appearance of nooks for the wealthy. These model parlors were pictured in advertisements and other promotional material. As the upper-class parlor diffused through the press, the male command of the newspaper was set before a large public as correct deportment. Social life for many was imitating the art of a few.[46]

The evidence about what men and women did with news in the home has to be read very carefully. The drama of men taking charge of the paper and making a single interpretation stick is well documented. These reading performances caught the eye of the Rev. William M. Baker in his serial in *Harper's Weekly* during 1866, "Inside. A Chronicle of Secession." Baker wrote the story while he spent the Civil War in Texas as a secret Unionist. As the pastor of the First Presbyterian Church at Austin, Baker was in a good position to observe home life. He hid the working manuscript in the ground and in his wife's clothing so that his Confederate neighbors would not see his "photograph" of the rebel community. Baker took careful note of the way neighbors and families fooled themselves with news dispatches. As men read the news, they cast a spell:

> Never in his life could the Colonel read a paper, or any thing else, except aloud and very slowly. In consequence of this his wife managed to get her news without much trouble on her part. Every syllable was believed by the Colonel as he read it, and by his wife with a double faith, because of the fact that it came together from the lips and backed by the comments and assurances of her husband.[47]

This was a man's story, but it squares with Caroline Gilman's *Recollections of a Southern Matron* (1838), a popular work pledged "to present as exact a picture as possible of local habits and manners." The spirited heroine of this story surrenders to her husband in the parlor: "If he was absorbed in reading, I sat quietly waiting the pause when I should be rewarded by the communication of ripe ideas."[48]

Without such broadcasts of news, many people said, the woman in Victorian America was cut off from journalism. In 1851 a woman's magazine reported that the American housewife was so busy that she could not seek knowledge herself and was fortunate if she had the energy to attend to her husband's reading of the news. Edward W. Bok, who made the *Ladies' Home Journal* the most successful magazine of the Victorian era, set his course on the observation that "the American woman was not a newspaper reader." This was an article of faith among top editors in the late nineteenth century, according to the women who asked them for jobs.[49]

The notion that newspapers were male discourse had a powerful hold on journalists of Victorian America. The division of reading by gender was the rationale for allowing things to be said in a news column that could not be said in a magazine or novel. Vernacular language and harsh realities were ruled inappropriate for the genteel literature addressed to women. But in the newspaper, supposedly guarded by the male, straight talk about the unfolding of American life was allowed. This is one reason why many of the pioneer realists and naturalists in American letters found their first outlets in the press and prized the freedom they had in the daily paper.

Daily papers enjoyed this freedom in part because both sexes participated in another display of deference, the division of the newspaper by gender. By mid-century, many newspapers were structured as if women had tunnel vision. Already by 1842 an editor spoke with certainty about the selectivity of females after they had waited for the man of the house to pass on the paper. The mother read the poet's corner, reviews of novels, notices of weddings and deaths. Her

COLONEL JUGGINS READING THE "SOMERVILLE STAR" TO HIS WIFE.

Illustration by Thomas Nast for [William M. Baker], *Inside: A Chronicle of Secession*
(New York, 1866).
Courtesy of the Bancroft Library, University of California, Berkeley.

daughters, in their turn, looked at fashions and entertainment. The women of the house read a newspaper by "perusal" and "glancing," but the man "devours its contents with an eagerness that shows how deeply his whole soul is in it." Gender determined what to read and how to read, so it seemed. This assumption grew stronger through the Victorian era. Edward Bok syndicated women's features to newspapers in the 1880s, and by the turn of the century the woman's page was a fixture in metropolitan dailies. These features preserved the appearance that the time women spent with newspapers was not an intrusion into the male sphere.[50]

There was some truth to the conventional wisdom that news was safely in male hands. When women read aloud, either in mixed company or to one another, fiction seems to have been their most popular choice. (Females were urged to read histories but often rejected the advice.) The solitary woman with a newspaper possibly did take less interest than men in the news of politics and business, for she could do much less than a man with the knowledge she gained. This is best understood as a bargain between the sexes. By the middle of the nineteenth century the moral care of children was passed from fathers to mothers. By disclaiming their interest in public questions, many women gained unquestioned moral sway in the home. The mother achieved emotional bonds with children just as a mobile society threatened to strip her of daily contact with kin. Through family letters, women of the nineteenth century controlled a good part of the household's communication with the outside world. A patriarch settled in with his newspaper might act the part of family ruler, but the woman of the house controlled her own network beyond the hearth. Like other forms of femininity, the acceptance of males as the proper custodians of printed news shows care in choosing the battleground rather than weakness.[51]

But access to a paper and the leisure to read it were not male prerogatives, despite the stage settings of so many pictures and novels. It was a myth that women did not see the crime news, political polemics, and local color that enlivened so many American papers. "The good women of Kentucky" monitored the press, according to a letter in one of the first papers issued on this frontier. "You have observed that in the many pieces which crowd our press, not a single sentence is addressed to our sex," this feminist of 1787 complained. Many diaries, letters, and memoirs of the early republic show women following the news, sometimes furtively, sometimes in frustration, sometimes in triumph (as in Spencer's canvas). James Gordon Bennett saw this market in the 1830s when he congratulated himself on supplying his penny newspaper to the women of New York City. *Peterson's Ladies' National Magazine* knew that women watched the newspapers in the 1850s when it sent out specimen copies to country editors, expecting new sales as women read about the magazine in their local papers. This leading magazine for women offered discounts on newspapers to its subscribers. All the evidence that women did not read the news for themselves is really evidence about their acting, the scenarios women followed so as not to upstage men.[52]

Women made no show of attending to news, especially when men were on stage. Fathers and husbands held dramatic dominance with the newspaper. Women stepped out of character when they gripped a paper. By that simple act they drew attention to themselves in the first half of the nineteenth century. Caleb Atwater, an educator, antiquarian, and busybody, was typical of male fluster. He announced the discovery in 1829 of women in Lexington, Kentucky, who read newspapers to each other rather than novels. He praised their seriousness, but he was not an advocate of leaving women alone with the news. In a Philadelphia boarding house he intercepted a religious newspaper intended for a female resident. While the subscriber and the residents watched, Atwater read the paper, then stopped: "I instantly tossed it from me, as I would a rattle snake, or a scorpion, had it fallen into my hands." He had found the paper unsuitable. As the parlor erupted in laughter and questions, the subscriber had to defend her taste in newspapers. Atwater showed his readers just who was expected to monitor the news in the early republic: the man.[53]

The move toward equality with the newspaper is clear after mid-century. *Harper's Weekly* published its first picture of a woman reading a newspaper in 1865 (eight years after the founding of this illustrated magazine). That woman was Queen Victoria. Writers on the home suggested that women should take command of spreading news in their household. Lilly Martin Spencer's canvas was a sign of that assertiveness. Julia McNair Wright's *The Complete Home* (1879) advised mothers to have a member of their household read newspapers and magazines aloud so that a busy wife would be up-to-date. Other guides to behavior made news seem bliss. Women were not to worry about the time they spent keeping up "with the truth of the present" in journalism. It was old-fashioned to believe that unbound meant unworthy. Women readers were dared to read the news for themselves. "A splendid feeling it is; like the swimmer's delight of riding forward on great waves in the sea," one authority said. The feminist implications of a woman with a grip on the newspaper were made clear in Charles Dana Gibson's satire on women who wanted the vote. The newspaper had crossed the breakfast table, and the republic (or at least the male) was in peril.[54]

4. Imagined Communities

Bars, post offices, and parlors may seem unlikely places to see a nation taking shape, but these varied displays of news reading add to our understanding of what knit this society together.

Literacy itself was nurtured in these settings through the constant reinforce-

Charles Dana Gibson, "A Suffragette's Husband," from *Other People* (1911).
Special Collections, Stanford University Libraries.

ment of people using texts in daily life. Theorists who believe that reading skill is not so much taught in schools as it is absorbed through social contacts ought to be ready to strike medals to commemorate the humble places where Americans first learned that they were bound together by print. Nineteenth-century readers and publishers also showed one way to tackle the challenge of readers with uneven abilities. "Readability" in modern America came to mean short sentences and limited vocabulary as well as arresting headlines and pictures . . . all features that the early press did not have. And yet this journalism won and held readers. What was missing in these dense columns was made up in the social setting. Americans learned to read the news with the talk and the gestures that brought stories to life.[55]

The early republic was the first society in history to test what would happen when the printed page carried news for all. No nation at the beginning of the nineteenth century had a higher literacy rate or more freedom to put facts and opinions before the public. Could the government—indeed, could society itself—hold together as thousands of journalists gave their versions of the truth? Conservatives in Europe thought that this American experiment with an unfettered press was a prescription for anarchy. Many Europeans believed that a society without a unifying church, a vigilant bureaucracy, and a habit of obedience could not survive. Americans did not even follow the time-honored measures of keeping domestic peace, such as opening mail to thwart conspiracies and censoring dangerous papers. Conservatives were right that there were startling ideas about. The abuse of those who governed was so shrill in the press that even democrats such as Thomas Jefferson despaired. There was certainly a cacophony of ideas in the newspapers in an era that began with Tom Paine's contributions and ended with the regular columns, in major papers, by Karl Marx and American socialists. There were newspapers for every political faction, editors who spoke for workers and editors who sought to comfort the commercial classes. The women's movement, antislavery, temperance, and many other reforms issued newspapers. Evangelical churches and other signs of religious ferment were continually in the news. The fear that the government and society of 1789 would fall apart in this new world of print was not far-fetched.

Some of the ways that the early press led Americans to pull together have long been clear. Tocqueville observed that the press functioned as a safety valve, keeping the caldron of democracy cool. Newspapers popularized political life and became agents of that party formation and national leadership that gave cohesion to politics. It is not time to throw out these familiar observations, but it is important to notice what they do not tell us: *how* texts reached people. The meaning of the news was not simply the facts and arguments put in print. The setting of news reading was itself a powerful part of the message.

Nationalism, the great homogenizing idea of nineteenth-century America, was strengthened by the way people got their news. Benedict Anderson, an anthropologist who has studied nationalism in both Western and non-Western societies, has observed that news in print was a key element in creating the "imagined communities" that make nationalism possible. Newspapers demonstrate that one is bound together with a multitude engaged in steady, simultaneous activity, sharing a common culture and symbols. Many forms of political loyalty were expressed before newspapers and related media appeared, but modern nationalism was only possible with their arrival. A page of news demonstrates a community by the stories it contains. These make people and institutions that the reader cannot see real. The press also creates community in the opportunities it provides to see *others* absorbing the text. In the performance of reading before one another, this anthropologist found, "the imagined world is visibly rooted in everyday life."[56]

Americans of the nineteenth century could see this more clearly than any earlier generation in North America. Reading the news provided what other anthropologists have identified as a key element of "nationness," the "daily interactions and practices that produce an inherent and often unarticulated feeling of belonging, of being at home." It is suggestive that the most popular pictures of news reading marked the unfolding of national power, in the war with Mexico and the settlement of California, for example. Spencer's painting, in which the artist, her children, her servant, and, she hoped, her public, had patriotic sentiments drummed in as they shared in a reading, was simply the logical extension of a nationalism implicit in the customary ways of getting the news.[57]

A sense of the nation was not the only civics lesson. Other social norms were reinforced as people read the news. Community ties were demonstrated in the simple act of getting news because, at a minimum, some cooperation, some surrender of privacy, some tipping of the hand was called for. Public spaces displayed the diversity of arguments, revealing who read what; in homes, readers were watched and knew their place. Often, the setting for news was part of its message, for the setting required that a role be played. A Revolutionary soldier called to hear Tom Paine's observations on equality read out by officers is getting one interpretation about what equality means. A woman who sits at attention to hear a man read the news is being given information, but also a message of her proper role in deferring to men. A village that is surprised by the latest paper to reach a post office or tavern is being knit together. It is in these performances and the acceptance by most citizens of their roles that antebellum society showed the ability to act together. News in print was cohesive and coercive.

To see this, we need not embrace any modern theory of how communities of readers are formed with common agendas. We need only look at the performances around news that were noted by artists and writers of antebellum America. More simply, we need only agree with Noah Webster's observation on newspapers in 1793. Webster began volume 1, number 1 of his own paper by noting that "newspapers are not only vehicles of what is called *news;* they are common instruments of social intercourse, by which the Citizens of this vast Republic constantly discourse and debate with each other. . . . in times of danger . . . a unanimity of opinion is formed, from Maine to Georgia."[58]

Webster claimed too much for newspapers, of course, for a terrible Civil War did come to a nation of news readers. Americans could agree on what to argue about but exhaust peaceful solutions. The spread of news in some circumstances heightened fear and distrust. As we shall see in a later chapter, where news in print extended its reach, it was more feared. Throughout the South, and among some Northern elites, the prospect of news for all triggered riot and revolt. In some social settings of antebellum America it was possible to believe that enemies possessed texts with diabolical power. The menace of news was to upset, for a time, the political equilibrium created by a free press. Eventually, the deference of one class to another, of one sex to another, and of one race to another would also break down as newspapers prospered. This, of course, does not make the equilibrium established in the first place by news less important.

The politics of the early republic rested on accommodations as profound as the famous compromises between states and branches of government that made the national government possible. The underlying question for this political culture was to define how a citizen should act in a democracy. One historian has drawn attention to the "deferential-participant" phase as citizens accepted older forms of political leadership before the mobilization of voters into modern parties.[59] The phrase is a good description of the structure of attitudes reinforced by news in print. Passivity *and* self-assertion, conformity *and* defiance: these contrasting roles were built into the ritual of getting the news. Whether the news prompted action or a shrug, there was reinforcement from fellow citizens. For women, for blacks, and for many citizens of humble status, the reading of news was one position of power that seemed within reach. News for all had the potential to free every American to go his or her own way, but the performance of reading the news bound the public together through much of the nineteenth century.

2

THE
OLD-FASHIONED
CIRCULATION
DRIVE

Journalists in the early republic faced obstacles to expansion that were as daunting as the mountain ranges that hemmed in the Americans. Pushing ahead with circulation looked to be perilous in most directions.

There was nothing to ensure that an underdeveloped ex-colony could build its own communication system. The United States of 1789 was backward in the production of paper, ink, and type, no match for the shops of Europe. To judge by the smudgy look of newspapers and magazines when the nation began, this form of printing was not an enterprise of great promise. News in print was born in the cities on the coast with their international trade and common life in market squares, coffee houses, and legislatures. As Americans of the nineteenth century spread across the land in small communities and isolated homesteads, they might have left this press behind. Few newcomers from Europe took newspapers as an entitlement. In the British Isles, popular journalism was discouraged by taxation; in the Russian Empire it was severely censored; in German-speaking lands, the tax man and other bureaucrats harassed readers and printers. African Americans had little heritage of a print culture, and their masters tried to keep news out of slave hands.

If the American press had failed in the early republic, historians would have no trouble explaining its demise. Had the press withered, we could point to the many peoples who came to this land with no habit of following

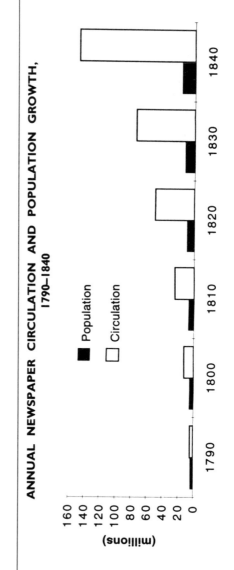

Chart 2.1 Source: adapted from Allan R. Pred, *Urban Growth and the Circulation of Information* (Cambridge, Mass., 1973), Table 2.1.

ANNUAL NEWSPAPER CIRCULATION AND POPULATION GROWTH, 1790–1840

Population
Circulation

(millions)

160
140
120
100
80
60
40
20
0

1790 1800 1810 1820 1830 1840

journalism. Had newspapers and magazines lost favor, we could point to backward technology and a wave of immigrants who discarded a cultural form of the eighteenth century as they did with powdered wigs and the minuet.

At the very least, a lag of newspapers behind population growth might have been expected as Americans filled the new land. But what happened in the first half century of the United States was something quite different. (See Chart 2.1.)

Magazines faced longer odds than newspapers when the nation began, for this form of journalism had never known success in North America. In 1800 British magazines seemed sufficient to meet the small market for belles lettres in the United States. No American publisher was able to make headway against these imports in the first quarter of the new century. But here too, Americans became a nation of faithful readers. A vast army of subscribers was raised that had never been seen before.

There are familiar and sound explanations for the triumph of both newspapers and magazines. Here is a synopsis of this good sense:

> The American republic, in contrast to Europe, was a nation of readers, with public education here pushing the literacy rate above 90 percent. At first, circulation gains came from upstart papers in new communities. A flat-bed press with a used set of type could be loaded onto a wagon or barge and set up in settlements of a few hundred. Land claims and sales, requiring legal notices, subsidized the printer's business until a full commercial life arose to support a paper. The nationalistic impulse for their own literature led printers of this period to risk bringing out magazines and steeled them against failures. In the 1830s new presses in the older cities boosted circulation. Publishers learned the manufacturing processes needed to produce the printed page in quantity, driving the cost of each issue down.
>
> The press won readers throughout the nineteenth century because Americans on the make had no better tool than the newspaper, with its ads, prices current, and advice on markets. Magazines were a gallery for the clothing, home furnishings, and tools that women and men prized. Most newspapers carried the mother's milk of politics: stories of party strife, the speeches of leaders, the hints about jobs or favors to be won. There were many other lures in the nation's press: agricultural information, fiction and sensational reports, religious news . . . the periodicals of the United States served every taste.
>
> Strangers in the land, even strangers to newspapers, quickly acquired the habit of following the news. In 1850 there were more German-language dailies in New York than in Berlin. In one decade, an average of one German newspaper started up each month in the United States. The number of weekly issues in this language frequently exceeded the number of German-speaking households. In 1894, the peak of this avalanche of ethnic journalism, the United States supported ninety-seven German-language dailies. As blacks won freedom, they won newspapers—both their own and the press of white America. Jews who had no tradition of news reading in the shtetls of Eastern Europe made a similar

discovery of journalism. Language, class, race, and religion set Americans apart, but all shared the habit of taking a favorite paper.[1]

This is not wrong. And it is known so well by students of the press that, like the smooth curve of the circulation figures, it sweeps other questions away. The readers, the people who made this revolution in journalism, remain hidden. It is the people we must understand, for the rise of the press cannot be fully explained by the familiar narrative of circulation given above.

Take the miraculous growth of printing technology. The first use of the steam press was to turn out tracts for evangelicals. The application to secular purposes and current events was an afterthought, a decision that was not inevitable. Technological innovation in printing news does not guarantee a larger public. Publishers of the second half of the twentieth century have learned this lesson.

However powerful the content of the press, this by itself does not explain the explosive circulation. Nothing forces people to be entertained and informed by journalism. Face-to-face communication and oral tradition have been sufficient for most people in most historical eras. Even a literate population in which following the news has become a way of life may backslide and lose interest in journalism. Americans of all age groups reported less use of newspapers in the 1990s than in the 1960s (and reliance on broadcast journalism went *down* as well for Americans under age fifty.) In the later half of the twentieth century, newspaper circulation failed to even match population growth. Why was the nineteenth century so different?

A history of consumer habit and publisher promotion is needed to see why newspapers and magazines became a part of everyday life. Rather than assuming a marketplace of eager buyers and rational sellers from the trajectory of sales, we must see just how the buyers and sellers treated each other. Circulation was driven by volatile readers, fickle in their tastes and steady in their resentments. Beyond self-interests, they found new forms of community through subscription. In this uneasy alliance between selfishness and concern for others, Americans became a nation of news readers.

1. Deadbeat Readers

The account books of Americans of the nineteenth century give a precise picture of the cost of news. In the 1860s the farmer William Lewis of Greene County, New York, paid $2.00 annually for the *Journal of Commerce*. This is what he made when he churned five pounds of butter. He paid $2.50 for the *Recorder & Democrat*, his price for a cord of wood from his farm. This was not the end of the expense, for Lewis had to pay the postage, amounting each year to the price of a pint of bourbon for each paper. Ella Clanton Thomas of

Augusta, Georgia, measured journalism in the same careful way. She began the year by selling three dresses in order to subscribe to *Appleton's Journal* and *Harper's Monthly*. She worried about extravagance and noted in her journal that the full cost of "cultivating my mind" included fees to a seamstress which allowed her time to read. Lewis and Thomas were typical in that a subscription was a measure of hard labor or sacrifice of another pleasure. In their dutiful budgeting and prompt payments, however, these were not true representatives of the American reader. This yeoman and matron were a journalist's dream; the reality gave journalists little rest.[2]

Publishers knew all too well that a great many American homesteads could not easily pay for newspapers and magazines. Before the Civil War, banks did not offer checks, the postal system did not issue money orders, and the federal government did not print currency. The haphazard issuing of notes from local banks often left citizens short of cash (William Lewis and Ella Thomas were both fortunate to get their hands on currency). Publishing was often a barter trade. Country papers announced they would settle bills for crops. Newspaper offices took in flax and wool, cheeses and feathers. Journalists came to accept cattle, hides, beeswax, and rags in payment for the news. "Pay in Any Thing" a newspaper in Maine printed on its first page. In 1845 the owner of the Memphis *Commercial Appeal* announced that he would accept payment for the paper in any product he could use in his household. William Dean Howells, the novelist, remembered his family taking a pig for a year's subscription to their small paper in Ohio.[3]

This flexible credit policy did not protect the newspaper from delinquents. The "persevering negligence of far the greater part of our customers" was as old a tradition in America as journalism itself. John Peter Zenger, after his celebrated trial for standing up to authority in the 1730s, complained in his paper that "some of these Subscribers are in Arrears upward of 7 years!" Even the alert Benjamin Franklin confessed that some founding subscribers of the *Pennsylvania Gazette* received the paper for eleven years *"without paying me one Farthing."*[4]

Editors of the nineteenth century told the same story. Of all American vices, non-payment of subscriptions was among the most egalitarian. It was the scourge of ladies' magazines and literary journals as well as newspapers. The bill for news went unpaid in both grand and humble homes. Former President James Madison fell three years behind in paying for a newspaper, to the despair of the editor. Former President John Tyler asked for an extension on his bill for the *Southern Literary Messenger* until his crops were in. This magazine for the planter class sent out a card with its issue of October 1855 pleading for payment, and the "disgrace" of these subscribers was widely noted in the Southern press. Gerrit Smith, a land baron in upstate New York, was never short of cash for his household accounts or for the cause of antislavery. But Smith fell several years behind in payments to the *Liberator*. "It is a long time since I have paid anything on my subscription," Smith confessed in 1853. William Johnson, a free black man of Natchez, Mississippi, noted in his diary the payment of twenty-seven dollars to a leading New York newspaper that he had taken for nine years. "I wish I had paid for it before now," Johnson said. (This was a month's wages for a white worker and more money than most blacks saw in a year.) Agricultural newspapers carried many readers on their books who were pushing toward a decade of non-payment. *The New England Farmer* announced receipt of forty-two dollars in 1845 from a subscriber who owed for twenty-one years.[5]

Howells said that the country printer of the nineteenth century learned to expect "a large and loyal list of delinquent subscribers." This is indeed what the surviving business records show. On some agricultural papers at mid-century, the delinquents on the books were growing to be as numerous as the current circulation.[6] (See Chart 2.2.)

These are not extreme examples of forlorn publishers. Early papers in the Midwest had little success in getting either cash or produce from subscribers. In 1822 the *Illinois Gazette* sang,

> How oft our *Editors* display,
> Their talents in the *dunning way!*

"The great majority of subscribers do not even *dream* of paying—their idea of *'taking the paper'* is merely *paying the postage,*" another printer said. Illinois "subscribers" were notorious in the office of the Springfield *Register*. Started up in 1839, the paper had more annual subscriptions in arrears than there were residents of Springfield in the mid-1840s. A Michigan printer recalled that the reader of this era would take a paper for three or four years and then become angry at being asked to pay up in full. He "only subscribed for the paper in the first place to help it along."[7]

The South's lower literacy rate and greater restrictions on blacks made reading the news more of an elite pastime, but printers learned patience as they waited for these privileged subscribers to pay up. The *Southern Quarterly Review*, which often took ten thousand words to warm to its subjects, printed a brief notice that, after five years of serious journalism, its circulation exactly matched its accumulation of unpaid subscriptions. Country folk who simply wanted the news of the day were also slow to settle accounts. The founder of the *Arkansas Gazette* was horrified to find that half of his subscribers in the first year had no intention of sending payment. In the decades before the Civil War, both the Raleigh *Constitutionalist* and the San Antonio *Ledger and Texan* said that just one subscriber in ten was paid up. After Thomas Ritchie of Virginia had spent three decades making the Richmond *Enquirer* into a Democratic Bible and given his party a lease on the White House he said, "Our cornucopias

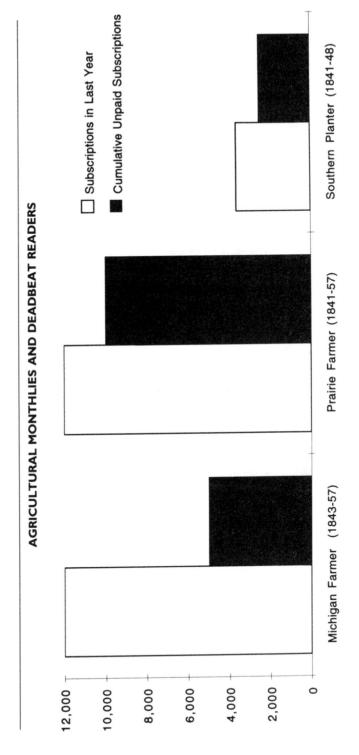

Chart 2.2 Source: note #6.

AGRICULTURAL MONTHLIES AND DEADBEAT READERS

☐ Subscriptions in Last Year
■ Cumulative Unpaid Subscriptions

Michigan Farmer (1843-57)

Prairie Farmer (1841-57)

Southern Planter (1841-48)

12,000
10,000
8,000
6,000
4,000
2,000
0

are filled, but not with gold and silver nor even with bank notes, but with our subscriber's bills." These were the equivalent of three million 1990s dollars when Ritchie left the paper. The *Arkansas State Democrat* collected nothing from nearly a quarter of its subscribers during its early years, 1846-50. The Nashville *Union & American* was forced to demand payment in advance from all subscribers in 1859. In doing this the editors thanked readers who paid with their subscription "or have not permitted their indebtedness to accumulate beyond one or two years, at most." This the editors called "punctuality."[8]

Whole classes of pious Americans showed cavalier disregard of subscriptions due. Delinquents bedeviled religious newspapers. The Salt Lake City *Deseret News* was sold by the Mormon clergy and priced so that everyone on the Utah frontier could make payment. The newspaper accepted prairie-chickens and bear, shingles as well as poles in addition to farm products. Subscribers could settle accounts by digging a canal for Salt Lake City. Nonetheless, delinquents troubled the Latter-Day Saints. After fourteen years, the circulation revenue was well below the debts run up by subscribers. Protestant editors in the Midwest also watched their bills to readers go unpaid.[9] (See Chart 2.3.)

No region, no religion, produced readers who could be relied on to pay for news from the clergy. *The Texas Christian Advocate* claimed a larger circulation than any paper in the state before the Civil War, but it also appeared to have the largest number of deadbeat readers: two thousand of its forty-five hundred subscribers failed to pay. *The Texas Baptist* reported that more than 60 percent of its readers had not bothered to pay for a year. The *Catholic Telegraph* of Cincinnati said that 841 of its 1,200 subscribers were in arrears. In the upper South, about a third of the subscribers to the official magazine of the Methodist Episcopal church refused to pay. These readers were unmoved by knowledge that their church paper provided income for widows and orphans of deceased ministers. The editor ran an announcement in 1839 pleading for five thousand dollars from subscribers: "More than this is due, but we will content ourselves for the present with the above, *if we can get it.*" Ministers of the United Brethren in Christ were told to ask every household they visited if their subscription was paid up to the church paper. The clergy could keep 10 percent of what they collected from delinquents. To no avail.[10]

The editor Luther Stone had won two thousand Baptist subscribers to the *Watchman of the Prairies* in 1851, but many of these required close watching. With the enterprise only six years old, Stone needed a hundred-page account book solely for delinquents. Stone's book notes some distinctive excuses ("refused: wants to read his Bible"), but the Baptist readers who had neglected this publication sound like their fellow Americans: "gone to California" and "left for parts unknown" and "impudent" and "irresponsible" and "honest, but poor & slack" and "hopeless & bad." The Rev. Stone made plans to sue some of these readers of the good news of Christ.[11]

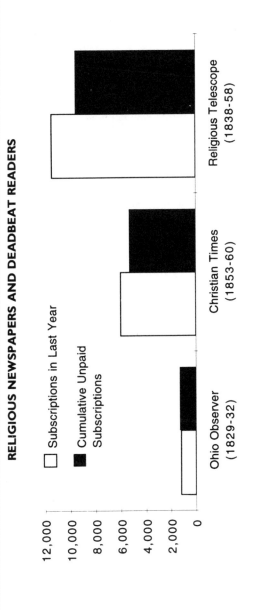

Chart 2.3 Source: note #9.

RELIGIOUS NEWSPAPERS AND DEADBEAT READERS

☐ Subscriptions in Last Year

■ Cumulative Unpaid Subscriptions

Ohio Observer (1829-32)

Christian Times (1853-60)

Religious Telescope (1838-58)

12,000
10,000
8,000
6,000
4,000
2,000
0

In the mature cities of the East Coast, courts were an effective threat to extract subscription debts, but the struggle with delinquents continued. In 1805 a New York editor working for Alexander Hamilton complained that "not one in a hundred" subscribers paid on time and 30 per cent never paid. In Philadelphia the *Franklin Journal* would seem to have attracted an attentive readership in the 1820s, for it was a digest of mechanical and scientific advances. Yet the editors sounded the alarm of American journalists everywhere: "that very few of our distant subscribers have paid us, and that more than one-half even of our Philadelphia patrons, owe for the year." Boston was no better. Joseph T. Buckingham edited a leading New England paper for four decades under the "distressing embarrassment" of readers who would not pay his bills. "Never had a periodical a better list of subscribers," the editor mused about the short life of the *Boston Quarterly Review* (1838–42). Orestes Augustus Brownson, a man of formidable erudition, admitted that his readers "were few, but they were serious, honest, earnest, affectionate." Brownson's towering intellect had not grasped a fact that his publisher's correspondence makes clear, viz. that his philosophical journal was stiffed in this period: "I have crossed off the list many (subscribers) who owed back debts & would not pay. This is very provoking."[12]

Two of the best-known editors of the early republic, William Duane of the Philadelphia *Aurora* (1798–1822) and Duff Green of the Washington *United States Telegraph* (1826–37), ran up astonishing uncollected subscription bills in the service to their political patrons. These journalists catered to every reader's budget, offering the news in editions that came out daily, two or three times a week, and weekly. They claimed a larger circulation than any newspaper of their time. Both men acknowledged about eighty thousand dollars in bad debts from subscribers. That sum was nearly twice the annual revenue from subscriptions earned by any daily paper in the early republic.[13]

So unpromising were the debts on the *Aurora's* books that the ledgers were used as fuel. Horace Greeley, who was to become America's most celebrated editor, sounded just as desperate as he piloted a small paper in New York through the financial panic of 1837. He filled columns with the "species of knavery" that allowed subscribers to evade his small bills. Greeley said that he would gladly give away his paper to anyone who would pay him half the money owed by readers. The few surviving subscription books of the antebellum period show readers in no hurry to pay. A Chicago *Democrat* ledger of 1836 had only 45 percent of subscribers paid in full for this newspaper. The New York *Star* found 54 percent of its subscribers delinquent in a two-year period. Court costs to try and wring payment from readers was a common entry on the books in New York. "Bad" and "Bad, very Bad" the accountants marked the readers. Other entries were evaluations of subscribers that must have been common oaths in the print shops and editorial offices of the nation: "good for nothing . . . ran away . . . gone west . . . never found." These worldly New

Yorkers behaved no better than the Baptists who took the *Watchman of the Prairies*. In Georgia, editors regularly went to public meetings, not to cover the proceedings, but to collect from the subscribers they would meet. The journalists of Boston, New York, and Philadelphia sent collection agents through the country looking for deadbeats, just as provincial editors came to the biggest cities to present subscribers with their bills. Newspapers threatened to humiliate their delinquents by publishing their names. Horace Greeley did this to survive in 1837. The practice spread west. In the 1840s the St. Clairsville (Ohio) *Gazette* ran a "Black List" of subscriber deadbeats and the La Porte (Ind.) *Herald* published the names of readers in its "Loafer's Department." Frontier editors of the next generation filled columns with the names of deadbeats.[14]

The dunning and delinquency cited here put subscribers in too kind a light. These are the sorry business records of the press that soldiered on, year after year carrying arrearages. What of the failed newspapers and magazines who did not survive long enough to complain? An Iowa editor, in his last issue, spoke for all disappointed printers:

> Would you know the cause, dear readers,
>   Why the paper stops to-day?
> 'Tis because so many of you
>   OWE THE PRINTER AND WON'T PAY.[15]

The cries from publishers, enlivened by sarcasm and exclamation points, caught the attention of foreign observers. In 1841 a London magazine reported that "probably in no other country where newspapers exist do the subscribers trouble themselves less about finding the means of paying their newspaper subscriptions when due, than they do in the United States." The negligent reading public in the New World became a national embarrassment. In 1826 *Franklin's Journal* used an insert slip to dun American subscribers which it kept out of issues sent abroad. The editors did not want Europeans to see the shame of readers in the United States.[16]

Critics of the national character missed the point. Readers could not slip behind for *years* without publishers willing to carry them into that hole. Publishers were force feeders. They did not cancel when subscribers turned away. The journalists extended subscriptions, hoping to shame the public into compliance.

Printers clung to subscribers in defiance of all obstacles. The *Southern Literary Messenger*, for example, threatened readers for seven years before finally deciding to stop sending the magazine. On January 19, 1807, the publisher of the *Ohio Gazette* noted that a good share of the readers, two hundred subscribers, had paid him nothing since he began publishing two years earlier and that he was out of paper. Still, there was to be no pruning of the list. The *Ohio*

Gazette reminded subscribers that "no person's paper will be discontinued until arrearages are paid up." Mastheads in the young republic defied the reader to turn away. "Failing to notify a discontinuance, at the end of an engagement, will be considered a wish to renew it," a paper in Delaware, Ohio, announced. This was typical. "The editor will reserve to himself the right to discontinue," readers learned. In 1854 an Ohio editor showed an uncharacteristic softening as his paper announced it would stop subscriptions when "we are satisfied that the subscriber is worthless."[17]

Publishing practices were codified into "Laws of Newspapers" and endlessly reprinted on mastheads at mid-century:

1. Subscribers who do not give express notice to the contrary, are considered as wishing to continue their subscription.

2. If subscribers order the discontinuance of their periodicals, the publisher may continue to send them till all arrearages are paid and subscribers are responsible for all the numbers sent.

3. If subscribers neglect or refuse to take their periodical from the office to which they are directed, they are held responsible till they have settled their bills, and ordered them discontinued.

4. If subscribers remove to other places without informing the publishers, and their periodicals are sent to their former direction they are held responsible.

The "Laws of Journalism" were a folklore of the printing trade, with no basis in postal regulations. But publishers abided by them. This meant that nothing short of a renunciation of the paper and full payment could stop the cascade of newspapers and bills. Like a sharecropper on the books of a calculating landowner, the reader had few chances to move on. It is not hard to understand why, by mid-century, some papers had a fourth or even half of their subscribers in arrears. Here were business transactions between pretenders. Readers pretended to be subscribers, and publishers pretended they had paying customers.[18]

Journalists sometimes acknowledged the self-deception here. James Wilson, the gruff Ulsterman who was grandfather to President Woodrow Wilson, thought that the newspaper business lived on empty hope. From his print shop in Steubenville, Ohio, it seemed to Wilson that "there are already more newspapers than can find readers and more readers than can pay attention to the terms of subscription." This was in 1818. Printers accused one another of a "forced and unnatural" newspaper circulation as the land filled with newspapers. The editors simply plunged ahead.[19]

Swaggering defiance united publisher and deadbeat subscriber. The journalist pushed the paper into the household that defied him. The reader accepted the dare. This battle was recorded in a survey of delinquents in the South at mid-century. One Aaron Sweatwell, a collection agent, spent three months calling on more than a hundred debtors for a South Carolina paper. Sweatwell found only one subscriber who had simply forgotten to pay and was willing to square the account. This man was "an oasis in the desert." The others filled the agent's notebook with a critique of the paper. A minister said that "he knows from the tone of your editorials that you drink, and paying you would only be the means of your ending your days in the kennel." A doctor cursed the editor for insulting his profession. An unmarried woman denounced newspaper references to old maids and "wouldn't pay you if she was rolling in wealth, and you hadn't cash enough to buy a crust of bread." A gambler complained of skimpy coverage of horse races and cock fights. "Liked the description of the prize fight most amazingly," the agent reported; "it redeemed a multitude of your faults." A policeman "thinks he has seen a considerable squinting towards the side to which he is opposed. Meant to have told you a year ago to stop his paper but forgot it. Tells you to do so now, and thinks you are getting off very cheaply in not losing any more by him." So it went on Aaron Sweatwell's travels. Insults and curses were the only substantial payment to the newspaper. The cash extracted was 3.12\frac{1}{2}$.[20]

Most deadbeats were not so angry as to stop reading, as their critiques demonstrated. The publisher, on the other hand, had been rubbing sores by continuing the subscription after the reader had taken offense. Agent Sweatwell placed most accounts under the general heading "mean as rot." The circulation of news in this young democracy was often exactly that.

The bad marriage of printer and subscriber lasted because it was curiously satisfying to each party. The publisher's commitment was built around stubbornness and pride. A reader who was piling up debts might someday pay something; to cut that household off was to lose hope in ever squaring accounts. The marginal cost of supplying a paper to a deadbeat was low, especially during the first half of the century when publishers did not pay the postage. Circulation numbers, however achieved, allowed a publisher to count for something. They were part of the bragging ritual of an expanding market economy.

The subscriber might also take satisfaction — in running up a bill. Social scientists have described debt as a career of passive deviance that many people enjoy, and the heady growth of American democracy surely made this tempting. "Solicitation appears to be agreeable to many of you," the printer of the Norfolk (Va.) *Herald* told his readers after dunning many of them for five years. The reader was inflicting punishment, not just getting something for nothing. Not paying the printer, like not paying the doctor, was a way of expressing resentment and leveling sentiment. Wisconsin printers of the 1840s told readers to "fork over immediately" and "cash in hand enter your names for subscriptions, and think yourselves happy for the chance." In the age of Davy Crockett and Andy Jackson, this was to wave a red flag before an American. The young republic wrote laws to make collection difficult, and penalties for debtors were notoriously lax. Mrs. Frances Trollope, in her study of American manners, amazed her British audience by publishing the pleas of a sheriff, no less, who begged delinquents for taxes long due. It was part of the democratic ethos to let debt slide and a dangerous step, politically, to asked to be paid up.[21]

This was a message that the professional classes were inclined to send, no less than the common folk. For if this elite was not being paid, why not join the game and show the common touch? In a note of good cheer written in 1839, an Alabama lawyer discussed his subscription to a paper being published by his classmate and friend. Keep the paper coming, this reader said, but don't expect payment soon: "Why should I pay the Editors when the people will not pay the Lawyers[?]" The circulation of news in print exploded in the United States at the very time that debt itself seemed an entitlement. Had publishers reached only those Americans who paid up cheerfully, journalists would have slept more soundly. But there would not have been a vast market to dream about. Without the willingness to carry deadbeats along, far fewer Americans would have made news in print a part of their lives.[22]

Journalism is information and entertainment that can easily seem a citizen's due in a democracy. The idea of news as a public good was promoted by the Founding Fathers and enshrined in the First Amendment. Let the means of collection be weak and Americans will take the media for free with a sense of entitlement they would not have in filching another commodity. The "cable pirates" of television at the end of the twentieth century were another expression of this "gallant banditry." Cable companies counted their losses as more than four billion dollars a year, a quarter of their revenues, and produced estimates of as much as 20 percent of "subscribers" in some communities who found a way to get programs for free. Cable operators echoed the cries of nineteenth-century publishers in expressing amazement that people from all walks of life would do this to them. They might also blame historians who have left the impression that the audience drawn to mass media in the first place, played fair. The standard handbook on circulation, for instance, tells the industry that newspapers "ended the bad debt burden" in the eighteenth century. This is not history; it is wishful thinking.[23]

Cable companies are cheated, in part, because the public finds them arrogant. Modern newspapers drill their marketing staff on this lesson: "People who like you pay you first." And as collector Sweatwell found out, a vague sense that the printer was up to no good made subscribers bad and bold. According to one doggerel verse of the young republic, subscribers thought of printers as hibernating bears, with no need for food or warmth. The renowned William Dean Howells agreed with Mark Twain (his fellow country printer) that their craft perplexed Americans. Howells said that villagers "cannot understand why he does not take up something else, something respectable and remunerative; they feel that there must be something weak, something wrong in a man who is willing to wear his life out in a vocation which keeps him poor and dependent on the favor they grudge him." A New England magazine put the matter more bluntly: the typical young printer who started a newspaper took on airs, sponged off creditors, "and then with a flea in his ear, and a lie in his mouth, makes a pitiable complaint about his misfortunes." The hostility to printers as over-reachers echoed through the Congress after the election of Andrew Jackson. The lawyer-legislators refused to "swallow the printers" whom this Democrat wanted to reward with political office. President Jackson had to make the difficult argument that it was not "improper to appoint printers to offices of honor or emolument." Ignoring the printer's bill was made easier because the newspaper sprang from a craft that seemed mysterious, misguided, and, sometimes, touched with both larceny and social climbing.[24]

The intransigence of publishers and readers yielded to the new business practice that swept the newspaper business after mid-century: payment in advance. "No man," Horace Greeley said, "need hesitate to subscribe from an apprehension of being dunned for arrears." Printers had dreamed of this since the eighteenth century, but now they managed the feat. Those blustering "Laws of Journalism" came off of mastheads, and subscribers who did not pay were dropped from the lists. There was delay and backsliding in enforcing the new rules for readers, and the South was the last region to tighten the subscriber's credit, but in the end the market was transformed. Readers now made a commitment to their newspaper, or they lost it. Publishers of metropolitan papers boasted that nearly every issue from their presses reached a paying customer. A trade journal at the end of the century called for a statue or painting to memorialize the American newspaper reader and specified that this hero *look like* he was paid up. Art would capture "the self conscious and self-approving look of the man who remembers that he has paid for his paper" as a glory of "the perfected American Newspaper Reader of to-day."[25]

2. Bonded Readers

Many Americans defied printers while taking their news, but there was more to the act of subscription than selfishness. "Subscriptions" in nineteenth-century America were demonstrations of civic-mindedness. Collecting names with the pledge to pay was the way communities built their lodge halls and churches, even their canals and railroads. It was no wonder that subscribing seemed a natural thing to do when the printer came around. A subscription to the early American press was a compact between equals which drew the reader into a community. "Subscriber" did not mean simply "customer." The term embraced both journalist and reader and suggested mutual obligation. A subscriber was, literally, a name entered on a piece of paper. Publishers referred to themselves as "subscribers" as they signed their names to a prospectus, "humbly hoping for suitable encouragement." The standard prospectus stated the terms and promised instruction, amusement, and unsparing efforts to please. A citizen who wanted this type of news signed a document, the "subscription paper," pledging to pay. This form was passed around, like a petition, and the list of loyal readers then returned to the printer.[26]

As newspapers grew larger and came to serve the interests of national parties, the publisher lost humility and the readership fell under heavier demands. With Andrew Jackson's campaign for the presidency in 1828, newspaper extras "lined, filled — inundated" districts as election day neared. Now the reader was pledging loyalty to a good cause with the subscription, and the publisher promised action. This was the subscription drive carried out by a journalist close to Jackson in order to keep the White House for the Democrats in 1836. Amos Kendall sought support for a newspaper "intended to reach EVERY NEIGHBORHOOD IN THE UNION. . . . Will you take the trouble for the sake of our good cause, *to raise a subscription.* [?]" Kendall elected his ticket. He was back at it for the Democrats in 1840. Using his office of Postmaster General, he instructed thousands of postmasters to get busy and sell the party's election special, the *Extra Globe,* to "every farmer, mechanic, and workingman." As the subscriptions rolled into Washington, government clerks opened the letters and enrolled the readers. This was as it should be, given the premise of nineteenth-century newspapers that government itself would be used to shepherd subscribers.[27]

Politicians of the nineteenth century used circulation to make their party conscious of itself. Region or religion, class or crop, faction or fellowship — these interests made distinctive kinds of party men. The circulation of news could inspire the fractious public to draw together. At mid-century, the Democrat's leading journal published the names of twenty-four hundred readers of the magazine's four thousand circulation. The *Democratic Review* had subscribers in thirty-four states spread out in more than five hundred communities. This subscription list was led by scores of congressmen. The long columns of names had a revealing heading: "Ourselves." The recognition by readers that they formed a community of the like-minded was one of the achievements of political journalism.[28]

Opponents of the Democrats in Congress were also busy creating a network of subscribers. For example, Rep. Elisha Whittlesey braved the March weather in Ohio to check on his constituents' reading in 1831. He supervised the circulation drive of his party's Washington newspaper through Trumbull County. This veteran congressman collected the names of potential subscribers and cooperative postmasters. "The people in this district are much a reading people," Whittlesey said, and he managed his constituents by paying close attention to their choice of news.[29]

The modern Republican party took shape in the 1850s with the help of newspaper subscription drives. Joseph Medill, one of the party founders, used his Chicago *Tribune* to give subscribers the sense that they were partners in party growth. The *Tribune* issued not one prospectus but many as the party faced new challenges. The reader was to renew commitment with a subscription. In the secession winter of 1860-61 customers were told that through the *Tribune* they could stand up to the "slave holding oligarchy." The 1865 prospectus said that "after four years of desperate conflict, the principles, for which THE TRIBUNE in common with patriotic soldiers and citizens has contended, have achieved their enduring triumph. The Union men and women of the great republic have won the most important victory since the dawn of the Christian era." The *Tribune* always detailed the valuable news and features it would publish in the year ahead, but it was clearly selling something beyond good reading. A subscription sealed a promise that the journalist would make the good fight (employing every weapon—Medill, like Kendall, enlisted postmasters in his circulation drive). One's name on the subscription rolls empowered the party. No wonder the paper received letters from surrounding states saying, "The thanks of all Republicans of this region are due to you."[30]

The compact between editors and readers of the nineteenth century was forgotten, at great cost to journalism. Publishers with ready capital did not need readers' names on a sheet. Partisanship and party work became an embarrassment to the profession of journalism. And so fewer promises were made by newspapers, and readers heard less often of their own ties to the journalist. Finally, both the public and the press forgot that a subscription had ever forged a community, and the bright new idea in publishing was to establish such a relationship. "The idea of a social contract that binds newspapers and their readers is itself new, " the *New Yorker* said as it reported on newspaper publishers' ideas for the 1980s. In fact, such a social bond had drawn mass readership in the first place.[31]

The tradition of community building through subscription drives did not make for a homogenized society. Just the reverse, it built diversity. The cultivation of readers in the field was a major enterprise of the dissenting press of the nineteenth century. The journalism for antislavery, women's rights, and socialism was sustained by agents who won an audience for new arguments. Elijah P. Lovejoy, struggling to find fifteen hundred subscribers for his new antislavery paper in Alton, Illinois, was cheered by the arrival of eighty subscriptions secured by agents in a single week in the fall of 1836. Abby Kelley, a feminist who lived her life on dusty roads and in lecture halls filled with curses, sustained antislavery papers with her skill at signing up readers. This indefatigable lecturer put seven hundred subscribers on the books of an abolitionist newspaper one summer. The agent could be midwife in the labor of changing minds. Few seem to have believed that the texts of the movement, by themselves, would be persuasive. J. T. Everett explained in a letter to the *Liberator*, the most famous masthead for antislavery, how others could win their neighbors to the cause. He did not place much stock in the power of the writing in the *Liberator:* "Before any minds can appreciate the matter of its columns, they must be, to a great extent delivered from the power and tyranny of sect—from the bewitching influence and idolatry of party politics—from the omnipotent sway of popular opinion." Everett asked abolitionists to watch for signs of their neighbor's enlightenment and then, "at the proper time, present the Liberator for subscription." The agent was to be the "moral thermometer" of the community.[32]

The radical press put its faith in the power of agents. The Chicago *Vorbote* (Herald), founded in 1874 by socialists, deployed twenty-four subscription agents in eighteen cities in its first two years. By 1913 the *Appeal to Reason* of Girard, Kansas, had fielded an "Appeal army" of about eighty thousand subscription agents in every state, an unparalleled effort to build a radical reading public. In Benton Harbor, Michigan, for example, the *Appeal* was known as "Southworth's paper" after the persistent agent who gathered seventy or eighty subscriptions each year from this corner of small-town America. One agent sold more than one hundred thousand subscriptions for socialist papers in two decades of work across seventeen states.[33]

Capitalism was on the march at the same time, of course. James H. McGraw, founder of the McGraw-Hill firm of business and technical publishing, found his calling after one summer as a subscription agent. In 1884, travelling by horse cars in the city and by stagecoach in the countryside, McGraw was able to sign up scores of readers every week for a new magazine that promised a new age of transportation. McGraw gave up his career as a teacher, concluding there was more money in journalism if audiences could be formed so easily.[34]

Subscription drives built up national networks of readers at the same time they created clusters of the like-minded in local communities. The cohesion here was sometimes political. Horace Greeley's New York *Weekly Tribune* was gospel to many who had moved west, and the paper was blamed for creating communities of heretics. Antislavery sentiment was the most dangerous bond between readers. In East Tennessee and trans-Appalachian Virginia, where many whites broke with Southern conservatives on slavery, there was a clandestine network of subscribers to antislavery publications. A Virginian was indicted in 1856 for forming a club to subscribe to Greeley's paper. The safer party struggles after the Civil War were guided by city papers with large outlying readerships. In Glen Falls, some two hundred miles up the Hudson, the leading Republican and Democratic paper of New York City had a quarter of the circulation of the party papers published locally.[35]

The "clubbing" of newspaper readers had a long history due to the economies for both publisher and subscriber. By 1800 many printers in New England had the happy thought of raising "companies" of readers in neighboring towns who would take turns in distributing their paper, a practice that became widespread. The postal law of 1852 that shifted most postage costs to publishers encouraged the pooling of subscribers by cutting rates for papers sent to a single address. Journalists slashed their subscription rates for these clubs. Political parties relied on them. "Send in Your Clubs," an Alabama publisher called in the 1860 election as he noticed that Democratic papers with "fratricidal designs" were spreading through the state. A circulation drive, the Montgomery *Advertiser* said, could save Alabama. Similar alarms rang out from publishers' offices in the North. "If the ascendancy of the Republican party is to be maintained," the Chicago *Tribune* advertised, ". . . a Tribune Campaign Club is needed in every neighborhood in the West, to supply the people with reliable facts and correct political information." In the closely fought Hayes-Tilden contest of 1876, the *Tribune* offered a weekly edition for less than three cents a copy when twenty-five copies were sent to a club. In turn, clubs boasted of their political zeal in the columns of their newspaper. Thus twenty-two Democratic readers sent in plans for a party barbecue along with their subscriptions to the Memphis *Appeal* in 1855. This club, eighty miles from the city, assured the paper that Democrats were prospering and asked, "Can't you come up and join us?"[36]

The result was communities of readers, many at great distance from the publisher, who shared in a common supply of news. Neighborly entrepreneurship and partisan zeal formed a large part of the market for papers from the Northeast. And not only here. From Washington, President Tyler's newspaper, the *Madisonian*, enrolled ninety-four subscribers in Zanesville, Ohio, a town of fewer than three thousand adults. The Memphis *Commercial Appeal* boasted of clubs through the upper South. In Florence, Alabama, a town of 835 free citizens some 150 miles from Memphis, a hundred-member club took the Tennessee paper. The Dubuque *Weekly Times* reported in 1861 that it had more than sixty good customers in East Waterloo, a town of about a thousand, nearly ninety miles to the west. Magazines and specialized papers also offered discounts to clubs and helped to form clusters of readers.[37]

This marketing practice completed the process of disclosure about reading that taverns and village post offices had always offered: Americans *knew* the tastes of their neighbors and who was up-to-date. Most of the seventy-one citizens who picked up mail at the Nashville, North Carolina, post office in 1833 must have known which five neighbors took the most popular magazine to come into the village: *Paul Pry*, the notorious compendium of Washington gossip. In 1852 a fifteen-year-old Virginian knew the thirty local subscribers to the *Illustrated News* published by the impresario P. T. Barnum.[38]

Editors thought of groups and networks of readers, not isolated subscribers. *Peterson's* hoped to sign up every family in Copperas, Vermont, during 1856 after hearing from a local that "we have only sixteen families in the place, and ten take your Magazine." The proprietor of the Brandon (Vt.) *Telegraph* found that his editing was under close scrutiny in a village of the Hudson River Valley in 1837:

> When I sign'd for your paper it was ripresentid as a rilegious one — and has been until you commenced editing it. but I am very sorry to say that it is turned into an anty Slavery paper we are all anty Slavery folks here and we like anty slavery papers but we want relegious one — and this one is pronounced anty slavery paper in every sence of the word — now if you persist in filleng your paper with anty Slavery — I must have mine discontinaed and there is 12 others that will do the same when I do — we met for to talk of it a day or two since and have come that conclusion — &c.

This reader said that if the editor would provide religious news in one paper and antislavery news in another, the locals would take them both![39]

Subscriptions were often born in negotiations among readers with a consensus about price and editorial policy. The antislavery press acknowledged its clubs of right-thinking readers, and this was a model for later reform journals. The Progressive Robert M. La Follette Sr. of Wisconsin, for example, founded a national weekly in 1909 simply by converting his admirers into subscribers and then getting them to buy subscriptions for their friends.[40]

Clubs gave readers a knowledge of one another and a common purpose, even if the magazine held back from political commitment. *Peterson's* spoke to its readers during the political campaign of 1856: "Ladies, if your husband or lover joins a political club, insist on your right to join a Peterson club." Often, to take a subscription was to make an alliance in this marketplace and to stand with others for a way of life. The *Ladies' Home Journal*, for instance, gained 90 percent of its subscriptions through clubbing plans as it sounded its call for domesticity in the mid-1880s.[41]

The back covers and editor's corners of the nation's press also tell of a different sort of community through subscription: getting the finer things in life.

3. Bounty Readers

The payment of a reward for convincing others to subscribe to the news seems to have originated with a hard-pressed printer in Dedham, Massachusetts, in 1799. Herman Mann took charge of the three-year-old *Minerva* and offered a free subscription to anyone who could round up nine readers and see that their subscriptions were in fact paid. In the next century the discounts grew into storied riches in the nation's magazines and newspapers. Art, books, and watches were favorite giveaways. *Emery's Journal of Agriculture* tempted subscribers with hundreds of exotic seeds. The *Prairie Farmer* offered a packet of tomato seeds to subscribers with the promise that the crop would be worth more than the price of the paper. After the Civil War, the Toledo *Blade* and the San Francisco *Chronicle* offered readers sewing machines for a small charge above the price of the paper. The "unexampled premium" for subscription-getters for the New York *Tribune* was a leather-bound dictionary. In Chattanooga, Adolph S. Ochs built the business that would allow him to take over the New York *Times* by offering free trips to the Chicago World's Fair to everyone who could gather a club of fifty subscribers to the weekly paper. The Boston *Globe* gave subscribers deep discounts on sets of encyclopedias. By the end of the century, the Medford (Ore.) *Mail* needed a wagon to display the bicycles, rifles and sewing machines it offered as premiums.[42]

At least two dailies offered readers a contest with a death benefit. "All a person had to do to win was to be found dead through some accident with a copy of that day's paper in his pocket," the business manager of the New York *Daily Mirror* explained.[43]

Demorest's Illustrated Monthly, a leading women's magazine, offered a double cornucopia of gifts. A regular subscriber paid $3.00 for the year and got the gift of her choice: stationery, needles, visiting cards, engravings . . . the premium list took up a page. The "getter-up" of a club of subscribers could offer the magazine for only $2.50 and keep a reward. Four subscriptions earned a mahogany writing desk; at six the desk jumped to rosewood. Watches were silver at twelve subscribers and gold with thirty readers. A clothes wringer was the reward for eight subscriptions, and the sewing machines began at twenty orders. A music box could be earned from only ten orders, but getter-uppers were lured with a melodeon for forty orders, a parlor organ for a hundred subscribers, and, at the end of the list, a piano organ for recruiting two hundred members of a club. Even for the reader who did nothing more than send in her own subscription, *Demorest's* wanted "to give, in short, such as will be worth the whole value of the subscription price, and even more, making it cheaper to take DEMOREST'S MONTHLY than not to take it; in other words, returning the full value of the year's subscription in a handsome article of use or adornment and sending the magazine as a *free gift.*"[44]

The premiums for nineteenth-century periodicals were usually a confirmation of the reader's place in society. Women were placed all the more securely in the parlor and kitchen. There was little talk of trips or excursions, educational or business opportunities. Even the *Woman's Journal*, the most successful suffragist magazine of the late nineteenth century, offered the conventional

Premium Wagon (1899).
Courtesy of the Southern Oregon Historical Society, Medford, Oregon.

premiums; its radicalism in this department stopped at croquet sets. On the other hand, Victorian periodicals certainly did address women as commercial operatives. In the shadow of a marketplace controlled by men, subscription gathering was a stock exchange for women, offering great rewards for hard work and luck. A woman controlled what she had earned and was not likely to share it. The gifts were rarely suitable for passing on to male members of the household. No amount of clubbing in women's magazines would produce a razor, a pipe, or a gun. (That croquet set for suffragist getter-uppers did carry a gentle egalitarian message, for here was a pastime open to both sexes.) The fruits of subscription drives might benefit all members of the family, but they entered the home because of the enterprise of women. Thus women's magazines neatly reversed the approved role of the male provider.[45]

Neither a woman nor a man would see cash from gathering subscribers. There were long lists of goods to dream over, but not a string of checks from the publishers. The tightfistedness of publishers does not explain the rarity of promotion by commission. Why not save the trouble and expense of shipping merchandise and simply pay the readers who signed up their neighbors? A market expert today might well avoid discounts for fear of cheapening the product, but this was not a problem for publishers a century ago. Free subscriptions were common. No doubt, many middle-class women (or their husbands) would have been discomforted if gathering subscriptions took on the appearance of a job. But notions of gender in Victorian society do not explain the cash taboo. *Scientific American*, addressed to men, found that its readers cared more for engravings of inventors than they did about the engravings of presidents on bank notes. In 1870 the magazine offered a print of the greatest nineteen inventors of the century for club subscriptions. At the same time, a top prize of three hundred dollars, and fifteen hundred dollars in all, was promised to the top fifteen subscription gatherers. (In current dollars the prizes were worth more than ten times as much.) Orders rushed in to win the inventors' faces, but few readers asked for a chance at the money. The magazine heard from only eight gatherers and awarded cash to all of them. *Scientific American* never offered money for subscriptions again. Well into the twentieth century, commissions were rare in the efforts to get readers to gather subscriptions. In the Great Depression, circulation managers noted that "for some reason, readers won't sell clubs of subscriptions to earn cash, but they roll in profitable circulation when merchandize prizes are offered." This has been found true in gathering subscriptions more recently. Americans have had an abiding reluctance to view information as a commodity with a price like other goods. The subscribers who would not pay were cousins to the subscription gatherers who did not take pay. Going into arrears or racing to win premiums transformed a business relationship into an adventure. Magically, the cold rules of a market economy were suspended: one got something for nothing, a pleasure without a price tag. During the birth of mass circulation, subscriptions were a transaction kept apart from the cash nexus.[46]

These communal approaches to merchandising were devised to correct scandal in individual promotion. Although newspapers and magazines published the names of their authorized representatives, charlatans made tours of rural America and collected money that publishers never saw. Clubs turned neighbors into agents and so enforced honesty. The apparent function of clubs was to get discounts, just as the apparent function of mail coaches was to transport passengers. A hidden function of clubs was to police collections, just as a hidden function of passenger service was to see that the driver did not plunder or lose the mail.[47]

The long lists of gifts for subscriptions only begin to suggest how readership was tied to bounty hunting. The ballast of giveaways and discounts that comes with the Sunday paper today was loaded into the mass media a century ago.

Susan Strasser, a marketing scholar, has observed that "every issue of every general-circulation magazine from the late 1880s through World War I offered readers the opportunity to send for samples of coffee, soap, complexion powder, canned soup, mucilage, toothpaste, varnish, or shirt collars." Coupons for special offers now came into the nation's press that could be clipped (and coded, to see which publications were most effective in reaching prospects).[48]

Coupons, like the offers to new subscribers and clubbing schemes, gave rewards to all readers who cooperated. Publishers increased the romance of their business with grand prizes that might transform the lives of a lucky few. These were games of chance or rewards for merit, not challenges to persuade neighbors what to read. Still, reading about other contestants did spread knowledge of the community and of the publication itself.

There were hundreds of lures to catch subscribers. Frank Leslie announced in 1856 that his pioneering illustrated newspaper would return the subscription money of every tenth customer. Further, he promised objects of gold and silver as well as rosewood pianos to subscribers who were enrolled on every hundredth line of his books. By the end of the decade, Herbert & Co., subscription agents in New York, decorated country weeklies with triple heads:

BEST OFFER EVER MADE
BEST OFFER EVER MADE
BEST OFFER EVER MADE

NO HUMBUG
NO HUMBUG
NO HUMBUG

Magazine subscribers here earned chances on pianos, sewing machines, even gold jewelry. A silver goblet, a prize hog, a new reaper, or a large check were some of the prizes offered to Americans who gathered subscriptions for the agricultural press at mid-century. The St. Louis *Democrat* offered a 160-acre farm to the Missourian who could sign up the most readers (smaller farms or city lots were offered to runners-up). At the turn of the century, papers in Tennessee and Virginia offered twenty thousand dollars in awards to subscribers who best estimated cotton receipts. During the winter of 1903, the Mansfield (Ohio) *News* numbered every newspaper, selected a winning number, and gave the reader who brought that newspaper in a ton of coal.[49]

The most successful contests were amalgams of neighborliness and prurience. This type of subscription drive swept the north central counties of Iowa during the first winters of the twentieth century. The weekly *Hardin County Citizen* held contests to find the most popular young woman in this region.

Coupons in the paper were ballots, and many more votes could be earned by paying up bills or taking out a new subscription. These expressions of admiration were not left to chance. Candidates and their supporters were given weeks of training on how to canvass, and the names and payment records of readers were turned over to all the teams. Then, for a month, the canvassers ranged through the townships. The editor recalled that the excitement eclipsed that of the presidential runs of William Jennings Bryan and Theodore Roosevelt. The running vote totals for popular girls were such big news that daily extras were issued. Bets were placed on women, and votes were bought and sold. This weekly paper tripled its circulation, and the editor credited the contests for his good fortune.[50]

City folk, too, were lured to journalism with contests. The Toledo *Bee* invited children to guess the number of votes cast in an election and promised the handsomest pony in Ohio to the young reader with the closest estimate. The New York *Evening Telegram* offered a gold watch to the woman servant longest in her family's service. A gold sword and a weekly cash payment for life were some of the prizes awarded before the end of the century. A Cincinnati paper gave away a city lot and the house to go on it in a circulation drive. Obviously, naked self-interest drove many contestants (one *Evening Telegram* reader purchased thirty thousand copies to clip the coupons that won him a trip around the world). But urban contests often pushed acquaintances, even strangers, to cooperate in the pursuit of prizes. The Boston *Globe* printed coupons which entitled readers to vote on the most popular war veteran, saleswoman, fireman, and so forth. Ties of affection or respect now were to be acknowledged, counted, and publicized. The paper reported five million entries in one contest. No reader could remain aloof. Many Bostonians left their homes with a pair of scissors, to clip the forms from stray copies of the *Globe*.[51]

This scramble for papers, anyone's papers, was one of the stunts conducted by the leading "yellow journalists" of New York City at the end of the century. The *Evening Telegram* ran coupons that were ballots for the most popular student and teacher. The winners got trips to Europe. During the campaign, schoolboys rode the trains carrying shears and besieged train stations for the coupons. An even more drastic mobilization in pursuit of circulation was condemned in the trade press: how Joseph Pulitzer "turned a number of respectable school children into beggars." This was the New York *World's* campaign to have children save their pennies (and extract them from soft-hearted readers) for a civic monument: the pedestal for the Statue of Liberty in New York Harbor. Beginning in the mid-1880s, Pulitzer inspired his rivals in New York and envious publishers across the country to run popularity contests.[52]

The contests were not madcap affairs but rather attempts to discipline readers. The glittering prizes offered to the nineteenth-century subscriber were offered because the typical reader was fickle.

To be sure, publishers celebrated subscribers who were loyal. The Montgomery *Advertiser*, for instance, found two Alabama families that had maintained subscriptions across six generations. But serf-readers, bound to mastheads, were rare. Readers played the field, stopping and starting periodicals as it suited them. The loyal subscriber is remarkably hard to find in the documents that have survived. Postal records for incoming periodicals show that a churning of titles was common. A sample of the readers in Calhoun, Missouri, shows that between 1851 and 1853 only 35 percent of the newspapers and magazines coming into the post office were taken continuously for eighteen months or longer. In this frontier county, readers tried out publications as diverse as *Prairie Farmer* and the *American Phrenological Journal*, and then gave them up. The postal records from Henderson, North Carolina, at the end of the 1850s are particularly revealing because the postmaster of this Piedmont county took the unusual step of distinguishing male and female subscribers. Seven women took seventeen periodicals in their own name in a two year period; seven men subscribed to twenty-nine. Only four of the women and three of the men were picking up these periodicals after two years. Only four periodicals had remained in the hands of a loyal female subscriber over this short period; among the men, just two titles were continuous. One way or another, seven of every eight subscriptions taken by post in Henderson ended in twenty-four months. Given publishers' willingness to carry deadbeats, these figures surely understate the number of readers who moved on or changed interests in periodicals.[53]

Local newspapers and some national magazines undoubtedly became fixtures in many homes. But the nineteenth-century reader wanted more and tried out a variety of publications. "'Stop my paper!' is the cry of terror" in American newsrooms, a British visitor observed, happily noting that English journalists had a more forgiving public. At the end of the century a veteran of publishing said that loyalty among readers was dead. He saw Americans walking the boulevards, gathering in different papers as if plucking berries from bushes. The "subscription fiend," who signed up for a month or two and then switched papers, troubled circulation managers. At the turn of the century, Edward W. Scripps, lord of a chain of small papers, prohibited all slick salesmanship, especially prizes and premiums. By close observation he concluded that circulation gathered in this way always melted away. Defection from the lists was also a nightmare of the magazine business: "It will be a surprise to the novice to learn that with many of the best established weekly journals the proportion of annual 'renewals' is less than twenty-five per cent."[54]

Circulation was much easier to build than to sustain. *Godey's Lady's Book* soared to one hundred fifty thousand readers before the Civil War and then, despite new premiums and discounts, sank below a hundred thousand in the

Gilded Age. *Demorest's* hit fifty thousand subscribers with its premium offers in the 1870s, but could not do better with further offers and a major cut in price. In a decade, *Frank Leslie's* circulation rose from nothing to more than a hundred thousand, then shrank by two-thirds. Guiding the circulation of a magazine was rarely a long, pleasant climb; here the journalist was cast onto plateaus and cliffs. Nineteenth-century readers were ancestors to the twentieth-century shoppers for American automobiles or air fares: the taste for a discount, a rebate, or a prize was in their blood. The "constant struggle" to supply premiums to jaded subscribers taxed the energies of publishers in Victorian America. What was true of the twentieth-century subscriber was true in the nineteenth century: "A universal principle of pricing is that discount offers create rapid increases but long-term instability by developing an expectation of discounted prices and by debasing the core of paid subscribers."[55]

Many publishers found ways to bind opportunistic readers to their publications. Contestants usually had to be paid-up subscribers. Longer commitments were necessary to earn the right to a chance at a prize. In a San Francisco contest, for example, subscribers could win a villa near Golden Gate Park only if they signed an agreement to pay the newspaper in advance for a year. "Prizes" were often mortgaged. Thus the Manhattan Novelty Company supplied dozens of papers with "an everlasting parlor ornament" to display pictures of family members. The papers sold the frames and pastel portraits at cost and collected on the installment plan for the premium as well as the paper. A loved one's face would not stay in the parlor if the reader was not careful, for the firm boasted: "You can regain possession of the premium if payments are refused or the paper is stopped."[56]

The heavy reading habits of Americans, so celebrated a part of their democracy, were not the spontaneous expression of a people seeking enlightenment. Self-interest and resentment stood behind mass circulation. News meant something for nothing for the numerous deadbeat readers. Often, readers begrudged printers their success. And the public wanted more: prizes lured Americans to take up the news. This said, the selling of newspapers and magazines complemented the work of community building carried out by editors. It was not simply that journalism boosted towns, sustained political parties, and drew together the like-minded for social betterment. The act of subscription threw citizens into one another's business and made shared interests visible. There was continual reinforcement for the habit of taking the news, for family members, neighbors, and even strangers created pressure to subscribe. To hold the news in the nineteenth century was to hold the membership badge of a club. As twentieth-century publishers have learned, there is no better way to gather up readers. The sell was often sealed by a bounty, a reward for taking the news.

Ad from *Circulation Management* I (1902–3).

Americans took to news, in other words, because the news business engaged their low motives as well as their high-mindedness, their desire to get ahead and also to stay in step with one another.[57]

What happened in the nineteenth century can be described in the twentieth-century language of marketing. Free samples blanketed the sales area, deep discounting built a customer base, affinity groups were targeted, promotional gifts and prizes were used to increase market share. As the marketing techniques accomplished their purpose, they were phased out. Deadbeats were dropped from the subscription lists. Party loyalists came to matter less to publishers by the end of the nineteenth century. Most publishers cut back on the prizes and premiums by the beginning of the twentieth century. What had made mass circulation in the first place came to seem unbusinesslike, disrespectable and . . . old-fashioned. The marketing strategy for news in the first century of American democracy had not been planned and was part of no one's grand scheme. Pushing the news into people's lives in these ways was simply the uncoordinated, pragmatic effort of publishers to get their wares out. But there was an underlying value, all the clearer today since it has become rarer in the news business. The common faith of publishers was that the broadest possible readership was desirable.

What was achieved here was nothing less than the formation of inclusive public discourse. Journalism of the nineteenth century made it difficult for anyone to stand apart from news in print. Publishers served deadbeats, exploited the faintest sense of community feeling among readers, and shamelessly bribed subscribers. This is not all they did to achieve a democracy of circulation, as the rest of this book will show. But these three marketing practices were basic to the formation of the reading public. The assumption was that everyone mattered and that no potential reader could be wasted. Publishers appealed to special communities, but they tempted everyone with agents, "clubs," and come-ons. The public was not confined, as it was to be in the twentieth century, to those who would always pay or to those who stood ready to buy the goods being advertised. The old-fashioned circulation drive was carried on with a vision of citizens who had infinite possibilities. They might change heart and join a good cause. They might rise in the world and use the news and the ads that they could not use now. They might pay their bill. American mass media sprang from this wildly democratic form of marketing. As we shall see, both its imprudence and its egalitarianism would be reformed in the twentieth century.

PART TWO

NEGOTIATIONS
OVER
MEDIA
IN TWO
CENTURIES

3

THE

MENACE OF

NEW MEDIA

Government in the United States has conducted a prolonged experiment with media that no society has matched. To a remarkable extent, it has left the press alone. Censors, an active bureaucracy on the continent of Europe, had no place in the young federal and state governments. There were no taxes on media (as there were in Great Britain) to see that debate was kept within the respectable classes. Faced with a foreign crisis at the turn of the nineteenth century, the United States did regulate the press with the Alien and Sedition Laws (1798–1800). These were designed to keep foreign radicals away from American shores (and print shops). The John Adams administration also struck down its domestic critics with this legislation, especially journalists. When Thomas Jefferson and his allies repudiated this use of state power, the course was set for unregulated growth of media. The notable exceptions were ad hoc efforts by civilians and the military to punish disagreeable newspapers during the Civil War era and the systematic crackdown on dissent through the sedition laws of the World Wars. But the hands-off policy was resumed after every breach.

Beneath this general policy of laissez-faire, government officials have tried very hard to encourage some forms of news and to discourage others. From the earliest days of the republic, the government used financial subsidy to play favorites. Administrations helped friendly papers, of course, but government also concerned itself with the *reach* of news. Beginning in 1792, the postal service charged a newspaper subscriber no more than one and a half cents, no matter how far the paper had been carried. In contrast, a one-page letter cost between six and twenty-five cents, depending on distance. Private communication subsidized the scope of the press, and the government helped to decide the reach of print media. When government opens a channel for distant voices to be heard in local communities, it challenges the structure of political power. Legislators who set postal policy in the early republic saw this clearly.

Jacksonian America frequently debated whether newspapers should be free of postal charges so as to encourage knowledge of government. The controversy arose with the birth of the federal government. The democratic promise of Jackson's era again focused attention on the reach of media. In Congress, legislators rallied in defense of local publications. Sen. Isaac Hill of New Hampshire saw the issue in stark terms. He warned that free postage for distant newspapers would mean that "instead of taking such lessons from our local newspapers, as the home-bred ideas, the honest, frugal and industrious habits of the yeomanry shall prompt, the people must be lectured by those who do every thing on a great scale." Hill had conducted a weekly paper in New Hampshire for twenty years before he reached the Senate, and his plea for the local editor was characteristic of the breed. The future senator Henry L. Dawes, when he edited a weekly in the 1840s, thundered against papers "published abroad" which were "gradually bringing the whole country under the influence and in some sense the control, of the leading cliques in the cities." This sentiment was not confined to the local printing trade. Sen. Felix Grundy of Tennessee, for instance, gave a vivid picture of the danger of papers with too long a reach, using language that was becoming commonplace. He said that there were two kinds of American newspapers, local and "foreign." A foreign newspaper was one published "abroad" — meaning outside the closest town. With postage free, the Senator said, the "prevailing curiosity" of Americans would lead them to drop their local papers, and republican virtue would perish.[1]

The guardians of "home-bred" ideas eventually won this debate. Congress decided that news, if it bore the imprint of a local editor, deserved free postage. In 1845 a law was passed allowing weekly papers to be sent free from a publisher's office for a distance of thirty miles. This meant that about a fifth of all periodicals circulated through the mail were delivered for free by the government. Lawmakers continued to argue over the subsidy to local editors, and for brief periods the privilege was withdrawn. The menace of the distant, metropolitan press remained the most resilient argument for local subsidy. At mid-century Rep. Abraham W. Venable, from North Carolina, called the city press a "cesspool" and saw "the simple, pure, conservative atmosphere of the country" as the antidote, if only local editors could be helped to circulate their news.

At the end of this debate Congress agreed to free postage for weekly papers sent within their home county. The United States thus attempted to achieve news for all within the local communities.[2]

The fear of a distant, "foreign" press has been a more profound theme in shaping reaction to the press than the much-studied episodes of government censorship. More than harsh words, the extension of journalism may produce new ways to read the news and change the political landscape. This has certainly been true in major confrontations over news of race in both nineteenth- and twentieth-century America. Defenders of the racial status quo felt the danger of new ideas, but still more they felt the menace of new media that changed the way the argument would be conducted. With new reach, news was no longer what it had seemed. Texts became twisted. A simple page of unremarkable copy looked as if it would explode. The watershed eras of racial news, the attacks on slavery beginning in the 1830s and on segregation beginning in the 1950s, were rich with subversive media.

1. Antislavery and Incendiary Publications

Attacks on slavery had small circulation before the 1830s. New organizations arose at the beginning of this decade that were determined to dramatize the injustice of bondage to a much larger audience. The American Anti-Slavery Society, formed at the end of 1833, united protesters from the West and from New England and found the money for a publicity drive in New York. The campaign was modest at first; in 1834, 122,000 single issues of newspapers and tracts carried the news of antislavery. But more than a million antislavery publications went out from New York in 1835 to a nation of fifteen million. There had been pamphlet wars in the early republic before this time. Questions over observance of the sabbath and the regulation of alcohol had shown that presses could be kept busy in a battle for public opinion. American evangelicals, in an effort to save souls, had shown a genius in spreading the printed word, a decade before antislavery forces mobilized. But it was the distinction of abolitionists to target the public with unwanted advice about fundamental political change. In this respect, the blizzard of paper from the North was the first sign of the power of news for all.[3]

Abolitionists issued tracts and circulars, but the majority of their appeals took the form of magazines and newspapers such as the *Anti-Slavery Record*, the *Emancipator*, and *Human Rights*. Other antislavery editors such as James C. Birney in Cincinnati and William Lloyd Garrison in Boston were sending their papers into the South by the mid-1830s. This news was the main body of "incendiary publications" that President Andrew Jackson denounced in his message to Congress in December 1835. The metaphor was more than that, for many towns burned antislavery publications, and Southern legislatures specified that this news be put to the flame.[4]

What was incendiary in the attack on slavery? There was the fresh heresy of "immediatism," the insistence that bondage end in this generation and on American soil, not through a return to Africa. But the "peculiar institution" had been vigorously debated in American slave societies since colonial times, and never before with pyres of reading material. In 1836 an attorney in the District of Columbia read from the works of distinguished white Southerners who had condemned slavery in print in a successful defense of a Northern man found with incendiary newspapers. Speaking to "southern friends" after the first bonfire of Northern papers in Charleston, an Ohio newspaper said that "if to denounce slavery be fanaticism, as they say it is, they have had fanaticism enough among themselves." South Carolinians were reminded that the white South did not speak with a single voice on race even as they formed their vigilance committees to stop the news. Angelina Grimké, a daughter of the state's governing class, published a letter in the *Liberator* of September 19, 1835, endorsing antislavery journalism.[5]

The publications were not addressed to slaves, the abolitionists insisted. "The right to send publications of any sort to slaves, or in any way to communicate with them, without the *express permission* of their masters, I freely acknowledge that I have not," said Elijah P. Lovejoy after hearing from the first white mob of angry readers. "Nor do I wish to have it," he said. Antislavery zealots noted, correctly, that few blacks in servitude could read (no scholar has estimated that more than one slave in ten was literate).[6] Abolitionists were pioneers in assembling lists of names and anticipated the modern world of direct mail appeals as well as mass circulation journalism. These reformers sent their literature to upstanding members of the white community. "If, therefore, our object is to excite the slaves to insurrection, the masters are our agents," the American Anti-Slavery Society said.[7]

It is axiomatic to conclude that Southerners who burned the antislavery argument acted in fear. But fear may open debates rather than close them. Virginia, the state with the most slaves, had openly debated abolition only a few months after Nat Turner's insurrection had massacred more than fifty whites in the state. Fearful Virginians circulated arguments for abolition in the press in 1832 — arguments so plausible that the Virginia House of Delegates declared slavery to be "evil." A Southern editor said then that he knew of no Virginia paper opposed to the eventual emancipation of slaves. Only three years later, in calmer times, white fears could not be contained. Why the obsession to burn this news?[8]

The habit seems more curious when we note that the fires often preceded the reading. The hated material was destroyed before it could circulate. This was true in Charleston, South Carolina, when the Southern mails arrived by steamboat on July 29, 1835. Antislavery literature "literally filled" the office, post-master Alfred Huger said. He discouraged anyone from calling for the publications, but word was out and the judgment on the mails was quick and universal. "Our whole population are deeply excited and exasperated," Huger wrote on the 29th; "indeed, there is a phrenzied and turbulent feeling." The Charleston post office was broken into that night, and the only thing taken was the antislavery papers. A mob burned this literature the following evening. Charleston was united in hatred of news that very few of its citizens had the opportunity to read.[9]

The key to understanding the Southern fear of antislavery publications is to be found in the response of the North to this literature. All across the free states in the summer and fall of 1835, meetings were held to take stock of the new antislavery press and its angry readers. Northern papers reported that Philadelphians in "an immense assemblage" resolved "that we regard the dissemination of incendiary publications throughout the slave-holding states with indignation and horror." In New York City, "the most numerous assemblage which we ever witnessed" condemned the shipment of abolitionist papers south. "We have never seen a larger or more respectable audience within the walls of old Faneuil [Hall]," the Boston *Atlas* reported as New Englanders agreed to condemn "the few, who in their zeal would scatter among our southern brethren firebrands, arrows and death." Feelings ran just as high in many smaller towns. A Rochester paper said that the meeting that damned the antislavery crusade was one of the largest in the history of that city. In Portland, Maine, the meeting to condemn the "incendiary machinations of Northern fanatics" was the largest gathering the town had ever seen.[10]

Everywhere, leading citizens took charge of these mass meetings. New Haven was swayed against the "incendiary documents" by the words of Noah Webster, the lexicographer. Harrison Gray Otis, a commanding figure in Massachusetts politics since the 1790s, gave a celebrated speech in Boston's Faneuil Hall. In New York and Boston the mayor chaired the meeting that drafted the censure; in Albany and in New Haven it was the governor.[11]

Mobs formed to turn back the surge of abolitionist meetings and tracts. The leading antislavery papers reported 209 hostile mobs in the North in the 1830s and 1840s. A Philadelphia mob tore abolitionist literature into pieces and dumped the paper into the Delaware in August 1835. There was more shredding of antislavery papers in Utica in October, and a local publisher who defended the right of abolitionists to assemble had his type thrown into the street. The same day, in Boston, a mob that grew to four or five thousand threw antislavery papers into the gutter and led the editor William Lloyd Garrison on a walk with a noose around his neck. Cincinnati dealt with incendiary publications in July 1836. A mob broke into the print shop of the town's antislavery newspaper, scattered the type set for the next issue, and dismantled the press.

When abolitionists repaired the damage before the end of the month, a second mob (which included the mayor) did the sacking again. July 1836 was a busy month for Northern censors of the antislavery press. Elijah Lovejoy's press was destroyed as it arrived in Alton, Illinois, that month. In the following year Lovejoy's press was wrecked by mobs two more times. It was in defense of his fourth press in Alton during November 1837 that editor Lovejoy was shot and killed. The mob did not scatter, but stayed to calmly dismantle the new press.[12]

The rage of Northerners subsided but never went too far below the surface. John Greenleaf Whittier knew this in Philadelphia, where the Quaker poet came to edit the *Pennsylvania Freeman* in 1838: "My paper is *beginning* to attract attention, and I should not think strange if it got pretty essentially mobbed before the summer is out." The Cincinnati mob rose up again in September 1841 and threw the presses of an antislavery publisher into the river.[13]

Many popular Northern journalists were leaders of suppression. Vigorous editorial attacks on the antislavery press were common in the North. Mordecai M. Noah, editor of the New York *Evening Star*, proposed a bill to punish anyone in the state who published anything with even a tendency to promote protests by slaves. Other journalists took more direct action. The mobbing of the first meeting of the New York City Anti-Slavery Society in 1833 was planned in the office of a leading commercial newspaper and supported by other prominent editors. The far greater riot in the city the following year was also encouraged by articles in several papers. In Boston, similarly, the Faneuil Hall assembly that damned antislavery agitation was organized by two leading newspapers in August 1835. In Cincinnati, newspapers prompted mob action into the 1840s, the decade that saw a decline in rioting in most of the nation.[14]

What did Northerners fear and hate in the antislavery press? Not simply the idea of a larger measure of justice for blacks. A minority of Americans had been left in peace to argue this unpopular cause until the middle 1830s. The North had no slaves to lose. Yet the suppression of this news was high on the agenda of the mobs. A city that sat astride a river of Southern trade, such as Cincinnati, had a good reason to rally for its customers, the planters. But what economic motive could drive the citizens of Rochester, Utica, and even Cooperstown to fill sweltering meeting halls? In any case, citizens took to the streets to damn the antislavery press before the South had even threatened economic retaliation.

Obviously, racism is a tempting explanation of what led Northerners to rally around the white South. Many Northerners were sickened by the "amalgamation" that they saw in the association of blacks and whites in antislavery. The "resolves" passed by community meetings shied away from this topic, but some who hated the new media of antislavery were clear in their taunts. "Shall we, to gratify the spirit of the incendiary . . . yield our daughters and our wives to that lust and amalgamation which he advocates?" the Boston *Gazette* asked. The link between abolitionist news and sexual surrender was clear in the lithograph issued in New York which showed a black man relaxing with the *Emancipator* in company with his white wife and mulatto children.[15]

But the communities that hated the antislavery press were not hotbeds of racism. Philadelphia with its Quaker heritage was not well schooled in racial hate. Cincinnati had been home to the organization of antislavery in the West through the Lane Seminary. Alton, Illinois, had the novelty of integrated schools, and just four months before Elijah Lovejoy was killed by a mob, his enemies assembled to insist, "We abhor and deprecate the evil of Slavery." Through the North, many of the leaders whose words mattered most on incendiary publications stood before their neighbors as moderates on racial questions. Men like Harrison Gray Otis did not deal in racial epithets. Noah Webster had denounced slavery as a young man and worked his sentiments into one of his school texts.[16]

Americans who believed that slavery was part of God's plan cannot have been comforted by the resolves of the enemies of incendiary publications. The Richmond *Whig*, in reviewing Northern support for the South, called these assemblies "impertinent." The editor had a point. In Portland, a giant meeting to condemn abolitionists declared that slavery was morally wrong. The Philadelphia meeting called emancipation a "happy result" that organized abolition threatened to postpone. "We hold this truth to be indisputable," the Faneuil Hall meeting declared, "that the condition of slavery finds no advocates among our citizens."[17]

The preservation of the Union was an incantation in the statements drafted in the North, yet this fraternal feeling, like the pull of white racial unity, does not fully explain why communities feared words and pictures on paper. If preserving the Union was the imperative, Northerners were the most forgetful of diplomats. The bones of contention between the sections—the tariff, internal improvements, and the addition of new states—were not addressed in the statements issued by assemblies or in the ritual of the street. If the North wished to make secession and nullification abhorrent, why did it follow the lead of South Carolina, the very state that had pushed a constitutional crisis at the beginning of the decade? Now again, on the interception of news it did not like, South Carolina announced that this was the eve of secession. An Ohio newspaper noted that "this continuous threat of dissolving the union, indulged in by our southern friends, is, to say the least of it, in *very bad taste.*"[18]

In his classic study of anti-abolition mobs, Leonard L. Richards has argued that the issues between the North and the South, indeed, the contents of the antislavery publications, were incidental to the feeling of crisis that gripped so many communities in the mid-1830s. The North and the South reacted so sharply because they sensed that political communication was changing. The "gentlemen of property and standing" who chaired meetings and often led others in the streets saw in antislavery a challenge to what they stood for. Recent scholarship has shown that the 1836 election campaign led both parties to summon up rallies and mobs in flamboyant answer to the new publicists of antislavery. Whigs and Democrats bid for votes by standing up to the radicals. The stage-managing of this political theater occupied regular politicians, up to the level of Jackson's Secretary of State. This was not business as usual in the politics of the early republic, and the innovations are a measure of how propaganda in print inspired drastic action. Reformers, in spreading news for all, were sweeping aside the old political leaders, the familiar newspapers, the established parties. The politicians and editors had carried the name and reputation of their community to the nation. No more. Now the masthead of a dissident sheet would stain the town's reputation as it circulated and upstart contributors to this press dared to assume leadership. Antislavery linked to mass circulation proceeded with a blind eye—or a nod of defiance—to local political leadership. More than race, more than union was at stake here. Local communities rose up against antislavery because it threatened to turn their world upside down.[19]

News in print, for the first time in the United States, was an invitation to citizens assigned no political role in the normal course of Whig or Democratic campaigns. The abolitionists' claims that they were not addressing slaves (even the few who could read) convinced no one. Otis said, "They may as well believe that they can set all the bells in Richmond ringing so as to arouse and alarm the white inhabitants, and affect the slaves only as a tinkling lullaby to soothe them to repose." In the patriarchy of American democracy, antislavery literature was diabolical because it also reached women and children. This notorious feature of abolitionism was highlighted by print with its special sections for the young and women. John Tyler, the future President, warned his fellow Virginians that the American female "is to be converted into a fiend" by the incendiary publications.[20]

The defenders of slavery were in awe of this new way of conducting political disputes. They denounced the pictures that made points that even the illiterate could grasp. The cheapness of this news seemed as alarming as its content. Tyler stood before his townsfolk and read them the low subscription prices of the leading antislavery papers. Residents of Harrison County, Virginia, petitioned Congress in 1838 to raise the postage on newspapers shipped great distances in order to preserve slavery and peace. Charleston citizens noted that *one* press in New York City had ten times the capacity of their town to answer abolitionists. It seemed that the North had a superweapon that left the South defenseless. Thus a correspondent to a Georgia paper wrote from New York of the elaborate organization of the enemy and said that the words of radical abolitionists "are thundered forth to the people at the rate of 200,000 papers per month. Such are not harmless weapons. THEY ARE ALL-SUFFICIENT TO DO DESTRUCTION UPON THE SOUTH." A Charleston editor saw abolitionists "hurling their moral firebrands of desolation and death, from their catapult in New York, into the very bosom and vitals of the South." "Some poisonous missile may yet pass the barrier," the Richmond *Enquirer* said. Mobs and their bonfires could not stop a press with this range. In a letter to a vigilance society in South Carolina, the president of the American Anti-Slavery Society taunted the South with an accounting: Charleston in July had destroyed only 1/175th part of the newspapers and pamphlets circulated that month. The vigilance committee reprinted this letter, saying that comment on the ongoing threat was needless.[21]

Why did the South not make ready powerful presses of its own? After all, this was what evangelicals had been doing, all the while denouncing the "satanic" presses of the worldly. That the devil could be beaten at his own game was the celebrated discovery of Christian publishers. How inviting a prospect for the white South, especially as it learned that the Northern public was turning out in great numbers to express sympathy. Proslavery had powerful themes: race prejudice, fears for the Union, nativist sentiment against British influence among the abolitionists. Why did the South not flood the Northern post with *these* incendiary appeals? In a celebrated pamphlet of 1836, a Northern statesman invited the South to fill the mails of the free states with their most candid and abusive observations. No one in the South took the dare.[22]

The South, of course, was handicapped technologically. It was not a publishing center, and the presses that "thundered" so ominously in Southern ears would have been difficult to build in this agricultural economy. On the eve of the Civil War, the fifteen slave states and the District of Columbia produced just 25 percent of the printing turned out in the state of New York. Slave states might have spent more to develop their own presses, but no such visionary scheme was necessary to compete with antislavery. The North stood ready to print the proslavery argument. This was a part of the publishing business that some Southern editors kept from their readers. *DeBow's Review*, the South's leading periodical and most militant defender of slavery in the 1840s and 1850s, was printed in Northern shops. James DeBow listed offices in Charleston and New Orleans on the cover of his elite magazine and gave no hint of its Northern origin until the Civil War forced his hand. The three thousand subscribers to *DeBow's Review* probably suspected that the South needed help to communicate. For some time Southern newspapers had lamented the work lost to their own print shops, noting that slave states had their laws printed in the very cities where abolitionists published. Proslavery publicists, backed by government and business, were in a better position to arrange mass circulation than the abolitionists, a despised minority in the North. But for all these opportunities, the white South did not put its heart into a battle for public opinion. Like the

Northern gentlemen of property and standing, defenders of slavery feared a broad public brought into politics by mass circulation.[23]

This was the hard lesson learned by the Southern journalist who was in the best position to answer the incendiary publications, the redoubtable Duff Green. His *United States Telegraph* in Washington championed the slave cause. This Kentuckian was living proof of the restless energy of the American democrat. Green had studied medicine, law, and land values. He fought Indians and had a hand in every form of speculation that the West offered. Green had run the first stagecoach line west of the Mississippi, founded a town in Missouri, and prospered as an editor and merchant in St. Louis. At first Green was a bulldog for Andrew Jackson, but he had gone over to John C. Calhoun of South Carolina by the time abolitionists picked a fight. The editor had defended slavery since the debates over the admission of Missouri to the Union in 1820, so his loyalty to the South was above question. His daughter had married Calhoun's son, if bloodlines were to count as well as conviction. In 1835, when abolitionist news filled the mails, Green used his paper to defend the white South. He dreamed of more work with powerful rotary presses and had a scheme to cut the cost of setting type by running a "Manual Labor School" for boys. But Green's enterprise went unrewarded. The editor was repudiated by spokesmen for the slaveholders. They feared he was spreading abolitionism by refuting its doctrines. Southern editors argued that only silence could stop the heresy. The *Telegraph* soon died, and Green's further plans to awaken the public to the danger of antislavery were damned by white Southerners who wanted fewer, not more, arguments in print.[24]

Green's patron, Senator Calhoun of South Carolina, the most brilliant strategist in the defense of slavery, hoped to show Northerners what was at issue in allowing new presses to bring unwanted arguments south. Calhoun asked Northerners if they could live in peace with an antislavery press carrying news for all:

> The incessant action of hundreds of societies, and a vast printing establishment, throwing out, daily, thousands of artful and inflammatory publications, must make, in time, a deep impression on the section of the Union, where they freely circulate. . . . The well informed and thoughtful may hold them in contempt, but the young, the inexperienced, the ignorant and thoughtless, will receive the poison.

Speaking in 1836, Calhoun looked ahead to a time when hatred would beget hatred between the North and South and the Union would perish. Northern institutions might come apart. The Senator invited those "who have a deep stake in the existing institutions of the country" to see themselves as part of the slaveholding class: "Reflect, whether there now exists, or ever has existed, a wealthy and civilized community, in which one portion, did not live on the labor of another." The Senator concluded with a warning: if the North allowed news for all and participation by all, the few who governed and owned would find this new democracy aimed at their own privileges.[25]

The papers furnished by abolitionists seemed to break an understanding of what the printed page should be. With the hated journalism before him on a table in Faneuil Hall, Otis noted the psychological damage of the news: "Men, women and children are stimulated, flattered and frightened," he said. In another of the emergency meetings of 1835, a judge told the friends of the white South in upstate New York that laws had not been properly drawn to stop the antislavery press because "it was not foreseen or believed, that men who could control presses and were able to write books, would ever engage in such enterprizes." Charleston called the news "missiles," Boston called it "fire-brands," and the universal metaphor of "incendiary" revealed how explosive news seemed to those who assumed that the printing was the exclusive concern of an elite for a limited audience that was schooled in what texts meant. The next publications from the North would please the slave South even less.[26]

2. Subversive Scrapbooks

In 1838 Theodore Dwight Weld, a tireless lecturer for emancipation, began work on a book to "thrill the land with horror" about slavery. He purchased the discarded Southern newspapers from the New York Commercial Reading Room, hauled at least twenty thousand issues out to his home in New Jersey, and set his household to work reading the news. Weld was married to Angelina Grimké of Charleston, and her sister, Sarah, lived with the couple. The three abolitionists settled down with Southern newspapers in the fall of 1838 and were hard at the reading through the winter.[27]

"Heart sickening as the details are," Sarah Grimké wrote, "I am thankful that God in his providence has put into our hands these weapons prepared by the South herself, to destroy the fell monster."[28] *American Slavery as It Is: Testimony of a Thousand Witnesses* (1839) was a subversive scrapbook. Almost all of the more than four hundred items taken from Southern papers had been published, literally, to keep blacks in bondage. These were notices of runaway slaves as well as accounts of slave catching and punishments. For example, the Montgomery *Advertiser* September 29, 1837, had printed:

> $20 REWARD. — Ranaway from the subscriber, a negro man named Moses. He is of common size, about 28 years old. He formerly belonged to Judge Benson, of Montgomery, and it is said, has a wife in that county.

Such newspaper items had been common in the South for a century. The white community needed this news if it was to police its labor system. Everyone knew how to read these notices, and no one had thought they undermined slavery.

American Slavery as It Is simply changed the context so that the news could be read another way. The South had long argued that the conscience of slaveholders protected black families. But this master thought nothing of separating Moses from his wife. Scores of items exposed the same callousness. The author of the notice for Moses was John Gayle, governor of Alabama when the incendiary publications first came south, a man who read the circulation figures of these papers aloud to the public as the strongest evidence of Northern malevolence. In the hands of antislavery editors, his own words had become incendiary.[29]

Many of the newspapers used in *American Slavery as It Is* had only a few hundred subscribers. The Welds made nineteen excerpts from the Charleston *Mercury*, noting that "the circulation of the 'Mercury' among the wealthy, the literary, and the fashionable, is probably much larger than that of any other paper in the state." This may have been true, but the *Mercury* had only about five hundred paying subscribers. The notices about slavery were, like all ads and news squibs, published for the moment, not posterity. When these items fell into the antislavery collection, the news found a vast, continuing audience. The pamphlet showed the talent for mass circulation that was the white South's nightmare. The American Anti-Slavery Society produced the 224-page collection just a few months after the last news item had been clipped. *American Slavery as It Is* came with an index of Southern sins against humanity and sold for thirty-seven and a half cents (or twenty-five cents if one hundred were ordered). Local antislavery committees presented free copies of the work to opinion leaders in their communities. The Southern newspapers used in the volume were sent a copy gratis with their unwitting contributions marked. Sales topped a hundred thousand the first year (this at a time when commercial publishers celebrated when a novel sold twenty-five thousand copies). The pamphlet proved to be the most popular item on antislavery lists until *Uncle Tom's Cabin* (1852).[30]

Press runs, however impressive, understate the new life given to obscure news items by the pamphlet. *American Slavery as It Is* began with an invitation to the reader to visit the clippings that the Weld household had assembled. They were on exhibition at the offices of the American Anti-Slavery Society. Stay-at-homes could order antislavery window blinds, decorated with scenes of blacks in bondage, "according to the descriptions which are given in the *Southern* papers." Abolitionist publications, which had a tradition of reprinting embarrassing clippings from the South, now featured this material. William Lloyd Garrison prefaced his life story of the ex-slave Frederick Douglass with a story taken from a Southern paper about a master's vengeance. Borrowing or imitating the Weld-Grimké collection of Southern news was a literary industry. In his *American Notes* (1842) Charles Dickens lifted forty-four items on runaways from the Weld-Grimké pamphlet. Harriet Beecher Stowe may have exaggerated when she said that she slept with *American Slavery as It Is* under her pillow while writing *Uncle Tom's Cabin*. But there seems no question that news items from the South fired her work for antislavery.[31]

In *A Key to Uncle Tom's Cabin* (1853), Stowe recycled six of the Weld-Grimké clippings and told the reader where to find more in the old pamphlet. She added her own clippings from more than two hundred Southern papers to support her novel. Stowe's scrapbook emphasized the callous listings of blacks for sale (items that *Slavery as It Is* had passed over). In a survey of two South Carolina papers over a single week of 1852, she found eighteen invitations to split up slave families. What did Southerners think was happening when their newspapers offered *"as fine a set of children as can be shown!!"* Southern critics of *Uncle Tom's Cabin* were told to spend more time reading their own newspapers.[32]

What she meant, of course, was that Southerners should learn to read their newspapers in a new way. This is not what the proslavery spokesmen cared to do. The *Emancipator* reported that when a slaveholder was read the news items from *Slavery as It Is*, the man changed colors and developed lockjaw. The South was slow to say anything about the charges. It fell to a Boston minister to argue in print that the notices of slaves for sale which "have often harrowed our feelings" could be read with a kinder construction about the motives of masters.[33]

In the quarter century between the incendiary publications from the North and the Civil War, no Southerner made systematic use of American news items to support slavery. Papers from the free states carried many items about troubles among their black citizens and the deprivations of white laborers. This is what the proslavery spokesmen sought to emphasize, and the material could be found in the exchanges coming into every Southern newspaper office. Very little of this was republished. Pamphleteers for the slave states mentioned news items that revealed Northern hypocrisy, but they usually apologized for resting an indictment on this evidence and never tried to be comprehensive. One newspaper editor noted that every Northern mail brought columns that might be used to condemn society in the free states, but told readers the stories would be suppressed for "we do not choose to abuse the position we occupy as a public journalist." To use this news to shape political debate was a turn that these journalists were reluctant to take. There was to be nothing like the regular column in the Chicago *Tribune*, "Items on the Progress of Treason," which reprinted secessionist fire-eaters from Southern papers. Again, the broad antislavery movement was in a vanguard of mass communications that left much of the press trailing behind.[34]

The white South was shy of the news because it lacked confidence in the whole enterprise of using print to rally a national public. Southern efforts to use the printing press against abolitionists were haunted by fear and defeatism. In

1835 the citizens of upcountry South Carolina gathered in the Barnwell District to mark the bonfire of news in Charleston. Edmund Bellinger Jr., a twenty-eight-year-old lawyer, gave his neighbors as belligerent a defense of slavery as any audience heard before the Civil War. But Bellinger was timid about printing the speech: "Although published, I have used proper precautions to prevent its being circulated among any but those who are Southern in sentiment, and Southern in conduct—*to none other is it addressed.*" Several proslavery writers said that they wrote with no thought to publication, and one even apologized for the "trouble" of publication. William Gilmore Simms, for instance, was a novelist and newspaper editor and certainly not the most timid about breaking into print of the proslavery spokesmen. But Simms apologized about agreeing to "extended circulation" of his defense of the morality of slavery. The panic of the white South in the 1830s did not drive many Southerners into print. In this decade, Northerners actually wrote twice as many books and pamphlets *defending* slavery as Southern authors.[35]

Authors and editors with this reserve were not on the same playing field as the abolitionists. Proslavery arguments were bound to the world of the regional review: journals in which fine arguments were spun for the South's better citizens. Circulation was minuscule. The *Southern Quarterly Review* of the 1840s set out "to protect the rights of our Southern soil from invasion" with a readership that never topped two thousand. *DeBow's Review* sought to capitalize on the excitement over the election of Abraham Lincoln in 1860 and ordered a press run of forty-two hundred. The editor claimed more readers and more influence than any other Southern periodical. Abolitionists began with small circles of readers but had managed to use the media of their time to encompass a whole society. Defenders of slavery were not sure they wanted to address a broad public through print in the South, let alone the vast reading public that lay beyond.[36]

The south had its "fire-eaters" on the subject of slavery, men who had no qualms about the level of the argument or the refinement of the audience. These Southerners were armed with new ideas such as the proposal that the importation of Africans, outlawed in 1808, be legalized. Though some of these radicals confined their words to the South's favorite political forum, the community barbecue, men such as Leonidas Spratt and James DeBow were anything but print-shy. They started their own publications and helped to invent new types of news stories. Commercial conventions in the South, for example, had a tradition of submerging political arguments. The militants of the late 1850s took over these meetings, lobbied for ultra positions, and then published news of these developments. By 1860 the South at last had a band of journalists who matched the audacity of the antislavery press.[37]

These radicals on slavery fumbled their chance with the press. They were obsessed with correcting the notions of other proslavery forces, not with recruiting new friends for the white South. The attention drawn to the slave trade embarrassed most secessionists, and the constitution of the Confederacy repudiated the controversy by condemning the importation of Africans. Fire-eaters never did educate the South to believe that trading in humans was morally above reproach. Presses stood ready, clever men stockpiled arguments, but the proslavery cause was not for export.[38]

Even those Southerners like Weld or Grimké or Stowe who burned to set the record straight in print did not have their appetite for news. In *Cannibals All!* (1857) George Fitzhugh dropped the genteel diction and magnolia scent that had marked the proslavery polemicist. From his beloved but fading estate near the Potomac, this Virginian indicted the North for a white labor system that was, he insisted, much harsher than slavery. Fitzhugh came north to debate leaders of antislavery and enjoyed the dust-ups. "We have whole files of infidel and abolition papers . . . ," he boasted; "good people give our office a wide berth as they pass it." Fitzhugh was one of the few proslavery activists ready for an age of mass communications. He blasted the reticence of Southern newspapers to justify bondage and dreamed of a slaveholding society knit together by cheap newspapers. But Fitzhugh, unlike the abolitionists, held back. He never found a popular format to defend the slave masters. And his own writings withheld the very material that the Welds and Stowe had proved was compelling. Fitzhugh engaged the ideas of the North, not its news. His documentation of the ills of capitalist society was drawn from Great Britain, not the Northern press. Fitzhugh talked of doing it, but did not in fact hold up a mirror for the North to read about itself.[39]

With its "wide berth" to Northern news, the Confederacy set a war course. The discovery of a Northern newspaper in the luggage of a traveller or the mail box of a resident called out mobs. The South's embargo on these "foreign" papers became a common practice across the slaveholding states.[40]

3. Civil Rights and the World Watching

The South lost the Civil War but won the argument over the attention to be paid to the argument for racial equality. By the end of Reconstruction in 1876, all mainstream publications gave up on stories that might bring black Americans into focus. African Americans refused to ride public transportation in more than twenty-five cities in the South, a half century before the celebrated bus boycott in Montgomery, Alabama, by Martin Luther King Jr. in 1955. This early protest was ignored by national media. Popular magazines rarely went near the subject of race until well after World War II. In 1953 *Editor & Publisher*, the weekly chronicler of the newspaper business, commended the Southern Newspaper Publishers Association on its fiftieth anniversary and issued a 240-page supplement, bound in gold, that celebrated the South. Segregation and integration were not mentioned, even in the lead article by the courageous opponent of intolerance, Mississippi's Hodding Carter. In these professional judgments, race tension was simply not a big story in the modern South.[41]

This changed in the mid-1950s. *Brown v. Board of Education* (1954) became an ongoing story as the forces of resistance took their stand. "A Wave of Terror Threatens the South," Hodding Carter announced in *Look* (22 March 1955), as he found powerful whites preaching hatred. In August 1955 the lynching of Emmett Till brought more than fifty reporters from across the nation into a courthouse in the Mississippi Delta. In December, the bus boycott and the Rev. King brought Montgomery into focus. These stories ushered in a national press corps that would stay in attendance on the race issue for a decade. For the first time since the nineteenth century, the mail from the North brought an abundance of incendiary material: "Approved Killing in Mississippi," William Bradford Huie wrote for *Look* (24 Jan. 1955); this account of the Till killing was picked up by *Reader's Digest*. "A Bold Boycott Goes On," said *Life* (5 March 1956) as it introduced its readers to the Rev. King. *Life* did a five-part series on segregation the following year, beginning with a slave auction on the cover. This attention came in the dizzying final years of growth in general circulation magazines. The publishers were now in a race with television for the mass public. Subscription drives were relentless. *Life*, alone, estimated that it reached more than a third of all American families; nearly sixty million Americans held a copy in the six weeks following the publication date. Never again would print be such a common denominator in American homes, for eventually this reach for readers put most of these magazines out of business. But no one foresaw this in 1955. The irresistible growth of the media audience seemed obvious to corporate strategists and to the public. Slick magazines sat on the 1950s coffee table. Nearby was the newest piece of furniture, the television set. That device would bring racial conflict into focus when the civil rights movement was a bit older.[42]

In telling the story of civil rights, the new media earned as excited a welcome as did the publicists of antislavery. Anti-abolitionist crowds had seized the papers they hated, but in the nineteenth-century South the mobs could only dream of catching the authors. At virtually every step in the civil rights struggle, angry white Southerners looked into the faces of journalists. The white South fought the press in courts and business offices by filing suits, pulling ads, and canceling subscriptions; but segregationists also fought the press in the streets.[43]

Every reporter who covered the civil rights movement has a crowd story; they were engulfed, insulted, and the unlucky were beaten. There were major confrontations in Arkansas, Alabama, and Mississippi, briefer skirmishes in

Tennessee, Maryland, Georgia, and Florida. More than fifty members of the press were beaten. This, despite reporters' best efforts to remain inconspicuous. Journalists chopped their notebooks so as to fit into their pockets, away from view. Reporters hid the stigmata of the professional. They removed their coats and even took off their shirts and watches so as to "just mill around with the boys" without detection. The efforts were often not enough.[44]

At Little Rock in 1957, a correspondent for the Hearst chain who had covered World War II and Korea said that the campus of Central High scared him as few battlefields had. Covering this, he said, was like standing next to an open gas jet, awaiting a flame to be struck. The beatings of four black journalists at Little Rock showed the murderous potential. Five years later, at the University of Mississippi, a mob proved that it could go all the way. Paul Guihard, of Agence France Presse, was taken behind a tree, made to kneel, and executed.[45]

Frequently the assaults and harassment took on a life of their own, independent of the crowd's hunt for blacks who dared to integrate. "We ought to wipe up the street with these Yankee reporters" was shouted at Central High in Little Rock. "Let's kill every reporter we can find" was the call at Ole Miss. On the May morning in 1961 when freedom riders protesting segregation by direct action reached Montgomery on a Greyhound bus, a mob delayed its attack on the passengers in order to finish off the press. John Lewis, the black civil rights leader, saw white men rush forward and smash the press corps, leaving his own group alone for the moment. The fury at journalists exploded before the whites turned their clubs on the freedom riders.[46]

In the tradition of mobs that stretches back to the American Revolution, these activities seemed an extension of legitimate authority in the minds of many in the crowd. "We've got permission to kick the — out of them," an activist shouted in Alabama. In many cities, this man was right. In Little Rock, Birmingham, Oxford, and Marion there was coordination between Southern police forces and the mob. Law officers condoned and even encouraged the attacks.[47]

Many of the citizens who formed mobs sized up the press with some care. This may be a hard idea to accept. The mobs that are best known today from the *Eyes on the Prize* television series do not look like students of media techniques; still less do they seem fortified by research. But many were. On several occasions there was method to the rabid press haters. White reporters with a Southern accent often had a shield. If that failed, they were more likely to win an apology from the Southerners who had beaten them. But mastheads mattered as much as regional loyalty, according to reporters at the scene. The *Arkansas Gazette* had staff beaten for the sins of its editorial page in defying Gov. Orval Faubus. Fred Powledge was slugged at Ole Miss, not when he was identified as a reporter, but after the crowd found out the Atlanta paper he worked for. Mobs settled scores with Southern news organizations that had crossed them on racial matters.

There was no surer way to become a press martyr than to work for the Yankee with the largest circulation and gall, Henry Luce. In the judgment of a Southern reporter who talked with the mob at Little Rock, Time-Life was made to pay for its early discovery of black America and its weekly criticism of segregationist heroes. It was a commonplace among segregationists that Time Inc. had spread the myth that Emmett Till was the son of a war hero (covering up the rape conviction of his military father). The scorn for Southern governors in the Luce magazines did not help. Nor did the performances of a rival journalist at whistle stops across the South in the 1960 presidential campaign. This man stole a Time badge and greeted the locals, "Look a here, yeah you. Henry Luce wants to know what you white trash are thinking about!" No wonder that Time-Life employees were frequently in harm's way. Mobs willing to pummel *Time*'s wry young staffer Calvin Trillin, twice, were clearly fed up. *U.S. News & World Report* devoted as much attention to integration as *Time*, but this conservative weekly deplored the civil rights movement and told the story the way the white South saw it. "There isn't a white man's magazine in print except the *U.S. News & World Report,*" a Klansman said in 1958. Employees of this magazine were conspicuous by their absence in casualty reports. In the opinion of a Justice Department official, this was more than luck: segregationists cooled down when one mentioned *U.S. News & World Report*. In Birmingham, this federal lawman used the magazine as his cover.[48]

At Little Rock, the hotheads wanted to edit, not just destroy. On assignment at Central High, Benjamin Fine of the New York *Times* accused a heckler of not reading the stories he filed. This segregationist sent away for a subscription and passed the paper on to friends. "Within a day, some twenty of the segregationists, who had been ready to tear me apart, and had given me a hard time, apologized," Fine said. This reporter noticed that his new readers now protected him at rallies.[49]

Crowds did their own reporting and were outraged by the prospect that what they saw and felt would not be what they would find in print. In Little Rock, shouts from the streets through the day told the story: "Oh, my, God, they're going in. . . . The niggers are in. . . . The niggers got in. . . . They tricked us. The niggers got in. . . . Look at that. They arrest a white girl and let the niggers in our school." This narrative was supplemented by segregationists' sheets, circulating through the crowd. "That's what we're fighting, you see," one man said as he pointed to a headline about a Communist conspiracy. In calling out their story, segregationists challenged the press to see the world as they saw it. In Little Rock, the moment after blood was shed, reporters heard calls to write stories that would confirm Gov. Faubus's claim that violence was inevitable if integration went forward. They would accept no other story: "If you Yankee bastards can't tell the right story why don't you go back where you come from?" "You won't tell the truth about us" was a typical taunt.[50]

Antebellum mobs wanted to smash presses and see the news in flames. Segregationists did not return to this ritual of impersonal bonfires and sackings. An Alabama mob did pile up the clothes of freedom riders and set them afire; it would have been easier to light up newsstands, or even newsrooms, across the South. But this did not happen. It was the embodiment of the press, the witnesses with their recording devices, that drove mobs to fury.

Segregationist mobs were smashers of the instruments that threatened the widest distribution of their activities: the camera and broadcasting gear. Cameras and all types of electronic equipment such as lights and tape recorders were invitations to mayhem in the South. This hardware, a reporter for *Newsday* said, is "often more dangerous than guns in the midst of race-baiting mobs." In the eight years of street violence against the press, cameras were often the first things a mob grabbed (and the only things they sprayed with paint). Blinding the press was the first priority of a Southern mob. These segregationists were charged with many things but rarely with pecuniary interests. These mobs were wreckers, not thieves. And at times, the Luddite impulse here seemed to compete with racist priorities. Thus men at Little Rock took time to smash a camera of a black journalist flat with their feet, rather than joining in murderous assault on their victim.[51]

Why, of all people, should friends of Jim Crow fear the camera and its record of their deeds? These whites assembled to *show* the South that blacks could be turned back and that federal forces were tyrants. They carried signs and placards. Photography could help, as Gov. Faubus demonstrated in the Little Rock crisis. "Evidence of the naked force of the Federal Government is here apparent in the unsheathed bayonet in the backs of school girls," he said as he held up a news photo during a television address. He also showed his audience a news photo of a bleeding mob leader, introduced as a martyr. Coverage of Little Rock, especially in pictures, helped to build resistance in the deep South, according to correspondents. Louisiana segregationists hired a photographer to take pictures of integrated schools in Washington, D.C., in 1960, asserting that "actual conditions" would show the wisdom of separating the races. George Wallace's stand in the door to bar a black student at the University of Alabama made no sense without cameras to record it. This may have been a reason that Col. Al Lingo, leading the Alabama state police in the preservation of segregation forever, gave cameramen a ringside seat for the Edmund Pettus Bridge at Selma in 1965. Standing up to defy integration and blinding the witnesses would seem to be self-canceling actions.[52]

There was a logic to people who were acting outside the law destroying the evidence that could lead to arrest or retaliation. But that is not how racist vigilantes had usually conducted themselves before the civil rights movement.

Posing for a photograph had been a venerable tradition of lynchers in the South. The posing stopped in the 1930s, but the dependence on the camera remained. In 1959, whites of Poplarville, Mississippi, pasted a news photo of the town's jail on their auto windshields, marking the cell of a black prisoner who had just been lynched. The purpose of the lynch photograph was to scare blacks and whites who questioned the American apartheid — was this less pressing when integrationists had come out in the open than it had been when they lay hidden? It is true that the Emmett Till lynching was part of a new accountability in the Southern justice system. But as the Till case had shown, even white bullies who killed could not be convicted in the rural South. More, they might make money off the deed, for this is what Till's killers did in selling their story to William Bradford Huie and *Look* magazine. Mobs in Little Rock and Oxford had nothing to fear from a jury. Prosecutions were rare, and penalties were light. In 1965 it cost a lumber salesman $53.75 to assault a UPI photographer; a service station employee was fined $78.75 for hitting Richard Valeriani of NBC in the head with an ax handle. It cannot have been the likelihood of trouble with the law or the penalties if one were caught that led mobs to assault photographers.[53]

At issue here was the reach of the stories told by still cameras and broadcasting gear. Like antislavery agitation in the 1830s, pictures of racial conflict were circulating too widely in the 1950s to live with in peace. Photojournalism for a mass market was only two decades old. Television was an infant (especially in Little Rock, whose residents waited until the Korean War ended for the broadcasts to begin). The number of television stations increased five times between 1953 and 1957. Television came of age largely ignorant of African Americans, especially in the South, where local stations would often drop network programs that had black entertainers. As late as 1960, the television networks cut away from black speakers at the national party conventions to spare the feelings of segregationists. Print journalism had never incorporated black Americans into routine coverage. In breaking this taboo with civil rights demonstrations, the mass media told stories that held talismanic power.[54]

Magic is not too strong a word. When a phalanx of white men in bib overalls rushed John Chancellor in a small Mississippi town, the broadcaster held up his microphone and shouted, "All right, come on, the whole world is going to know what you're doing to me." The mob backed off.[55]

A sure sense that the whole world was watching raised the stakes for everyone following civil rights. In leading magazines, *Brown v. Board of Education* had been welcomed for its effect on foreigners, no less than on Americans themselves. The conflicts that followed in the South were inevitably lamented because of what the world would think. With good reason. Cables to the State Department from U.S. embassies were a chorus of alarms about how news of racial discrimination in the South hurt the image of America. The white South was aware that it was being humiliated abroad. Southerners noted that there were more than ten foreign reporters at King's trial during the Montgomery bus boycott. The mobbing of freedom riders in Birmingham was a picture on the front pages of papers in Tokyo and an embarrassment to a touring Alabama business delegation. A Memphis paper hated those cameras because with them the South was "held up as an object of scorn around the globe."[56]

The civil rights movement itself believed that the right media outlets had magical power. John Lewis of the Student Nonviolent Coordinating Committee saw that television was transforming the protests that he began without regard to press coverage. During the Birmingham demonstrations, Lewis and his friends at Fisk University pinned the stories from the press on trees so that students would mobilize. Both the Congress of Racial Equality and the National Association for the Advancement of Colored People Legal Defense Fund issued handbills in the early sixties that were reprints from the national press, prominently displaying the source. Across the spectrum, activists sought the imprimatur of prestigious media to tell their story. This was precisely what segregationist mobs seemed to know instinctively, that images let loose by the national media were deeply wounding.[57]

Mobs were not simply guardians of their community's image; they were protectors of its means of intimidation. Isolation and a sense of impotence were required if blacks were to remain second-class citizens. Too many witnesses complicated the abridgment of rights. Lynch photographs were meant to be private, and press photographers of the crowd were not welcomed. These scenes were memory pieces for a small audience who shared assumptions. The racist rationale was sometimes memorialized in notes written on the back of the photos. Stripping away this context and creating a vast audience for the lynching scene spoiled everything.[58]

The victims learned they had allies. The number of marches, sit-ins, and freedom rides grew in tandem with the national coverage. Always before these tactics had played out without being carried by the mainstream media. Photojournalism and broadcasting, especially, kept issues alive. This may explain why the truck-stop answer to the movement, *Sex and Civil Rights: The True Selma Story* (1965), sounded more outraged at people who had stayed north to edit rather than protesters who had come south to fornicate. Segregationists could visualize an audience conscious of its strength and willing to persist in these protests. As a worried planter told Theodore H. White, "Every one of those Negroes on my land has a television set in his shack, and he sits there in the evening and watches." "Bloody Sunday" in Selma, as filmed by the television cameras that Alabama authorities had welcomed, was a public relations disaster for segregationists. The Wallace administration's explanation was that there had been "too much film," too graphic a record for too large an audience. This supply of images was the new, fearful breach in the defense of the segregated

South. In attempting to terminate photojournalism and broadcasting, mobs were astute.[59]

4. Alabama Deconstructs

"A great body of opinion here is against the printing of race news," Hodding Carter observed in 1961. "The mob is just an extreme form of this view." Thus the white South was true to its fears about the media of 1835. Again, there were formal denunciations of the emblems of mass communications (as when Carter's contribution to *Look* magazine was condemned by a vote of the Mississippi House of Representatives). Again, the media of the region were not able to produce a counterpoint news weekly or network. But this time there were strong voices who took on the Northern press, capitalizing on the resentments felt against it and even subverting its reporting.[60]

The Southern editor most successful in taking the fight to the Northern press was a cordial antagonist of Martin Luther King Jr., Grover Cleveland Hall Jr. This stylish bachelor made the editorial offices of the Montgomery *Advertiser* into a club for Northern reporters during the bus boycott of 1956. His hospitality extended to a black reporter from the New York *Post* who came south to indict Jim Crow. Hall, a card-carrying member of the American Civil Liberties Union, thrived on controversy. "King is a souped-up Swami," he said. The editor was a segregationist committed to peaceful resistance. Hall's tactics against the civil rights movement caused more disarray in the ranks than any mob achieved.[61]

Hall turned to reporting, daring the Northern press to explore racial feelings at home. He goaded the New York *Post* to send reporters to see how black and white New Yorkers were getting along. When an open exchange of letters with the liberal editor James Wechsler did not yield these stories, the Alabama editor produced his own. Hall turned to the Bible for the running title, "Tell it not in Gath, publish it not in the streets of Askelon." This was a mischievous encyclopedia of Northern failures to report on race, unless that story lay conveniently in the South. The Montgomery *Advertiser*, the paper that the Weld household had clipped to expose the South, now picked apart the Northern press to vindicate the South. The *Advertiser* asked Yankee editors when they had last printed the picture of a black bride on their society page. A box score, printed under the famous mastheads of these papers, showed that black citizens were invisible to society editors of urban America. The New York *Times* could point to only one African American bride in its whole history. Detroit papers that featured series such as "Thunder over Dixie" were caught hiding the news of a white mob that demanded segregation in the Motor City. The Montgomery paper found the NAACP eager to talk about a story that Northern editors would not touch, of systematic discrimination in their towns.[62]

The series was syndicated in the South to great praise and summarized in national magazines with pained admiration. The Alabama legislature commended the Askelon stories and challenged the Northern press to report on their own communities. Hall had charted a safe course for the editors of Dixie. Memphis papers, for example, followed Hall and featured reports of street crime where Northerners had their way on the race question. Segregationists in Little Rock produced their own pamphlet filled with horrifying news stories and pictures from northern cities. Harry S. Ashmore, fighting a lonely struggle for integration on the *Arkansas Gazette*, saw that Hall had built "a moral escape hatch" for Southerners who could not face their own sins.[63]

The mobilization of the press of the white South to embarrass the North would be of limited interest if Hall's indictment had gone no further. But Hall was the voice of the paper that John Lewis, Ralph Abernathy, and Martin Luther King Jr. read. Indeed, blacks of this region followed the *Advertiser* (and praised the paper) because it was more likely to give respectful attention to African American life than most other white papers. King, in his account of the Montgomery bus boycott, shows that the movement followed the *Advertiser* closely. He commended Hall for condemning violence and called the editor a "brilliant but complex man." These African American leaders did not need Hall to tell them that racism was a national curse and that the Northern press was selective in its attention. But the Montgomery *Advertiser*'s point cannot have escaped their notice. The NAACP actually commended the Askelon series at the same time that segregationists cheered it.[64]

Hall had a friend who took this story north and waged a counter-revolution to the civil rights movement. This friend called Hall nearly every day and asked the editor for help on some of his most important speeches. His name was George Wallace. "You and I together will be able to make this nation see that it's not just the South that's so terrible," the Governor told the editor.[65]

Wallace had learned early in life of the power of national magazines. He travelled through the upper South and the Midwest during the Great Depression as a magazine salesman and found that even the illiterate and the blind wanted their homes furnished with these publications. Television fascinated Wallace, and he was quick to use it in his rise in Alabama. When the Rev. King marched on Montgomery in 1965, the Governor sat and watched sets tuned to every channel. Wallace was obsessed about what the press, especially the national press, thought of him. Wallace's loyal press secretary found that his boss "uses no discretion at all" in attacking journalists to their face and "never missed an opportunity to lambast the press" before a general audience. The record bears this out. A third to a half of Wallace campaign speeches were a gloss on news coverage, according to a reporter who sat through this hunt for demons. "We got the Newsweek and the Time travelin' with us today," he would say at the beginning of a rally. "They're lookin' us over. Smile and look pretty today," he continued, "because you may wind up on national television." The Governor had a stock vocabulary for the people who provided this coverage: "intellectual morons" and "sissy britches editors" and "slick haired boys" and "TV dudes."[66]

Wallace said this even as he seized every chance for coverage in the media controlled by these creatures. At rallies he bragged of appearances on the networks and held national magazines up, proudly, that had written him up. Indeed, when his wife ran for governor in his place in 1966, her chief function at rallies, after introducing him, was to hold the archive of clippings that he wanted in easy reach. "See here, they got a picture of yo guvnuh in this magazine that goes all over this nation," Wallace said. "The national press now, anything's that bad about yo guvnuh, oh yes, they gonna run that." National correspondents were granted access to the Governor that local journalists could not hope for. When Col. Lingo, head of the state troopers, barred these visitors from the confrontation at the University of Alabama, Wallace made sure that the reporters most likely to hate him could see him send the blacks away. Wallace newsletters prompted followers to look for him on national programs and in famous magazines—occasions for him to be misrepresented and to scorn this media. It was as if a gambler who knew the dice were loaded should insist the game continue and the stakes be raised. Wallace was clear about why: the crooked media conferred honor. "I took 'em all on," the governor would remind his audience, ". . . and they are more respectful now. They say MISTER Wallace. And when they say that, they're sayin' MISTER Alabamian, and MRS. Alabamian, and MISS Alabamian." By putting stories in his own context before his own audience, Wallace was as bold and as successful as the Welds with their scrapbook. He, too, subverted an enemy press.[67]

Wallace was not the first Southern leader to court a national press while he let loose on them. Huey Long, the "Kingfish" of Louisiana, had done this in the 1930s. Wallace was the first Southerner to take his argument north and play on the lapses in Northern reporting and the hypocrisy that Grover Hall had helped to place at the center of segregationist argument.[68] Wallace broke with many other segregationists in his studied refusal to make public statements about race. The Governor decried racism while he managed to make a strong racial appeal through allusions to crime and federal interference. The conservative white South never had a more effective salesman. In 1968 his presidential campaign won nearly ten million votes. Wallace did what the slave South had never dared to do, lay out a program to the widest possible audience by embracing the media . . . on his own terms.

New media have no more powerful function than the sense they give that the whole nation, indeed, the outside world, is watching. The comfortable haven of local elites is shattered. The meanings of words and pictures seem up for grabs. When the audience expands, locals not only lose the power to silence the press; they lose the power to attach a meaning securely to a text. Leaders may now make their own selections from the enemy media, helping to change the meaning of texts that they have appropriated. What happens, whether Weld or Wallace makes the clipping collection, is that stories become cues to social action unforeseen by the journalists who created them. An interest group that shrinks from this task, as the slave South did, must rely solely on raw power to make its view prevail.[69]

When revolutions in the media accompany revolutions in society, they force new readings and create new bases for legitimacy. In three centuries of debate on race in North America, social action has been quickest when new media allowed words and pictures to reach new people and simultaneously created a new range of meanings. The paired growth of audience and interpretive choices is both the opportunity and menace of new media.

4

DISCRIMINATING

READERS

The middle of the nineteenth century produced news readers of greater independence and larger appetite. Their enlarged freedom and tastes came with the expansion of news in print. Publishers raced ahead of the three-fold increase of population between 1850 and 1900. Periodical titles grew nearly tenfold. In 1900 there were twenty daily newspapers in circulation for every one at mid-century. Even modest households found that news fit their budget. Some papers sold for a penny or two, a third or even a sixth of the cheapest price for news in the early nineteenth century. By the 1890s even the quality dailies cost only pennies, and some of the best magazines had become similar bargains. With more copies about, the reader was freer of the social contacts that had been necessary to see news in print. Borrowers were replaced by buyers. The news itself expanded. Human interest and other specialized beats such as crime, sports, and society news were the hallmarks of the popular press. With the coming of the telegraph and the daily paper to all substantial towns, the press could often outpace word-of-mouth in delivering news. Print journalism was distributed so widely and cheaply that even isolation or poverty did not necessarily take the American out of the flow of news. The daily paper and the weekly periodical became a common denominator in American life.[1]

The growth of the news-reading habit was the subject of worry and advice in the nineteenth century.

Pathologies of reading were examined by many experts. Evangelicals, those relentless purveyors of reading material for ordinary citizens, worried that newspapers had helped to create a nation of skimmers. Along with their popular tracts, Christian publishers issued injunctions against "cursory reading." Distinguished journalists believed that reading bad newspapers—or reading good newspapers the wrong way—could harm Americans almost as much as paying no mind to the press. "Mental desultoriness" was the fate of readers who flitted from story to story, according to E. L. Godkin, editor of the highbrow New York *Evening Post*. Walter Williams warned his fellow editors about the "over-indulgence in newspaper reading, with its attendant mental results, enfeebling of memory, dissipation of mind and thought." Williams, already a worried man, became the founding dean of the nation's first journalism school in 1908.[2]

The popular author Julia McNair Wright commended the reading of newspapers while she condemned the way many people read them. She did not issue a general warning about scandal and frivolities, for she had something else in mind:

> What is the use of reading the marriages and deaths in cities where you are unacquainted, advertisements where you do not mean to purchase, time-tables when you do not mean to travel, accounts of gay weddings, interesting only to the friends of the contracting parties, police news of strange places, tit-bits of scandal about strange people, doggerel rhymes by nobody [?] . . . This reading *everything* in the paper is dangerous, as filling the mind with disconnected trifles, and rendering almost impossible a *continuous* train of thought and study.[3]

This obsessive reading of news was common enough to have deserved Wright's attention. The reading aloud of whole newspapers, not forgetting the ads, had gone on in frontier settlements. Many rural Americans had warm memories of time spent going over every inch of newsprint. Whittier's celebrated poem "Snow-Bound" (1866) pictured a household feasting on everything in a weekly paper: far-off wars, marriages and deaths, goods for sale and property lost, criminals caught and weather recorded. In the Rev. Baker's serial for *Harper's Weekly* on family life during the Civil War, a Confederate husband read every word of the newspaper to his wife, repeating the stories with encouraging political news several times. Unionists in the South treated a paper from the North even more obsessively, the author confessed: "We carefully unfold and read the precious paper aloud to wife or sister, to say nothing of all the Union people in the neighborhood cautiously summoned in to hear. The editorials, dispatches, items, advertisements of hair oil, and the like—with greedy hunger we let no morsel or crumb of the paper escape us." And it was not only the isolated or the desperate who needed to be saved from obsessive news reading. Whitelaw Reid, successor to Horace Greeley at the New York *Tribune*, felt that peaceful, urban life was producing readers who were hopelessly mired in the news. Could we expect more from these compulsive readers, he asked, than "an intellectual state of oyster-like consciousness?"[4]

Whatever that might be, it sounded bad. The voracious appetite for news that startled these observers is one of the few passions of Victorian America that has gone without study. When noticed at all, the reader of the popular press has usually been pitied as a victim of press lords or the commercial culture they represented. But to make readers into dupes (or oysters) is to miss much. The first Americans who lived with an abundance of news in print had something important to say about how media were changing their lives. They talked back; they made choices. Their discriminations stand today, often unrecognized, in writing, art, and documentary photography that has been celebrated in other contexts. Mass communication was not incidental to these observers. They were its students, both advancing and rejecting the spread of news.

The testimony we must hear about journalism is nothing if not diverse: a journal keeper who had limited patience with society, an artist who obliterated words, and sharecroppers who were the media's connoisseurs.

1. News at Walden Pond

Henry David Thoreau often said that he hated journalism, root and branch. Frequently he scorned the very idea of news and said that coverage of even the most important public questions corrupted readers. In his beloved town of Concord, Massachusetts, he saw the dawn of instantaneous communication in the coming of the telegraph. He was unimpressed. Thoreau addressed his personal journal, and then his fellow citizens, with his doubts about mass communications.

In *Walden* (1854) Thoreau's wit surpassed his scorn and he was polite: "We are in great haste to construct a magnetic telegraph from Maine to Texas; but Maine and Texas, it may be, have nothing important to communicate." "I am sure I never read any memorable news in a newspaper," Thoreau said. "If we read of one man robbed, or murdered, or killed by accident, or one house burned, or one vessel wrecked, or one steamboat blown up, or one cow run over on the Western Railroad, or one mad dog killed, or one lot of grasshoppers in the winter,—we never need read of another. One is enough. If you are acquainted with the principle, what do you care for a myriad of instances and applications?"[5]

In his journal and in essays published after *Walden*, Thoreau was frequently more direct. "Do not read the newspapers," he told himself. "If you chance to live and move and have your being in that thin stratum in which the events which make the news transpire—thinner than the paper on which it is printed,—then these things will fill the world for you." There was a conventional side to his hatred of the press. Like most nineteenth-century Americans, he singled out those papers that defied his politics. In the 1850s his journal explodes with criticism of a "mercenary and servile" press that was blind to the evils of slavery. Finding apologists for the white South in the Boston press, he asked, "Is there any dust which such conduct does not lick and make fouler still with its slime?" Thoreau said that when he read Boston papers, "I have heard the gurgling of the sewer through every column." The same summer that *Walden* came from the press, in the heat of the slavery issue, Thoreau told a New England audience that those who read the periodical press "are in the condition of the dog that returns to his vomit."[6]

Many of Thoreau's words on mass communications are famous; most are savage. They are also misleading and deserve a second look. At times, newspapers fit into his pastorale. The spread of news could be as sensual for him as the life of Walden Pond. He was an agent in making mass communications possible. And it was the journalism he professed to hate, in the end, that set his political course.

In the journal, the telegraph is an object of wonder. On his walks around Concord, Thoreau heard the wind hum in the bare wires of the first lines strung near the village, and dozens of passages celebrate this "American lyre." When he built his cabin at Walden Pond he rested with newspapers, reading the pages that had wrapped his dinner. Deep into the Maine woods, Thoreau's travelling party distributed newspapers, "than which nothing can be more acceptable to a backwoods people," he said. "Reporter" was one of the identities Thoreau chose to explain his life with nature. He said that Concord was his "news room" and felt its pull: "Every day or two I strolled to the village to hear some of the gossip which is incessantly going on there, circulating either from mouth to mouth, or from newspaper to newspaper, and which, taken in homeopathic doses, was really as refreshing in its way as the rustle of leaves and the peeping of frogs."[7]

Only rarely did Thoreau tell the reader that his knowledge of mass communications was based on more than casual contact. He knew this trade. It is not simply that Thoreau's first published writing was a newspaper article, that he edited one issue of the *Dial* and once tried his hand at selling magazine subscriptions. Thoreau was a conscious though unskilled player in the literary marketplace who calculated his audience and sought circulation in the most popular journals. He was grateful to be taken in hand by Horace Greeley, who served as his agent and boosted this Transcendentalist in the columns of his New York *Tribune*.[8]

And Thoreau had an even more practical grounding in mass communications. In the decade before he built his cabin, his family had become the most successful manufacturer of pencils in the United States. Thoreau's uncle had found a graphite deposit, and his father had organized the manufacturing and selling of pencils. The pencil was the product of mining and manufacturing advances in the seventeenth and eighteenth centuries, but the essential step of extruding a graphite mixture that could be smoothly encased with wood was not managed until the 1830s. This was an achievement of a German firm. Thoreau managed to figure out what the Germans had done, and, adding improvements of his own, he made the family's plant in Concord a success. None of Thoreau's careers, not his writing, his surveying, nor his inspecting of snowstorms, kept him from giving his best to graphite. Thoreau told his neighbor Ralph Waldo Emerson that when he worked in the family business he dreamed about pencil manufacturing. It was his research and tinkering on the processing of graphite and the shaping of wood that gave his family its first sustained prosperity in the 1840s. Thoreau's skill in handling the fine, black powder helped to make American pencils the equal of imports.[9]

The humble pencil will never be cast, like the steam engine, as a supernatural force in Victorian society. But this piece of wood accelerated the way people communicated. Pencils were carried by the first European explorers of the New World for sketching, and by the end of the eighteenth century the pencil was a common tool of artists, surveyors, and engineers. Thoreau pencils were welcomed by these specialists, but the quality and price of this line made them attractive to the general public. It was the start-up firms like the one in Concord and the manufacturing process Thoreau advanced that democratized the pencil. This simple, inexpensive device became the most convenient way to put words on paper. (Sales of pencils in the United States are about double those of all forms of pens.) American writers popularized "pencillings" or "pencil sketches" as metaphors for prose at about this time. Words set down at lightning speed might capture the moment. Thoreau came to sleep with a pencil under his pillow so he could awake and record his thoughts. Soon, the pencil industry in America gave everyone this easy access to words on paper.[10]

Thoreau graphite proved to be both the support of the family and the agent for mass production of the printed page. Before the second decade of the nineteenth century, American publishers had but two ways to produce more copies of a work after the first printing: they saved the original type as set, or they did the whole job of setting type over again. Publishers hated to commit their limited supply of type and crowd their shops with old printing forms. New editions were a gamble with high stakes. Stereotyping changed printing in Thoreau's youth. Plaster, and later papier-mâché, took the impression of the type-metal and formed a mold for a new plate. One hundred thousand impressions could be made from the stereotype. The original type was freed for use, and storage was much easier. "Stereotype" had no pejorative meaning. The term suggested only that print could now pass more easily to the people. In 1841 an American magazine introduced electricity into the production of a plate. The electrotype process deposited copper held in solution over a wax impression made by the original type-metal. Graphite on the wax mold was essential to the electroplating. The Thoreaus had learned of this secret manufacturing process by 1850, alerted by a switch of orders for their raw material instead of their finished product. The family thought less about pencils and more about the lucrative trade in graphite for printers. *Walden* was produced by the older stereotype method, but by this time the secret of electrotyping was out and publishers could get plates yielding sharper images. The new plates were good for half a million impressions. Thoreau, who knew only frustration in the publication of his own work, had helped American printers to realize the dream of texts and pictures for all.[11]

In the nineteenth century, Yankee scourges of modern media frequently found themselves advancing the new forms. Albert Brisbane, another Transcendentalist, carefully trained his son to hate commercialism and produced the crassest and most effective editor of the yellow press at the end of the century. "The press is overstepping in every direction the obvious bounds of propriety and of decency," Samuel D. Warren wrote with his co-author Louis D. Brandeis. This famous *Harvard Law Review* article of 1890 established the modern right to privacy, spurred by recognition that "gossip . . . has become a trade, which is pursued with industry as well as effrontery." The Warren family of Massachusetts manufactured newsprint and led the way in the technical improvements that made cheap and prying dailies possible. They were substantial investors in what one press historian has found to be "the most audacious" of the major Boston papers, the only one with a gossip column. A Warren and a Brisbane, much like a Thoreau, denounced cheap papers with the same standing as a du Pont would have denouncing bombs.[12]

Thoreau, who is forever asking the reader to make choices, also makes the reader choose about Thoreau. Is he an assassin of news . . . or its poet? Did he live by mass communications or defy it? The answer is: both, and at once. The dilemma occupied much of Thoreau's public life after *Walden*.

The attack on slavery was the one news story to fully engage him. Indeed, the story of John Brown's raid at Harpers Ferry during October 1859 seems to have been the only news from outside of New England ever to mean much to Thoreau. (Thoreau's journal and correspondence show almost no attention to national news before John Brown's attack. The entire surviving journal, 1837–61, more than seven thousand pages as published, mentions only one contemporary American President. Congress is mentioned twice; the Supreme Court not at all. In a lifetime of letter writing, Thoreau rarely acknowledged national leaders and referred to Abraham Lincoln only once.) News of John Brown helped Thoreau to decide the value of mass communication itself.[13]

Thoreau knew John Brown. The guerrilla fighter from the Missouri border came to lecture in Concord in late winter of 1857. Would Kansas join the

Union as a slave state and open the West to bondage? Thoreau was in step with some of New England's most celebrated writers and politicians in caring about this issue. Brown's host, the Concord schoolmaster, brought the old soldier into Thoreau's home for a long conversation. Later, Thoreau turned out for Brown's lecture on the hard fighting that had kept the Slave Power down. In 1859, five months before Brown took an armed band to Harpers Ferry, he gave his second lecture in Concord. Again, Thoreau attended. Through this two-and-a-half-year period, Thoreau said not a word about this friend of the slaves in his journal or in his correspondence. It was only the news of Harpers Ferry that sent Thoreau to write and speak out about John Brown.

Brown and his twenty-one recruits attacked Harpers Ferry on Sunday, October 16, 1859, and held the federal arsenal until Tuesday. The next day, Wednesday the 19th, Thoreau heard of John Brown's raid while visiting Emerson's home in Concord. The news that reached Emerson's must have been one of the early rumors that sprang from the telegraph reports, for the story had it that Brown was dead. The journal entry for the 19th assumes the truth of the rumor that Brown was dead. But this sense of immediacy is a false note. In fact Thoreau was not willing to commit his thoughts to his journal until he could fashion them around newspaper stories.[14]

The first entries in the journal, dated the 19th, include passages from issues of the Boston *Journal* and William Lloyd Garrison's *Liberator* of October 21. This shows that the diarist, however quickly he examined his soul, hesitated until he had seen the papers. Thoreau may have scribbled his first thoughts in pencil, but he waited for the newspapers before he touched pen to his journal. Much of his energy went into a search through the press. He boasted, "I read all the newspapers I could get within a week." The journal condemns the paper with this "pregnant news" of the raid for bothering to cover routine political speeches. Republican and even abolitionist editors are rapped for failing to rush to Brown's defense. On this subject, Thoreau could not speak in his journal directly. What he wanted to say he could only say in reaction to the press.[15]

"A Plea for John Brown," the address that Thoreau first delivered in Concord on October 30, continues this mission "to correct the tone and the statements of the newspapers." There is irony in this search for news. Thoreau found Brown's most revealing words in a publication that wanted the rebel hanged. On October 21, the fiercely pro-South New York *Herald* gave Brown's dialogue with his captors to the nation. Thoreau centered his "Plea" around this unexpected testimony. (He seemed almost to pinch himself at finding the New York paper useful, for he wrote "Herald!" as he made extracts in his journal.)

In many ways, Thoreau was not helped by news. The rush of information into Thoreau's life made reality harder to grasp. In the journal he complains that nature itself eludes him as he thinks about news of John Brown. The story of John Brown in the press also eluded Thoreau.[16]

After Harpers Ferry, newspapers focused on a story from the battles between free soil and slavery men in Kansas three years earlier. What had John Brown done at Pottawatomie Creek? Here in May 1856 five proslavery settlers had been killed in the middle of the night. It was Brown's doing. He commanded a five-man raiding party, which included two of his sons and a son-in-law. Brown had roused the families from their beds, decided which males were to be taken, and marched them into the dark. Brown's men hacked the prisoners to death with swords. Brown himself shot one corpse through the temple.

Nearly ten months later, Thoreau first met Brown. By that time some newspapers (including two in Boston) had told the story. A U.S. government report (printed in one hundred thousand copies) had given official status to the atrocity story. Harpers Ferry revived the story of Brown's earlier, inglorious raid. The New York *Herald*, the paper that Thoreau pored over for news of Brown, ran an account of the massacre on October 19. During the rest of 1859 the Boston and the New York press that Thoreau followed gave ample demonstration that there was blood on Brown's hands. Thoreau turned a blind eye to the evidence. In "A Plea for John Brown," Thoreau cleaned up a remark that the abolitionist had made in Concord. Emerson's journal had caught Brown saying that his enemies in Kansas "had a perfect right to be shot." These were the words of the man who had pulled the trigger. Thoreau put some distance between the vengeful patriarch and Pottawatomie Creek by recalling that Brown had said proslavery fighters "had a perfect right to be hung." In Thoreau's last memorial to Brown, a published address in the summer of 1860, the hero had no blemish.[17]

Thoreau acquired the new errors of journalism between Brown's capture in October and his hanging in December. Thoreau swallowed Brown lore, especially as it came from the paper that had toasted his own literary productions, Greeley's New York *Tribune*. The Brown apocrypha, dismissing the charges against him on the Kansas border, endowing him with military cunning, passed from the press into Thoreau's journal and addresses. At Brown's execution in December, Thoreau could *see* his hero bend to kiss a slave child held up by its mother—a scene invented by a reporter in the New York *Tribune*.[18]

Thoreau followed Brown to the grave two and a half years later. His death, at forty-four, from tuberculosis, was probably hastened by the years spent inhaling graphite in his work for the industry of mass communications. After John Brown, Thoreau had retreated from the spread of news. There was no more in his journal on the music of the telegraph lines. Even the Slave Power faded from his view. In the spring of 1861, the South took over federal installations: the systematic steps toward war that John Brown had begun with a Quixotic

raid on an arsenal. Thoreau addressed all Americans as he wrote to an abolitionist of his disdain for the news. "As for my prospective reader," he said, "I
hope that he *ignores* Fort Sumter, & Old Abe, & all that. . . . I do not so
much regret the present condition of things in this country (provided I regret it
at all) as I do that I ever heard of it."[19]

Thoreau had stepped forward and exposed himself to news, allowed it to
color his imagination, acted on what he had learned . . . only to stand, in the
end, detached from the course of events. Was he deceived? Was he inconsis-
tent? There is good reason to think so, but perhaps not if we think like Thoreau.

Facts and exact observation were not his preferred path to the truth. Thoreau botched things as an observer of nature (he was particularly prone to error
on bird life), but no sensitive reader of his journal can reject his meditations on
the fields and ponds because of the mistakes. It was a person's intuitive grasp of
nature, achieved in solitary contemplation, that mattered to him. Similarly,
Thoreau wrote to lift eyes above the transactions of political life so that the
truth of antislavery would be clear. Information, he suggested, could not rouse
the public, and in the "Plea for John Brown" he reviewed both the secular and
religious press in order to illustrate "the all but universal woodenness of both
head and heart." Language must be used to awaken, not to report prosaic facts,
and Thoreau, it seems, scanned the press only for the inspiration to unleash his
own emotive arsenal:

> The slave-ship is on her way, crowded with its dying victims; new cargoes are
> being added in mid-ocean; a small crew of slaveholders, countenanced by a large
> body of passengers, is smothering four millions under the hatches, and yet the
> politician asserts that the only proper way by which deliverance is to be obtained
> is by "the quiet diffusion of the sentiments of humanity," without any "out-
> break." . . . What is that that I hear cast over-board? The bodies of the dead
> that have found deliverance. That is the way we are "diffusing" humanity, and
> its sentiments with it.[20]

The journal shows us that the function of press opinion was often to inspire
such provocative passages, that he saved items and copied the public prints to
answer journalism with a higher language. What Thoreau most wanted to say,
then, had on purpose only a distant correspondence with the facts.

Thoreau's political life was a series of emblematic acts, not of commitments
or sustained interests. He used the news to allow himself to teeter between
passivity and action. Communication was short-lived, for the individual must
soon lose touch with the story. In the "Plea," Thoreau said of slavery, "I do not
think it is quite sane for one to spend his whole life in talking or writing about
this matter, unless he is continuously inspired, and I have not done so." News
was valuable as an incitement, nothing more. News was not worth questioning
if it led to moral revelation. But news could not anchor a soul; it would soon

drag it down. The individual shared his revelation and moved on. Thoreau's active political life was set in motion by news, but he never lost control of where or how far the news would take him.[21]

2. News on Canvas

Just over a century ago an American artist spent much of his career painting newspapers without readers. William Harnett produced canvases in which newspapers lay at hand . . . but people were gone. The newspapers were folded and set on a table or cabinet, pinned in place by books, tableware, and food. Between 1875 and 1890, Harnett painted more than sixty still lifes of daily papers.[22]

Judged by earlier American paintings, this gallery devoted to newsprint is compensatory. It was the books, the maps, and the manuscripts of written culture that had long fascinated artists. The merchants and public officials who dominated the portrait trade had this older media spread out before them. But not the newspapers of their day. Even the men and women who made newspapers often avoided posing with these sheets before Harnett's time. There is no eighteenth-century illustration of Benjamin Franklin with the newspapers that made his fortune. Sam Adams, the firebrand contributor to the Boston papers during the Revolution, posed with his manuscripts, not his columns. Isaiah Thomas, who published a newspaper for sixty-one years, cradled books, not the news, in his portraits. Genre painters did of course show newspapers being read in a great variety of social circles. Here too Harnett struck a new balance, making the readers disappear. To view news as a serious subject, free of human contact, was a bold turn.[23]

Harnett was famous for tricking the eye. At his exhibitions, a guard had to be posted to keep the public from trying to touch the objects on the canvas. The invitation in this art was clear to U.S. Treasury agents who saw Harnett's paintings of banknotes. They arrested him on suspicion of counterfeiting. The newspapers, too, make us want to take them up and to become the missing readers.

This is understandable given Harnett's meticulous technique. There were few limits to his love of detail. He painted messages that are only visible with nose pressed up near the canvas. Hairbreadth features of texture must be found with a magnifying glass. (Harnett painted his signature on the canvas as a gouged line, varying the depth of the "cut" the way a real knife would make curves.) Further, Harnett's paintings are usually informative. We can read some of the objects on his table tops: the address on an envelope, its postmark, even a sentence from the letter. Reproducing news stories, then, would seem a natural step for Harnett. But here he tricked his public again. Harnett had no interest in news. The dates of these papers are without significance. The pages he painted hold no comment on public affairs. Nothing substantial can be read except the masthead. Harnett transformed news copy into a gibberish of precise cross-markings. Here is the artist of disembodied news, as free of ideas or events as he is of readers.

Harnett invited the public to make sense of these canvases. "I endeavor to make the composition tell a story," he said in his only known interview.[24] This has come to sound like a dare and an added deception. After all, Harnett gave titles to only two of the newspaper still lifes. The canvases have acquired titles that mix the prosaic with the antic: *New York Times, November 9, 1879; Philadelphia Public Ledger, March 2, 1880; Staats-Zeitung and Pretzel* and *Lobster and the New York Herald*. Elegant and apparently impenetrable, Harnett's paintings of newspapers seem a trick played on society and on social historians.

It is a useful trick, for it raises questions that the genre paintings of reading ignored. By removing people from the news, Harnett asks what we really know about the Americans who took newspapers into their lives. In painting gibberish amidst a jumble of objects, Harnett asks how Americans made sense of news. Harnett's work raises the questions that most need answering about the spread of news in this society.

Harnett encoded his own answers in these paintings. It is quite clear that he pegged news as a male vanity.

In the first place, he carried on the tradition of news as a sign of dominance and made newspaper reading into a man's business. Only his earliest three newspaper studies are tables at which a woman would have fit as appropriately as a man. The threescore newspaper canvases that followed marked the table off for a man in Victorian America. Pipes or cigars now lay close to the newspaper in the still lifes. Once, a pocketknife alone gave the scene male ownership. Twice, an envelope addressed to a man lay at the center of the picture. Harnett's news was not for women.[25]

Harnett turned this piece of sentiment into a subversion. Other still life painters presented newspapers as part of comforting bachelor nooks. Not Harnett. He painted the vanity of male wishes. In the tradition of *vanitas* paintings, the pleasures of life are surrounded by symbols of transience. Harnett's inviting reading tables hold matches, ashes, and embers (some smoldering on the newsprint).[26] His favorite object in the newspaper studies was the meerschaum pipe, which appears more than three dozen times. The German word means "sea foam": a clay easily broken. As with the pretzel and the lobster, one does not feel that many things in a Harnett painting are going to be around for long. The prominence of dated newspapers adds to this mood of the passing moment. Further, the newspaper is usually the only link to public affairs on a table filled with artifacts of private life. This one chance for communication is the

William M. Harnett, *Emblems of Peace*, 1890.
The Springfield Museum of Fine Arts, Springfield, Massachusetts.
Gift of Charles T. and Emilie Shean.

false hope, for Harnett's newspapers make no sense and proclaim that one cannot know the world at large.[27]

Harnett's life work was the smashing of the neighborliness and civic-mindedness that had carried the newspaper into American art. The genre painters of the nineteenth century assumed that citizens read the news in company to pass judgment on public questions. American art had recorded deference, to be sure, but it had also proclaimed participation. Harnett's work shifted the focus of artists to news taken in private and alone, away from others and divorced from public questions. In this respect, he was not eccentric. Social historians have shown us a transatlantic Victorian culture that attempted to make the home a "fortress of privacy" in every social class. Pictures of reading in the nineteenth century reflect this turning inward. The self-absorbed news reader came to the forefront of American art in the first century of the popular press. The woman in an Ammi Phillips portrait of 1817 holds out the masthead toward us, and the reader meets our eyes. In contrast, Eastman Johnson showed a woman reading her paper in 1872 who did not engage the viewer in either way. Male readers, too, now seemed more oblivious to others, as in work by Johnson and John Harrison Mills. The news reader found sanctuary, not company. The creation of a sanctum for news runs though the canvases of women reading by William Paxton and Mary Cassett. Taken to its logical conclusion, this tradition ends with the self-absorbed commuters and apartment dwellers, hunched over their newspapers, painted by Reginald Marsh and Edward Hopper. At the historical moment that publishers were filling America with news for all, artists in Harnett's tradition proclaim that mass circulation is an illusion. Masses of people do not know more about one another or the outside world. The artists suggest that news now brought solipsistic reverie.[28]

The making of news reading into anomie goes too far as social history, despite the power of this art. Newspapers and magazines connected Americans to one another. Journalism forged ties between city and country, gathered in immigrant groups, sustained political movements, and created markets where buyers and sellers met. But Harnett had a point about the *discriminating reader* who arose in his century. The prodigious supply of new titles, scattered across the land, meant that individuals could stand apart with news for their own taste. The Victorian wish for the reading sanctum or nook was the natural outgrowth of a distribution system that brought the unique title for the special individual into nearly every community.

The private sphere of the subscriber has been documented by the postmasters of nineteenth-century America as they jotted down the postage on news that it was their duty to collect. The worn and faded postal account books show that many subscribers enjoyed a privilege that has been lost to modern readers: the distinction of being the only person in town to take a particular newspaper or magazine. Postal records from five communities in the three decades before the Civil War show that on average 43 percent of all the titles coming into these towns had a single subscriber.[29] (See Chart 4.1.)

These figures reflect a diversity which must have been obvious in the community, as with the single subscriber to the *Jewish Chronicle*, or the *Methodist Preacher*, or the *Journal of Medicine*, or the *New York Public Schools*. Others enjoyed an exclusive subscription because of where they had grown up. In Abraham Lincoln's town in Illinois, there was one customer for the *New England Farmer*, one for the *Connecticut Courant*, and one for *Le Courier des Etats Unis*. Other titles spoke of special interests and tastes: *Scientific American* and *Gleason's Drawing-Room Companion*, for instance. Many citizens had news not available to their neighbors. Whether one considers politics, religion, or geography, the journalism sent into American communities was diverse and differentiating. These were texts that allowed individuals to retreat into the self, just as Harnett wished.

Publishers bragged about their singular subscribers, presenting them as evidence of their reach into American society. The *Democratic Review* did this at

Chart 4.I Source: note #29.

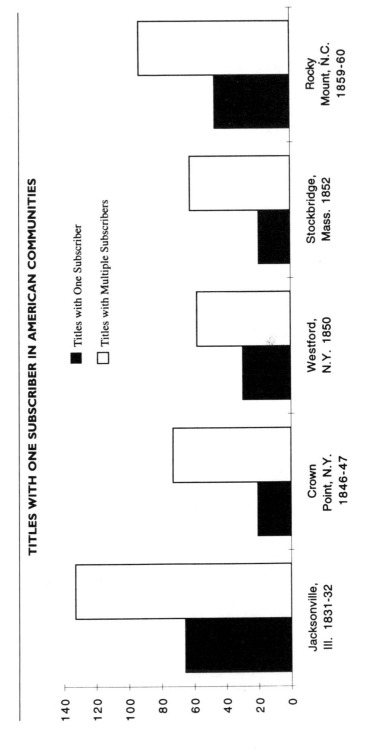

TITLES WITH ONE SUBSCRIBER IN AMERICAN COMMUNITIES

■ Titles with One Subscriber

□ Titles with Multiple Subscribers

Jacksonville, Ill. 1831-32

Crown Point, N.Y. 1846-47

Westford, N.Y. 1850

Stockbridge, Mass. 1852

Rocky Mount, N.C. 1859-60

140 120 100 80 60 40 20 0

mid-century. The publishers showed that more than 60 percent of the communities it reached had a single subscriber. In both Centre Sandwich and in Great Sandwich, New Hampshire, just one subscriber took the magazine. In Blackface, Virginia, Lumpkin, Georgia, and Oswichee, Alabama, the *Democratic Review* had a single customer. Similarly, in Boonville, Missouri, and Blufftown, Indiana, only one person took the paper. This was more of a philosophical than a partisan journal; its contributors included Nathaniel Hawthorne, Edgar Allan Poe, and Walt Whitman. On the dusty main streets of small-town America, a subscriber could commune with these great minds with the delicious sense that no one within sight had gotten these words.[30]

Editors who sought fellowship were troubled by this state of affairs. Yes, they could speak to readers and put them in the larger current of opinion and events, but was this enough? J. A. Wayland, the Kansas editor who produced the most successful radical publication in American history, worried over the loneliness of his readers. Wayland's *Appeal to Reason* reached a quarter million subscribers at the turn of the century with news of the coming triumph of socialism. But at more than fifteen thousand post offices, he noted, the *Appeal* had only one subscriber. William Harnett was not the only person to see that the cultivation of every taste with news placed a great burden on the individual. A page of news, like all print culture, is both an invitation to a community and a prompt to turn inward. The press may push the reader either way.[31]

3. News on the Walls

Surely no body of work by artists has spread as much uneasiness about citizens and the media as this documentary scene from the Great Depression: newspapers and magazines on the bare walls of the American shack. The conventional elements were battered furniture and people in hand-me-down clothes in the foreground, set against headlines, magazine covers, and ads showing the larger world.

The pages on the wall revealed the pathos of the home: see the poor people who have put up the images of goods they do not have and of events they cannot control. This was an icon of the 1930s. The image was prominent in the work of photographs taken by the Historical Section of the Farm Security Administration. Other documentarians hung their stories of America around this same scene. Margaret Bourke-White, for example, had six pictures of media in lowly households in the best-selling book she did with Erskine Caldwell, *You Have Seen Their Faces* (1937). When Twentieth Century–Fox made *The Grapes of Wrath* in 1940, the Joad homestead was papered with the news (an emblem of poverty that John Steinbeck had not used in the novel).[32]

The photographers knew that the paper on the wall had a practical purpose.

Newspapers and magazines kept out the weather. The insulating quality of cellulose was understood by a rural people who had to make do during cold and damp. Some homesteaders of the mid-nineteenth century had used newspapers for the same purpose. In the South of the 1930s, the news may have mocked these people, but it at least made them more comfortable.[33]

Investigators of the Great Depression have left the matter there. In 1936 Rubert B. Vance simply noted "the gaudy display" in his sociological classic, *Preface to Peasantry*, and in his pictorial record, *How the Other Half Is Housed*. When the Federal Writers' Project sent interviewers into sharecroppers' homes at the end of this decade, the writers paid scant attention to such decor. One interviewer cited the media on the walls only as evidence of a "despairing picture" of poverty. When, in the 1970s, the Smithsonian Institution installed a farm tenant house off the Capitol Mall, museum-goers saw bare walls. More than a decade passed before the Smithsonian learned that the home lacked its vernacular wallpaper of newspapers. This same shack, without the pages of news, has now been drawing visitors on the Mall for a generation.[34]

To view the news as an incidental building material is to ignore the plain evidence of the photographs and the historical record. Several of the surfaces so patiently covered were partitions between rooms, not outside walls, and the decorators did not bother with the ceiling. What kind of insulation was this?

The media were something more than a weather guard. Magazine pages filled the walls of many a black family at the end of the nineteenth century. Although the photographic record of these rooms is slender, there seems no doubt that a strong decorative sense controlled the papering. The most colorful pages, for example, often appeared above the mantel. Arthur Rothstein captured some of this living decorative tradition in a black home at Gee's Bend, Alabama. Here the quilters by the hearth face a maze of magazine pictures, and one is not sure where the cloth ends and the wall begins. A Historical Section photograph such as Russell Lee's picture of a fireplace in Transylvania, Louisiana, can easily be misread as a sign of desperation or pathos. In fact Lee has recorded a Southern heritage. This is what a home was *supposed* to look like to many rural Southerners. "Most every room I's had I's been able to pretty up with magazine pictures," an old black man told an interviewer from the Federal Writers' Project. Newspapers, too, were put up with pride and forethought. New black residents of a cabin in North Carolina cited the hanging of newspapers as proof that "dis house is in tole'ble good shape."[35]

For some African Americans, pasting a newspaper on the wall was a way to protect the family from ghosts. It was folk wisdom that these evil visitors would have to count every letter before they caused trouble. Sharecroppers could not easily follow the tested ways of preventing a haunting by building new steps or putting in a new floor. One of the few things they could change was their

Arthur Rothstein, Gee's Bend, Alabama, 1937.
Collections of the Library of Congress.

wallpaper, and this may help explain why a seasonal renewal of media on the walls was common.[36]

In this matter of decoration there was no color line. Tenant farmers, black and white, cycled through the same housing, and so it is not surprising that photographs from the 1930s show very similar wallpaper for families of both races. It is a safe assumption that tenant farmers of the Depression would not have used newspapers and magazines for wallpaper as often if they had the money for something better. It is wrong to assume that they were embarrassed about what they could afford. When Arthur Raper revisited tenant homes in the economic boom of the war years he noted that now "curtains and shades, a table cloth and paper flowers, and mail-order wallpaper can be bought if you have a little money to spend." But the photo of a home he chose to illustrate this decoration shows a magazine ad for Karo syrup proudly hung up in the center of the mantel, in front of the new wallpaper.[37]

The interior decorators of shacks gave newspapers and magazines a privileged position. Posters, cardboard boxes, and the pages of mail-order catalogues are remarkably rare considering how well fitted they were for the job. As Bourke-White noticed, billboard posters might wrap the outside of a share-

Russell Lee, Fireplace in Transylvania, Louisiana, 1938.
Collections of the Library of Congress.

cropper's home like a cocoon, but it was magazines and newspapers that lined the rooms. The decorators chose publications that had been paid for—by someone. Free-circulation publications were ubiquitous in the Great Depression. *Simplicity Fashion Forecasts*, for instance, reached nearly nine million Americans every month, at a time when the largest weeklies, such as the *Saturday Evening Post*, had only about a million circulation. Another free paper, *Rural Progress*, addressed the dreams of sharecroppers. But these free publications are rare in the documentary record of poor people's walls. Caldwell and Bourke-White believed that the homes they visited did not take papers or periodicals. A careful study of two Southern counties shows that only one black household in eight subscribed to the press. Yet, there they were, on the walls.[38]

They are not posted in a casual way, as one might put up pages over a room to be painted. Almost all of the media in the shacks can be read. Usually, the pages are horizontal, straight, and do not overlap. This decoration was not a distant echo of cubists who, for a generation, had popularized the arrangement of banal fragments of news pages, avoiding any striking graphics.[39] In poor homes of the Depression, covers and display ads are prominent. The attention to national rather than to local publications is remarkable. Certainly the most convenient wallpaper for these people was the daily newspaper, a cheap product and a quick discard. These papers were a mainstay of home decorators, but in many homes national magazines dominated the sight lines. One had to tear these pages out or bend staples to remove the full leaf. Either way, these pages covered a smaller area than newsprint. Why go to this trouble?

In Belmont, Florida, East Feliciana Parish, Louisiana, and Marshall, Arkansas, Margaret Bourke-White took pictures of magazine wallpaper that help us sort out what was going on with the decorating. The white men in Arkansas sit in front of the *Saturday Evening Post*. So too do the black children in their Florida home. The boy and his dog in Louisiana are in a doorway framed by pages from both *Collier's* and the *Post*. So much use of one magazine may suggest that the decorators simply took up issues at hand and indiscriminately covered their walls. But there are many signs that this was not so. Little of what we can see is sequential: the pages do not follow one another as they would if one worked through a magazine forwards or backwards. Indeed, if covering the walls was the single objective, the decorators made extra work. The leaves from the magazines were not often pasted up whole; they were usually torn at the crease. These were large-format magazines, fat with ads in the Christmas seasons of 1935 and 1936. One of the magazines on each wall had enough pages to cover all of the area revealed by the camera. But the Florida home used at least two issues, the Louisiana home at least four, and in Arkansas at least seven different issues filled the space. In a life that left them few options, these poor people made choices, at least about what would appear on their walls.[40]

Margaret Bourke-White, Marshall, Arkansas, from *You Have Seen Their Faces* (1937).
By permission of the estate of Margaret Bourke-White, *Life Magazine,* © Time Warner.

Margaret Bourke-White, East Feliciana Parish, Louisiana,
from *You Have Seen Their Faces* (1937).
By permission of the estate of Margaret Bourke-White, *Life Magazine,* © Time Warner.

The collages they created have some clear aesthetic appeals. Graphics were chosen over text, bringing color as well as figures into the house. The Arkansas home, for instance, had a gallery of *Saturday Evening Post* covers. "We ain't got no colors," complained one sharecropper child to a social scientist who visited his cabin. That lad did not have the good fortune to live with media wallpaper.[41] It was probably just as important that the pictures were large. Ever since the high cotton prices of World War I, the farm tenants had been condemned for spending earnings on family photo enlargements of the type that hangs in the Marshall, Arkansas home. Magazine pages were the cheapest way to fill a room with large pictures.[42]

Margaret Bourke-White thought that the ads on the wall showed the things these people wished to have, such as warm clothes. There is not much evidence of this. There were clusters of favored goods, such as the automobile ads taken from an issue of the *Post* that crowd one side of the doorway in the Louisiana home. But the ads themselves do not support such a literal interpretation. On the other side of the same doorway this household placed bedside scenes: the five pages that run down the side of the doorway (taken from two issues of *Collier's*) feature sleepers in tender or romantic poses. If the pages are a catalogue of wishes, they are surely figurative and symbolic. As a black man explained about his magazines on the wall, "Flower and tree pictures rest a body jest to look at them. They ain't never had to work hard."[43]

The early public for mass media in America wanted a good supply of ads. This is what William Randolph Hearst found when he started his newspaper empire at the end of the nineteenth century. "Don't have enough advertisements" was one of the most common complaints of people who rejected the paper he edited for the ordinary citizen. Decades later, Americans of every social class were fascinated by advertising appeals. At the end of the 1930s a broad survey of newspaper readers in fifteen communities showed that the public did not merely glance at advertising; a median of 78 percent of men and 94 percent of women read the copy in display ads.[44]

The attraction here was not simply the wish to possess this or that product. A poor mother who subscribed to a magazine told the Federal Writers' Project that her educated daughter would "read me the little stories and then turn over to the ads and read them too." Ads are a vicarious way to participate in society and to find assurance that times will be better. The sociologist Michael Schudson has observed that advertising is the socialist realism of capitalism in the sense that ad copy shows an ideal world of happy spending and builds faith in this economic system. The point needs to be expanded to include the picture ads give of humanity as a healthy lot. Harry Crews, the Southern novelist, grew up in a sharecropper family of the 1930s with black and white boys who dreamed over the Sears, Roebuck catalogue.

All the people in its pages were perfect [Crews remembered.] Nearly everybody I knew had something missing, a finger cut off, a toe split, an ear half-chewed away, an eye clouded with blindness from a glancing fence staple. And if they didn't have something missing, they were carrying scars from barbed wire, or knives, or fishhooks. But the people in the catalogue had no such hurts. They were not only whole, had all their arms and legs and toes and eyes on their unscarred bodies, but they were beautiful. Their legs were straight and their heads were never bald and on their faces were looks of happiness, even joy, looks that I never saw much of in the faces of the people around me.[45]

Unlike public housing projects in later decades, the homes of the poor in the Depression do not scan for political heroes or causes.[46] These households of the 1930s were close to grass-roots organizing projects. Here in the South there was open warfare between reformers in Washington and reactionary state governments. Yet to read the news these people displayed, there is little hint of this charged atmosphere. The glossy magazines, of course, did not often seek to inspire the forgotten or the disinherited. These were steady, Republican publications. They did not issue portraits of FDR suitable for framing by his admirers, and they reported that the New Deal was a road to bankruptcy. Certainly there was no advertising that encouraged social protest. One of the regular advertisers sold time clocks. For cautious tenants decorating the property of a landlord who was probably their boss, these popular magazines were nearly risk free.

The walls caught by documentary photographers are tame but not reactionary. The time clock ad (and others glorifying factories) do not show up on the walls. Neither do the cartoons aimed at the New Deal. Specifically, the Louisiana home used *Collier's* of October 10, 1936, but not its large cartoon showing Works Progress Administration money being sprayed from a fire hose and going down a sewer (p. 66). The family used *Collier's* of December 12 that year, but not the featured cartoon of FDR as a Lilliputian (p. 86). A half-page cartoon of the U.S. Treasury being raided by New Deal constituencies does not appear among the six pages chosen from the *Post* for the Arkansas home (Nov. 2, 1935, p. 23). While chance surely played some role in how these rooms were decorated, it seems clear that these poor people were editing the news.[47]

Indeed, the decorators of the home in Marshall, Arkansas, did exactly what editors had done and created a wide black border for one of the most affecting news photographs of this decade: the picture distributed in hopes of finding the kidnapped baby of Charles Lindbergh.

Next to the doorway in the Louisiana home there is a piece of furniture that can be identified as a hall stand from one of the prints not used in *You Have Seen Their Faces*. Hall stands were pillars of Victorian respectability, the first thing a visitor saw past the front door, the last chance to adjust one's appearance before meeting the world. This hall stand has a substantial seat, graceful lines, and the requisite mirror at eye level. The older children in this family do not have shoes, but they had a substantial piece of furniture. Time spent around the hall stand could also be informative, for its low arms framed an article from *Collier's* of October 10, 1936, illustrated with the sketch of a powerful black man, the full length of the page. A visitor would not be likely to notice this picture tucked away, and only with difficulty could anyone follow the article, "Do like de Man Say," pasted to the wall. The decorator seems to have taken care to get this story, however, for page 15 of *Collier's* was put up next to page 62 so that the beginning and the end of the article were saved. The story centered on field hands in Louisiana, their wit and their power. These blacks were prospering on the complicated system of agricultural subsidies, *Collier's* reported. The main source for black thinking was one Zeke Whittington of West Feliciana Parish, who "had a few ideas about the way the white folks in Louisiana run things and he had found an audience."[48]

In only one American community, a steep hollow in Appalachia, has there been a systematic study of what the media on the wall meant to the people who pasted up pages. Hollybush, in eastern Kentucky, resembled the crater of a volcano and sheltered white farmers from the 1880s until 1960 when the settlement died. Their simple structures are a shambles, and the newspapers and magazines they attached to walls have long since been ruined. But the men and women who grew up in Hollybush remember how news was displayed. A family's walls might change dramatically every time they were papered, and never look like walls on a neighboring farm. Still, there were rules and thought behind the selection of pages. It was not proper, for example, to mix newsprint and magazine pages on the same wall, unless the newspaper was a neutral background for magazine pictures. Some pages were chosen because they offered a good lesson for the children. A woman recalled that she selected magazine pictures because they reminded her of still lifes she had seen in homes away from Hollybush. Pictures were clustered by theme, and some walls were meant for dreaming. A car picture symbolized the places outside of Hollybush a resident wished to see. Glossy magazine pictures of exactly the right color would make the reflected coal fire dance at bedtime.[49]

The long association of men with the control of news seems broken by this use of media. The whole family worked at papering, but women seem to have had the most to say. When the pages were put up, each family member had favorite stories or pictures to wonder over. The subject matter was vast, and the point of view was one's own.[50]

Many societies have enjoyed the display of pictures with storytelling, adapting news and new types of illustration to the cultural form. Picture recitations have an ancient history in China and India, for example. In recent centuries, an Italian could look to the *cantastorie* for news with pictures. The

Bankelsanger sometimes spoke of topical illustration in German lands, the *crieur de journeaux* in France. These traditional practices have not everywhere been killed by the mass media. The rural homes of the South are evidence of the human need to incorporate images of events into oral narrative. Yet these rural Americans stand apart from this tradition in their insistence that stories be followed in a private space. Here are people not reached by street performers, people who have turned inward. They do not depend on outsiders for meaning.[51]

The appeal of papered walls must have resembled the delight with mass media in more affluent homes where magazines and newspapers sat on the table, inviting young and old to take them up and make of them what they could. These walls are signs that the inhabitants are taking notice of the press, that these citizens count for something because they are in the news stream. The walls make the family's claim for attention as readers . . . or in some cases as a family with merely a respect *for* readers. (This was George Wallace's insight in his career as a magazine salesman to the illiterate and blind: folks who could not read wanted to be hospitable to the more fortunate. The anthropologist Shirley Brice Heath has found evidence for this in the contemporary South.) Furnishing with media is a declaration that one is connected to a society. Here are Americans who have gained stature and pleasure with news. These walls proclaim hope, not despair. On the other hand, the folk decorators are in touch with the mood of Harnett and other serious artists. The fragility of communication is on display.[52]

Thoreau, Harnett, and the anonymous Americans of the South were early students of mass communications. They span that period, from the middle of the nineteenth century to the middle of the twentieth, when the press learned to supply news for all. This ascendancy of mass media has produced an accounting of readers that is long on pathology and pathos. From the "phantom public" of Walter Lippmann to the "narcotizing disfunction" described by Robert Merton and Paul Larzersfield, social science has found citizens unable to cope with information. One literature review showed six fundamental arguments, produced by scholars across the political spectrum, all demonstrating to their satisfaction that new media have worked to create a helpless audience. The Americans considered here stand as a corrective and point toward a fresh scholarly appraisal of the audience for news: the "transgressive, ironic or poetic activity of readers."[53]

Arguably, Thoreau, Harnett, and the decorators were victims of mass media. But they also shared the excitement of its use and exercised control over the texts. With news pushed into their lives, they never stopped making discriminations. Their strategies and comments were surely distinctive, but they were indicative of general practices by readers that we turn to next.

The discriminating reader was one of the great dreams to come from the age that first produced news for all. The futurist Edward Bellamy published a short story at the end of the nineteenth century in which the morning paper had become an electronic box connected to an ear trumpet. Bellamy imagined that by turning a dial, Americans would select stories, sit back, and hear them read. But that was not good enough, even in 1898. There was a "skipper" knob handy so that the user of this electronic newspaper could speed past unwanted details and dull paragraphs. It was not a fantasy to dream of this appropriation of texts by ordinary citizens. The use of news for one's own purpose was well under way among a broad public in the early stages of mass circulation. Taking just what one wants from the news has turned out to be a major activity of the reading public and a great challenge to the journalists on the eve of the twenty-first century.[54]

5

EVERYONE AN

EDITOR

Journalists have not been the only ones who circulated news in print. The public itself has passed along these publications, across great distances and time periods. Editors have not been the only ones who have edited news. Readers who are not (as in Whittier's "Snow-Bound") desperate for any printed words may pick their way across stories or ads, blind to what a journalist wants them to see. The tailoring of a magazine or newspaper according to what readers say that they want puts readers in charge of the news. Journalism, then, may have the life that readers choose to give it and the meaning the public imposes.

Journalists have long been uncomfortable with this state of affairs. Gifts of news can get out of hand and hurt business. Type is set and pictures chosen to gain attention; it is humbling to have readers go their own way, oblivious to an editor's priorities. If a publication is edited according to market surveys, then the journalist's work is reduced to filling orders. Still, this is where journalists find themselves after three centuries of the craft. That great abstraction, "the public," has taken more control of the printed page. Market forces suggest that journalists should let everybody be his or her own editor. Signs of this assertiveness were clear in the first uses Americans made of their press.

I. The Gift of News

Circulation has always been in part a giving of gifts. When Americans chose the news, they were often not simply thinking of stories they wished to read; they were thinking of another reader. The practice was as old as the earliest papers of the colonial era. John Campbell left blank space in his Boston *News-Letter*, the first successful newspaper in the colonies, so that subscribers could add information when they sent issues on to friends. Subscribers paid a premium for wrappers on later Boston papers so that they would have a generous writing space as they sent the paper along. Samuel Sewall, a Puritan gentleman, favored the widows he courted in the 1720s with Boston papers. During the Revolution, John Adams carried newspapers from his travels home to his learned wife Abigail. Josiah Bartlett, representative to the Continental Congress and New Hampshire's first governor, also sent papers to his wife. He kept posted through a lifetime exchange of papers with his allies in New Hampshire politics.[1]

Politics inspired a great many Americans to ship newspapers to their friends. Congressmen sent Washington papers in the post to inform and inspire constituents. Fisher Ames, a grumpy Federalist during the Jefferson administrations, was cheered by sympathetic newspapers sent by two of his Massachusetts representatives. The ambitious Henry Clay of Kentucky, noting that favorable stories about himself "never find their way into the papers of New England," sent Yankees a vindication of his record from his hometown paper. The habit spread well past officeholders. An undergraduate at Yale in 1819 complained of the conservatism of the place and found his father, in Connecticut's hill country, to be sympathetic. The young man regularly sent democratic papers back home, to keep the family spirits up.[2]

Accounts of natural wonders, too, were passed from one reader to another. *The Unearthing of the Mastodon*, one of the best-known paintings of the early republic, was inspired by a single clipping sent to the artist Charles Willson Peale by his daughter who had read about the discovery of strange bones in her local paper.[3]

In the nineteenth century, the habit of newspaper and magazine gifts took hold in all regions and classes. A dutiful Southern father sent his daughters magazines so that they would have relief from school books. A newspaper from a city with grand holiday celebrations was sure to be passed around among country families. A young woman in New York saved the papers from the July 4 celebration, for instance, so that friends in New England could share the excitement. The opening of the West provided constant encouragement to share news. Frontier editors insisted that the newcomer had an obligation to send the local paper to friends left behind so that they could read of the promise of the new land. Gift subscriptions for people who would never see the town on the masthead were common on the frontier.[4]

The *Deseret News* of Salt Lake City announced that ten subscriptions for friends in the East had already been taken out in its first issue of June 15, 1850. The editors spelled out the psychological import of circulation: newsprint might preserve the reader's place in history. The *News* itself was not an imposing institution at this time. The paper consisted of a Ramage hand press (about the size of a rain barrel) in an adobe hut which was as easy to stand on as it was to enter. The key business concern of the editors was to find enough rags among the four thousand settlers in the Mormon territory of the Great Basin to manufacture newsprint. But in that first issue of the *News*, emigrants to Utah Territory and travellers headed farther west were urged to pay twenty-five cents for a future issue with their travels recorded.[5]

It was so much easier to send a newspaper than a letter through the mail that many Americans let the printed page do the work of the letter. Papers taking the place of letters bothered Josiah Bartlett as he sought to lead New Hampshire through the War for Independence. He skewered a friend for writing no more than what was required to forward a newspaper. "This I Esteem as a favor," Bartlett said, "but if your More important Business & your other Correspondencies would give time for you to write me more fully of the Situation of affairs it would be much more agreeable." "Save frequent correspondence" was the sales pitch of many a Western publisher in selling gift subscriptions. The poorer the writer, the more likely the gift subscription seemed a good idea. Indeed, an editor in Washington state convinced an illiterate settler that he owed his friends a subscription so they would know how he was getting along.[6]

Many readers who wished to share the news could not be led to take out subscriptions for their friends. They found cheaper, shady ways to use the news. Americans often added their own text to the printed page of news and snuck this in at the trifling postage charged to the papers. To outwit postal inspectors, readers circled words in the text to get their message across. They sketched pictographs. The "cabalistic mark" was a commonplace of newspapers in the mails by the 1840s as American ingenuity flowered. In 1846 the Postmaster General ordered postmasters to take the wrappers off of papers sent by individuals to inspect the pages for marks. This was not easy work. To fool the eye of the postmaster, some readers made a pinhole stencil of words. The Postmaster General condemned "the extensive practice of carrying on a business or friendly correspondence by writing on the margin of newspapers," to no avail. Sanctions against these scribblers were put in postal laws, but the communication could not be stopped. To discourage the recycling of newspapers so that they became a message from the reader, the government charged three cents for "transient papers," two or three times what publishers paid. The three cents on the gift newspaper was denounced as "one of the most obnoxious and unreasonable taxes ever laid upon knowledge, and [it] has created more dissatisfaction and ill feeling towards the Post-Office Department than any other tax ever laid upon the people." Still, Americans favored distant kin and friends with newspapers in the mail.[7]

This flow of newsprint was a substantial addition to regular subscriptions. In 1850 the postmaster in Palmyra, Tennessee, recorded only ninety-six annual subscriptions in his village, but four or five transient papers came through the mail each week. In the fall of that year, some families got as gifts twice as many papers as they had paid for.[8]

This was not simply the recourse of the hard-up. A congressman from Illinois observed in 1850 that "nothing is more common than for a man coming from the eastern States on landing from a steamboat in one of our western cities, to go to a newspaper office, purchase a paper, and send it to his friends at the East, to let them know the he has arrived there."[9] Isaac Mickle, a privileged young Philadelphian, received distant newspapers from old schoolmates every few days in the 1840s. This was not a crowd that watched its pennies. The reason the gift of news was followed in all social classes is that no matter what one's station in life, it was easier, emotionally, to send a newspaper than a letter. One's own news may be difficult to set down and disappointing to those who receive it. "How are things?" is a hard question for a people who have pulled up roots. As Americans left the farm for the town and the settled communities for the frontier, they found in newspapers a natural greeting card. And the newspaper did not tip the hand in that most unsettling of all communications, romantic friendship. The gift of printed news was an expression of affection that did not reveal too much.

The traffic in newspapers to one young man in the Upper Connecticut Valley makes the social functions of news clear. From the spring of 1844 to the summer of the following year, Edward Jenner Carpenter kept a diary, noting weather, work, and social contacts. Carpenter was a country boy who had come to live in town, and he enjoyed the doings in taverns, workshops, and lecture halls. As an apprentice cabinetmaker he could not expect much contact with those he called the "big bugs" of the town, but he had wide contacts among artisans. He recorded the getting and giving of newspapers as social highlights. Once or twice a month he received papers from kin or artisan friends who had moved on to opportunities in the West. In return, Carpenter sent a local newspaper out to the people who had sent him distant papers. To judge by his diary, Carpenter did not often receive letters from these people, or write to them. He mentions only one exchange of letters. In this circle, composed of fifteen- to twenty-one-year-olds, the newspapers kept friendships alive without further words. Carpenter found the printed page a substitute for letters, and remembrance by newspaper seemed to brighten his life. On a cold fall day he noted, "I received a paper this morning from Eliza A. Whitney dated at New Orleans. I cannot hardly believe she is there, but I suppose I must." The next day was warm, and he remarked on the moonlight, then added, "I did up a paper tonight to send to Miss E. A. Whitney, in answer to one I received yesterday."[10]

Friendship, even courtship, was frequently advanced by an exchange of printed news, calling for careful judgments about what was to be circulated and to whom. With menfolk away in the Civil War, Lucy Breckinridge was delighted by the visit of a handsome army surgeon to the family plantation in Virginia. The Confederate taught this twenty-year-old how to make ivy wreaths and crowned her with one. The doctor returned to the front but renewed the friendship by sending Lucy copies of the *Southern Illustrated News*. The magazine "was full of poetry and an allusion to vines, of course," Lucy noted in her diary. She thought of sending the doctor her local newspaper in return. But the women of the household told her that this was not appropriate.[11]

Sustaining human relationships through newspapers may have its drawbacks, but it is more revealing than a greeting card. Each party learned something about local conditions. Familiar names and scenes came back to those who had moved on. People contemplating a move might get some picture of their prospects. The newspapers sent home by New England mill girls before the Civil War allowed the families they had left behind to see that independent wage earners still valued family ties. Sometimes the families were confused. "My Dear Girl," one father wrote, "we received a couple of [news]papers last Thursday & suppose they came from you. I hope you will find time to write soon as the papers were quite silent as to your whereabouts, business or health." But this father was grateful for the papers, and in the next month his wife noted the significance of the exchange: "Your paper reaches us weekly. We look upon it as a token of your kind regard for us." The loving father was still puzzled, for the papers arrived so promptly that he was sure his daughter had not had time to read them herself. He declined her offer to supply the family with yet another periodical, for "we now have eight different papers which certainly ought to be enough."[12]

In passing on newspapers, Americans sometimes shared family achievements and moral convictions. These were not necessarily tied to anything so prosaic as printed words on the page. In 1861 a new mother in Lynn, Massachusetts, sent a crumpled local paper to her father in Vermont "for a message." The grandchild had "laid violent hands on this one," the mother noted. A Midwestern newspaper, which had nothing to say about race, was treated as a relic in 1874 and made a gift when it was discovered to have been printed on the press once used by the abolitionist Elijah Lovejoy. Usually, of course, the text gave the gift its significance. A Whig or a Democrat might be won for the cause by entering a subscription in his name. It was not necessary to own up to the attempt to change a neighbor's mind; publishers agreed to keep the names of benefactor-propagandists a secret. But making the gift of news was satisfying.

The *Sunbeam*, a workingman's paper, pleased a reader in Boston enough to send in an order for fifteen people. He was delighted in 1841 to find an alternative to "the *hypercritical, clique-bound, egotistical, self-styled people-loving press.*" On a plantation in Mississippi before the Civil War, a New England woman thanked her mother for sending her just the right, conservative paper from home, "like a gleam of sunshine from my native land, now so wrapped in the *blackness* of Abolitionism." On an Iowa farm in 1872 a young woman gave visitors twenty back issues of a suffrage newspaper "with a hope they may see rightly & understandingly." Elsewhere in the Midwest, suffragists took out gift subscriptions to the *Women's Column* for the most influential men in their state. Turnabout was fair play: the Iowa woman received an anti-suffrage paper in the mail from an unknown correspondent.[13]

Such exchanges were probably as important in nineteenth-century political life as the arguments that filled taverns, lecture halls, and courthouse squares. Women, in particular, could step into politics with the gift of news without physically entering spaces that men had claimed as their own. By circulating other people's words, women and men were doubly concealed. One said nothing directly, to an audience completely of one's choice. This was the path to socialism of two Missouri families according to the leading paper of the movement, the *Appeal to Reason*. A Republican father and a Democratic father would not allow their children to cross party lines and marry. The young man left home in despair. He converted to socialism and sought romance through political re-education. He first tackled his own father: "I wouldn't have dared hand him a copy of the *Appeal*, but I was willing to risk sending it through the mail to him." Month after month, the paper did its work, and the old man converted. The son next sent the *Appeal* through the post to his sweetheart's father. Again, hearts were changed by circulation, and this time a marriage was brokered in newsprint.[14]

Carpenter, the New England apprentice, subscribed to papers that printed exciting adventure stories, and he mentions sending these to his young friends. Recycling this kind of newspaper had risks. A book on letter writing of 1845 condemned the circulation of unsuitable newspapers tainted by "novels, love stories, and slander." If the warning didn't work, the model letter was designed at least to stop young people from sending the newspapers home.[15]

Magazines were safer gifts at this time. Edited to high standards of respectability, as newspapers were not, they could be given with little thought of compromising the morals of a reader of another generation or sex. At the end of the nineteenth century, *Literary Digest* represented the best of Victorian moral concern and cosmopolitanism. Just before announcing the "Topics of the Day" the editors announced the terms for "presentation copies," since so many of their readers sent subscriptions to friends.

Handing over a newspaper, the reader in urban America walked a fine line between benevolence and fraud. Red boxes were fixtures on New York train platforms, and a commuter could leave the paper here for hospital patients. This was a serious endeavor. In one year of the mid-nineties, the Hospital Book and Newspaper Society distributed more than 150,000 newspapers to readers in institutions. The sharing here amounted to one of every twenty-five daily and Sunday papers produced in the metropolis. But others begged for newspapers at these stations with even greater success. Perhaps seventy-five thousand newspapers a day went into the hands of children who met the commuters. Twice that number of daily papers were simply left on the cars, where they were collected by guards and conductors. So as much as 10 percent of the dailies in circulation were given up by commuters. "Do the readers of these papers know what becomes of them after they are thus discarded?" a trade journal asked. "Some may think . . . that some little family circle somewhere gets the benefit of the paper after the first perusal." The truth was that this was organized crime. Tens of thousands of papers were on their way to a criminal enterprise that ironed the day's papers and presented them as unsold "returns" to the publisher through crooked news carriers and agents. The larcenous recycling of the news went on in every city in the 1890s and drove publishers to desperate measures. In Denver, for example, street copies of papers were sold with yellow or blue paper bands that broke when the reader opened the fold. With this seal torn, the paper could not be returned. In New York, publishers experimented with hooks and even rivets. American determination to share the press was hard to contain.[16]

For magazines, this remains true at the end of the twentieth century. Gift subscriptions are a major part of circulation. Across the cultural spectrum, *Reader's Digest* and the *New Yorker* heavily promote giving the magazine to another person with the same special taste. Among *Smithsonian*'s 2.3 million subscriptions, one in eight is a gift from a friend or family member. It is about one in ten at *Rolling Stone*. *Southern Living* trades on the sense of place that was so important in the nineteenth century, appealing to the locals and to the homesick with gift promotions. Sixty-five percent of the subscribers to *New Mexico* live outside the state, and a quarter of the ninety-six thousand circulation is gifts from one reader to another. Bonds of belief are apparent in religious periodicals, with more than half of subscriptions for some magazines going out as gifts from the like-minded. Publishers love gift subscriptions for cool business reasons. Donors pay up out of fear that their friend will hear of their delinquency. Donors can be prompted to renew easily with notice that "your friend will be without his magazine." Again, the gift of news calls for careful judgment. *Weight Watchers Magazine* and *Psychology Today* contain news that can be used, but not, perhaps, as gifts.[17]

The gift of news, at the end of the twentieth century, continues to be a way for Americans to make arguments and express feelings where a more direct approach seems impossible. *Ebony*, a magazine about successful African Americans, has been commended to whites by blacks, to open their eyes. Taking up this invitation, a white family in Wisconsin read the magazine together and sent gift subscriptions to friends who they thought would be improved by this news. There are ominous gestures as well. Gift subscriptions have been used by abusive partners to let the family members they have terrorized know that the emotional bond has not been broken.[18]

2. News to Save

Hanging on to newspapers for later reflection was a common practice in the young republic. When Isaiah Thomas started a new paper in eastern Massachusetts in 1783, he courted subscribers by reminding them of the value of an archive of news in the home. Preserving the weekly paper, he wrote, "will afford knowledge and entertainment to the rising generation." This was a common appeal as Americans settled new lands. "A paper that is worth printing, is worth preserving; if worth preserving, it is worth binding," the *Deseret News* in the Utah Territory said in 1850. In homes, newspapers were sometimes stitched together into folios for handy reference. The taverns had their archives of news, with iron contraptions to keep old papers in order. Even without this care, yesterday's paper was easily saved. Newsprint was made from rags until the 1840s, and the fiber made pages wear like cloth. It was the modern practice of making paper from pulp that turned old papers into a crumbling ruin. As newspapers first spread across the young nation, they were taken in and remained a part of people's lives.[19]

There is confirmation of this in an extraordinary personal statement left by the self-trained scholar William Manning. "I am not a Man of Larning my selfe," this New England farmer confessed in 1798, ". . . & I am no grate reader of antiant history for I always followed hard labour for a living." Manning testified to the durability of pages of news as he explained how he had learned about the classical world and the nature of republics: painstaking study of series of articles in his favorite newspaper. The farmer spent a dozen years or more with these articles, never wearing them out, before he sat down to write his own views of America's destiny.[20]

Magazines, too, were saved. Many subscribers had their collections bound. This was encouraged by publishers, who often undertook the job themselves for a fee. The *American Farmer* had lured 90 percent of its subscribers to return the issues for binding by 1822. That same year, subscribers to the *Genius of Universal Emancipation* could have a handsome volume made up with a title page and an index provided by the publisher. Women's magazines were worried over as the latest issues were shared: would the borrowers return them in good shape for the bindery? Inside the cover of *Demorest's* for January 1871, subscribers were promised "a splendid volume for binding for the center-table at the end of the year." *Scribner's Magazine* of the 1890s lined up agencies across the nation to bind reader collections. Quality magazines boasted that they offered stories, art, and even advertisements that would be "preserved."[21]

The preservation of the press was a business as well as a hobby, and the titan of this industry in the nineteenth century was an African American, Robert M. Budd. "Back Number Budd" was a name known in every newsroom, for there was no surer way to get yesterday's news. From his warehouse in Long Island City, Budd presided over some fifteen million papers and every American magazine published since 1833. With little education, Budd had devised a cataloguing system that allowed him to retrieve any issue within a day. The enterprise was started with the capital of eight dollars when Budd sold papers during the Civil War and noticed that soldiers prized the old papers that reported on their battles. This trade in memorabilia was vigorous until a fire in 1895 wiped out much of Budd's archive.[22]

Scissors and paste gave a boost to the circulation of news through the humble vehicle of the scrapbook. The preservation of news in this way goes back to the eighteenth century. One Harbottle Dorr, a Boston shopkeeper, assembled four volumes of newspaper pages as he lived through the early years of the American Revolution. Abolitionists, as described earlier, made press clippings into an effective exposé for a mass audience. Before the Civil War, politically active people, including abolitionists, sometimes sent their clippings, along with other evidence of party service, in application for patronage jobs in Washington. Abraham Lincoln campaigned by throwing open scrapbooks of his press clippings. Aside from political gain, the frankly sentimental collection of news was commonplace. Transplanted Americans, for instance, kept scrapbooks of news from their hometowns. The keepsake value of news cracked some very hard hearts. Oliver Wendell Holmes Jr., the "Yankee from Olympus" and enemy of sentimentality in law or social policy, treasured some carefully chosen news columns. Justice Holmes was famous later in life for his boasts that he did not read newspapers. But he preserved clippings of his campaigns in the Civil War in a scrapbook. Floating upon that new ocean of news that went out to all Americans from the 1860s to the 1930s, Holmes attempted to ignore it, save for his one bottle.[23]

The Proust of scrapbook makers lived in Kosciusko, Mississippi, and labored over the press between 1847 and 1890. Jason Niles was a Vermont lawyer who chose the geographical center of Mississippi for a career in state politics and on the bench. He edited the town's paper for brief periods both before and after the Civil War and was one of the doomed Republicans of Reconstruction. He served one term in Congress before the Democrats drove his kind out of politics. Somehow, in this busy public life, Niles found the time to make at least sixty-eight hundred pages of diary entries. And this was a warm-up for his scrapbook making: fourteen volumes, bursting with clips. Niles must have used the exchange papers coming into the office of the Kosciusko *Chronicle*, for his reading covered the nation. His main theme was his own career and Republican affairs, but he saved all of the delights of newspapers: travel letters, reports on foreign crises, sentimental poetry, literary essays, and exciting murder stories. Markets, alone, did not seem to interest him; ads, crop reports, or business stories are rare. But nearly everything else was cut and plastered. There are many signs that this was difficult labor. Niles used old ledger books that he must have picked up cheaply, and some scrapbooks are volumes from the Government Printing Office that were probably the fruit of his congressional term. He simply pasted his text over the ledger accounts and the government reports. The pages of this motley library are filled to the edge, and Niles was usually able to fit three columns on a page. Thus in these fourteen volumes, on nearly two thousand pages, the columns of news total a mile in length. A quote has been written on the cover of one volume that sums up Niles's philosophy: "Many remembrances make an experience."[24]

In the pre-history of news clipping and scrapbook making, familiar worlds were re-created by amateurs in the preservation of memories. As we hold these scrapbooks, with their personal marks of the makers, we have little clue as to what lies ahead.

In the 1880s and 1890s clippings became a very big business. Burrelle's Press-Clipping Bureau, started in 1888 with twelve subscribers, had thousands of customers at the turn of the century and sent out 12,000 items on an average work day. "WIDE AWAKE people want to know what the Newspapers say of them, and the subjects that interest them," Burrelle's said. A dozen clipping bureaus, founded as Burrelle grew, were still going strong through the Great Depression, four decades later. Many other firms had briefer success in the market. With branch offices and regional specialization, Americans everywhere had access to a company that would scan the press by proxy and deliver news on a favorite topic. By the turn of the century, these bureaus were reading factories. Burrelle's New York office occupied sixty-five hundred square feet and processed as many as two thousand dailies and six thousand weeklies. During World War I, Hemstreet's in New York clipped thirty thousand newspapers and magazines every day.[25]

In 1901 a trade journal noted that "today there is hardly a professional man who does not patronize a clipping bureau." Thousands of women kept scrapbooks on domestic matters, the Chicago *Tribune* reported in 1912. The paper sold the blank volumes by mail and at its office to meet the demand. Clipping bureaus fed the appetite of every type of entrepreneur. In Minneapolis, for example, a bureau offered clippings on bond issues, hotels, creameries, and amputations—there was money to be made supplying all of these wants. Elsewhere, an exterminator paid for news about rats, a lightning rod maker for news of lightning strikes, a steel bar company for news of jails. This was not a trivial pursuit. At its century mark in the 1980s, Burrelle's claimed half of the five thousand largest U.S. corporations as subscribers.[26]

Vanity, both vulgar and refined, made clipping services seem indispensable. On a visit to America, George Bernard Shaw wandered into the Hemstreet bureau and grew lyrical about the work he saw in this "dynamic factory, where history is compiled for individuals every hour of the day." Shaw advised Americans to have their clippings and other mementos arranged into one of Hemstreet's beautiful scrapbooks. "It isn't vanity at all, it is just an orderly way of keeping tabs on your own life, and not letting things go helter skelter and just any old way." Elbert Hubbard, sage to millions of American magazine readers, subscribed to Hemstreet's so that he could check his "cosmic bank-balance." Without press notices, Hubbard confessed, he felt bankrupt. The celebrities of the new, twentieth century amassed clippings to guard against such dark thoughts. John Philip Sousa, the March King, patronized the clipping bureaus and filled eighty-five volumes with the news of his career.[27]

The mania for clippings was a departure from the days when people bound beautiful sets of the news or kept heirloom copies. Preservation had come to mean cutting into the page and taking things out (a practice that Shaw or Hubbard would never have recommended for passages in books). This gnawing away at media was further institutionalized at the end of the nineteenth century with a new form of marketing, the coupon. Instead of merely inviting a customer to write in for information or the product itself, advertisers printed a form: CUT OUT—MAIL TODAY. The pioneering coupon was for sales of the *Century Dictionary and Encyclopedia* in the 1890s. This invitation to tear into the news page was unprecedented and unsettling. An advertising trade journal of 1896 called the cutting an "injury" and a "mutilation." By the early years of the new century, however, the surgery was commonplace. Magazines were filled with rectangles and triangles, ready to be pruned and filled in. Newspapers had coupons, too, as with the ballots for popularity contests that, we saw, led some contestants to carry scissors as they walked the streets. On the eve of the explosion of government forms—for the military draft and income tax, driver's licenses and Social Security forms—commercial media accustomed the population to put information in the right space and to send the paper on to the correct office. Coupons were information-gathering devices. They asked not simply for the names and addresses of sales prospects but also for their age, travel plans . . . all data that might help make the sale. The coupons were frequently keyed, so that advertisers could tell which publication the prospect had read. The press, literally, bore the mark of the reader as never before, and the reader was growing accustomed to a more bureaucratized society in which unseen agencies would gather information.[28]

The couponing of America was one of the unheralded revolutions of news in print during the twentieth century. As a general rule, it has been the readers with lower incomes who were the most likely to reach for the scissors. Publications with a broad audience offered coupons as a sort of entitlement. For instance, in the 1930s *McCall's* had coupons in nearly 40 percent of its large ads. By the end of the century, researchers found that more than half of all newspaper readers were clipping along the dotted lines.[29]

The talismanic power of clips was becoming especially dear to journalists themselves. Editors had always known what other publications said through the free exchange of papers in the mails and the practice of sending magazines to local editors gratis. The digest was a familiar form of journalism in the nineteenth century, as with the weekly *Niles' Register* (1811–49). News that one journalist thought well or ill of another's work was frequently noted. But early journalists had no systematic way of collecting compliments or insults, and so readers were spared a full accounting. The efficient collection of press comment allowed editors to show readers that the very publication they were holding had impact across the country. *Peterson's*, for example, demonstrated in 1858 that "our January number took the country by storm. . . . Newspaper notices pronounce it the handsomest number of a Magazine ever issued, at any price." Week after week the magazine quoted from local papers that commended an issue, no matter how trivial the notice. *Collier's* did this after the turn of the century in a regular feature, "Brickbats and Bouquets," that demonstrated that *Collier's* name had come up in many columns. (Letters from readers were printed as well, but these were drowned out by the flood of notices.) This was editing of the news to confer authority on the very paper that the reader was reading. As the public found ways to select and preserve articles that met their special interests, journalists countered by becoming their own clipping bureau. What both enterprises had in common was the further transformation of printed news from a perishable commodity in limited distribution to a permanent record in a showcase.[30]

Press comment has been turned into a fetish with the institutionalization of the blurb. Testimonials from famous people have long been used to sell American media. But in the craft of promotion, the imprimatur of a masthead has grown since the nineteenth century. Book publishers, theater producers, and film makers have all courted an audience with lines of adjectives, separated by dots, wrenched from the nation's press. For instance, prior to the paperback revolution of the 1950s most books were issued before their praises had been sung in published reviews. The modern merchandizing of books now looks like a revival of the passion for scrapbooks. A 1976 printing of the reporters' view of Watergate, *All the President's Men*, had sixteen testimonial clips from newspapers spread out at the front and the back of the book. The first paperback edition of David Halberstam's study of imperial media, *The Powers*

That Be (1980), contained twenty-two press clippings on his story. One did not have to read these authors to know that the press was powerful; the blurbs made the point.

Press clipping could do more than gain attention or fortify an ego; it could build political movements. The twentieth century has made squares of newsprint into paladins for a variety of causes. The flood of photographs into the press made possible by the half-tone process created work space for graffiti comment. Thus a reader of the Chicago *Tribune* in 1913 alerted the editor to the appointment of a "Papist rat" to the state government by clipping the man's photo and inking in a cross on his forehead. There was much encouragement for this type of clipping that year among Protestants. The million readers of the weekly *Menace* published in two neat columns the "Rules" set by Catholics to control daily papers. These guidelines required that news of lascivious, gun-toting priests be suppressed while every blemish on Protestant America was put on the front page. "Cut this out," the *Menace* directed, "send it to the daily newspaper you subscribe for, and ask them why this rule is followed." Many readers did just that. The Chicago *Tribune* received so many that it drafted a standard letter of reply.[31]

Advocacy by clipping has been the mainstay of some of the most successful social movements of the late twentieth century. Civil rights workers were sustained by the coupon as well as by the march and the sit-in. "Heed Their Rising Voices," the full-page ad that appeared in the New York *Times* on March 29, 1960, contained language that was at issue in the celebrated Supreme Court decision four years later of *Sullivan v. New York Times*. But the language that counted most to the movement in the days after the ad appeared was "Please mail this coupon TODAY!" The Committee to Defend Martin Luther King was testing conscience and marketing at the same time. Similarly, conservationists have sewn newspaper coupons like seeds. This began in the 1960s with the Sierra Club's campaign to stop a dam at the Grand Canyon ("Should we also flood the Sistine Chapel so tourists can get nearer the ceiling?"). Environmentalists have pioneered in creating coupons that declare that other coupons have been properly sent to political leaders. David Brower, the advocate for wilderness, has broken fresh ground for the political memoir by reprinting ads and "the all-important coupons." The square of newsprint is destined for a role in many autobiographies. For nearly a month in 1982, the New York *Post* printed a small pair of scissors and, inside the dotted lines, "I think Ed Koch is the best person to be governor of New York." The paper said that a thousand clippings were returned every day for the paper's favorite politician. New Yorkers needed to buy the *Village Voice* to vote "no" in the plebiscite. Their "Impeach Governor Koch" coupons filled mail bags; sixty-two thousand clippings arrived one morning. In the 1992 presidential campaign, the state of Texas received forty-five thousand coupons from readers of

Gary Trudeau's "Doonesbury" six weeks after the cartoonist provided a form to apply for residency in that state. Trudeau argued that if President George Bush could dodge taxes with this claim, newspaper readers should have the same privilege.[32]

The annotated clip and the sheaf of articles have remained handy weapons for the reading public in the last decades of the twentieth century. Sexist clips from the nation's press have been one of the most popular features of *Ms.* The editors could have filled their magazine with these discoveries sent in by their readers. The Congress is showered with clips. Constituents have made sure that their representatives read the news about the savings and loan failures, threats to Social Security, and the perks of office. Whether the destination of a clip is Congress, a distant friend, or the family circle, newspapers at the end of the twentieth century have encouraged this disassembly and display. *USA Today*, for instance, waged a national advertising campaign: "The Paper People Love to Tear Apart." Editors speak with increasing respect of "refrigerator journalism," as they have come to see that a story held up by a magnet is one of the best ties to a reader.[33]

Reporters and columnists who write on sensitive subjects often receive their clips back, with insults on them. A reader of the Raleigh *Times* carefully wrote the word "Tripe" five times on an editorial criticizing George Wallace, and this paper frequently received annotated texts from Southerners who did not care for its moderate racial stand. Decades after the breakthrough for civil rights, stories about African Americans are likely to be returned to reporters in the mail with scrawled racial epithets. Clips, though, are just as easily marshalled by the other side. African Americans have been encouraged to scan the press for stories of their triumphs in order to educate a younger generation. In settings of urban decay, clips may be a weapon to defend the neighborhood. The working-class community of Kingsbridge in the Bronx was surrounded by squalor in the mid-1980s but saved itself through a variety of local initiatives. Kingsbridge residents (three-quarters black or Hispanic) used clippings in virtually all of their organizations. Saving the news is such a ubiquitous form of communal expression that it survives among groups of Americans who are notorious for anti-social behavior and poor reading habits. Urban youth gang members frequently clip and preserve stories of their exploits. They are known to be demanding readers, and gang banging in one Midwestern city has been traced to anger over incomplete coverage.[34]

People at the bottom of the social system who keep track of their clips are doing no more than people at the top. In the 1990s lawyers in New York gained permission from their bar association to tout themselves with their press notices. Howard Kurtz, press critic of the Washington *Post*, observed that in the race for the White House in 1992, headlines were being used by some candidates so frequently as props and talking points that "read my clips" was becoming a campaign theme.[35]

All of this news that Americans wanted remembered, beginning with the eighteenth-century collections, required active readers who selected and preserved what they found in the press. The clipping bureaus and entrepreneurs like Back Number Budd merely took orders to do this monitoring. But nineteenth-century America devised a way for readers to preserve news that they had never seen; indeed, these were newspapers that few people had read and almost no one had saved. The ersatz newspaper memento was created by reissuing historic papers on commemorative days. In 1876, for example, the nation was flooded with the papers that had carried news of the Founding Fathers. One man who looked back on a village parade that year remembered getting his fill of Continental soldiers, lemonade, and sandwiches and recalled that "everybody got a copy of the Ulster County [N.Y.] *Gazette*, which were sold very cheaply, and everybody went home tired and happy." This reissue, January 4, 1800, carried the news of George Washington's funeral. The original paper cannot have had a circulation of more than a thousand at the time, and, indeed, no copies of the paper were in archives in the hundred years after Washington's death. (To date, only two original copies of the paper have been found.) But beginning around 1850, print shops of America issued scores of reproductions; a millon copies of the venerable Ulster County *Gazette* had been circulated by the beginning of the twentieth century. Only five of the first issues of the New York *Sun* (September 3, 1833) seem to have survived the nineteenth century, but this paper flooded its subscribers with reprints. On its fiftieth anniversary in 1883, a third wave of souvenir editions of the 1833 paper hit New York, 160,000 copies.[36]

Colonial papers were fruitful and multiplied. There are more than a dozen different reissues of the Boston *Gazette*'s news of the Boston Massacre, about as many copies of the town's first successful newspaper from 1704, and nearly that many imitations of Benjamin Franklin's first paper, the *New-England Courant*. A Maryland *Journal* of the Revolution has more than eight commemorative editions, and the first issue of the *New Hampshire Gazette* in 1756 has won five reissues.

When it came to the Civil War, publishers manufactured mementos as energetically as for the War for Independence. No Chattanooga *Daily Rebels* survive for August 9, 1862, but two reissues tell the news. No one has been able to count all spurious editions of the New York *Herald*'s report of Lincoln's assassination, a vehicle advertisers used to sell their wares through the rest of the century. The fall of Vicksburg, celebrated with such vehemence on the canvas of Lilly Martin Spencer, was remembered in more than thirty reissues of the town's *Daily Citizen*.

Roughly 150 daily newspapers from the eighteenth and nineteenth centuries lived on in commemorative editions, often taken for the original news sheet. When S. N. D. North assembled his *History and Present Condition of the Newspaper and Periodical Press* for the Census Bureau in 1884 he reproduced nine pioneering papers, four of which, he probably did not know, were fakes. For more than a century, archivists have been consoling families with heirloom papers that their value lies only in sentiment. Beginning in the 1950s, the Library of Congress has handed out circulars on seventeen early papers, breaking this news.

3. What Readers Read

The large public that saved the news for display and dispute were not the only readers who actively edited what journalists had put in print. For as long as there have been newspapers, readers have played with texts. "Ned Lovefun," for example, told readers of a Boston paper in 1786 to read across column rules, viz. "A warrant is issued for the execution of"—"The whole order of lawyers, to a man we hear." Skipping and skimming seem to have increased as Americans tried to manage the nineteenth century's flood of news in print. Would the reader or the editor get the upper hand?[37]

The 1890s began a century of struggle over the reader's habits of paying attention. Newspapers made some impressive moves. The front page became the place to look first, replacing the inside pages (which usually had the latest news in the eighteenth century). Advertising was swept back from its common position on page 1. Banner headlines stretching across columns became more frequent. Joseph Pulitzer put his most important story of the day in the right column of the front page. He had reversed the visual field for reading the English language and created a lure that people accepted, without knowing why. Electrotyping allowed whole pages to be prepared for the printing press, further banishing the vertical column rules that had controlled newspaper design up to this time. Photoengraving, including the new half-tone process for photographs, added visual interest that had been impossible for earlier publishers to achieve. The publisher's effort to manage the attention of readers with pictures and other graphic devices spurred efforts to find out exactly what the audience was doing.

The first answers to this question came from university laboratories at the turn of the century. Here elaborate mirrors and scopes were created to watch the eye movements of readers. Researchers were not content with merely looking at the reader's pupils. With the aid of cocaine or other narcotics, delicate cups of ivory or plaster were attached to the cornea. A pointer attached to this disk traced eye movements while the head and eyelids were held steady.

Charts of these reading sessions showed the sweep across the page to the right with pauses to take in words and then the smooth sweep back to the lower line. Readers paused at least three times as they read a line in a newspaper column, many fewer stops than for the wider formats of magazines and books. Journalism had produced Darwinian victors: without quite knowing what they were doing, editors had shaped text "near an optimum" for easy, fast reading.[38]

The verdict on magazine readers was less clear-cut. These publishers were slower to encourage studies of reader behavior and more perplexed by what scholars told them. The reference point for dailies was yesterday's paper, but interviews testing impressions of a magazine that was read last week, two weeks ago, or last month could not be expected to achieve the same recall. Magazine surveys could be quite strange. Agricultural editors, for instance, learned that regular readers showed more interest in covers that put farmers in the foreground, hogs in the background, than the reverse. On the other hand, new readers were better attracted by covers on which hogs loomed larger than farmers.[39]

No doubt much news reading was done by racing straight down narrow columns, but the laboratory setting made no allowance for distraction and assumed that the text of stories was what the reader was after. We can only imagine the eye movements of these human subjects had they been given the yellow press of the era, with its insistent headlines and drawings. Did readers follow the stories of mayhem and wonder sequentially, or jump to the best parts? For that matter, we cannot be sure that stolid readers of the most respectable financial papers took in the news in the orderly ways suggested by the first laboratory findings about reading. Perhaps their eyes darted off to the ads that told them how to spend their money. The newspaper reader had yet to be studied in anything like a native habitat with a full range of the pleasures of the printed page.

Gentle questioning about recall, rather than a regimen with eye cups, seemed the best way to figure the reader out. *Life's Continuing Study of Magazine Audiences* began in 1938, bringing subjects into an office to page through issues and talk about what they remembered. A similar *Continuing Study of Newspaper Reading* began the next year. This was funded jointly by advertisers and publishers and relied on the professional staff of the Gallup organization to examine what adult readers noticed in their daily paper.

The newspaper survey got Americans to page through yesterday's daily and to point out the stories and ads that they remembered. A glance at headlines was not enough to count as "reading." Researchers probed to make sure the reader had gone further. The staff dismissed comments about what was "worth" reading or what was "usually" read. Only what *had* been read counted. The resulting map of "reader traffic stops" was drawn up in communities across the land. Readers shared their time and tastes, sometimes too enthusiastically. In Memphis researchers found "the most difficult problem for the interviewer is the desire of the respondent to prolong the interview after all necessary information has been obtained."[40]

An equal number of men and women were used in the newspaper survey, and some gender differences in taste were evident. Men were much more likely than women to read sports, financial stories, and editorials. Women read the society features, health and beauty stories, and death notices that men passed by. The gender map of reading was probably influenced by the readers' sense of what was appropriate. What man would tell a stranger that he noticed models and socialites? How ready were women to talk about investment advice or dashing male athletes? (Slightly more than one man in three reported a traffic stop on the society or women's page, the same percentage of women who said they had read something in sports.) Examined closely, this Gallup survey showed that men and women had at least a passing knowledge of the whole paper. While men recalled reading editorials far more often than women, the two groups reported equal attention to the editorial page. Women simply fastened on other things here such as editorial cartoons or letters to the editor. In most papers, at least twice as many men as women said they had read financial *news*, but on half of the fourteen American papers, more women than men looked at the financial *page*. The Gallup survey showed that the news page was a common ground for men and women, with men averting their eyes from some items, women from others. This study found what later researchers have confirmed, that however jerky the path through a paper, adult readers shared most of the same pages.[41]

The *Continuing Study* of newspapers lasted eight years; of the magazines, a decade. But projects of this type have remained a measure of news reading to the present day. Trust in this method did not grow. Might readers be deceivers when they spoke about their tastes? Alfred Politz, a German statistician, dreamed of bringing rigor to these marketing tests. This refugee from Hitler prepared for a career on Madison Avenue by promoting a headache remedy and teaching judo, surely useful subject areas. With his English improved and his mathematical skills recognized, he went into marketing. He waged war against sampling techniques that were not truly random. This gadfly, who once rented a hall to denounce sloppy questions in marketing, said that publishers were spending their money to measure what people thought they *should* read, not their true behavior. (In the most dramatic confirmation of this theory, Politz found 4 percent of respondents insisting they had read issues of magazines that had not yet been published.) In 1947, the year Alfred Politz Research was incorporated, the director told publishers that all their survey efforts were so flawed that "no knowledge about the real audiences of various magazines is available." He was paid well to do better. To cut through deception, Politz had interviewers look through magazines with a careful sample of readers to find the most interesting features. "Each interviewer," Politz explained, "was trained to use instantaneously carefully contrived comments in such a manner as to maintain a natural rapport-inspiring atmosphere."[42]

Now the finding of good reading material did not interest Politz at all. He simply wanted his staff to be able to ask, seemingly as an afterthought, whether the subjects had already read the issue they looked through. This way he would get an honest answer. To prevent the interviewers from tipping off readers, he told them that this really was a survey to see what readers liked. No one knew the real game, except Politz. The detective work continued in a study of newspaper readers in New York. He would not count people as readers unless they could tell a plausible story about where they bought a paper. Eventually, Politz studies used the methods of a spy: one-way mirrors to observe the reader, and light-sensitive emulsions or microscopic drops of glue to see if the reader had really opened a page.

Did readers even know what they had taken in during their hurried journey through the paper? More contraptions were brought into the study of reading to get at the truth. By the 1960s eye movements could be roughly correlated with a page of text so that one could "see" at least the general area on a page that people read. Cameras, mercifully, did the work of pointers attached to the eye. Still, the reader's face and whole body were clamped down, and the setting was wildly different than the easy chair or breakfast table. In the 1980s the headsets became bicycle helmets, freeing movement at last. With the aid of optical fibers on the helmet, researchers could narrow down what readers were seeing and how much time they spent on different parts of the page.[43]

Research designed to learn exactly how Americans read the news took a new turn in the 1980s with the arrival of an apparatus that watched the reader's eye and choice of text at the same time. The Eye Trac system was worn like a fencing mask. One miniature camera was set on the headband and aimed at the news page; another camera cantilevered out from the forehead to monitor the reader's pupils. The headgear weighed only eight ounces and allowed free movement. A single screen showed the exact lines of type or figures the reader was taking in while paging through a paper. One could see every "processing opportunity" (that is, what might have been read) as well as what was actually "processed" (that is, looked at long enough to be absorbed). The camera could tell a vacant stare from the movement of the pupil across print from left to right. If the subject's eye did this, the behavior was logged. It was a simple matter to see how Americans took in each page of a newspaper.[44]

Eye Trac research shows that the public does not, as editors had long thought, enter the front page through the lead story in the right column of the first page. Although a digest and index appears below the fold of most front pages, very few readers ever look here first. Even a color photograph will not draw readers to take their first look at the bottom of the page. Headlines and graphics are the points of entry for page 1 as they are for every following page of a newspaper. The public looks right on a two-page spread to see the dominant graphic or headline and then repeats the process on the left-hand page. These findings suggest readers who are sometimes steered by the purely formal qualities of a news page but more often go their own way. No graphic, no headline will lure the public to enter a page at an ad. (Printing an ad in color where all else is in black and white does not change this visual habit.) The reader looks at more than half of the headlines in a newspaper and decides to look at the text of half of these stories. A reader then makes another cut, reading most of just one story in eight. Again, newspaper readers cannot easily be led to change their ways. Highlighting text with color, for instance, makes little difference to the public. This research supports the back-handed compliment to editors that comes from the Media Lab at the Massachusetts Institute of Technology: "One of the things the newspaper does so well is it makes it easy to disregard 90 percent of the information."[45]

Research on the habits of magazine readers is less precise, but personal and idiosyncratic paths through this news have long been noticed. (Again, knowledge was not easily won: a camera was concealed in the shoulder pad of a researcher's suit for candid shots of commuters turning pages.) *Time* has concluded that only one reader in three begins with the first story or picture in the magazine "book," and other surveys have found an even higher rate of people who refuse to begin at the beginning. Promiscuous paging, fanning a magazine with the left hand and alighting on a page, seems to be a practice of up to 40 percent of all readers.[46]

Research studies document hopscotching, but they have never paid much attention to the social game a reader may play with the news. The chatty newspaper readers who showed up in the Politz research and the *Continuing Study* of newspapers were demonstrating that talking with other people was a part of reading the news. The sociability that grew up around the printed page in the early republic did not cease in the twentieth century. Yet research on modern readers did not explore this social context. The subject in the lab was almost as isolated as the self-absorbed readers that artists, following Harnett, put on canvases. In reality, Americans read in company, noting other people's taste and sharing their own.

The pictures of news readers taken by the documentary photographers of the 1930s and 1940s captured this world that other researchers missed. This vast enterprise with the camera was an effort by the Roosevelt administration, through the Farm Security Administration and related agencies, to show America to itself (especially as this vision would aid the New Deal and mobilization for World War II). The government had no point to make about news reading, but in seeking to catch the texture of homes and public spaces, the photographers of this project left a telling record of newspapers and magazines in a natural habitat. A sample of more than a hundred such scenes shows that fully 40 percent of those seeking news joined company with another, sharing the page or reading while a household member or neighbor also read the news. These Americans scanned newsstands, opened their papers on their way home, and sank down in the living room with a paper or magazine. The cameras caught nearly twice as many news readers in company as they caught readers alone. About one reader in four was sharing a text by reading together, pointing to stories, and even by embracing one another with their papers.[47]

There are, then, two sets of editors for every newspaper and magazine; the people who decide what to print and how to print it, and readers who glance, skim, and stop through the pages to meet their own needs. The better experimental techniques have gotten for the study of reading, the more freedom has been measured in the response to text. Over time, surveys show more picking and choosing by readers. Stunning graphic effects do not seem to control the public eye (though they may increase pleasure spent with a newspaper). Indeed, page make-up in the future may strengthen readers' ability to bend texts to their own interests. Icons, like this ℭ, have begun to appear in major papers, to indicate where more detail is available from an electronic database. Californians using one of these resources, the Mercury Center at the Knight-Ridder

John Collier, Childersburg, Alabama, May 1942.
Collections of the Library of Congress.

paper in San Jose, are encouraged to use print journalism to access statistics, speeches, and other stories the editors could not fit into the paper. These readers now edit this news, using the same technology that the editorial staff used a few hours earlier.[48]

In three hundred years of journalism, publishers have cultivated a vigorous reading habit. They have not disciplined readers to accept a professional judgment of what is most important. Editors do not have the confidence they once had about what the public *should* know. The New York *Times* confessed this in 1989 in killing its "Saturday News Quiz." The quiz had ranged over every news section. The problem for the editors was that this "seemed to suggest that there is a right or a wrong way to read The Times." But this was impossible, readers learned: "The paper may occasionally fail its readers, but its readers cannot fail The Times." Picking and choosing without regard for the editor's judgments was blessed. In 1995 the *Times* sales campaign was "Read What You Like." This may not be the noblest sentiment known to journalism, but it has been an attractive proposition to millions of readers at the end of the twentieth century who see publishers asking them what they want and delivering publications edited just that way.[49]

4. Hogs and Humbled Editors

American journalism did not begin with editors who were discriminating in what they printed. In the eighteenth century, the men and women who conducted the press were likely to excerpt whatever was new in publications coming out of the mail sack and every pronouncement that a friendly government or supportive political faction expected to see in the paper. These first editors barely imposed order and looked to others for editorial direction. Zeal to interpret events for the reader was rare. Brief notes of remarkable occurrences filled columns, rooted in a worldview that God worked in mysterious ways and that citizens should ponder the record and sort this out for themselves. Benjamin Franklin spoke for his trade when he confessed, in a famous defense of printers, that they "acquire a vast Unconcernedness as to the right or wrong Opinions contain'd in what they print." "Miscellany," a common term in early magazine titles, was the strongest editorial theme of the early press. Scholars have described the front page of the American daily as a "dense jungle" until the end of the nineteenth century, for "it gave an impression of diversity, randomness and complexity, leaving it to the reader to make sense — or draw a map — of the world." Mark Twain, an apprenticed printer who grew up in the offices of rural weeklies before the Civil War, did not stand in awe of editors. The weekly was the typical fare of Americans and, as Twain recalled, a publication "just as well off with a sick editor as a well one, and better off with a dead one than either of them."[50]

The laissez-faire days of editing ended in the nineteenth century when men and women in charge of what was published cut back the jungle of stories, imposed editorial philosophies, and enshrined originality as a virtue. The simplification and amplification of stories on the modern front page was one sign of this, but in all forms of journalism a catalogue of novelties and wonders was no longer enough. The press promised an independent judgment on the public good. Editors took on the new challenge of reflecting public taste. Samuel McClure, magazine impresario of the 1890s, praised a colleague because what she liked was liked by thousands, praised himself because what he liked was liked by millions, but saved the laurel wreath for a rival editor because what he liked was liked by everybody. This gift to connect with the public was not enough, however. The editor of the modern age must improve readers. McClure was also proud to have started the social criticism that came to be called "muckraking." This sense that the editor had a trustee's responsibility to watch the readers' true interests, not simply to answer their whims, was the emotional basis for many careers. "Come down to the level which the public sets and it will leave you at the moment you do it," Edward Bok said, as he created the magazine with the largest circulation at the beginning of the twentieth century.[51]

These two roles for the editor, that of representative and of trustee for the reading public, often conflict. Note that they have one assumption in common: that editors had *some* type of genius that allowed them to serve readers. Editors of the *New Yorker* and the *National Enquirer*, of the New York *Times* and *USA Today*, publish very different things. But we are used to thinking that these editors have the gift of finding stories that make these publications a success. For a century, editors have boldly claimed credit for managing the attention of readers. Of all the heresies in journalism, the rarest in recent American history is Mark Twain's mischievous hypothesis that editors don't matter much and that readers will put news together as they please. There are signs that this is now happening.

The unraveling of the assumption that great editors knew best began with hogs. Farming has been the most volatile work performed by the American people, the occupation of 97 percent of the country at its birth and of 3 percent at the end of the twentieth century. This is one reason why agricultural periodicals have had to be adept in meeting demographic challenges and particularly curious about what their readers were thinking. While other large-circulation magazines died, *Farm Journal* (founded in 1877) adapted. It cut its circulation from 3.7 million in 1953 to a profitable three-quarters of a million in the 1990s. Agricultural editors did not always know what to do when they studied their public (witness the baffling study of hogs on magazine covers), but they have led the industry in experimentation. The *Farm Journal* went beyond its regional editions to become the first magazine to customize by precise demographics. A "Hog Extra" was bound into copies of the magazine that went to the nation's top hog-raising counties in 1962. Readers sent in a card and a dollar to customize their magazine. In the late 1970s the R. R. Donnelley printing firm that had printed *Life* magazine found in *Farm Journal* its first opportunity to use its selective binding technology to produce a press run with different stories and ads keyed to different types of farmers. Donnelley, in a further break with five hundred years of publishing history, also learned to incorporate printing in the binding process so that every issue could be customized. *Farm Journal*, in the early 1990s, appeared in as many as 9,315 versions each month.[52]

Readers of this book, who probably missed all of these editions, may well have seen this technology demonstrated in the Thanksgiving-week issue of *Time* in 1990. This magazine came to four million homes with the subscriber's name as part of the cover design: "Hey . . . Don't miss our really interesting story on the JUNK MAIL EXPLOSION!" The issue after Memorial Day in 1994 had a personalized political feature that reported on the subscriber's representatives in Congress and had a postcard for readers to send their views to Washington. At this time, by coincidence or possibly in homage, *Time* saluted its readers with a full-page close-up of a rooting hog. "In this environment of high reader involvement, your advertising takes on real added value," the publishers told Madison Avenue. Even the hog seemed surprised by this endorsement.[53]

Magazines for parents followed the lead of *Farm Journal*, producing different editions as children grew older. Like the farmers, one family living next to another, subscribing to the same magazine, might find very different things in it. One executive at a mass circulation magazine blessed selective binding as "the idea of marketing to one." *Newsweek* marked a new direction for mainstream publications on April 27, 1992, when it began to offer editorial supplements, bound into the magazine, to those who wanted to know more and who were willing to pay more for this material. The next year, *Sports Illustrated* led the *Time* family of magazines in this direction. Publishers have had trouble getting software running to make a profit with customized press runs. But the technology is ready. In 1994 each magazine coming off a production line could be different, at a rate of fifteen thousand copies an hour. Magazines could now throw a different light for their different readers. Publishing, like cable television, could let its audience choose a basic service and also sell a premium channel to those willing to pay.[54]

Cable provides a basic service because regulators demand it. In a free market, would print media find it in their interest to provide news for all? Magazines saw the general interest publications die and could confidently position themselves around strong special interests. The number of such magazines, and their total circulation, exploded in the last third of the twentieth century (sto-

ries to be told at length in this book). In their new, segmented markets, magazines had confidence that they knew what their readers wanted. Newspapers
did not. When dailies woke up to their circulation crisis in the 1970s, they
found a new way to listen to readers: the focus group. This was a sea change
from the sort of large, random sampling pioneered by Gallup and Politz and
carried out by the American Newspaper Publishers Association. Columns of
figures are cold and mute to most editors. The stories that readers tell are more
easily taken to heart. The editor can sit with the guests (or eavesdrop behind a
one-way mirror). Interviews with passers-by have been a staple of most journalist's lives; how natural to make editorial decisions the same way.

Under the confident direction of Ruth Clark, focus-group wisdom on the
news page drove a transformation of many newspapers. In the "Changing
Needs, Changing Readers" report issued in installments over 1978-79, focus
groups said that they wanted an emotional bond with the newspaper, that they
wanted news that was relevant to their lives. Clark told publishers that their
readers considered "self" a vital news beat and reported reader interest in "the
importance of 'me.'" Distant events and complicated stories were found to
endanger circulation. Clark announced that newspapers needed a new social
contract. "The old contract between editors and readers was clear," she said.
"Editors decided what readers should know and readers read what editors
thought they should know. The rules have to change."[55]

There were at least as many methodological problems in Clark's research
(and in focus-group pronouncements of the 1990s) as in the weakest of the
quantitative work. Focus groups are not representative samples of readers, and
so results do not have general statistical validity. "No one has yet devised a way
of making a focus group representative of anything," a distinguished researcher
cautioned his fellow journalists in 1985. One might as well be guided by the
proverbial, grass-roots sentiments of cab drivers or callers to talk radio. Indeed,
a reporter could have bettered Clark's sample in one day at a taxi stand or radio
station: "Changing Needs, Changing Readers" listened to only about 120
people (Clark rushed into print after hearing from about seventy). Americans,
as Politz saw, like to please people who ask them questions and remember
reading, mostly, that which makes them look good. What people say in discussion about reading may not at all be what they take from the printed page in
private. Even representative, candid readers may not be able to specify their
interests, as everyone knows who has ever been pulled into a strange article by a
talented writer or a chance association. But the stories from the focus groups in
the late 1970s, with their pleas for self-help and news-to-be-used, registered in
editorial decision making across the nation. Called the "hot book" for newspaper editors of the 1980s, the Clark report was probably the single most
influential statement ever made about the news reader and literally put editors
behind glass, those one-way mirrors that these journalists used to follow the

dialogue of focus groups. This ritual of editors spying on their readers has survived all criticism. "Today's editors have become focus-group groupies," Howard Kurtz wrote in 1993, after years of study of these professionals for the Washington *Post*. The uncritical acceptance of dicta from focus groups is one of the most curious practices of journalists in convention.[56]

Taken simply as suggestions, the ideas from focus groups are unobjectionable. Listening to readers can put new life into news, especially if people are asked what would make them fulfilled citizens, not simply happy customers. The Wichita *Eagle* and the Charlotte *Observer* set their coverage of the 1992 presidential campaign by polling readers on what was important to them. (The *Observer* went so far as to have their reporters ask candidates the readers' questions.) For every instance of journalists renewing themselves by listening to their readers, there are many more cases where news has been dumbed down or made less coherent because "we wanted to see what happens if you do *everything* with the customer in mind." Erik Larson, who covered the marketing beat for the *Wall Street Journal*, has concluded that the obsessive attention to audience has "crimped the national imagination." Looking to readers for editorial direction has proven to be an easy way to get lost. A few years after Ruth Clark had sent editors scurrying to please the "me" generation she released a new report, claiming that recession and international crises had "transformed what used to be a narrowly self-involved audience into a far more sophisticated, cosmopolitan group." Editors were told that readers now liked them but were hungry for more hard news stories. Editors were cheered by this announcement. Few noticed that Clark's second report had a new feature: a projectable sample. Clark was returning to the conventional findings of readership surveys because she was moving closer to their methods.[57]

Even *sound* reader research is often a Cheshire Cat, inviting editors to rush ahead in opposite directions. Susan Miller, the director of editorial research for Scripps-Howard, said in 1987 that "thanks to market research — and to the increased hiring and promotion of women — editors realize that women do not require a separate section of the paper filled with anything and everything that might interest the members of their sex." These certainties led to the transformation of women's sections into "style" or "home" departments. But focus groups and female editors have brought women's sections back to life. "When women tell newspaper editors they do not see themselves in the newspaper, they suggest that the newspaper does not see life complete and whole, the way they see it, live it," an editor of the Chicago *Tribune* found in 1991. Colleen Dishon has revived the women's section as a mini-paper within the *Tribune* because "newspapers, to save themselves from becoming irrelevant to women readers, must reflect what's going on in women's lives. Women must see themselves reflected in the newspaper in general and in specific places."[58]

One of three things must be true. First, the reading public may change its mind, fundamentally, every few years. Editors were willing to believe this in the case of Ruth Clark. *Strategic Newspaper Management* (1988), a reference tool for the newsroom, accepts this view as gospel. The second possibility is, to quote an editor of the New York *Post*, "readership surveys are a ripoff." This is heresy in a field that is eager to adopt modern business practices. A third conclusion about listening to readers is the best documented: given a chance, the public will ask for wildly contradictory things. The American Society of Newspaper Editors, in their "Future of Newspapers Report" (1990), showed the patience and good manners of Alice in Wonderland, trying to find the way. The editors listened to a dozen focus groups, spread across the country. These readers sounded a great deal like the Cheshire Cat:

> People want complete news coverage, but they don't want to have to spend too much time with the paper. The [*sic*] want in-depth stories, but they want jumps [to inside pages] to be avoided at all costs. They want the important news, but it has to be personally relevant. . . . They want news coverage that is to-the-point, but they decry superficial "headline news." They want a newspaper that is progressive and innovative, but that is also comfortable and familiar.[59]

Perhaps the only certainty about reader research is that it is humbling exercise for editors. They can listen to these surveys and rush ahead in opposite directions, or they can take their own counsel and earn the reputation of being unresponsive. To date, the wisest advice that editors have heard about letting readers help edit the paper is Philip Meyer's *The Newspaper Survival Book: An Editor's Guide to Marketing Research* (1985). Meyer, who came by his knowledge both as an academic and as an executive at Knight-Ridder Newspapers, found that after many years of toil on reader attitudes he could not produce a respectable list of certainties. ("'Give me a week,' I said, 'and I might be able to come up with three.'") This handbook has eight "homilies" ("Remember the Importance of National and International News," "Do Something for the Kids") drawn from the full range of sophisticated polls and focus groups. "And on some days," Meyer says, "I'm not too sure about these eight."[60]

Apostles of the "tailored newspaper" hold out the promise of giving the editor's job to the reader, without further studies of readership. This term became fashionable in the 1970s, when dailies first realized the economies of computers to set type and to store information. Many publishers targeted groups of readers with special supplements and increased the number of zoned editions. A publisher (not an editor) had the happy thought that readers would soon be phoning in their order for what would appear in the next day's paper. The nightmare among editors was each reader demanding a special edition with news "about only what they want." But this would be welcomed by some in publishing today. *Editor & Publisher*, a trade journal, has carried the praises of the "Personal Newspaper" which would put readers in charge of content.[61]

Business plans for a customized daily are proceeding, including provisions for miners' lamps so that carriers can read the subscriber's name on the paper and select it from their load. Financial and logistic challenges remain, however. Americans were safe from a narcissistic daily paper arriving on the front porch in the twentieth century. But the electronic off-shoots of the newspaper were a different matter. America On-Line, Dow Jones News Retrieval, CompuServe, and Prodigy sought a market for news that a customer could put together by his or her own light. In the early 1990s firms such as Comtex Scientific, Farcast, and Infoseek allowed their subscribers to "see stories . . . without an editor getting in your way!" The selection was done by computer programs, sometimes called "Droids." Often, the role of flesh-and-blood editors in this industry, former editors, was to help the client create the profile of interests that would then be used to search the database for stories. "It restores control to the individual," said a leader in the race to sell an electronic, personalized newspaper. At the Mercury Center of Knight-Ridder, new editors at the electronic division of the newspaper are called "senders." They order and supply information for the databank. Tribune Media Services in Chicago believes that "tight writing and good story selection are . . . less prized in the interactive world" and that the editor should become the "host" to newspaper readers. In 1994 the Tribune Company bought *Farm Journal* (including *Hogs Today*), in part to acquire its skills in targeting readers. No one who becomes an editor today can be sure that, blessed with a long career, the word "editor" will make sense when he or she retires.[62]

Many metropolitan papers offered the custom delivery of news via fax, phone, or electronic bulletin boards. About 40 percent of all dailies established "audiotex" services by the mid 1990s; about a third had some type of 900-number program. This is the decade in which papers, literally, found their voice. In a three-year period at the beginning of the 1990s, the number of papers with a voice service multiplied sixty-four times. The Baltimore *Sun* started up with nearly three hundred thousand calls coming each month. The Washington *Post* logged eight hundred thousand calls a month, only three years after starting the service of recorded announcements. The Atlanta *Journal and Constitution* topped a million calls a month on its phone services. Roughly a dozen papers ran electronic supplements which allowed subscribers to browse the news and gain access to information that the editors had not put in the paper. The Kansas City *Star* hopes to become a "navigational tool" for readers to sail through its recorded messages. The weekly Boston *Phoenix* uses audiotex to sell the voice messages of people who have placed personal ads in the paper. Some of these come with music to set the mood. In 1991, three years after it began this service, the paper earned more money from readers calling up to hear the sound tracks than it did from the ads themselves. Nearly two hundred other publications used this same system. A modern reader may find a job listing in the paper, call in a voice résumé, and hear back in the voice mailboxes of the press: yes, no, maybe.[63]

When readers see the newspaper as a device that allows them to listen or perform, editors have granted them a new license. CityLine, the leading audiotex service, offers the promise of "personalized information" from the newspaper. Callers program the service in advance to give them just the reports they are looking for. The computer bulletin boards in the metropolitan dailies, with their invitations to open conversations with reporter and editors ("Give . . . a piece of your mind"), have further expanded what an active reader may do. Readers could talk to one another, computer to computer, through programs like "Windy City Chat" run by the Chicago *Tribune*. It was easy to see who the newspaper believed was the editor of the service: "You can schedule your online time to take advantage of the information and activities that interest YOU!" Magazines, led by *New York* and *Time*, joined this effort to allow readers to range through the files and talk to one another. More than 125,000 searches were made through *Time* during the first three weeks the magazine went on line in 1993. (Here the editors learned to master their most persistent readers, the "Bandwidth Hogs.") *Wired* attracted more than a hundred thousand subscribers in its first year and a half, and nearly that many electronic mail inquiries flooded into the magazine every *week* at the end of this debut. The press began the twentieth century with the street cries of headlines, the journalist's priorities. The press ends this century with the sound of the dial tone and keys clicking out the reader's orders.[64]

Media companies have wagered huge sums that text would someday be delivered on portable, interactive screens that would complete the dream of customization (with appropriate bills). At the Media Lab of MIT the name for this future edition is "The Daily Me." This new age, if it was dawning, was really a return to the forgotten day when scrapbook makers checked their cosmic bank balance and entrepreneurs ordered their clippings on rats, lightning rods, and jails. What was different was the spectacle of the whole public, not just a few, editing what was published. Also, the editor's desk did not look the same when the reader sat at it.[65]

Many editors were not pleased by the specter of readers ordering up the news. Katherine Fanning, who has edited dailies in Alaska and Massachusetts, believes that "there is a point at which there is information people should have, even if they don't know they want it and even if they don't tell you they want it." Ray Cave, managing editor of *Time*, said in 1987: "I hate reader surveys, and may be the only editor alive who has never attended a focus group." This is indeed an eccentric view at the end of the twentieth century. Shouts that the reader is always right come from the center of business thinking in journalism. "Know Thy Reader" managers plead, "There's no reason not to give readers what they want—even if it means diverging from tradition." Up-to-date editors of metropolitan papers, even in monopoly markets, told the profession that "the surest way to editorial failure is to impose upon readers our own sense of what they ought to know." That rising force in the American press, Rupert Murdoch, has tackled electronic publishing with the determination "to put the 'me' back in 'media.' "[66]

It is not clear that the "ed" for editor is to be given more importance. The logic of marketing at the end of the twentieth century often seems to leave little room for an imaginative editor. Mark Twain's modest proposal that dead editors be favored over live ones could come true. Theorists of "mass customization" urge the press to move in step with other industries, looking away from general audiences and toward smaller groups with narrower interests. The editor's domain seems ever shrinking. The chairman of the American Newspaper Publishers Association roused his colleagues to the challenge of the 1990s by informing them that Nine Lives cat food now came in twenty-three varieties. "The niches are becoming the market" was a commonplace of business planning of the mid-nineties, a maxim publishers took to heart. The talisman of editors went from pet food back to the barnyard. A smiling, inflated pig crouched on issues of *Pig Life* in an ad taken out by the Cowles media conglomerate. The proposition is to use subscriber lists "to create another significant profit center" by holding conferences and exhibitions. Convention-prone pig fanciers, one of a galaxy of Americans who knew what they wanted, were waiting for editors to serve them.[67]

If the past is a guide, some editors will have the last laugh over such marketing wisdom. The value of a point of view and a genius to organize information has never before been diminished by changes in technology or merchandising. These were skills that grew in the nineteenth century, uniting Americans with news in print. The explosive growth in information through new media can only increase the value of perceptive judgments for more people. What is likely to fade is the value of a pedestrian ordering of facts and ideas. Readers can now assemble these things for themselves with less help from professionals. With everyone his own editor, her own editor, journalists have to prove, all over again, that they know their job.

PART THREE

THE
DURABLE
DREAM
OF A
READING
PUBLIC

6

UNWANTED

READERS

At the birth of journalism in the United States, public policy and business practice lived by a simple maxim: readers wanted. Americans saw no limits on the audience for the press. Newspapers (though not yet magazines) were viewed as a free citizen's birthright. Thomas Jefferson knew that many people could not afford a subscription, but he still hoped "to contrive that those papers should penetrate the whole mass of the people." A generation later, in the age of Andrew Jackson, reformers and conservatives alike used more affordable papers to win over the common folk. News, like politics, was for "all" in this discourse. True, news of race as well as upsetting ideas about gender and class provoked efforts to limit the audience. Home-bred news was favored in the postal system over publications sent from distant cities. But these were off-key notes in a chorus of rejoicing about the spread of information. Claims that the whole public was to be enlightened and improved by a free press rang out. Evangelical Protestantism, the moral voice for the nation, repeatedly called Americans to recognize equality before their maker. Manufacturers and farmers found that larger markets paid better than smaller ones, and in businesses as diverse as meat packing and sewing machines, gun making and floor milling, size was the way to wealth. To be frankly elitist was bad faith, bad politics, bad business. Popular taste and elite taste in the nineteenth century were often not far apart. Mechanics and professors took common inspiration from a lecture by Emerson (who travelled incessantly to meet the demand). Dickens, Whitman, and Twain enjoyed audiences that cut across levels of education and social standing. Shakespearean drama and Italian opera were staged for everyone, attracting vast audiences as broad as those drawn to a baseball game. Journalists inhabited this mental world in which truth and beauty seemed accessible to the mass of Americans and profit seemed ensured by increasing the scale of a business. The intoxicating thought that news was for all guided a press that reveled in its democratic spirit. The crash of this faith as journalists came to see multitudes of readers they did not *want* has been an unexpected and momentous change in the media of the twentieth century.[1]

I. A Democracy of Circulation

The early republic faced this policy issue: if news was vital to its health, why not allow newspapers to circulate for free? This subsidy for public enlightenment had powerful friends. George Washington and James Madison spoke up for the idea in the 1790s, and Jefferson proposed the free distribution of newspapers in his First Annual Message in 1801. In every decade of the nineteenth century, publishers supported some version of this reform. The Senate came within one vote of abolishing postage for newspapers in 1832. A senator from Delaware at this time equated the postage paid by "the yeomanry of the country" on vital newspapers with the tyranny of English and French governments. Senator John Holmes of Maine, in three days of speeches, compared the postage on newspapers with the injustices that had brought down the Roman Republic. Toward the end of the century, Canada set a shining example by allowing all news to circulate for free through the mails. Over and over Americans asked themselves: did the logic of democracy not require that the government bear the cost of keeping citizens informed?[2]

Publishers liked this idea, and most journalists of the nineteenth century believed that Americans of every rank in society could be and should be their readers. Looking out at the audience, publishers spoke, by second nature, of inclusion. James Gordon Bennett Sr., the most successful operator of the penny press of the 1830s, grew breathless as he promised to gather in "the great masses of the community—the merchant, mechanic, working people—the private family as well as the public hotel—the journeyman and his employer—the clerk and his principal. . . . There is not a person in the city, male or female, that may not be able to say, 'Well I have got a paper of my own which will tell me all about what's doing in the world.'" It is no surprise that Walt Whitman shared this sentiment when he sat in an editor's chair. "We really feel a desire to talk on many subjects, to all the people of Brooklyn," he announced as he took charge of the *Daily Eagle* on the first day of June in 1846. But better businessmen also shared this dream. The New York *Times* began with the same wish at mid-century. In its first issue, Henry J. Raymond, the founder, damned New York's "*class* journals, made up for particular classes of readers." In his prospectus he promised "*the best and the cheapest newspaper in the United States.*" The *Times* celebrated its first birthday with pride that "it is made up for all classes."[3]

This was not simply the talk of upstarts, clamoring for attention. Builders of strong newspapers spoke this way in private and in their memoirs when they defined accomplishments. Joseph Pulitzer told his staff that "nothing is worth printing . . . that is not sure to be read by the masses, the many, not the few." Florence Kelly joined the staff of the Boston *Globe* in the 1880s and celebrated a newspaper dedicated to a "democracy of circulation." Into the 1890s newspaper business managers often struck the same romantic note, even when speaking to one another: "A paper must be made so big and broad in its scope as to interest and hold the attention of the dweller in the hovel as well as the owner of the brownstone front." The conventional business judgment of nineteenth-century publishers was that a paper aimed only at an elite would weaken and die. Many publishers claimed to have affluent subscribers whom advertisers should prize. But most of these papers insisted that they wanted the ordinary citizen too.[4]

If a choice was to be made, powerful voices in the press advised that the elite be ignored. "God damn the rich and God help the poor" was the cry of Edward W. Scripps as he built the first modern newspaper chain in the 1880s and 1890s. He acquired thirty-four dailies before World War I, quarreling with everyone he did business with, including his relatives in the newspaper world. Bruised and brooding, he made a splendid exile on twenty-one hundred acres, perched above the Pacific near San Diego. Like Hearst on his California mountaintop, Scripps fussed with his papers and ruminated on the public during the last decades of his life. Scripps called himself a snob at heart and admitted that he fled the company of plain people. Yet he expected nothing but trouble for his papers from the wealthy of his *own* class. And so he would have his papers depend on nothing but this circulation to plain people. He instructed his editors "to serve that class of people and only that class of people from whom you cannot even hope to derive any other income than the one cent a day they pay you for your paper." Scripps did not have the clear mind of the abstemious Hearst, and he built part of his media network while drinking, he said, a gallon of whiskey a day. Scripps cannot be trusted on his bottle count. But he had every right to boast that "the first of my principles is that I have constituted myself the advocate of that large majority of the people who are not so rich in worldly goods and native intelligence as to make them equal, man for man, in the struggle with individual of the wealthier and more intellectual class."[5]

"We must get right down with the people," the publisher George Booth told the editor of his new paper in Chicago. Booth had married into the Scripps family and been touched by their shifty populism. Appealing to businessmen was not enough, Booth explained: "I have felt disposed to go as far as seems wise on the side of the workingmen. Be honest with them and ourselves, and yet calculating to please and to win them by securing their confidence with the methods we may adopt. We are not in a position to be very dignified as yet." Booth was in good company and held up Hearst and Pulitzer as models. Few publishers at the turn of the twentieth century could afford to concentrate on polite society.[6]

Plain citizens were in fact the routine guests of publishers. In small towns, newspaper offices had open doors and anyone might drop in to place an ad, to browse the out-of-town papers in the pile of exchanges, or to set the editor straight. Some publishers turned a profit by fitting out reading rooms. "A good glass, an interesting paper and a pleasant cigar may always be found at the Star," the editor of this Houston paper boasted in 1840. Newspaper offices grew too comfortable to please some publishers, and visitors who were "loungers and boors . . . complacently occupying your easiest chair" were cited as occupational hazards. Big-city dailies, with their cavernous presses and honeycomb of offices, were not as easy to visit, but they tried to be hospitable. Shortly after the Civil War the Philadelphia *Public Ledger* built a headquarters open to all people at all hours, with the amenities of a hotel lobby. Even citizens passing by on the street could put their head in the mouth of the *Ledger*'s marble lions for a cool drink. By 1876 the paper could report that a hundred thousand people had come, "scrutinizing the establishment."[7]

Metropolitan dailies had other ways of gathering in Americans. Their contests and sales promotions assembled citizens. The Washington *Post*, for instance, drew a crowd of twenty-five thousand to meet the winners of an essay competition in 1889. In the pre-radio age, newspapers were already broadcasters of exciting sounds and sights. Thus the Chicago *Daily News* startled the lakefront in 1885 with cannon volleys to celebrate a circulation of one hundred thousand. Other civic gestures memorialized the publisher as the people's servant and host. Some of these affairs were frankly partisan, as when the Chicago *Tribune* illuminated its office with a thousand lights and invited the public to come and see rails that had been split by the new Republican nominee, Abraham Lincoln. But in the last quarter of the nineteenth century, political zeal took in whole communities. Headline news was spread across the ornate facade of press buildings. War bulletins from Cuba and the Philippines, for instance, went up in giant script outside newspaper offices in 1898, to the delight of large crowds. Regularly, on election days, newspapers held an open house for their town. The Providence *Journal* deployed megaphone men and gargantuan banners outside its building to announce the vote. Citizens filled the downtown in Rhode Island, serenaded by the paper's thirty-four-piece brass band. The crowds outside the newsrooms in Indianapolis were "a surging mass of people with upturned faces . . . shouting themselves hoarse." In 1896 Joseph Pulitzer took over City Hall Park in New York and projected vote totals in a light show on his building. William Randolph Hearst countered by opening Madison Square Garden for the public. In 1912 the Chicago *Tribune* displayed the latest vote counts in twelve of the largest arenas and set up six additional displays on the streets. More than forty-seven thousand Chicagoans followed the three-way contest between Teddy Roosevelt, Woodrow Wilson, and William Taft in the *Tribune*'s centers. The whole city watched the paper's spotlights signal the likely winner.[8]

In the minds of many publishers, their audience knew no limits. Under what one editor called "the policy of preposterous brag," they stretched circulation figures, creating a race of phantom subscribers. Desperate men, fighting for the lives of their publications, invented readership. But so too did publishing geniuses who had a growing share of the market. At mid-century, *Scientific American* posted a circulation figure of fourteen thousand on its front page. In his private diary, the publisher recorded an "actual" circulation of about eight thousand. After Joseph Pulitzer had conquered St. Louis, he published circulation figures for his paper that were as much as 15 percent more than what appeared on his books. The Chicago *Inter-Ocean* was caught starting its press run with the round number of twenty-five thousand, and other major papers were accused of larger exaggerations.[9]

The modern advertising industry, born in this era, fought these fantasies and sought to reveal what clients were getting for their money. Publishers bristled at the suggestion that real people be found to stand behind a journalist's sense of the audience.[10] George P. Rowell, the pathfinder of circulation audits, probably held more frigid conversations about readership than anyone else in America, and his appraisal of his adversaries, the publishers, is revealing. He did not think that the men with closed books or the habit of making 60,000 into "about 100,000" were dishonest. He found that men of high character could be the most secretive. "What was meant by circulation was not as well understood in those days as it is now," he said after the turn of the century. The quantification of the market according to averages of paying customers was simply a foreign concept to publishers who lived on hope that their "true" reading public had to be a vast multitude.[11]

The power of wishful thinking was captured in sales pitches and orders for new presses. In the last decades of the nineteenth century the Boston *Herald* was "A Newspaper Made for All." The Chicago *Tribune*, not yet "The Greatest Newspaper in the World," was "The People's Paper." This was also the boast of the founder of the Cox media group, James M. Cox, as he built up an Ohio paper. Even the crusty Charles A. Dana retained the legend "It Shines for

All" on the masthead of his New York *Sun*. Other papers boasted of their endorsements by ordinary citizens. "Everybody who can read at all, reads the Eagle," editors in Brooklyn heard citizens saying. "Every body in the District of Columbia who can read, reads THE STAR" was the claim of journalists in the capital in 1876. Publishers put money on the table to cover their boasts, ordering expensive new presses to "confirm" rising demand. The new models would churn out papers for the new readers that publishers believed it was their destiny to serve.[12]

In an era without survey research, it is impossible to pin down what readers thought of the journalists who kept embracing them. A coin given up for a newspaper, like small change given to a panhandler, is no sure sign that a citizen likes the paper or the person very much. Circulation figures or attendance at civic fetes, after all, may hide a degree of resentment. We cannot forget the legion of readers in the nineteenth century who stalled in paying their subscriptions. But there is evidence that even Americans at the bottom of society valued the press.

There was a good deal of news reading in the workplace, for instance. Artists pictured this in such works as William Page, *The Young Merchants*, c. 1834; William Henry Burr, *The Intelligence Office*, 1849; John George Brown, *The Longshoremen's Noon*, 1879; and Benjamin West Clinedinst, *An Idle Moment*, c. 1898. Shoemakers read aloud to their fellow artisans and made their shops a cacophony of hammering and talk. In both Cuban and Jewish cigar shops the workers pooled money to buy newspapers and books, and one person was elected to read them aloud while fellow workers rolled leaves. Samuel Gompers, founder of the American Federation of Labor, gained stature and knowledge as a reader in a cigar shop in the late 1860s and 1870s. James Weldon Johnson, the black poet, had close ties to Cuban cigar workers. In his novel *The Autobiography of an Ex-Colored Man* (1912) Johnson captured the heady sense of being elected a reader by shopmates and showing that one is "well posted" in talk of literature and the news.[13]

Working-class neighborhoods were, like communities of more affluence, enthusiastic followers of the news. Jane Addams, a pioneer charity worker among the immigrant poor of Chicago, noticed at the turn of the century that papers were a center of attention in these homes. In the tough seventeenth and nineteenth wards of this city, more saloons provided newspapers than tables or chairs. When Rocco Corresca, a bootblack, could afford four chairs in a Brooklyn basement, he "took the papers that have pictures in and made the place high toned." Working-class Americans were often critical of the press. But they loved many features and created galleries on their walls of what they most cared for. A newspaper was not a joyless record. The pop music idol John Philip Sousa performed the "Washington Post March." There were many newspaper marches at the turn of the twentieth century, and this one was a hit that sparked a dance craze. The fact that Frank Sinatra, Elvis Presley, and Barbra Streisand were not even tempted to sing about the press is a sign of America's change at the end of the century. Publishers had a place in popular culture that they do not have today.[14]

Journalists (in all eras) are likely to credit the appeal of news to the words and pictures they put on paper. But the democracy of circulation that was achieved a century ago owes just as much to the distribution system. It was by staging a pageant of selling, as well as by knowing what to print, that journalists achieved news for all.

2. Newsies and the Allure of News

A newsie, in nineteenth-century slang, was a person who sold a newspaper or magazine. The coins might be pocketed by a boy or girl who worked the street, or put in the till by the proprietor of a newsstand. Either way, the reader got more than reading material. Sales agents created a setting for news that guided taste and reinforced the democratic character of news.

Hawking newspapers in the streets was as old as the first penny dailies of the 1830s. But it was not until the end of the century that the system dominated sales. Horatio Alger's newsboys of the 1870s were patient fellows who worked all day to sell the pack of papers they picked up each morning; they were not representative of the newsies who made circulation take off in urban America. By 1890 two-thirds of the dailies were published for city folk at the end of the work day, opening a twilight blitzkrieg on the reading public. There was no shortage of troops. In Boston at the turn of the century there was one newsie to solicit every seventy male adults in the town. Three thousand newsies assembled on Bunker Hill Day in 1908 to announce their solidarity.

Newsies were marked by their "sauciness." The signature of the newsboy, a New Orleans paper said, was that "he shocks nervous people by screaming like a steam whistle." This was the announcer's voice, introducing the most powerful papers to the mass readership of urban America. When William Randolph Hearst launched the Chicago *American* on July 4, 1900, the streets were filled with cries, "De new pape', 'Merican; here's yer 'Merican!" Hearst and Pulitzer, the most influential publishers of this era, were dependent on these children. When newsboys and girls struck in 1899, these publishers were devastated.[15]

Newsies anticipated the age of broadcasting as they used stories in their sales cries. "The boys who shouted the loudest and twisted the headlines most creatively earned the most," according to one historian. For better or for worse, this made for excited readers. The first win of an American crew at Henley in England unleashed the newsboys on Broadway one evening in 1878: "Git dat ex-tor!" "Every man grabbed his paper as if it were the bulletin of his

Wagons Distributing Evening Papers at Union Square, New York. *Scribner's* 22 (1897): 455.

own individual good fortune, and read it with dancing eyes and once in a while a few excited jig-steps," one observer said. Shouted news on the streets reached an alarming level during World War I when publishers and city governments cracked down on these broadcasts. The newsies' reports of disaster scared Americans with loved ones in the service. Faked news summaries to boost sales were an everyday hazard. The more slurred the cries, one authority said, the more likely that the carrier was making the story up. But better diction did not ensure straightforward dealings. One customer, finding no story of a conflagration the newsboy had been yelling about, was told, "I know, that's such an early edition the fire hasn't started yet!"[16]

The children who swarmed though the metropolis with papers to sell were making news everybody's business. There was no escaping the most sensational of developments. (In homage to this era, the film *Citizen Kane* has the press lord's first big idea for a sensational story shouted through the streets by a carrier.) Editors at the turn of the century relied on the "gee-whiz emotion," not simply as the reader explored the paper, but also at the point of sale. There were messages here that went beyond the text of the story. First, here was a demonstration of diversity, of the kind of country the United States was becoming. A writer to the New York *Times* in 1911 stated the obvious: "Newspapers are sold here almost exclusively by young foreigners, whose pronunciation and whose voices are offensive." Iowans reported the same scenes on their streets. News was now called to public attention through the vernacular of the ghetto. Readers of a Hearst paper in Chicago were bullied by Max and Moe Annenberg (rough operators who founded a family dedicated to mass media and the arts). In New York the yellow press was translated by budding entertainers such as George Burns and Joe E. Brown. As these examples may suggest, the demeanor of these messengers was different from that of the white, Anglo-Saxon Protestant newsboys popularized by Horatio Alger. Ethnicity and accent was not the only disturbing development. The shortening of the selling day meant that more children attended school before venturing out in the rush hour. They often dressed well, played hard, and met the commercial classes more as equals than as supplicants. News for the first time was shouted in your face by young people who aspired to be your social equal. Some of the public took alarm (as some would a century later with rappers).[17]

Newsie and news reader were in a symbiotic relationship, even before the coming of immigrant hawkers. The enterprising lad was an answer to the fears that arose from reading the news of the city. The display of audacity and signs of success fit well with the reader's dreams of how to succeed in the world and underscored the enterprise that popular papers commended. Just as the dress and speech of the door-to-door salesman or evangelist were designed to signify the advantages of the product, the rough-and-ready newsie suggested that a world of opportunity might open through the daily paper. Newspapers of all political persuasions, with their ads and contests, were not selling gloom. The poor but game newsie was a reminder that some started with very little in America but that all could make good. Fraternal organizations of "old news-boys," backed by a celebratory literature of the lads, suggested that news taken on the streets was a door of opportunity for both carrier and reader.[18]

The amplification of adult texts by *children*, news reversing the order of things, was one of the reasons for the rise of the *Saturday Evening Post* at the beginning of the twentieth century. This weekly was seventy-six years old in 1897 when the Curtis Publishing Company took it over. The *Post* liked to say that it had been started by Benjamin Franklin, but it was, at best, a withered monument with a circulation of only about twenty-five hundred copies. Curtis set things right with sales promotions and stories that spun a romance of business and offered practical steps to success. In three years, Curtis won a hundred new *Post* readers for every one the company started with. The Boy Department at Curtis, six thousand strong, was a key to both the distribution and the salience of the magazine. Curtis taught children to buttonhole every-one they met through their family: relatives, neighbors, shopkeepers, even doctors, lawyers and bankers, "don't let a single one escape you." After paying a cut rate in advance for the *Post*, the boy would sell his pile at the cover price. Just as important, readers now had a messenger who illuminated the road to success that the *Post* was writing about. Scholarships and other prizes offered to the boys were talked up across America. The sale of news in order to "work my way through college" apparently began with the *Post*'s scholarship prizes for the boys at the turn of the century. In 1903 exemplary *Post* boys stared out from full-page ads, with the news of their sales feats. Here was Jay Johns, about ten years old, selling near Pittsburgh, "who has apparently absorbed some of the spirit of its gigantic business combinations." Another boy was a "Captain of Industry" and a "Money King." These terms seem appropriate. Though a scheme of sub-agents, an eleven-year-old in Seattle was selling twenty-five hundred copies of the weekly in 1905, the total output of the magazine just eight years earlier. At this rate, this boy and his young business friends were supplying this one magazine to one out of thirty-three people in the city. Jan Cohn, the historian of the *Post*'s rise, has noted that these boys were not recruited merely for their diligence: these newsies were supposed to be "small-scale buccaneers." Citizens were solicited by the *Post* boys and reminded of their sales contests and prizes though the Great Depression (when this sales force was forty-seven thousand strong). Self-improvement, optimism, and an eye for the main chance was the editorial line of the *Post* during its first decades of popular success. It was not merely the text that sent this message. It was the newsies as well.[19]

One institution that seemed to confirm the people's access to the press was the counters where the news was sold. The "periodical depot" became part of city life in the 1830s: galleries where men and women of all stations in life went to get the first look at the newspapers and magazines coming into town. These retail establishments had the drama of country post offices with citizens caught up in the excitement of news and the chance to watch one another. Newsstands as a large-scale, continuing business were born with the railroads and William Henry Williams's creation of the Union News Company in 1864. By 1930 this company was part of the empire of the largest distributor, the American News Company, which serviced more than sixty-five thousand racks, stands, and counters. Independent distributors, such as the network run by Hearst publications, had even more outlets for magazines. In the view of these professionals the reading public was seventy-five million strong in 1930. There was, roughly, one newsstand for every five hundred potential customers. Real customers crowded around. In the mid-thirties, 39 percent of the urban work force bought a paper on the street.[20]

Just as newsboys and girls made news inescapable with their shouts, the newsstand contributed to pageantry by putting news on display. The cover of a magazine had not been its selling point until the middle of the nineteenth century. Before the 1890s, in fact, most covers changed no more from issue to issue than the coins handed over for the sale. This was economical (art need not be commissioned) and dignified, as it suggested that the magazine was not purchased on impulse. *Harper's Weekly*, with its illustrations of the Civil War and cartoon work by Thomas Nast, was one of the early efforts to attract readers with a fresh face every issue. The newsstand encouraged this sort of merchandising. Now the public could be lured to look at a periodical on a whim. A new illustration, frequently in color, beckoned the reader in each issue. Top stories were revealed on the cover. Set on racks, beside scores of other tempting issues, journalism at the newsstand looked like an expanse of treats, waiting to be picked up. This simple change in merchandising, like the mobilization of newsboys and girls, was probably as important to circulation growth as any underlying change in society.[21]

The contribution of newsstands to mass readership went beyond the ways they sold news in print. At the hub of American journalism, New York, newsstands made it difficult for publishers to target elite groups. Newsies hid the class of customers. In many cities, such as Chicago and Philadelphia, the business office of a newspaper could report sales block by block, and tens of thousands of subscribers were on the paper's books. New York publishers were left in the dark about who was buying what. The morning papers, including the Hearst and Pulitzer circulation wonders, had no subscription lists and no sales figures by neighborhoods. The American News Company, a monopoly, handled virtually all sales. In the 1890s, if a naive New Yorker walked into the office of these newspapers to subscribe, the customer was directed to the nearest newsstand. The newsie handled everything just as his boss, the American News Company, picked up almost all the papers printed. What the trade called a "'cat in the bag' uncertainty" of newspaper sales left publishers to guess about their audience. They knew how many papers they printed and crowed about this as this grew. But publishers had no figures to show how the paper was doing in the ethnic enclaves of the Lower East Side, the silk-stocking district, or up in Harlem, where Jews were moving out and African Americans were moving in. They could not chart their appeal in affluent neighborhoods, even if they wanted to. Untroubled by data, New Yorkers led the field and fell easily into Whitmanesque claims that they spoke to all.[22]

The nineteenth-century newsstand was a colorful but sedate place. Pulitzer's New York *World* reported the goings-on at dozens of locations one day in 1885, and no agent claimed salesmanship beyond telling customers which paper had the most help-wanted ads. Dealers of this era might display a poster or two supplied by a publisher, but no effort was made to mesmerize readers. The principle of display was that of plentitude. The merchant put the full line in view, inviting the public to make a selection. Newsdealers were more inventive than most American shopkeepers, who were just acquiring the rudiments of a "display aesthetic" in the 1890s. But newsies had not yet learned to be set designers. Nor did this seem possible. Newsstands thrived in the tight spaces near transportation points and at the edges of crowded walkways. The news was a side business for stationers, tobacconists, and druggists, and a rack of publications was tucked into the expanse of other goods.[23]

The most adventurous of these newsdealers scanned the tables of contents when publications arrived to see which magazines might sell out and order more in time. Then they struck up conversations with customers about what was worth reading. By knowing their line they could make sales to customers who did not know where to find an article that was being talked about. In the 1890s dealers read special magazines telling them what would be in magazines for the public. With this advance word they could steer readers and increase sales.[24]

These synopses for newsdealers were relentlessly approving and improving:

> "Madcap William" is the irreverent title given the Emperor of Germany in an article quoted by the "Review of Reviews," which reproduces Madcap William's celebrated picture as a frontispiece. "The Sultan of Turkey" is the subject of the character sketch in which is given a capital map, showing Turkey past and present, and enabling one at a glance to see the contraction of the Mussulman power in Europe. There is a handy map of Venezuela, showing the various ideas of proper boundary lines—nine all told.

Newsdealers of the nineteenth century could be sneaky. They sometimes hid the ads that would enable readers to get big discounts directly from the publisher. Black sheep in the business discounted papers if the reader quickly brought them back to the stand to be sold again. Newsies profited at the publisher's expense from this lending library. Still, most of the salesmanship at the Victorian newsstand would not have troubled the conscience of a good librarian.[25]

In the opening decades of the new century newsdealers took readers more firmly in hand, matching the enterprise of newsboys and girls. In 1920 Col. E. H. Armstrong reported on his campaign to sell more news at the Artesia Pharmacy in Pleasanton, Texas. "In these six years I've been trying to get these fellows to use their heads for other purposes than to eat with them," he told his fellow newsdealers. "I'll get some of these mossbacks to reading magazines yet, or break my neck doing it." Short of wrestling matches with readers, the trade went into aggressive displays of the news. "Pulling People Into Your Store Through Your Window" was typical of the tough talk in the new tip sheet of the American News Company. Each month the *American News Trade Journal* published a gallery of exemplary newsstand displays. Publishers paid "newsstand boosters" to see that titles were featured in splashy displays. There were battle slogans: REGULAR ROTATION. COVER CONCENTRATION. POSTER PROCLAMATION. INSIDE INFORMATION. SELLER STIMULATION. There were two main trade secrets: "Full frontal display" and "the dignity of a pile." "The full-front cover gets in its deadly sales work much more easily than a display wherein the covers overlap," experts insisted. Covers should be strung out along the stand, mounted on special racks or hung at the customer's eye level. Some dealers were willing to try clickers and buzzers to draw attention to the news, but the main effort went into putting magazines and newspapers in the face of the American people. A thick, neat pile was an essential way to bring a cover into view. Quantity proclaimed quality, for customers could see that a huge readership was expected. They would not want to miss out. In the folk wisdom of newsdealers, a single copy of a publication was the hardest publication to sell.[26]

The street-learning of dealers was the sole guide to putting single copies of magazines into the hands of the American people. There was no research on selling at the newsstand (and there is little today). Unaided, the newsies accomplished much. Between 1925 and 1945 the largest category of general magazines increased their subscribers by only 34 percent. But newsstand sales went up 366 percent in these decades.[27]

In the 1930s the newsstand imperative led to magazines designed to please newsdealers, not just readers. (Circulation managers of the 1930s counted some four hundred magazines fighting for space, with room for only forty at most newsstands.) The president of the Kable News Company concluded that selecting covers to please readers was a waste of time; it was the person who stocked the shelves who must be reached: "Our cover must come up to his idea of attractiveness before he will push it forward at the expense of some less eye-catching magazine." This was not a call for sensationalist stories or bizarre graphics. This was not a reliable formula in the tough world of the news racks. A red cover, for example, would not stand out amidst other red covers of rival magazines. Better to see that each cover had a contrast of colors and balanced design with restraint on the copy. The newsdealer would be watching, and "he cares not if President Roosevelt or John Whoosis is writing for you if you ruin the scheme of your cover in telling about it." It was a commonplace in the business offices of magazines that newsdealers were demanding reviewers. Often, the public approached the newsstand not knowing what they wanted. The newsdealer laid out the attractive choices.[28]

Again, this is a pageant that Americans have lost. In the second half of the twentieth century, newspapers and magazines have struggled to remain convenient by taking refuge in vending boxes and supermarket stands. By nearly every measure, single-copy sales have gone down and impulse buyers have become rarer. Except in airports and a few rail stations and big-city neighborhoods, newsstands play little role in the delivery of news. On most streets, they are as unexpected as shouts about a newspaper story. The plentitude of titles and the social reinforcement to read them are no longer provided by the newsie. The marketing of news now takes different forms, but these are seldom as egalitarian and successful as the insistent display of journalism at the beginning of the century.[29]

Of course the geography of print media has changed in other respects. Taverns and post offices are not the haunts of readers that they were when newspapers and magazines captured the attention of the American people. Passing the day at a publisher's office has little appeal, even when momentous news breaks. Pageantry that suggested every citizen had a need for news (while allowing readers to show off) had a great deal to do with establishing a democracy of circulation. As these symbolic interactions around texts became rarer, publishers did not find new ways to reinforce the habit of news reading. Indeed, the marketing wisdom in journalism was to cast many readers adrift.

3. Dollars and Sense of Circulation

The institutions and habits that were in place to build circulation at the beginning of the twentieth century were in poor shape before the century was half over. The publisher who dreamed of the income of a Carnegie or a Ford with their methods of mass production awoke to find that the news business was different. Higher circulation was not always profitable. The Whitmanesque hope that an editor could speak to all faded. The twentieth-century press came to believe that it could only deliver news for a few.

Manufacturing costs were basic to the change. The steady curve upward of newspaper circulation at the end of the nineteenth century rested on a cheap mush of boiled trees. For the first time in the 1880s, papers were printed on newsprint composed exclusively of this abundant material. More expensive fiber such as rags was no longer needed. Across the nation, newsprint that had cost more than ten cents a pound in 1880 cost only two or three cents a pound in 1900. For the major papers in New York, the cost dropped even more sharply. Whitelaw Reid of the *Tribune* began his career in the Civil War when newsprint fetched twenty-two cents a pound and retired from management at the turn of the century when he paid a penny and a half a pound. Every decade he worked, the price of paper was cut in half. Pulp allowed publishers to add pages, increase press runs, and drop prices.[30]

Magazine publishers enjoyed a similar economy and ballooning readership. By the end of the century, illustrations could be made ready for the press through the half-tone process at one tenth the expense of the engraved pictures of the Civil War era. Quality magazines had commonly sold for thirty-five cents until the 1890s, then prices fell to fifteen and even ten cents as entrepreneurs such as Samuel S. McClure, Frank A. Munsey, and William Randolph Hearst gathered in millions of citizens who could now easily afford this news. Even small magazines prospered as tumbling prices brought more readers into reach. *Forum* magazine, for example, cut its prices to readers in half in 1893 and immediately realized a threefold increase in sales. At century's end some in the magazine world were beginning to think, like newspaper publishers, that their audience need not be confined to an elite with special tastes and liberal household budgets.[31]

The problem was that all of the economies of scale were not enough to make the huge public drawn to the news profitable on what the reader paid. Hearst's Sunday New York *Journal* ran fifty-two pages on average in 1896 and eighty pages in 1897; even at the best prices for newsprint, the paper itself was worth more than he netted from readers. Hearst and Pulitzer, who did not yet have advertising lined up, lost more money the more papers they sold. Ad revenue could not easily right a business determined to sell goods below the cost of production. When the *Saturday Evening Post* went on sale in the last days of the prosperous 1920s, scrap dealers eagerly paid the nickel at newsstands to get their hands on the nearly two pounds of paper. Had things continued in this way, publishers might have found recyclers a greater threat to the First Amendment than government.[32]

Ego, not economic logic, drew publishers of this era into the search for readers. As the new century opened, the men who commanded great presses wanted to be bigger than their rivals. In reaching for circulation, publishers lost sight of profits and inspired employees to add readers heedless of the cost. Hearst's arrangement with the boy wonder of circulation, Arthur Brisbane, is a model of this reckless business plan. Brisbane, the son of founders of the Brook Farm socialist community, grew up in wild country play with stern instruction

not to read. He was schooled in France to be kept safe from American material-
ism. Brisbane's English was as rusty as his grasp of business when he tried out as
a reporter in New York at the age of nineteen. The brilliant pet of Dana and
then Pulitzer, he became a master at editing a Sunday edition for the reader
who wanted to see comics, undraped women, and scientific oddities. He was
hired away by Hearst in 1897. Then thirty-three, he signed a contract that
added a thousand dollars to his salary each time he brought in an increase of ten
thousand in the circulation of the evening edition of the New York *Journal*.
Brisbane pounced on the Cuban story, and for a time he put more editions on
the streets than there were hours in the day. One issue of the evening *Journal*
reached more than 1.8 million customers. The reader paid a penny. Hearst was
delighted to sink his mother's money into this mad race to be number one.
Brisbane earned nearly $140,000 in 1898. That dwarfed the $75,000 that
Adolph Ochs paid for the New York *Times*, the entire paper, just two years
earlier.[33]

The spendthrift path to circulation made economic sense only if the publisher could afford the loss of millions in hopes of gaining a hold on local
markets that would, in time, pay. Hunting down every citizen made psychological sense only if the publisher had sufficient altruism, vanity, or political
ambition to afford it. Thus a democracy of circulation was precarious.

Advertising revenue might change the equation, of course. Publishers were
slow to see that this could subsidize the costs of reaching larger audiences.
Display ads, for example, were shunned by many newspapers until after the
Civil War because they seemed to cheapen a publication, and no one yet saw
that they could greatly enrich the journalist. Magazines viewed ads the same
way. No American periodical employed a full-time advertising manager until
1870. Well after that date, national magazines turned down reputable ads
because they went against the grain of their business. However, publishers got
used to the idea of taking the new money. Their revenues jumped as they
offered more space and delivered larger publics. Ads earned 44 percent of
newspaper and periodical revenue by 1880. In 1920 both forms of journalism
were making about two-thirds of their revenue from ads. The twenties was the
decade in which many journalists conceptualized stories as "written bait," to
make the public take in ads.[34]

Heavier reliance on advertising was not invariably helpful in making news a
democratic product. The journalist who saw this with crystal clarity was the
plebeian rich man Scripps. In his media empire, he placed editors in charge
who were not to spend money on soliciting ads. Circulation should grow
because people wanted the news, not because advertisers wanted to reach more
customers. A Scripps paper was to be four pages. No more. Ads were supposed
to be the scrimshaw work of locals. Display ads and national advertising campaigns were not welcome. A rise in newsprint prices would never drive a

Scripps editor to depend on advertising. Large advertisers would not dilute the editor's sympathy with the working class. The reader's penny, alone, was all a Scripps editor was to dream about.[35]

The commercial limitation of mass circulation was grasped by another of the most successful journalists of the 1890s, Lincoln Steffens. This Californian grew up rich, in the house that later served as the governor's mansion. Steffens lingered, to age twenty-six, at American and European universities. He knew little about the common man and less about earning a living. He quickly learned about both when he was forced to take his first job at a New York paper. As Hearst and Pulitzer set circulation records, Steffens looked on and took note of the devices that won millions of readers. He knew that fortunes were being made in democratizing news. But the frantic promotions to build greater numbers were not the future, he said in 1897. The "character of the circulation" was likely to set the course of newspapers, he argued. The coins taken in from readers would not pay for much more than newsprint. Profits came from advertising, Steffens saw, and a broad audience with little to spend could not interest the most lucrative advertisers. At a time when circulation manager was an office so new that Steffens had to explain it to his readers, he saw that the race for greater numbers already made little sense. Indeed, Steffens interviewed some of the earliest business managers who tried to make this clear to publishers. The top bosses did not grasp the logic of commercialism. More could be less.[36]

What Scripps and Steffens saw would later be called the segmented market. In marketing terms, most of nineteenth-century production and retailing was fragmented: businesses sold a low volume of goods at high margins for a local market. American newspapers and magazines, with their strong regional appeal, began the century in step with general stores, soap makers, and breweries that operated in this way. Journalists at this point recognized only one set of customers, the readers. National businesses and brands emerged at mid-century, appealing to a mass market thrown open by the improvements in transportation and communication. Whether the product was soap or beer, it was likely to be produced in high volume and at a lower price. Chain retailers such as A&P and catalogue sellers such as Sears, Roebuck now competed with the local merchant and helped to unify the nation's business. This is what Hearst, Pulitzer, and Scripps were doing as they drove the price of news down and consolidated the gathering of stories through their own wire services, syndicated features, and chains. Their newspaper businesses were more local than that of Procter & Gamble, Anheuser-Busch, or Ford, but these publishers were attempting the same economies of scale. Magazines, for the first time in the 1890s, made the same breakthrough to a mass market, free of the local ties that still anchored the daily press. The Curtis Publishing Company that brought out the *Saturday Evening Post* was on its way to become a massive, vertically integrated company, managing everything from trees to *Post* boys and *Post* girls. Publishers were pulled in this direction by the example of other big businesses. With national brands and retailers in a unified market, the press was a necessary platform for their ads.[37]

But the logic of American capitalism moved on, taking journalism into special difficulties. Producing a standard product at a cheap price for the largest public was not the road to corporate health in the long term. Henry Ford learned this in the 1920s when he gave up on his single product, the Model T, available in any color so long as it was black. A segmented market was more rewarding because the high volume of production was combined with premium pricing. Happily for manufacturers, prices float more easily above the cost of production when customers can be targeted. General Motors, Henry Ford's nemesis, introduced a variety of models and annual styling changes aimed at segments of the market and won high prices from the groups it courted. This "segmented" marketing was not named and celebrated by theorists until the 1950s, but it was the direction that much of American business took from the beginning of the century.

Most manufacturers have only one set of customers: the people who buy their products. It is tough enough to make a profit in mass production serving them. Henry Ford's brilliant system of turning out Model T's yielded a return of just two dollars a car in 1924. Print journalists of the twentieth century have had two sets of customers: readers and advertisers paid them. Unlike manufactures who were fully compensated when a customer purchased a car, any car, publishers were at risk of having one class of customers ensure that another class of customers will not pay. If people who are not potential buyers of a product are readers, the manufacturer will not pay the advertising rate asked to reach them; if readers are asked to pay more for a publication to allow cheaper ad rates, these readers will balk.[38]

Advertising trade journals at the turn of the twentieth century rang with news of the discovery that money was being thrown away on unwanted readers: "The questions always to be asked are: What class of person does this publication reach, and are they likely to be purchasers of my goods?" This was the moment that circulation began to be shaded with adjectives. "Mushroom circulation." "Mere circulation." "Cheap circulation." "Worthless circulation." The talk of the newspaper trade was that readers who were unlikely to be good consumers had been swept up by the press and that the wise advertiser would not pay to reach this public. Marketing experts spent the twentieth century repeating these incantations, warning the media and media buyers about "unhealthy" readership and "waste circulation."[39]

Most publishers were slow to learn this lesson. Market research on readers, aimed at potential advertisers, was under way at the *Saturday Evening Post* and the Chicago *Tribune* before World War I, with some breakthroughs in finding unwanted readers. Charles Coolidge Parlin, director of research for Curtis, distributed maps with poor neighborhoods colored blue and recommended that magazines not be sold in these zones. But this was the extreme, and the indefatigable *Post* boys and girls were not interested in administering a means test to their customers. Other publishers merely joined the effort to prove that their readers were good consumers in the inter-war years. There was a strong inertia of egalitarian sentiments in the business reports that journalists commissioned. Two separate *Continuing Study* projects on magazine and newspaper readership were launched in the late 1930s with this interest in the common citizen. At first, neither showed any particular interest in the "quality" of readers. The well-off were simply a small quota of the interviews, in proportion to their place in Depression-era America. In the newspaper study, "Business and Professional" was only 9 percent of the sample. These massive, well-funded projects did not directly inquire into the special reading habits of the more affluent readers. The results were blended together so that only a picture of the general public emerged. Most publishers were not yet thinking of their readers as segments of a market.[40]

The last sheet of the first magazine study did note what percentage of reader's homes had electricity, gas, and a telephone. On this final page, the researchers also reported whether readers owned cars, and how good a car they owned. The camel of marketing now had its nose in the tent. The "buying power" of readers occupied most of the *Life's Continuing Study* after World War II. Page after page reported how magazines captured readers according to the money they had to spend and the general products they bought. In the 1950s Alfred Politz filled substantial books with the proof that magazines and newspapers were being read by important groups of consumers. He broke down the eleven million readers of an average issue of the *Saturday Evening Post* in segments such as "Conversation about the Post by Electric Food Mixer Ownership" and "Satisfaction with the Post by Whether Someone in Household Fishes" and "Conversation about the Post by Linoleum Tile Ownership." The reading public, charted by marketers, was being put into niches.[41]

Drawing boundaries for an audience was an uncongenial task for those planning the future of American news media. "The economic logic of private enterprise forces most units of the mass communications industry to seek an even larger audience," the commission headed by Robert M. Hutchins of the University of Chicago declared in *A Free and Responsible Press* (1947). But these distinguished academics waffled on what the market was doing to make media inclusive. They had struck the phrase "each unit" from their draft of this report and substituted "most units," weakening the claim about size ensuring profits. "Specialized targets" based on income was the key, the Hutchins Commission said, in a footnote that undermined what they said in the big print above. The democratic imperative of the media marketplace, so clear in the early drafts of the Hutchins statement, was merely a hopeful notion when the report reached the public. The first half of the twentieth century had been the dawning of the idea that the publisher could have too many readers; the second half of the century put this threat in blinding light.[42]

4. "We're Pretty Particular About Who Subscribes"

General circulation magazines were the first victims of the traditional wisdom that bigger was better. They enjoyed the prosperity of a unified marketplace of the first half of the century, and then became the biggest losers to the logic of segmentation. The *Saturday Evening Post* emerged near the head of the pack in the magazine boom of the first years of the twentieth century with two million readers by World War I. *Life* (1936) and *Look* (1937) were experiments by publishers who sensed that the public was ready for more imaginative photo-journalism. The Luce and the Cowles organizations sold their new magazines in the face of the Great Depression and were astonished to find that they could not meet the demand. By the end of the decade, surveys said that 31 percent of Americans over the age of ten read at least one copy of *Life* each month. In 1948, when there were some 150 million Americans in about 40 million house-holds, researchers counted a combined audience of 71 million readers of these four magazines. The tens of millions who picked up one of the weeklies formed a bigger audience than any television program, in the early years of that new medium. Television led magazines to issue what Mark Twain would have called "stretchers" about their reading public. In 1957 the *Post* published a survey showing that of all Americans over the age of ten, nearly one citizen in seven read an average issue. *Look* marched toward its grave with the confidence that one of every four American adults read every issue. By *Life*'s reckoning, it had 48 million readers in 1968, "larger than any other single communications medium." These publishers were heirs to nineteenth-century journalists who saw no limit to their audience. Luce, in the prospectus for *Life*, spoke of reaching "half of mankind." "The power of *Look*," its last publisher said, "is that it spans the whole universe of interests. It is a platform for all Americans to turn to."[43]

The words and pictures that Americans were most likely to have in common did appear here. In the middle decades of the twentieth century, these maga-zines were the shepherds of politicians, as when *Life* got the fifty governors to come into a studio and take their places on a sprawling map of the United States. The deaths of Presidents Roosevelt and Kennedy were mourned in these magazines. Ranging the world, they delivered the memoirs or last scenes of Winston Churchill, Charles DeGaulle, Nikita Khrushchev, and Mahatma Gandhi. These media introduced much of America to Martin Luther King Jr.

and Malcolm X (whose *Autobiography* appeared in the *Post*). Here were the covers of Norman Rockwell, the mysteries of Agatha Christie, the stories by Will Rogers. The star-making machinery of Hollywood could not have worked without these nickel-and-dime outlets. Detroit's new models were sold on the dreams spread across the glossy pages of these magazines. Chrysler dealers, for example, reported that customers came to their showrooms carrying *Life* with its full-color picture of the car they wanted. For decades, aspiring national brands introduced themselves to consumers in these magazines.[44]

The weeklies were masters of the irresistible, insistent invitation. Their subscription offers reached virtually every mailbox and suggested that non-readers were unprepared for civil society. Life's "Summer 1963 Family Up-dater," for instance, was a quiz that asked who was "the next Gary Cooper," who had discovered DNA, and who headed the NAACP. This "enables you to get a quick reading of your knowledge of the subjects most people are talking about these days . . . [and] how well you can hold up your end of the conversation. . . . In short, you have a measure of how interesting a person you are to others." All test results showed a need to subscribe to *Life*, since the best informed were bound to like the magazine and those who flunked had a pressing need to become "interesting." Such mailings stressed that the cost was negligible. The price was one of the best deals in the history of publishing. *Life* started out a dime weekly that cost fifteen cents to publish. In its last years, a subscriber could get an issue for about ten cents at a time when the magazine cost more than forty cents to produce. The *Post* and *Look* were similar bargains.[45]

The business history of this journalism has been carefully studied because of the intriguing link between their popularity and doom: at a time when readers swarmed to these magazines, they crashed as businesses. The *Post* folded in 1969; *Look* quit in 1971, and *Life* was killed the following year. (The first and the last to go have had an after-life as scaled-back monthlies.) (See Chart 6.1.) Autopsies of the magazines have found many causes. Costs were simply too high on over-staffed publications such as *Life* with its legendary expense accounts. The *Post* was as quaint as a Rockwell cover, supporting a fleet of electric buggies, built in 1913, to move paper around Philadelphia.[46]

In the summer of 1968 the *Post* did what no famous magazine had attempted: it dismissed the majority of its subscribers. To cut a sale of 6.8 million copies to 3 million, the magazine told 2 million paid-up readers who lived in counties not attractive to advertisers that they could not have the *Post* any longer. They were offered a choice of five other magazines that were willing to risk serving a public that was, on average, less affluent. Another million *Post* subscribers in desirable communities were given over to *Life* (these good consumers were the only names that weekly would accept, the *Post* had offered more). In 1970, *Look* aimed to lose a million subscribers who lived outside the major metropolitan

Chart 6.1 Source: *Magazine Circulation and Rate Trends.*

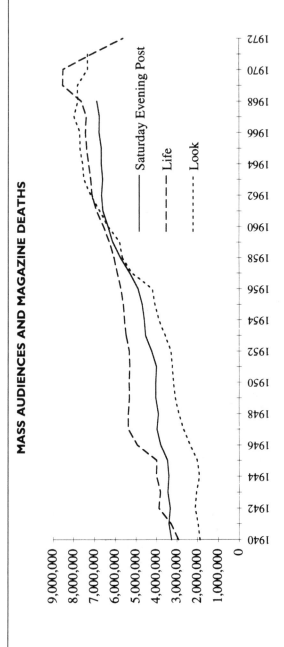

MASS AUDIENCES AND MAGAZINE DEATHS

——— Saturday Evening Post

– – – Life

·········· Look

areas. *Life* soon doubled this goal and attempted to shed two million rural subscribers.[47]

Beyond the economies, these cuts were designed to create a cachet for the magazines. The president of Curtis said he "hoped that the cutback in circulation would upgrade *The Post's* image, with everybody clamoring to be among the magic three million." *Look* took out four full-page ads in the New York *Times* in the spring of 1970 to give the advertising the good news in bold letters: **CONCENTRATION**. The magazine reminded Madison Avenue that it had been putting out an edition for subscribers in high-income zip codes since 1968 and said that the new cuts in the subscription rolls would deliver "readers who earn more, want more, and spend more." The last ad in this series was comments made by ad executives in phone calls, letters, and lunch-table conversation applauding the magazine for eliminating "inefficient sources of circulation." "Look, for your best customers" was the magazine's last campaign theme on Madison Avenue.[48]

Did cold economic facts make many readers unwelcome? The income of these legions of readers bothered advertisers. In 1964 *Life* had the most affluent readers of the large magazines, but at that, it was read by more people who earned less than five thousand dollars than by those with incomes above ten thousand. But these publishers were going upscale, as the advertisers wished. Why didn't the strategy to please advertisers work?[49]

If advertisers *knew* which appeals in which media would sell products, then the demise of the general circulation magazines would be the logical unfolding of the market. But there was no such science of marketing during in the magazine die-offs at the beginning of the 1970s . . . nor is there such a science today. The sociologist Michael Schudson has observed that on fundamental questions such as how often to repeat an ad, "advertisers and their agencies operate by hunch, by taste, by level of anxiety." Advertising decisions about print media came out of the same school of intuition.[50]

The "numbers" in media marketing are, significantly, matters of taste. For instance, some magazines have many "pass along" readers. Other magazines of the same class are not widely shared. The rates can be calculated by interviewing a sample of readers. But what to do with this figure has always been a matter of judgment. Some believe that a reader who has borrowed a magazine should count as a .5 reader; others choose to count this reader as a 1.0. The figure one chooses will determine the circulation ranking of competing magazines as well as the audience "delivered." As early as 1968, "this tangled morass of figures" was proverbial on Madison Avenue. The issue swirled through advertising literature in the last half of the twentieth century, confusing quantitative measures and leaving agencies and clients to pick the numbers they liked to explain their decisions. Chris Welles, who interviewed media experts at a dozen advertising agencies while the fate of *Look* and *Life* was being decided, concluded that all close calls were based on feelings. *"Ex post facto,"* Welles wrote, "numbers are then mobilized to lend the decisions weight and credibility." A Dutch publishing executive who lived in New York during the die-offs of general magazines and who wrote a dissertation on the subject at the University of Amsterdam concluded that empirical evidence about magazines did not change minds on Madison Avenue. "Grapevine rumor," he wrote, often sealed the fate of the American press.[51]

Soon after the big magazines were gone, the emperor's lack of clothes made news. William R. Simmons, a protégé of Alfred Politz and founder of a leading firm that measured the reading public, pointed out the "obvious conflicting and irreconcilable audience results" in the study of magazines. "In almost forty years no practical way has been found to make any appreciable improvement in the accuracy of this procedure." Indeed, the mass circulation empires fell in large part because Madison Avenue could no longer believe the stories about their reach and could not think of a reason to use their component parts. Publishers did not really seem to have their hearts into downsizing (all Americans needed the magazine, they insisted) and the costs of reaching the best parts of the old circulation seemed high. Advertisers knew where to go to find tight, attractive audiences, and they simply gave up on print (no matter what figures said) as a way of appealing to the mass. A democracy of circulation seemed impossible; that franchise had passed to television.[52]

So it has seemed in the last decades that followed the end of these general magazines on public questions. One prominent ad of the 1960s courted the right type of subscribers by stigmatizing the wrong kind:

> Dear Sir: Over the years the idea has gotten around that we're pretty particular about who subscribes to Business Week . . . the management man who holds a position of responsibility in business, industry and government. Along the way we've alienated lots of housewives, ferry boat captains, barbers, basketball players, and affluent jockeys who don't seem to understand the publication is not for them. Last year we turned down [so many] subscriptions representing a potential income of [so many] hundred thousand dollars.

This was the most effective ad in generating subscriptions, *Business Week* found, no matter how broad or narrow the audience. The unwanted readers were carefully chosen. The original copy mentioned disc jockeys and authors. But they complained to McGraw-Hill, the publisher, and got the ban lifted. Arguably, in 1968 the millions of women about to enter the work force (not to mention affluent sports stars) would have been well served by a subscription to *Business Week*, and the magazine would have profited in the long run by signing them up. It is certainly true that the magazine would have stood on higher ground, in its frequent laments that Americans do not understand the needs of American business, had it not dismissed eager readers. Controlled circulation of this type betrays a conservatism rarely seen in the nineteenth century: the notion that people cannot rise from their station in life and that print media need not bother about ambitious people if they are poor.[53]

Publishers with much broader targets have also narrowed their aim. "Our philosophy is not to go after every reader available," the general manager of Hearst's magazine group said. Women's magazines, the most popular category of magazines, have purposefully tightened their circulation. The largest publications, *TV Guide* and *Reader's Digest*, cut hundreds of thousands of readers. Smaller magazines have also become more selective. *Black Enterprise* shed readers in the mid-eighties, as did the financial guide *Changing Times*. Macho and machisma talk about cutting off subscribers echoes where magazine publishers gather in the 1990s. "We can no longer afford as an industry to support the circulation levels we had in the past" has become the conventional wisdom.[54]

The publisher of *Harper's* has compared the hunt for tighter audiences to the red-lining of poor neighborhoods by banks. It is not quite that simple, since what a publisher is shedding is not necessarily poor people, but subscribers who are expensive to maintain on the books: they must be showered with renewal notices, discounts, or prizes. But in practice, publishers who begin to shed difficult subscribers often see that poorer consumers are thrown out at the same time. *Time* in the late eighties cut its subscriber list from 4.6 to 4 million using a computer program that first screened for readers who were expensive to keep . . . then for readers who would be unattractive to advertisers.[55]

Newspapers did not begin purposely to get rid of readers until the last third of the twentieth century. To be sure, race and language had always been barriers, and it was the exceptional publisher who made practical efforts to appeal across these lines. But journalists usually spoke the language of inclusion, even when they did not meet the challenge of diversity. What changed in the 1970s was frank talk that the reading public could be separated into groups on the basis of lifestyle as well as demographic data and some readers, then, written off. This strategy meant putting aside the considerable body of research that showed that people with strained budgets were careful and loyal readers of the daily paper and in some ways better informed than the affluent. New surveys produced a different map of newspapers' best and worst customers. Market Opinion Research, for instance, offered newspapers a breakdown of their audience on the basis of phone interviews with readers. Though the interviews lasted less than eight minutes, the conclusions were breathtaking. Publishers learned to think of their readers as "Vanguards" and "Winter Affluents" and "Agribusiness Actives" or "Upper Rungs." There was bad news in these surveys, as with the uncovering of "Past Prime Passives—They were never good newspaper readers and aren't going to become so now." Worse were some of the "Ms. Coping" types: "The poverty, unmarried mother group who permanently interrupt their educations and chances to live on more than ADC or

minimum wage . . . will, at best, always be marginal readers and spenders."
Like the view of the public in *Business Week*, this was a blueprint for walling off
classes of people as unwanted readers.[56]

The confidence that a survey could measure ambition and predict mobility
was the truly revealing part of this research. Newspapers were buying short-cut
methods to classify their readers, oblivious to the subjectivity that serious
researchers confessed. The findings also violated common sense. After all,
categories of this type drawn up during the Great Depression would have
written off most of the American people. The boyhood homes of Ronald
Reagan and Bill Clinton would have been red-lined. Newspaper publishers had
never dared to pick the winners and losers from among the reading public.
Now this changed. A handbook of the 1980s on newspaper management cited
the alarm over "unprofitable circulation in areas having little corporate, editorial, or advertising value to the newspaper." Though it is hard to know how a
citizen falls below a standard of "editorial value," this would seem to be a
complete list of all the reasons a reader may be unwanted.[57]

Distant subscribers, the pride of the nineteenth-century paper, were let go.
Readers living outside of a metropolitan trading area (the basis for ad rates)
were cut off to save delivery costs. Gannett, the largest newspaper group, led
with these cutbacks in the 1970s. Strong regional papers did the same thing.
The Atlanta *Journal and Constitution* eliminated fifty thousand subscribers in
south Georgia. The Cowles papers in Minneapolis matched this surgery in the
upper Midwest. The Chicago *Tribune* cut more than half that number in
Illinois at the end of the decade. More recently, the Des Moines *Register* ("the
newspaper Iowa depends on" according to the masthead) gave up a commitment made since 1903 and discouraged readers outside greater Des Moines.
The Los Angeles *Times*, which lost 120,000 circulation in the early 1990s, shed
its San Diego edition and gave up its dream of regional dominance.[58]

Local poor folk were targeted for neglect in business plans. The Los Angeles
Times battled for the suburbs while it let the working-class sections of the city
get away (a loss it has not made up with a Spanish-language edition and
attention to African Americans in the wake of the L.A. riots of 1992). The
Nashville *Tennessean* (despite its record of concern for black America) will not
supply the paper to some ghetto neighborhoods. "Look . . . we are a newspaper for all the people, period," Katharine Graham of the Washington *Post*
said in 1987. Her son and successor as chief executive officer and president of
the Washington Post Company charted the same course. But the Grahams'
director of circulation and marketing has claimed credit for "eliminating sales
efforts with households that are too costly to attract and renew." The executive, Candace Medd, told a publishers' group in 1991 that the *Post* now concen-
trated its sales efforts in census tracts with high incomes and rents. A veteran
editor pointed out in 1993 that dailies have yet to try cutting the cost of

subscriptions for people with low incomes. (Discounts of up to 50 percent would be compatible with Audit Bureau of Circulations rules.)[59]

The industry's own outlook does not take in a vast new public. In 1991 a study group drawn from the nation's leading papers (including the Washington *Post*) reported to the American Newspaper Publishers Association on the marketing choices in the next decade. After three years of study, these analysts found mass appeal to be only one of four business plans that might work. And in their model, striving for mass appeal was a holding action, until better ways to target customers proved themselves. The most profitable plan the publishers came up with would shed one-third of the households in the year 2000. No marketing scholar has yet stepped forward as a revisionist on this point: "The newspaper can no longer be a mass medium."[60]

Business plans are normally a secret (when they are not theoretical), and in the face of newspaper pledges to serve their total community, it may seem uncharitable to charge that the nation's press is discarding readers. But a growing body of executives in the industry say this clearly. The trade press suggests cutbacks in distribution, subscriber service, and marketing to new readers to meet tighter budgets. Lee B. Templeton, who had been vice-president of the Detroit *Free Press*, said in 1990 that this was a business strategy for newspapers that "amounts to a conspiracy to keep them out of reader's hands." In 1994 he was joined by Otto A. Silha, past chairman of the board of Cowles Media, in noting the trend to "rationed circulation." These authorities said that "few papers really want to increase circulation." Critics of corporate media such as Ben Bagdikian and Noam Chomsky have been arguing for some time that readers are manipulated. These critics have now lived long enough to find their acerbic view of management supported in testimony published in the *Newspaper Financial Executive Journal*.[61]

The alternative to this winnowing, a paper with broad demographic appeal, was conspicuously rare. This despite demonstrations that the hocus-pocus of segmenting is not necessary to succeed. *Details Magazine*, one of the most successful ventures of the Newhouse operation, was launched in 1980 without any audience research. The editors simple assumed that a fresh point of view would draw plenty of readers and ads. The editor, James Truman, has told newspaper publishers to save their money on the expensive quest to segment and simply serve the whole community. This old-fashioned idea has not been popular.[62]

The largest new paper, *USA Today*, was launched in 1982 with a frank purpose of gathering together an audience of mobile and affluent readers. As the paper headed toward two million circulation, its chief problem was in convincing advertisers that it was in fact connecting with these desirable readers. Downscaling was attempted in New York City. Here the modern Scripps has been Rupert Murdoch, the most celebrated newspaper proprietor in the last quarter of the twentieth century. On taking up the battered New York *Post* in 1977, this Australian announced that the American press had gone wrong in looking for the "minority quality audience." He wanted the men and women from the assembly lines, the gas stations, the back offices.[63]

The story of Murdoch's egalitarian strategy has been encapsulated in a single conversation, one of the well-worn anecdotes of the business. The publisher asks Bloomingdale's, then New York's elite department store, why they don't advertise in the *Post* and hears, "Your readers are our shoplifters." It is most unlikely that this conversation ever took place. All of the people who have been identified in the exchange have denied the story. Bloomingdale's signed an advertising contract with the *Post* when Murdoch bought the paper. Nevertheless, the anecdote, sometimes labeled "legend," sometimes taken as a fact, appeared in Murdoch biographies and in a dozen other profiles of his newspapering. The story became a substantial barrier to the paper on Madison Avenue. The willingness to recycle the "obviously untrue" observation that people who follow a popular newspaper might be expected to pilfer, not to buy, says much about the cramped view of marketing that afflicts journalism. In a city with hundreds of thousands of high-salaried blue-collar workers, it was wise, as Bloomingdale's knew, to pay attention to a newspaper these citizens might read. Behind closed doors, department-store executives are likely to dress publishers down for ignoring growing young families, especially minorities. But the idea that a paper must reach the affluent to be worth an advertiser's time prevailed. Murdoch was not a Scripps; he lost money being popular. One reason for this was what Scripps had foreseen: advertising forces were beyond his control.[64]

Marketing pressures of the type that struck Scripps and Steffens a century ago have not been the only force discouraging publishers to think that their news was for everyone. In most forms of communication in this century, specialized audiences have displaced a mass public. Once broadcasting, film, or print appealed to nearly everyone; then newer media dispersed the crowds. Thus movies and radio found narrower audiences with the coming of television, and the audience for the networks shrank when challenged by cable and VCRs. Competition often makes media companies expand, but it usually makes the public for an established outlet grow smaller. This may make for better, not poorer, entertainment and art. But if citizenship is what is wanted, there are many costs.[65]

7

VANISHING

CITIZENS

Readers of news disappear in two ways. They sometimes flee from the publications that would like to have them as customers. This exodus has been dramatic and selective, with newspapers losing and magazines gaining readers. There is a second way that readers vanish, and this has nothing to do with circulation figures. The press may cease to think of its public as citizens and view them simply as people to be rented to advertisers and marketers. When the editorial content of a publication is incidental, a newspaper or magazine may live on and hold an audience, but its readers as citizens are gone. This slower death of the reading public is under way as news in print begins its third century.

I. Newspapers Down, Magazines Up

The era of daily papers in all American homes lasted less than a century. The production of dailies matched the number of households for the first time shortly after 1900. There was a daily in circulation for every family during the next six decades. But the one-to-one ratio was lost, apparently for good, around 1970. This is the great slide off the mountain of daily circulation. (See Chart 7.1.) Through the first decades of the twentieth century, the habit of reading *some* newspaper was universal in all income groups. The reach of this news across class lines

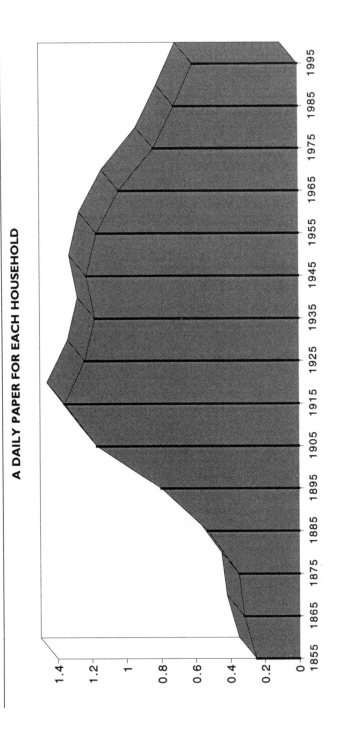

Chart 7.1 Source: U.S. Census reports and *Editor & Publisher.*

A DAILY PAPER FOR EACH HOUSEHOLD

was remarkable. A government survey after World War I showed that for low- and medium-income white families in urban America, more than nine in ten took a paper. (At this time that ratio held in other studies of people who had not finished the eighth grade of school.) Half of those news buyers slipped away in the low- and middle-income groups by the 1970s. This despite the fact that the daily paper was cheaper (allowing for inflation) than it had been when people on tight budgets helped publishers set circulation records. This century ends with only an economic elite showing the loyalty to newspapers that was once shared by blue-collar workers, small farmers, and clerks.[1]

Just under sixty million Americans took daily newspapers when John F. Kennedy was in the White House. During President Clinton's first year in office, circulation again was just below sixty million. But in these thirty years, the population of the country had grown by more than seventy million. Newspapers were one of the few institutions to miss the demographic ride of the last decades of the twentieth century.[2]

Any way one looks at it, the fall of the daily paper is impressive. Tighter accounting of circulation did not affect the trend: the supply of papers kept pace through the 1920s, the first full decade of rigorous checking through the Audit Bureau of Circulations. Chart 7.1 does reflect the explosive growth of households in the last decades of the twentieth century. However, a graph of the percentage of adults who read a daily paper would be nearly as steep (80 percent of Americans sampled said they had just read a paper in 1970, but only 62 percent gave that answer twenty years later).[3] Circulation figures for magazines in households show that news media could keep pace with new living patterns. There was no *general* turning away from print journalism. The major newsweeklies (*U.S. News & World Report*, *Time*, and *Newsweek*) held their audience far better than newspapers. These magazines were frequently called troubled in the 1990s, but even so, their circulation represented a much higher percentage of American households than in the 1950s. The most general category of magazines tracked by the industry does not show the anemia of newspapers. Indeed, the supply of these magazines for households increased smartly. (See Chart 7.2.)

Many social trends of the twentieth century helped magazines and should have helped newspapers. In most respects, this has been an era of better education and new opportunities to use information. Only 6 percent of Americans over the age of seventeen held a high school diploma in 1900. In 1925 a quarter of all adults had graduated, and in 1950 that figure went above 50 percent. In the 1990s high school graduates totaled more than three-quarters of adults. College training has mushroomed in the same way. In 1950, for instance, there were only 125,000 black college graduates; in the 1990s more than two million African Americans held degrees. (That is a larger number than the circulation of any daily). The twentieth century provided new calls to be informed as well

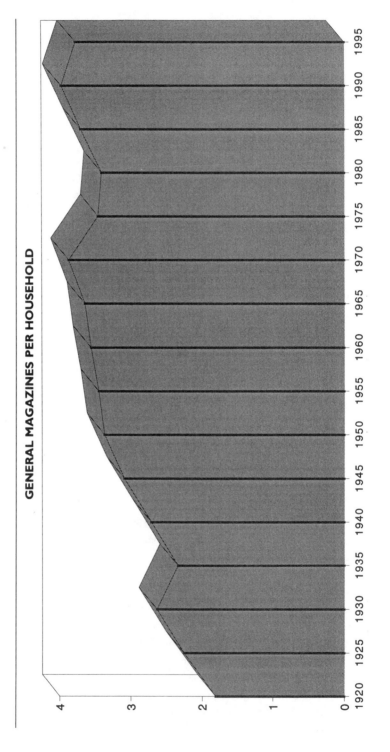

Chart 7.2 Source: U.S. Census and Magazine Publishers of America. Estimate for 1995.

GENERAL MAGAZINES PER HOUSEHOLD

as the added years of schooling. Women, blacks, and Hispanics gained the vote. Jury duty and military obligations became far more democratic than in the nineteenth century. A variety of entitlement programs, especially Social Security and Medicare, touched every family. A more promising foundation for mass circulation could hardly be imagined.

More than general knowledge, the modern public has had a need for specialized information that newspapers, uniquely, supply:

• In 1950 fewer than five million Americans owned individual stocks or security mutual funds, one out of thirty citizens. In 1990 fifty million Americans were in this market, one out of five people. Short of visiting a broker's office or making a call, investors needed a paper to keep close watch on their money. The age-old feature of stock quotes on a financial page was not yet surpassed by electronic media, and a vast new public was interested in these columns. But for all this, newspapers reached a shrinking share of the public.

• The growing number of women in the work force directed millions of Americans to a unique newspaper feature: the want ads. Magazines and electronic media carried only a small fraction of employment opportunities. When newspapers had their greatest reach into American households in 1930, less than a quarter of women worked outside the home; the female offspring of these families have joined the labor force at more than double this rate. Half the population, then, *needed* newspapers at the very time the papers lost their hold on the public.

• The audience for newspapers declined in the era when sports leagues expanded across the country, creating networks of fans who used daily papers to follow results. "Rotisserie leagues" and similar fantasy sports contests made daily reports particularly exciting for millions of Americans in the 1980s. But all these readers, too, could not prop up the drooping readership line.

• Newspapers lost their grip in the era of suburbanization when the paper itself was the primary medium for advertising these tract homes and furnishing them in shopping centers. The automobiles that made this expansion possible were bought and sold through newspapers in steadily increasing numbers.

The decline in circulation in the face of social change that made newspaper features more valuable shows that simple explanations as to why readers vanished will not work.

Television, the temptress in the story of how readers were lured away from dailies, has been given too much blame. Circulation fell before the viewing habit took hold, well before the success of local and national news programs in the 1960s. Television created new opportunities for newspapers to hook readers with program guides and stories on the personalities in the new medium. At the end of the twentieth century, tabloid papers key their coverage to television and win an enormous public. Some magazines have done this, and even titles that ignore television have demonstrated that print media can meet the challenge of the video age.

Similarly, it is hard to argue that any change in daily life led to the anemia in newspaper circulation. Mass transit declined in the age of freeways that followed World War II, taking away millions of commuters who had been prime customers for papers. But the drivers were not able to read magazines at the wheel either. Americans found more time for many types of reading, but not for newspapers. Why?

Did the marketplace deal a poorer hand to newspapers than to other media? In most markets, newspaper subscriptions continue unless canceled (or not paid for). Magazines have always faced the need to win new commitments and have envied the involuntary element in selling newspapers. Magazines had distribution problems to rival those of the dailies. Single-copy sales of best-selling magazines declined by more than a third in the 1980s as traditional newsstands disappeared from city streets. Newspapers coped by filling public right-of-ways with more than six hundred thousand vending boxes and racks; magazines did not build this obstacle course to snare their readers. Costs did not force readers to let go of newspapers and reach for magazines. In the 1970s and 1980s magazines went up in price much faster than papers. By the middle of this decade, magazines were drawing half of their revenue from readers at a time when the public was still contributing only a fraction of what newspapers earned. There has to have been something distinctive about the way newspapers were conducted to explain the fate of dailies in the second half of the twentieth century. What happened here?[4]

2. Monopoly and Enterprise

The most skillful hunt for the fleeing reader was conducted by the Newspaper Readership Project (1977–83), which was sponsored by publishers. Leo Bogart, a sociologist with a background in advertising, showed newspaper people what was happening to their audience in scores of reports and a comprehensive summing-up, *Press and Public* (2nd ed. 1989). This is the most comprehensive body of research ever done on reading habits, but it did not please its sponsors, and the project ended just as the decline in newspaper use became unarguable. In a memoir of the bruised feelings and cross-purposes of this investigation, Bogart noted that the departing newspaper readers were not noticed for a very long time. The industry assumed that "everybody" was their audience and had not bothered to track who was reading the paper. Flourishing the right quotes from Thomas Jefferson settled most worries about the importance of newspapers to the nation. Nobody on the project wanted to emphasize bad news about readership, and early work invariably showed that declines had been exaggerated or were self-correcting. When "four out of five" could no longer be claimed as readers and the data hovered near three out of five, "nearly four of five" was the phrase marshalled up. When baby boomers, those born to the new families after World War II, did not share the news-reading habits of their parents, researchers told publishers what they wanted to hear: that maturity would bring them into line. Journalism was a can-do enterprise. Editors lived by the faith that better stories could solve any marketing problem. It was the common wisdom of circulation departments that they could generate any increase in subscribers the publishers were willing to pay for (through discounts, premiums, or prizes). Democratic talk about the public might be rare in the rooms where ad buys were negotiated, but it overflowed where journalists met the public. Newspapers' hired hands (Bogart's term) who studied readership kept the faith that the newspaper was for all.[5]

The Newspaper Readership Project, and later industry studies, put more emphasis on the *convenience* than the *content* of the product to explain the loss of readers. Crowded highways made timely delivery of afternoon papers especially difficult, helping to weaken a form of news that had, in any case, been better suited to the work schedule of blue-collar rather than white-collar America. Security-conscious communities were another bar to readership. "Penetrating them with newspaper delivery is like attacking a fort," circulation managers have learned. When locked gates and vigilant guards block carriers, the newspaper perishes, for most readers give the news only one chance in their day. Because many neighborhoods are less safe, the perils of delivery and collection make publishers wonder why they should keep trying for circulation here.[6]

These findings were accurate as far as they went and useful correctives to the notions (often floated in focus groups) that if only journalists could strike the right *tone*, the right *look*, then the public would come back. But the research financed by publishers paid far too little attention to structural complacency and the indifferent salesmanship of daily papers.

"Uneven" is the kindest word for the corporate strategies of newspapers during their long hemorrhage of readers. Newspapers of the last third of the twentieth century made some wise decisions. The computers in the newsroom and printing plant were a vanguard for American industry. But in few other respects have the business plans of the dailies inspired respect. A 1978 report to the Federal Trade Commission by a Stanford economist put the point across that "the usual approach of newspapers to the business of management is positively ante-diluvian." One aspect of this is the failure to reinvest profits in gathering news and readers. Newspapers are among the most profitable of American enterprises. In percentage of return on sales, they are roughly twice as profitable as the mean figure for Fortune 500 companies. Many newspapers lost their grip on households at the time they became public corporations.

They faced a choice of investing for their long-term success or reporting steadily higher returns to their stockholders. This was a dilemma that the older newspaper barons such as Hearst, Pulitzer, and Scripps never faced. The defining trait of most modern publishers has been their failure to plough profits back into editorial or marketing, or research or development. (Bogart made this point, but very gently.) Given this, the wonder was not that newspapers slipped, but that they managed to keep steady readers.[7]

"The Hershey company worries a hell of a lot more about the content of its Hershey bars than we worry about the content of newspapers," Eugene L. Roberts Jr. told his fellow editors in 1994. Roberts, who had led the Philadelphia *Inquirer* to national distinction, was about to become the managing editor of the New York *Times*. He recognized that some papers had protected the budget to gather news. But this had not been the rule in his working life, he said. Metropolitan newspapers that used to have 10 percent of gross revenues as a budgetary floor for the newsroom had seen this shrink to 8 percent, to 6 percent, or less. "Newspapers are terribly short-sighted about the way they're constantly squeezed in newsrooms," Roberts told press executives. The people who take risks with chocolate bars and with newspapers—investors on Wall Street—heard the same warnings. The most respected market newsletter had an appropriate obsession with the bottom line, but looked to the future and saw "that newspapers should spend more of these profits in improving editorial quality."[8]

The figures in marketing the product look no better than the investment in content. In 1980 few newspapers were spending even 2 percent of total budgets for promotion in the broadest sense, including research, public relations, and community service. In the middle of that decade, newspapers spent no more in advertising themselves than America's *licensed* monopolies, local cable television franchises. As a percentage of their sales and of their profits, the manufacturers of pens and pencils spent more than twice as much on advertising as the nation's newspapers. In 1988 the American Newspaper Publishers Association complained that its members were contributing less than a penny for research from every hundred dollars they earned. At this time, the publishers' organization pointed out, auto companies spent two of every hundred dollars they earned on research, and computer companies spent eight dollars.[9]

One reason that magazines kept pace with the growth of the nation is that they have promoted circulation with more vigor and imagination than the newspaper industry. For every dollar in sales, magazines have spent roughly twice as much to advertise themselves as newspapers spent in ad campaigns. Papers were poor at carnival barking in the last half of the twentieth century. Giveaways were rare among serious newspapers. The circulation-thumping contests of a few urban tabloids were embarrassments to most journalists.[10]

This dignity stemmed in part from a restraint of trade. Ninety-eight percent of the roughly 1,550 daily newspapers had no competition from another daily. Joint Operating Agreements under the Newspaper Preservation Act of 1970 meant that "rival" papers in cities such as Detroit and San Francisco had no economic reason to win readers away from their business partners. In 1994 only sixteen cities had independently owned dailies, freely battling for customers. That was 1 percent of the nation's newspapers.[11]

This is a business structure designed to shrink the number of readers, even in the best of circumstances. One need not demonize concentration to see this. Monopolies may keep costs down because of their efficiency of scale. Competition from broadcasters and weeklies in the local market can limit what a surviving daily charges. The challenges from the other media may even keep the lone daily editorially sharp. These strokes of luck do sometimes happen. But even with such rosy outcomes for the public served by monopolies, many readers lose the habit of reading a daily when there is only one around. "Audience levels are highest where readers have a choice," Leo Bogart has observed. Would we watch as much television news if ABC, CBS, CNN, and NBC combined into one mighty service? Would one superb newsweekly hope for a reading public as large as *Time, Newsweek,* and *U.S. News & World Report* share? Taking the news is one part the inertia of familiar reading material. But another part of the reading habit is triggered by curiosity about what other journalists are saying. We take cues from other citizens who model the act of reading the news and worry us that they may know something that we do not. Just as it is very difficult to read just *one* magazine on personal finances or fashion or sports, it is easier to ignore these subjects if just one specialized magazine has a lock on a subject.[12]

The magazine business, in contrast to newspapers, has had a growing number of competitors, who have been eager poachers on the readers of their competition. Magazines offered the bounty and a sense of community that had helped to establish mass circulation in the first place. Newspapers may have convened more high-minded meetings of their readers, though even in this they have impressive competition: twenty-thousand people have joined Utne Neighborhood Salons, organized by this bi-monthly digest of new ideas. It seems certain, however, that magazines have led the way in making subscriptions fun. For instance, at the end of the twentieth century, fully half of all consumer magazines were offering readers premiums or sweepstake prizes. This was in the tradition of the nineteenth century, and, once again, it brought a harvest of readers.[13]

The modern carnival for magazine circulation came out of the basement of the Mertz house on Long Island in 1953. Charles H. Mertz and his daughter did two new things at once. They expanded the field of magazines a subscription agent could offer to hundreds of titles, and they went after customers through mass mailings. Soon, thick envelopes from Publishers Clearing House offering discounts on a galaxy of magazines became a fixture in the American mailbox. Good prospects might receive twenty-five letters a year. Deep discounts and pledges of customer service were the main sales pitch, but the "kit" made the choice of reading itself seem a pleasant game. Customers pasted handsome stamps onto the order forms. Beginning in the 1960s, money was part of the fun. *Reader's Digest* pioneered the subscription sweepstakes in 1962, and Publishers Clearing House topped this effort five years later. This agency alone issued checks to two million winners. Together with American Family Publishers, started in 1975, these subscription drives gave away more than $125 million in prizes by 1990. The Magazine Publishers of America has estimated that the contests through direct mail bring in at least 10 percent of all subscriptions and about 25 percent of new subscriptions. The public theater of the sweepstakes is designed to build fantasies that magazines are good luck. The audience is enlisted through "involvement devices" to make this connection. Publishers Clearing House, for example, had its "prize patrol" that encouraged potential subscribers to plan their big celebration. The contestants were put to work, not only pasting the stamps that would bring the magazines, but also drawing sketches of their neighborhood so the patrol can find them and filling in a guest list for the party. Very few Americans are visited by the prize patrol, but everyone who watches television may see the ecstasies of the big winners as a subscription offer turns into a "miracle." Every household gets the message that taking a magazine opens a door to excitement.[14]

The direct mail campaigns do more than this; they also reinforce the idea that there is a magazine for everyone. The kit from Publishers Clearing House has offered a hundred titles (at times, many more) printed on colorful stamps. This direct mail does not rely on the tired theme that reading will make you a better person. Never mind the reading, these appeals suggest, a subscription is a ticket to opportunity. Though by law a person need order nothing to enter and win, magazine agencies sell the idea that the household will be dropped from future mailings if the residents hold back. "DON'T RISK IT," warned Fred C. Shotwell, president of American Family Publishers: "If we haven't received a new magazine order from you in some time, your name is in danger of being dropped from our regular mailing list—soon!" In the trade this is called the buy-or-die letter. Newspaper promotions have usually been hit-or-miss affairs, with few ways of improving the appeal mid-course or making this season's campaign better than the last. In the direct mail world of magazine selling, there is constant testing of approaches with batches of letters with different appeals sent to sample groups to see what works. Good letters acquire the names of the people who thought them up and inspire work along the same line. Indeed, there are direct mail legends, kits that the trade talked about the way the newspaper world once celebrated heroic newsboys. "Who has five eyes and eats her mate for dinner?" *Natural History* asked on the envelope of a mailing of the 1980s. The only way to find out was to open the envelope and peel off a token . . . and the token was most easily gotten rid of by putting it on the sheet where it stood for a subscription order. Careers are made on such work in the magazine business, but not in newspapering.[15]

These blizzards of magazine promotion, sweeping through the postal system in all seasons, should be compared with newspaper use of the mails. Industry surveys of the late 1980s found that only 4 to 8 percent of dailies had even tried direct mail. Though newspaper companies have sought to beat the direct mail industry at its own game by packaging circulars and coupons for every address, the newspaper itself has not been promoted with any flair in these packets. Magazines buy lists of people with special interests and tempt them, repeatedly, to subscribe to a title that fits that interest. Newspapers lead not into that temptation. No matter your hobby or cause, newspapers do not fill your mailbox with word about their terrific coverage of your interest with an irresistible invitation to subscribe. Perhaps it is a sign of the dignity of the press that newspapers can not bring themselves to write a buy-or-die letter. But it is also a sign of the marketing savvy of a monopoly product.[16]

The daily paper has also lost ground with its public because it has allowed other media to do its job better. *TV Guide*, one of the largest circulation magazines in the final decades of the twentieth century, might have been beaten in the market by daily and weekly program listings of daily papers. In the 1980s "car trader" and "swap" papers outclassed traditional want-ad sections of dailies. These specialized papers organized the goods more clearly and took simple steps, like offering pictures of cars, that newspapers did not use their resources to provide. Similarly, in recent decades metropolitan dailies have been the laggards of journalism in the visual display of information. Stock tables in these dailies have often been fuzzy, cramped, and off-putting to the uninitiated. These papers have had to catch up with the clarity and convenience of the tables run by the *Wall Street Journal* and *Barron's*. *USA Today* showed that features even more neglected than business news, like the weather reports, could be reported with great visual impact. Only in a setting of local monopolies could a business grow so vulnerable to entrepreneurs who would steal their customers.

Magazines have found the most elusive readers, the customers that newspapers have given up on. Hispanic males between the ages of sixteen and twenty-one, for instance, were successfully targeted by *Lowrider* in the 1980s. This magazine brought news of hydraulic systems that allow a car to bounce and cruise just a few inches from the pavement. Most feature articles have pictures of young women in bikinis. There are at least as many opportunities for community feeling and personal expression here as there are in *Country Living*. *Lowrider*, like other magazines keyed to a minority culture, has addressed broader concerns such as urban renewal, street violence, and schools.

"La Raza Report" and spirited defenses of Aztlan nationhood from readers are regular features. This English-language monthly has been used in school districts to help Latino children build reading skills. In principle, a newspaper should reach this subculture in cities such as San Jose, Los Angeles, and Miami where young Latino men are a great untapped market. Automotive sections, after all, are a standard part of metropolitan papers, and regular lowrider features could be used as an entry point for new readers. *Lowrider* has a circulation of two hundred thousand, about double the number of subscribers to the most successful Spanish-language edition of an American daily. As a magazine, that circulation is about the combined audiences for the *New Republic* and the *Nation.* This circulation was built up by doing things that newspapers have not thought to do. *Lowrider* agents copied down license numbers at car shows and contacted these hobbyists. The publisher sent representatives from the *barrio* into liquor stores to talk up the magazine. At the end of the twentieth century, this is the kind of marketing necessary to maintain a reading public. Magazines, much more than newspapers, have been willing to do it.[17]

3. Fables and Franchises

American journalism was born as a commercial medium. But it was not until the nineteenth century that journalists feared commercialization, the dictation of news content by advertisers. Alarms sounded after the Civil War as advertising replaced payments from readers as the chief source of revenue for newspapers and magazines. The stories killed by advertisers became part of the talk of the trade. Around the turn of the century, thousands of small-town newspapers had signed contracts agreeing not to support the regulation of patent medicines so as to keep the lucrative ads for these elixirs. Silence on this topic could be purchased, even in Boston, that bastion of genteel values. Running stories for a price was a much-denounced practice of newspapers and magazines at the beginning of this century. "Reading Notices," commercial messages disguised as news, were so notorious that the postal regulations restricted them in second-class matter in 1912. That same year, a socialist magazine made the gentle point that the capitalist press was a whorehouse, with the advertiser the best customer. Upton Sinclair's *The Brass Check* (1919) was a tome on the prostitution of the press, and he was able to update the book with new instances of advertisers getting their way over the next two decades. It was not hard to spot pay-offs in the press of the 1920s and 1930s. Hearst newspapers, for instance, were notorious for printing good theater and movie reviews for advertising space or a cash payment.[18]

Journalists have continued to cry out against the way money influenced what they printed. Recent studies of editors, using large samples and collecting data

Art Young, drawing for *The Masses,* December 1912.

anonymously, have shown that advertising pressure on editorial decisions is a common headache. Nine out of ten newspaper editors cite this occupational hazard, and nearly that many of their colleagues at magazines suffer. In all types of newspapers and magazines, the surveys show that about four of every ten editors believe their work has been compromised.[19]

There has indeed been egregious censorship by market pressure. The suppression of the bad news about smoking through most of the twentieth century is the best-documented case. But not all of the alarms about commercialization are as important as journalists are apt to think. In the first place, anxious news people have plenty of company. Many professional groups are worn down by commercial pressures: scientists, lawyers, physicians. All of these occupations are shaped by the tension between internal values and the pressure of outsiders who command their services. It is revealing that recent memoirs of news values sacrificed to gain larger profits sound very much like the reflections of advertising executives who speak with conviction about how commercial considerations have degraded *their* calling. Market forces tear away at the values of many guilds. Journalists probably do not deserve special sympathy.[20]

Is the reader the victim?

The history of the American press provides little evidence that readers can be discouraged by publications with too many ads. Those sharecropper-cabin walls with their selections of good things for sale are a reminder that ad-weariness is not a universal complaint. Gannett, the largest chain of newspapers, believes that one reader in twenty takes the daily *for* the ads. In the 1990s the American reader is deluged by ads in newspapers and magazines that earlier generations did not face: the loose inserts that are stuffed into the Sunday paper and every issue of magazines. The National Lampoon's *Loaded Weapon I* (1992) exaggerated, perhaps, in showing a reader trapped by falling inserts as he picked up something to read. (This hazard has been created by new technology and publishers' need to win advertisers away from direct mail. Inserts cost less than the "run-of-publication" ads and have a higher profit margin for publishers.) The detritus of this new advertising has not driven readers away, though they may be responsible for a jump in complaints about "ad clutter." Not only are magazines, as a class, a success story of the late twentieth century; the Sunday papers that carry most of the inserts have had more success with readers than the tidier dailies.[21]

Nor is it clear that the sacrifice of editorial integrity in order to court advertisers will, automatically, repel readers. Consumer magazines are notorious for lulling their readers into a buying mood by uniting ads and "compatible copy." Gloria Steinem has given convincing testimony about how traditional women's magazines became cheerleaders for the cosmetics, clothes, and leisure activities that advertisers wanted to sell. But this has been a formula for holding a large audience in this field, as Steinem's *Ms.* magazine learned to her sorrow. Travel magazines never seem to write about lousy vacations, gourmet titles rarely do hard-hitting reports on food, and bad news about car companies is seldom in the journals for auto enthusiasts. Yet this type of journalism has found more favor with readers than daily papers in recent decades. The young Mexican Americans who enjoy *Lowrider* are representative of a large body of modern readers who find compatible copy rewarding: ads tell them to buy things, and stories tell them how great it is to have these gleaming beauties. Similarly, most pages of *Vogue* and *Gourmet*, advertising and editorial, offer something on the pursuit of stylish affluence. Such boosterism may form a bond between the reader and the press. "Consumption communities" have been identified in the flowering of nineteenth-century capitalism and they live on. Some readers have always wanted the press to be fascinating, not inquiring, and to play out commercial fantasies. In some circumstances, dropping editorial standards satisfies this taste.[22]

There is sometimes an element of the pharisaical among those who would root out commercial considerations in putting news before the public. The folklore of publishing has a "church/state separation" between the editorial side and the business side . . . in the distant past. Henry Luce made this distinction in his forty-year reign over Time Inc. Journalists commend this tradition, and its concrete representation at the Chicago *Tribune:* separate elevators for the sacred and the profane employees. People who cling to the metaphor of church/state separation seem to forget that main functions of most churches at most times have been to collect money and to win public favor. Luce himself made the key business and editorial decisions for his publications, as did Col. Robert McCormick, high in the *Tribune*'s Gothic tower in Chicago. Some of the most adventurous and successful journalism of the late twentieth century has been produced by people who made the business and editorial decisions at the same time: Jann Wenner at *Rolling Stone*, Edward Kosner at *New York*, Mortimer B. Zuckerman at *U.S. News & World Report*, for example. Tina Brown, at *Vanity Fair* and the *New Yorker*, has shamelessly combined marketing and editorial decisions. It is a fair point to argue that these journalists are "dangerous," but it is also fair to say that they have produced some of the most interesting journalism of their time. Many wish it otherwise, but the scrupulous separation of editorial judgment and the lust for profit has not been the defining mark of all of the most successful journalists. Nor is it clear how the press is improved if journalists meet the demands of the fastidious and cancel lunches with the marketing staff, avoid shaking hands with advertisers, and refuse to provide an index for ads in the paper. Advertising imperatives may have terrible effects on journalism, and the people who condemn them often have good evidence of this harm. But *exactly* what is wrong with news that is shaped by business pressure is not made clear in the chorus of complaints.[23]

There are two main reasons why the public and the press have been ill served by commercialization.

The first is that publications run this way usually cannot extend the reach of journalism across the lines that separate people with special interests. Commercialization may sustain consumption, but it will not support citizenship. It is true that even the narrowest of publications will sometimes address public questions. The much-maligned women's magazines had a role in spreading ideas of modern feminism. *GQ* and *Sports Illustrated* have done serious reporting on American society. *Lowrider* is a voice of the *barrio*, not just the sales pitch of car customizers. But a society needs common talk about issues among people who *know* they have been brought together for this purpose. Much of print journalism has a franchise to form a common discourse, to truly make it seem that the world is watching. It is business folly to give up that franchise.

Most niche publications offer a sense of refuge. There is great appeal to a press that makes readers feel that they are moving in their own crowd and that outsiders are not watching. This is why parents who read their teen's magazine are courting trouble and a woman who conspicuously reads a men's magazine (and vice versa) is likely to make other people uncomfortable. Readers have different expectations for the publications that engage them in their full role as citizens, the newspapers and magazines on general topics of the day. Americans expect to adjust their minds to new facts and to arguments that are surprising, even upsetting. This is what the best editors of news for a broad public hope to achieve. In this part of the press, most notably in metropolitan newspapers, readers poach on the territory that has been set out for other groups. Those studies that have readers page through yesterday's paper and even monitor eye movements document these roaming habits (chap. 5, part 3). Readers do not always want to be confined to their own crowd. They seek encounters with people who do not think the way they do. This is one reason that this country, in contrast to many European nations, has rarely supported a powerful, focused media for Catholics, for labor, or for a racial minority. Americans have a history of doubting the value of words and pictures on paper that do not reach a broad public and of discounting the print medium when it preaches to the converted.

There is wisdom in this habit of mind. The journalism that is bound by the assumptions and enthusiasms of readers (as niche publications usually are) leave their audience unprepared for the real world. The view is too narrow. Chapter 3 was one such case study: the slave South was undermined by the stories of fugitive slaves that its press took for granted; the segregated South could not understand its own black residents by reading the press of the local white establishment. In the 1990s a press that ignores the underdogs of American society because these groups do not much interest advertisers puts readers in the same position.

There is another reason why a common press is important. The publications we read and expect others to have seen are a sort of compass for discussion. These mark the directions that citizens are willing to travel. Their power, as communication scholars have made clear, is to help set the agenda for a society. There is no quicker road to eccentricity than to champion a cause that has not gotten noticed under familiar mastheads. The publications that address a mosaic of small causes cannot set this agenda until the press that connects citizens picks up the story. If the focusing is left to other institutions — broadcasting, for instance — print loses much of its power.[24]

The second problem with commercialization is that most businesses need an audience that is larger than those people who are already fascinated by a subject. The pressure to segment markets in the last third of the century has made it increasingly difficult to meet this need, and since the print media could not do this job, marketing has turned elsewhere. In the end, the commercialization of the press may contribute no more to consumption than it does to citizenship.

This is why newspapers and some serious magazines have been hurt by reducing their readers to marketing targets. Allowing advertisers to do the storytelling erodes the competitive advantage that critical journalism has over the general run of advertising vehicles. Readers resent this when it is done outside of the hobby or fantasy publication that they have chosen for themselves.

Consider a typical innovation of daily journalism in the past decade, the AutoZone section of the jointly operated San Francisco *Chronicle* and *Exam-*

iner. This advertising supplement contains only good news about new cars and is relentlessly chirpy ("What's a Suburban? Whatever you want it to be."). Most dailies have tried this approach for real estate, schools, and camps as well as consumer goods. This is the netherland between news and sales pitch, the "advertorial." The AutoZone carries stories with bylines that look like news stories, and, despite the public disclaimer, "advertising supplement," it is acknowledged by management as "the result of a combined effort" with the editorial staffs. The San Francisco papers have congratulated themselves in the following terms: "A true 'Customer Connection' was made with both the sales reps and the advertiser as 'customer.'" Perhaps so, but God help the reader, whose interest in getting a candid view about an automobile was sold out when this deal was struck.[25]

There are cases of big commercial interests demanding complimentary copy or pushing advertorials with the swagger suggested by Art Young's brothel cartoon. The women's page of the New York *Times* was run this way in the 1950s. During the rise of feminism in the 1970s and 1980s, editor Gloria Steinem of *Ms.* faced advertisers who wanted stories and ads that nurtured "a kept woman mentality." But seduction in the 1990s has become part of the newspaper publisher's business. In the mid-1990s the new trade group, the Newspaper Association of America, was busy soliciting advertorials, and the happy features appeared in many papers. The NAA urged sponsors to buy space for a campaign called "Mexico: Everything You Ever Dreamed Of." It seems that these features were not to mention anything to worry about south of the border. But we will never know, for this was too much for the Mexican tourist authorities: they would not pay, and to the disappointment of the publishers, these stories on paradise never ran.[26]

An important element of the press has a different franchise than the selling of cheerful news. This is print journalism that appeals to our taste to know what happened, not to feel good about our fantasies. Its comparative advantage over all other messengers is that it is trusted. Readers will not stay loyal to a publication of this type that does not look out for *their* interests and give them intelligent direction. Lose that critical edge, and the public will slip away. Howard Kurtz of the Washington *Post* has identified the element that is killing interest in newspapers:

> The problem with dumbing-down newspapers is that we're talking down to people, and they know it. Instead of capturing their attention the hard way— with well-written stories about schools and taxes and crime and culture and other things that matter in their lives—we take the easier (and cheaper) way out.[27]

Indeed, there is evidence that when the sales puffery is wrung out of a newspaper, more people will make time for it. When the Miami *Herald* put hard-hitting news in its real estate section, after two decades of printing softer stories on that subject, it attracted more readers and more ads.[28]

The dead end of placing commercial goals above service to citizens has been illustrated by the campaign that has a slogan with superficial resemblance to the motto of dailies a century ago: Total Market Coverage. In order to compete with saturation distribution of advertising by mail and the home delivery of circulars, newspapers use their mailing facilities or carrier force to do this job. More than eight of ten dailies had a program for non-subscribers at the beginning of the 1990s. But this is not news for all, it is ads for all. The industry has found that "short, punchy, soft news items" make these giveaways work. Hard news is not recommended. The Milwaukee *Journal*, for instance, gave no taste of its best work in the *Express Line* it delivered to all non-subscribers in seven zip codes west of the city. The *Journal* wraps ads around entertaining filler, supplied by a syndicate.[29]

A newspaper that uses its resources to supply non-news to its non-readers is almost certainly in a bad business, no matter how much money comes in the short run. When readers don't seem to care, advertisers don't either. Magazines learned this when they saw that stuffing mailboxes with the *Saturday Evening Post* would never impress Madison Avenue. So too with Total Market Coverage. After the contraption was built and made to work, advertisers decided they did not want it. One advertising director noted that a publication that cannot engage the reader on any serious level is not likely to put Americans in the desired "coupon-clipping mode." Kmart, then the nation's second largest retailer, asked for this service at the beginning of the 1980s but announced, ten years later, that it preferred papers with paying customers.[30]

The most compelling fear in the news business is that all publishers will reconceptualize what they were put on earth to do, deciding "they are in the business of building advertising markets, rather than the business of delivering information." It is not hard to see why editors and reporters feel this way, for they are often told that the readers are consumers and only infrequently reminded that readers are citizens.[31]

4. Readers at Retail

Readers of this book may not know that their most routine contacts with news organizations make their names an item of commerce. In the 1990s subscribing to magazines or newspapers, taking out a classified ad, entering their contests, writing a letter to the editor, even using the information services they offer by phone, may well begin a chase. Contact with news has made the reader the prey.

A glance through the trade journals of the magazine business will reveal just what you are worth. Your name on the subscription list of an upscale magazine is worth a dime or two, every time it is sold. A single magazine may sell your name twenty-five times a year. All readers of periodicals are up for sale, from some of the most specialized to some of the most inclusive. Cowles sells the subscription lists of eight historical magazines ("Put history to work for you . . ."). The *Smithsonian* magazine list promises Americans who are "financially secure," "well-educated," and "mail-mannered." "The Atlantic subscribers can afford to be selective in their tastes and fervent in their interests. . . . And they're direct mail enthusiasts!" according to another sales campaign. Even Eustace Tilly, the *New Yorker's* cartoon dandy, is a pitchman, selling the magazine's readers to sales forces and fund raisers, so much per thousand. Seemingly, no publication and no group of readers stands outside the trade. "MAIL TO NAMES THAT RESPOND! You want to talk about responsive . . . then let's talk about outstanding lists from *Biblical Archaeology Society.*" Progressive politics are a selling point in the list business. The dream is to "harness the buying power of *The Nation* for your company." *Ms.*, *Earthwatch*, and *Mother Jones* ("They share a passion for worthy causes that goes unmatched") are also for sale. In closing down his publication, I. F. Stone, the maverick political writer of the Cold War era, sold the names of his subscribers to the *New York Review of Books* for more than a dollar a reader.[32]

Stone's readers probably were in friendly hands, but in the list business, the trusting reader may fare no better with new owners than did Black Beauty. For more than a decade, historians have been targeted by propaganda denying the Holocaust, courtesy of the sale of subscription lists. The databases that magazines have for sale can undermine their editorial message. Readers of *Time* magazine, in recent years, found coverage of the dangers of smoking. But Time Inc. led the publishing field in revenue from cigarette advertising in the early 1990s, and to hold its place, Edward McCarrick, associate publisher of Time, suggested that "if a tobacco company asked us to match our subscription base with its list, we could target some niches those companies want to reach."[33]

Lists are not yet making publishers rich, but since these records have to be kept anyway, list sales represents an attractive part of their business. And with no additional expense, publishers easily imagine that the revenue will grow. The direct marketing industry said in 1993 that it had total revenues of $350 million. The lure of that business is likely to be irresistible.[34]

The scale of the record keeping is impressive. In the early nineties, Condé Nast had collected eleven million names; Times Mirror had fifteen million; Hearst had fifty million; Meredith had fifty-six million; and Reader's Digest had data on line for one hundred million people, worldwide. PUBLISHERS FIND GOLD IN DATABASES was a headline in *Advertising Age*. These unsuspecting readers were being targeted (often with the aid of other databases on what they bought). They were for sale, and they were the basis for new ads, new features and new publications. The Ziff-Davis magazine group has a slogan for their list services that is an industry goal: "People who know how to live right." This marketing imperative seals the pact that journalists have made in the last half of the twentieth century (and that they rarely cared about when they invented mass circulation): to supply news to the right sorts of people.[35]

The database gold mine that newspapers sit on consists of information that the public may never have thought of as a commodity: their own names when they write letters to the editor or pay for their subscription with a credit card; births, deaths, marriages, and divorces that come into the news; job switches; degrees and licenses that people have earned; donations to local events and charities. Seen this way, a great deal of local news is saleable data that marketers would like to have. Crime reports can become names and addresses of people on carrier routes who will be good customers for burglar alarms and security lights. Why not collect the name of everyone who takes a position on the abortion issue and sell those names to interest groups who are looking for new members? This is no more fanciful than what has already been done, the combing of subscription records to find good candidates for mortgage offers: "Banks Zoom In on Customers." Firms that handle "antiliberal media donors" as well as "Democratic liberal donors" are likely to be good customers for the names that journalists collect.[36]

List building is the new imperative of the newspaper business. Major dailies such as the New York *Times* have gone to court to pry subscribers' names out of independent distributors of the paper who were given exclusive control of this information in the days when record keeping was seen simply as a burden. Now these names and addresses have great value because they can be combined with other data to provide the basis for marketing. Harte-Hanks, one of the most profitable newspaper groups, has a subsidiary that helps papers use reader data for direct marketing. The Washington *Post*, like other papers with the City-Line audiotex, gives information to readers for free and in return builds a valuable database. The names and numbers of callers with specific interests— stock quotes, skiing conditions, sports scores—are used in the paper's own promotions and sold to advertisers as well as direct mail entrepreneurs. The Denver *Post* achieved the same result by hiring a consultant to integrate its subscriber list with databases on the lifestyle and credit history of people in the metropolitan area. Name an interest, and the *Post* can offer the names, addresses, and income levels of readers who fit the bill in Denver. *Editor & Publisher* has opened its pages to the revolutionary declaration that "newspapers are really in the database business, no more, no less." This is not what most publishers believe. But give them time.[37]

The "inland empire" market of Spokane, Washington, has a brave, new horizon on news readers. The Cowles Publishing Company dominated this hub of commerce for four states with a joint operating agreement between the

Spokane *Spokesman-Review* and the rival *Chronicle* in 1982. The *Chronicle*, the afternoon paper, was closed in 1992. The era of coordinated management produced a net loss of readership. But Cowles was a model to the industry for innovative marketing approaches. Shaun O'L. Higgins led this campaign as a pioneer of audiotex in the early 1980s and of database marketing in the 1990s. Higgins finds that "household-level data is empowering because it enables us to home in on individual moments of truth in the purchasing process." Readers of the Spokane paper were hard pressed to avoid the cross-hairs of this marketing. Higgins sent out 136,000 questionnaires with the papers and rewarded those who returned the self-profiles. (The seven thousand dogs of *Spokesman-Review* readers also benefited, for as they were identified, attractive offers came to their owners.) Fishbowls were put in shops for business cards, with the lure of a prize drawing. The paper offered books to the public and premiums to subscribers, noting what the choice revealed about the interests of each customer. There was a chance for circus tickets from the paper for a little information, a good way to flush out young families. "Read the paper (what could be easier)," Higgins told other marketing executives: news itself could add new people with new interests to the lists. In thinking about its readers' buying habits and linking these people with those with something to sell, the Spokane story inspired many publishers.[38]

Another marketing pioneer, the Cedar Rapids (Iowa) *Gazette*, has continued to use the news it gathers in databases and has shown how the effort may take journalists and readers into the unknown. The *Gazette*'s marketing proved so promising that it was made a separate operation, seeking local merchants as clients. The newspaper tries to report what is newsworthy about these businesses. Gazette Database Marketing uses the full resources of the paper for a different mission, which is in part to "help bring the customer into the store more frequently and spend more money." Information that a reporter gathers and information the reader may disclose to the newspaper are being marshalled to produce this busy cash register. In Iowa, there is talk of enlisting carriers to feed the database: the condition of the reader's patio or screen door or roof could be reported and the names of these potential customers sold to advertisers. There is no reason to condemn transactions between willing buyers and sellers. But it is far from clear that readers know that every contact with the press may put them at retail.[39]

The *Gazette*'s MediaStar software allows reporters to use customer profiles in writing stories and the marketing staff to use news items in the search for more customers. With a click on a desktop computer, any street in Cedar Rapids can be summoned up, and every dwelling will glow with a color that reveals the resident's social and economic position. A nest of environmentally conscious college students can be found in a few clicks. They are non-subscribers, and special offers will go out to lure them to the paper. And there may be a story here about Greens. A reporter can have the students' telephone numbers with another couple of clicks. When something blows up in a MediaStar neighborhood, an editor can send reporters in the direction of the smoke and supply them with a profile of the residents they might talk to by the time the journalists pull up to the curb.[40]

More uncharted territory lies ahead when papers have comprehensive, detailed databases on their community and can trade this information for good will — a process that has begun. Which charities, which religions, which political interest groups will be favored with this information? Citizens may feel that their voluntary association is being guided by the press. With the integration of news and marketing, the press will know more than anybody else about everyone's business. And journalists will also gain the suspicion that goes with comprehensive knowledge. The press will have the public relations problem of credit agencies, motor vehicle registries, and tax collectors.[41]

The trade journal *Editor & Publisher* has noted that "when readers call a phone number for a survey of information, it gives newspapers an unprecedented opportunity to capture information about who those might be and what the key might be to their wants and desires." Editors and publishers have rarely thought this to be of interest to readers. The Chicago *Tribune* and the Spokane paper have allowed the public to check a box on their promotions that will keep the information from being passed on to other databases. Privacy is not made to seem a very attractive option, however. Here is how it was put to Spokane readers:

> Your answers will help your daily papers serve you better. This survey also provides you the opportunity to receive offers and information from companies whose products and services match your interests. Please check here if you would prefer NOT to take advantage of this opportunity. □

Most of the new marketing devices do not come with consumer warnings, and the subject of reader privacy rarely surfaces in the news the public sees. Trade journals, so lyrical about the "limitless acquisition of information" in the new databases, give terse assurances that privacy is "handled with extreme care." It would be just as accurate to say that the subject has been locked up and kept away from the public. In the most systematic survey of marketing practices at newspapers, Doug Underwood found "a virtual blackout of information" for the readers about the enterprise of gathering information from this public. A 1994 survey conducted by the database marketing industry found that only 20 percent of magazines published information about the lively trade in their subscribers' names. The respected trade journal *Folio* suggested in 1995 that magazines simply lie when gathering data from readers. A survey shows that ethical concerns are on the decline among MBAs, the core decision makers on databases. Many researchers have found that in the buying and selling lists, data has the recombinant properties of a virus and can easily slip out of the best efforts to confine its growth. Business executives themselves are not sure what they have in database marketing, this "mystifying concept" with its "veil of secrecy."[42]

Vigorous cultivation of lists and databases must produce a good harvest in mailboxes. Direct mail marketing has long been a feared rival of the press, winning advertising dollars that journalists thought were rightfully theirs. But the modern news corporation has moved into the junk mail business. To some extent, this may diminish the pejorative term. A mailing list that uses reading habits to gauge interests will address fewer people who have no intention of trying a product or contributing to a cause. On the other hand, do Americans want a world in which more mail arrives each day tempting them to buy things that they really might want? To give to causes that they endorse? Pertinence is probably not enough to make such mail welcome. Notions of a right to be left alone turn solicitations into junk for many people, and they are going to stay mad as the press unleashes its growing power to mind their business.

The historical lesson that is most frequently heard when publishers get together is a warning tale about the railroads: they declined when they thought only of cars and tracks and did not realize they were in the transportation business. Like the church/state separation, the analogy is curious. Economic historians agree that the railroads' insufficient investment in cars and tracks weakened this once-proud industry. It is not enough to know that you are in the transportation business (as scores of airlines and bus companies found out) if you lose touch with your customers. An obsession with marketing does not guarantee a clear view of business interests. The founder and president of Applied Segmentation Technology, who has guided many publishers into this enterprise, has been shocked by the preference of some of them for "a path of least resistance and immediate gratification." Tom Ratkovich found journalists who have been content to develop a profitable direct mail business, choking off the advertising that would support their newspapers. By taking their eye off their core business of news and information, Ratkovich says, the press is asking for trouble. As newcomers to direct marketing, newspapers can be beaten by the veterans of this industry. When they weaken their commitment to reporting, they lose their competitive advantage in the marketplace.[43]

Similarly, when the press fastens on the discovery of "Winter Affluents" or "Upper Rungs" it writes off readers without economic logic. Marketing texts are clear on this point: "There is no one correct segmentation." Readers can be selected more on the basis of their outlook than on what they are able to buy at present. Segmented markets need not favor the haves; they can reach out to discover those have-nots who are on the make. It makes just as much sense to screen for ambition and talent as it does to find people who are currently in the market for a BMW. In what American city do newspapers canvass people who take out business licenses, pass civil service tests, or improve their property? These strategies have been hinted at by visionaries in the trade press, but if any American newspaper is pursuing this inclusive marketing, it has kept it a secret. Every day, papers receive news of people who have won recognition on the job or in fraternal organizations: loyal secretaries, prize-winning choirs, bowlers heavy with trophies. Nowhere is there a system in place to make sure these people are taking a paper. American dailies could draw a bead on people who have graduated, gotten their first positions in civil service, or started military careers. Advertisers, especially those with a long-term outlook, find these people attractive. There are no guarantees, but this would be a market strategy more in line with the history of the press . . . which is to offer hope and to bet on the future.[44]

The spurious logic of market segmentation has found support from journalists who have lurid visions of privileged subscribers and a doomed majority that print journalism does not want. "As the gulf widens between the rich and poor, between those who are inside the palace and those outside clawing at bones, the paper for those in the circle of the privileged will continue to have an audience," says editor Lewis Lapham, deploring the times from his editor's chair at *Harper's*. "Society is bifurcating between the upwardly mobile and educated and the downwardly mobile or inert," according to Ed Kosner, the editor of *New York*, and he doubts that this second group can be won over to newspapers. These fin de siècle musings are likely to look just as silly as the predictions of an American catastrophe in the 1890s.[45]

Enterprise and success are spread much more widely in America than these publishers seem to think, and so is the interest in hard news. People of all racial backgrounds, economic beginnings, and national origins are good candidates for what serious journalists have to say. The plain, documented lesson of scores of newspapers that failed in the 1960s is that they did not supply as much information about their community and the nation as their successful rivals. Christine D. Urban, who heads a firm that has been hired by scores of papers to assess their audience, has been shaking publishers by their lapels to see that "study after study has proven that . . . blue-collar, working-class, middle-class folks are excellent newspaper readers. They're interested, involved and experienced—often *better* informed about local, national and world events than 'yuppies' or other subgroups prized for their buying power." Similarly, Bill Kovach, ex-editor of the Atlanta *Constitution and Journal*, has described the untapped market for "the daily report of hard news: the events and ideas that directly affect people's lives." Kovach points out that long ago, publishers repeatedly fashioned such papers in the polyglot cities and prospered. "Such a newspaper might create and enlarge an economic niche among a new kind of mass-market consumer," Kovach said.[46]

There can be no dispute that daily papers have been slow to target one of the fastest-growing segments of the American people. In 1990 researchers at the University of Missouri drew up fifty demographic and lifestyle groups and asked managers of the press which they had gone after. Immigrants were fiftieth on the list, though there had been more than thirteen million of these newcomers in the 1980s alone. Strangers to the land, most non-English-speaking, had engaged the imagination of Scripps and Pulitzer and Hearst a century earlier. They won that battle for readership. Editors and publishers of the 1990s, with many more powerful weapons, were in danger of losing the new battle without putting up much of a fight.[47]

It is telling that this conspicuous failure of the press was with non-citizens. A press that cannot engage Americans, native-born and newcomer, *as citizens* will have lost its place in commerce and in governance that it has held since the birth of the republic.

8

"THE PEOPLE!

TRY AND

LICK THAT!"

I. Humphrey Bogart's Hypothesis

For most of its history, the American press has had little trouble picturing the people it reached. Readers were neighbors, townsfolk who easily came into focus. As William Allen White, sage of the Emporia (Kans.) *Gazette*, walked Main Street at the end of the nineteenth century he made the only demographic and psychographic survey he would ever need. He looked into the faces of readers and heard their compliments or insults. Before the twentieth century, a paper or magazine might range far afield for readers, yet keep a comfortable sense that it knew the audience. Readers were all patriotic Americans—or at least all true Democrats, all improving farmers, all diligent housewives. Editors believed that they understood these folks. The memoirs of nineteenth-century journalists are free of the worries that preoccupy the profession today: Where is my audience? Who am I writing for? What news do people want? Journalists of William Allen White's era did not search for the answers, for they did not yet have to face these questions.[1]

As we have seen, economics forced the press to take a fresh look at its audience. But accounting and marketing were not the only new vantage points. The discovery of "professionalism" gave journalists a sharper picture of the reading public. Members of the press argued about this among themselves. But more important, the reporters and editors took their worries about professionalism and the reading public into the new medium that touched every American, the movies. The lively traffic from America's newsrooms to Hollywood defined both the press and the public.

Free of the notion of a profession, the journalist would have a much simpler view of the public. "Professionalism" means duties and standards over and above what the market demands. A journalist could happily give readers what they want—like a jeweler or a chef—if professionalism disappeared. But a professional gives the public what it needs, not simply what it asks for. This is a distinction much studied by social scientists; it is an intellectual divide that emerged in great complexity with the shifting positions of elite groups in both eighteenth- and nineteenth-century America.[2] This is also an analytical construct drawn by Humphrey Bogart after a hard night of drinking in *Deadline U.S.A.* (1952). Bogart is a managing editor, lecturing a newcomer:

> *Bogart:* Newspaperman is the best profession in the world. Know what a profession is?
> *Newcomer:* Skilled job.
> *Bogart (wincing laugh):* Yea, so's repairing watches. Nope! A profession is a performance of a public good. That's why newspaper work is a profession.

Bogart's parting advice as they leave the tavern is: "It may not be the oldest profession, but it's the best." This lesson in *Deadline U.S.A.* was written and directed by an ex-newspaperman. He was doing what came naturally. In the twentieth century the American press has been obsessed with gaining the status of a professional, which has meant that it has talked endlessly about what the public needs. The press has fallen short in its race to join doctors, lawyers, and engineers. But, as an outsider, the press has challenged the secure professional groups for the public's trust. Indeed, it is as a marginal figure, never quite the professional, that the journalist has won public attention. In the mass media, journalists frequently introduced themselves to the public as their saviours and put a vision of the reading public at the center of American popular culture.

2. The Blocked Professional Path

Journalists began talking about their craft as a profession after the Civil War. The journalists' dream was not far-fetched. True, the occupation was not ancient (the term "journalist" became common usage only at the beginning of the nineteenth century). But in profession making, age was not in all ways an advantage. The field had been spared the ravages of egalitarian sentiment in the age of Andrew Jackson. An American elite, at this time, lost many prerogatives associated with the old order of the colonial period. Men of property and standing no longer monopolized careers in government. The clergy lost their last ties to the state. Doors were opened to let almost any white male practice law or medicine. In the decades after the Civil War, medicine, law, and engineering successfully pressed claims for renewed privileges and respect. Occupational groups with greater handicaps than journalism were granted the status of a profession. Dentists performed manual labor, pharmacists bought and sold goods — the very things which a professional, by tradition, could not do. Victorian journalists no longer needed the printer's skills that had marked the field for more than a century, and in modern news organizations the journalist was supposed to be insulated from the business side. It was surely no harder to glorify gentlemen of the press (as they called themselves) than the Americans who fixed teeth or sold potions.[3]

Furthermore, journalists acquired special legal status before the end of the nineteenth century. Reporters had assigned seats in America's legislatures and courts. They crossed police lines by showing their press cards and sat at executions as the public's witness. Journalists gained their first "shield law" in 1896, allowing them to keep information confidential in court. A lawyer sounded the alarm about "a statute making the most irresponsible tramp reporter a privileged person in the matter of communications the same as doctors and lawyers."[4]

American literature had not been kind to journalists, it is true, and novelists such as James Fenimore Cooper and William Dean Howells were no gentler with journalists in their day than Tom Wolfe has been in ours. These attacks in fiction were the most damaging kind — based on close observation. Some newspapermen had joined the harangue, as when E. L. Godkin, editor of the New York *Post*, said that he "would nearly see a son of mine opening a faro bank or an assignation house" as become a journalist. But journalists produced a counter-weight in a celebratory literature of reporting and editing. By the 1880s journalists' lives frequently required more than one volume for the telling. The engravings were lavish, the pages thick and smooth, and these proud memoirs were insistent reminders to the public of the dignity of the press. Most cities of any size had best families associated with the leading papers. A statue, a building, even a park were the tangible signs of journalism's service to the community. A craft that could tap memories of Benjamin Franklin, Horace Greeley, and the ex-slave Frederick Douglass had a call on the nation's imagination.[5]

The fame and privileges of individual journalists of the nineteenth century convinced journalists, but not many others, that this was a profession. As one national magazine said in 1906, "Outside of a newspaper office, a reporter has no professional standing." William Allen White said that commercial pressure had weakened the professional temper of the press. For all its promising early steps, journalism had not yet managed to cross the lines of established professions.[6]

By 1918 journalism did have new ways to win acceptance as a profession. The First World War gave to reporters new visibility and official blessings. The most honored role of the journalist was to sell the war. George Creel and other veterans of the newsroom ran the Committee on Public Information in the Wilson administration. Reporters thus directed the work of subordinate professional groups (including four thousand historians). The daily *Official Bulletin* became America's first newspaper established by law. Jobs and favors to journalists had been handed out since the nation began, of course, but never before had the federal government put a spotlight on their skills and given them so much authority.[7]

Service in war was important for journalists because it was of a piece with efforts to institutionalize respect that had begun just a few years before the mobilization. Universities had been enlisted to legitimate the field. (There was a scattering of courses in the 1890s, the first program at the University of Missouri in 1908, and then, auspiciously, Joseph Pulitzer's gift of a journalism school to Columbia in 1912.) The Pulitzer Prizes, first awarded in 1917, were signs of the parallel process of establishing instant traditions and honors. "The Honorary Fraternity for Journalism," Sigma Delta Chi, was born on campus in 1909. No wonder that Pulitzer was carried away in the bequest to Columbia saying "journalism is, or ought to be, one of the great and intellectual professions . . . exactly as if it were the profession of law or medicine." Younger hands embraced the professional ideal almost as eagerly before the war. The college men who started Sigma Delta Chi removed "honorary" and inserted "professional" on their stationery before the organization was even three years old. They seemed to agree that the blessing given by that word was more up-to-date.[8]

If insistence could make it so, journalists had become professionals. "The Journalist's Creed"—widely circulated in the 1920s—began, "I believe in the profession of journalism." Knopf published *The Ethics of Journalism* in 1924, one of the most agile demonstrations of the progress toward professionalism. The author even took encouragement from prior restraint on the press in the colonial period because "licenses were not required or were required under much less strict provisions for other occupations."[9]

For all the brave talk about professionalism, there were many signs that the elevation of the journalist would be most difficult. Journalists complained of a suffocating anonymity. On daily newspapers, where most of the jobs were, reporters rarely had bylines, and so it was difficult to build a reputation. Men like Ray Stannard Baker left newspapers for muckraking magazines in part to make a name and forge a personal link with the public.[10]

It had long been true that journalism could support few of the Americans it inspired. In nineteenth-century America it was common knowledge that few writers could live on the proceeds from non-fiction books and that it was folly to expect a decent income writing magazine articles. The press corps was noted for its resort to cheap restaurants and dirty shirts. The great majority of reporters and editors on the nation's newspapers were paid a clerk's wages in the first decades of the twentieth century.[11]

Social institutions were no more helpful than the marketplace in giving the journalist the autonomy of established professions. The journalism degree was very slow in becoming either a ticket for entry or a credential for career advancement. The model set in medicine, law, and teaching did not work. Even the simple fellowship of journalists proved counter-productive. By the 1920s most large cities had a press club, originally conceived to exalt the journalist's calling. Some of these were started before the state's bar association. But the clubs proved of little service in profession building. The clubs prospered by attracting outsiders: politicians, advertising and public relations people, as well as business executives who joined to ensure "good press relations." As professionalism in journalism came to be defined as independent judgment and objectivity, the clubs looked subversive (from the reporter's point of view) or useless (in the eyes of citizens who wanted a say in shaping the news). The forms of professional life in journalism often turned out to be empty.[12]

The problem ran deeper, to the mercurial culture of the practitioners themselves. The working press often fancied themselves as bohemians: detached, mocking critics of respectable society. No scholar has actually measured the wildness of this occupational group, but we are on safe ground in concluding that the press was different. There was no other profession whose most visible elite (Washington's Gridiron Club) organized for the purpose of scoffing at authority. Surely no other budding profession celebrated Jack the Ripper (as reporters in Chicago did in their Whitechapel Club) or convened in "the bucket of blood" (a lair for the Denver press corps).

Drinking toasts from skulls (a habit of reporters in Chicago) was less harmful to professionalism than working conditions. Theodore Dreiser, in his account of newspaper days, said that city rooms were jungles in which reporters "had a kind of nervous, resentful terror in their eyes as have animals when they are tortured." Journalists were too busy and too scared to cooperate with one another, Dreiser said. He was talking about Joseph Pulitzer's newsroom under the spell of that publisher's drive for circulation. The very professional standards Pulitzer talked about as an old man were the ones his early methods of success ruled out.[13]

The most serious students of journalism bestowed the title of professional on reporter and editor, but nothing much more than the title. According to Walter Lippmann, the task of journalists was to be a sturdy conduit between a policy elite that thought through important matters and the citizens who would ratify decisions of the best minds. In influential books such as *Public Opinion* (1922) Lippmann taught deference to most of the working press: "There is no discipline in applied psychology, as there is a discipline in medicine, engineering, or even law, which has authority to direct the journalist's mind when he passes from the news to the vague realm of truth." Lippmann spent the 1920s running the editorial page of the New York *World*, the newspaper that Joseph Pulitzer's will installed as a beacon to lead the press to the highest standards of professionalism. Lippmann did defend the press against many detractors, but he also demonstrated that journalists could not come into professional harbor.[14]

Against all of these discouragements — and sometimes because of the forces that upset professional development — the ideal of professionalism remained strong among the working press. The people with the most power in America's newsrooms were the first to organize on a professional basis. The American Society of Newspaper Editors, open only to top editors in cities with over fifty thousand population, was founded in 1922. Their code of ethics said that journalism was in essence a "high trust," and the ASNE preamble mentioned "profession" or "professional" eleven times in thirty-five lines. Its annual conventions in the 1920s and 1930s heard calls for the journalist to emulate the standards set by better established professions. The newspaper itself was to be the citizen's "lawyer without fee."[15]

By the mid-1930s there were signs that journalism had closed the lead held by established professions. More than fifty colleges and universities had full programs in journalism by 1930. Shield laws, seen by *Editor & Publisher* as a test of whether the press "will have the rights enjoyed by other professions," spread to more states. When Allen Nevins wrote the article on journalism for the *Encyclopedia of the Social Sciences* in 1937, he organized the survey around the promising ways journalists had patterned themselves after established professions in order to serve the whole nation.[16]

This was an inspirational but not a realistic outlook in the mid-1930s. The field was in a quandary: the more institutions journalism turned to for support, the more uncertain journalists became about professional ideals. This was a lesson learned in the greatest organizational achievement of the inter-war years, the American Newspaper Guild.

The Guild, formed in 1933, was an unanticipated outcome of section 7a of the National Recovery Act, a New Deal measure aimed at blue-collar labor. The NRA was the legal foundation for the organization of newspaper editorial workers. At first, the Guild made many efforts to enhance the professional standing of news people. The name itself was auspicious: in choosing "guild" the journalists chose the mother institution of several English professions. The charter cited the need for confidentiality backed by shield laws. There were schemes for in-service training, a code of ethics, and prizes for distinguished reporting. The president of the New York Guild, Allen Raymond, faced the question of professional entry requirements without flinching. He called himself "an old tramp reporter." But Raymond told his fellow journalists that he wanted standards "raised high enough and restrict entrance so that we would not have been able to meet it when we came in. . . . The law and medicine have done that. Just because I couldn't qualify under this new thing and still am hanging around doesn't indicate it is wrong."[17]

Talk like this in the Guild was rare after the first two years. Bread-and-butter issues were all-important by the late 1930s. The employers discredited the ideal of professionalism in the conflict over organization. Publishers attempted to negotiate themselves out of the NRA codes on wages and hours by gaining the status of professionals for their editorial employees (a loophole in the President's order enforcing the act). The NRA accepted the employers' proposal that any reporter earning more than thirty-five dollars a week was a professional. Reporters and editors complained of this self-serving use of the term, and their own talk of professional standards waned. As the historian of the Guild has observed, it did not take much time for reporters to see that they could not get what they most wanted by pretending to be the American Medical Association.[18]

For many observers of the American press, the gates to professionalism seemed blocked by the mid-1930s. The press possessed some outward signs of the established professions, and some of their expertise was respected. But there was wide agreement that the term "professional" needed quotes if it was to fit a reporter. Leo Rosten, in a discerning study, *The Washington Correspondents* (1937), gave strict advice on usage: "Newspaper work . . . is a profession with no professional standards, no professional discipline, no examining or accrediting bodies, no agreement upon norms for testing competence." Rosten found "increased personal and professional insecurities" in the 150 reporters he studied. Several recent students of the press corps of the inter-war years have reached the same conclusion.[19]

What qualified a citizen to be a journalist? There were few occupations in America where the answer was less concrete. In the 1930s no one seemed to have a confident answer. The two most admired journalists in America in the inter-war years were Walter Lippmann and Edward R. Murrow. Neither man had received a day of training in a school or in a newsroom to be a journalist.[20]

3. Surrogate Professionals and Their Faux Public

Journalists did not step out of the public eye as doubts about their professional standing persisted. Ex-reporters brought the newsroom to the Hollywood studios. Journalists did not win the argument over whether they were a profession; instead; they changed the terms of the debate. Most movies found an equivalent for professional standing in the bohemian ways of journalists. A few movies had a darker vision of the press, seeing it as an institution that had captured the hearts of the American people, only to betray this trust. Whether the journalist was a good or a bad surrogate for the established professions, these films had a common vision of the reading public. In the dominant entertainment form of the twentieth century, the American public saw itself as consumers of news who were credulous, impulsive, and dependent. Journalists cannot blame Hollywood for this story. They made it up themselves.

Telling the story of journalism to movie audiences was a new turn for popular culture. The American theater had done little with the newsroom before World War I. Stage lawyers, stage physicians, and stage ministers came easily to mind, a newspaper editor said, but audiences, he regretted, knew nothing about *his* job.[21] Newspaper life became a main theme of popular entertainment with the success of the 1928 play by Ben Hecht and Charles MacArthur, *The Front Page*. This became an early talkie in 1931. Reporters and their attentive public were constantly before movie audiences in this decade: *Five Star Final* (1931); *Blessed Event* (1932); *I Cover the Waterfront* (1933); *It Happened One Night* (1934); *Libeled Lady* (1936); and the technicolor *Nothing Sacred* (1937). Clark Gable, Cary Grant, Fred MacMurray, James Cagney, Humphrey Bogart, James Stewart, Edward G. Robinson, and Spencer Tracy had all begun their string of roles as reporters. By 1941 Jean Arthur, Rosalind Russell, and Barbara Stanwyck had established a woman's place in the Hollywood newsroom. The Second World War did not push the beat reporter from the screen. The most celebrated fetishes of the Fourth Estate were created in these films: Joel McCrea's trenchcoat in *Foreign Correspondent* (1940); the fedora Jimmy Stewart won't remove in *The Philadelphia Story* (1940); and Orson Welles's incantation "Rosebud" before a crystal ball in *Citizen Kane* the following year. Hollywood faced the challenge of television with stars in the newsroom: Stewart in *Call Northside 777* (1947); the newcomer Kirk Douglas in *Ace in the Hole* (1951); William Holden in *The Turning Point* (1952); Bogart's performance in *Deadline U.S.A.* (1952); and Burt Lancaster in *Sweet Smell of Success* (1957).

The number of newspapers has declined, and the percentage of Americans who read them has gone down, but Hollywood has persisted in thinking that the newsroom would win at the box office.

It is not possible to make an exact count of films about journalism, but rough figures make the point well enough. In 1991 one researcher built a list of a thousand American movies about news. Many scholars have noted the obsession with the newsroom in the first decade of talking pictures. During the 1930s and 1940s the nation's movie houses frequently sold eighty million tickets a week and some four hundred films had a large role in shaping the public's notions about the press. More than the dashing reporters, the moviegoers saw themselves, for Hollywood supplied a picture of the audience for news.[22]

The Americans who have made movies have usually viewed their previous employment as a poor subject matter for the screen. MGM and Warner Brothers had no interest in the work of their founders, who were furriers and tobacco salesmen of the Lower East Side. Nor did Hollywood recruit experts to work on genre films. It proved possible to supply the public with an endless string of gangster films without hiring criminals or lawyers or cops. But journalism was different. Ex-journalists controlled the genre. The writers, producers, and directors of these films were frequently doing something more than repeating success with a proven formula. Here were ex-reporters and ex-editors, speaking from the heart. Behind Hollywood's newsroom stood a corps of lapsed journalists. Ben Hecht (ex-Chicago *Daily News*) brought the newspaper game into *Viva Villa* (1934), *Nothing Sacred* (1937), *Foreign Correspondent* (1940), and *Comrade X* (1940). He also helped perform the gender change on the character of Hildy Johnson that made *The Front Page* into *His Girl Friday* (1940). Charles MacArthur (ex-Chicago *Herald-Examiner*) was a script doctor on newspaper films. Myles Connolly (ex-Boston *Post*) contributed to Frank Capra's vision of the press (the character played by Clark Gable in *It Happened One Night* was a chemist, not a reporter, before Connolly got his hands on the script). Herman J. Mankiewicz (ex-New York *Times*) became Hollywood's highest-paid writer and the collaborator on *Citizen Kane*. Herman's younger brother, Joseph, was an ex-reporter turned producer of such biting portrayals of the press as *Love on the Run* (1936), *Philadelphia Story*, and *Woman of the Year*. Maurine Watkins (ex-Chicago *Tribune*) helped write *Sob Sister* (1931) and *Libeled Lady* (1936). Her broadway play of 1927, *Chicago*, went through the typewriter of Nunnally Johnson (ex-New York *Tribune*) to become *Roxie Hart* (1941). Other names will be added to this tally later, but the list is long enough now to make the simple point: far more than other occupational groups, the popular film version of journalism was shaped by people who had been practitioners.[23]

The apparent jumble of newspaper stories in the movies is really not chaotic. At the Ur-level was the Ben Hecht–Charles MacArthur property, *The Front Page*. This examination of reporting did not fit Allen Nevins's picture of a young but maturing profession. On stage the journalists competed in telling lies and double-crossing each other. The press celebrated its liberation from an alien world where citizens believed what they were told, took out mortgages, and got married. Both on Broadway and in cinema, *The Front Page* was a breakthrough in profanity. The fast, overlapping dialogue seemed to mark American journalists as clearly as if they wore white coats.

The simplest idea that *The Front Page* got across was that a good American journalist would do anything to get a story out to the public and that these readers would swallow anything. Anything. Hecht and MacArthur's play had the reporters bribe sources, hide a convicted murderer, then blackmail the sheriff and the mayor. Hildy Johnson and his editor, Walter Burns, reminisce about writing the diaries and confessions of criminals for their paper and embellishing disaster ("Even the telegraph operator was crying!" Johnson re-called). With renewed imagination on the front page, Burns says, "Why, they'll be naming streets after you. Johnson Street!" Hecht and MacArthur did not stretch the record much of what had been accomplished in their day on Chicago newspapers. *Editor & Publisher* admitted this when the play was on Broadway. But now audacity was to be a norm, not the boast of a few wild reporters. Screenwriters settled down to see if they could top *The Front Page*.[24]

Hollywood did not fail. In *I Cover the Waterfront*, a film based on a popular memoir, the reporter deposited a drowned man on the table in front of his editor to show that the story was coming along nicely.

This element of calculation in rash action goes to Hollywood's central message about journalism as a profession. The movies were Jacksonian in the sense that freedom from high culture and a touch of the barbarian often made the journalist wiser and more trustworthy. At the beginning of Alfred Hitchcock's *Foreign Correspondent*, the managing editor rejected the members of his staff who knew something about Europe, disqualifying one reporter because he had written an academic book on the subject. What was needed, the editor said, was a reporter who "doesn't know the difference between an ism and a kangaroo." The editor found a reporter who was unaware that Europe was in crisis but had proved his mettle by assaulting a policeman. It was "the fresh, unused mind" that made the journalist.[25]

Frank Capra's *State of the Union* (1948) telescoped what Hollywood had said about journalists for two decades. Reporters rose from their gin game to ask if a publisher would die on deadline with time for pictures of his last moments. The publisher used his last breaths to fire an editor who dared to show an independent mind. All this happened in the first sixty seconds of *State of the Union*. The everyman reporter, Spike, cheered as he lost *two* jobs in the last minute of the film. Capra's work gave the game away. Firings and resignations were the sublime moments of these stories. Capra's ace reporters were splendid quitters, and in such very good company. Hildy exploded as he/she quit (an act of exquisite complexity that took up the whole evening in the theater). Jed Leland's partings from Charles Foster Kane made much of the story of *Citizen*

Kane. A publisher and editor begged for the help of their rogue ex-reporter through *Libeled Lady.* (Ten years later in the remake, *Easy to Wed* (1946), the journalist again tortured his old bosses before quitting the newspaper game in triumph.) It is hard to view these partings as simple plot turns. They are too prominent, and sometimes they are the central tension in the movie. What Hollywood offered was an idealization of becoming an ex-journalist: the thrill of telling the publisher off, gaining integrity, serving the public by telling the truth. Again, the screen version of a life in journalism was not so much a slap at professionalism as it was a grasp for those things a true profession was supposed to deliver.

In the Hollywood version of the newsroom, the journalist was fenced off from the respectable professions but still got the fruit. It is not simply that heiresses and heirs dropped before these rugged, lower-class reporters—*Platinum Blonde* (1931), *It Happened One Night* (1934), *Love on the Run* (1936), *Mr. Deeds Goes to Town* (1936), and *The Philadelphia Story* (1940). No person of privilege was a match for the beat reporter. The journalist, however frantic, was wiser than the so-called experts and more trustworthy. Lawyers, business-men, doctors, politicians . . . nearly everyone the public is supposed to trust is shown up in these films. Jean Arthur of *Mr. Deeds* shouts, "My opinion's as good as these quack psychiatrists," and, this being a Capra film, the news-woman is right. Pancho Villa (in Ben Hecht's telling) is married by the omni-scient, gringo reporter, not a priest. The untutored tough guy of *Foreign Correspondent* discovers the fascist menace, while respectable people look the other way. Experts hide knowledge. Journalists tell the town. The journalist's dream of professional standing had more to it than higher education, higher standards, and higher salaries. What the journalist wanted was what all profes-sional groups have wanted: higher social standing and trust. On the screen, the reporter ascended to this level. Hecht's summary of the Front Page era was the celebration of a profession that had conquered all:

> No other profession, even that of arms, produces as fine a version of the selfless hero as journalism does. . . . A good newspaperman, of my day, was to be known by the fact that he was ashamed of being anything else. He scorned offers of double wages in other fields. He sneered at all the honors life held other than the one to which he aspired, which was a simple one. He dreamed of dying in harness, a casual figure full of anonymous power; and free.[26]

Hollywood's screwball comedies and breathless adventures of the newsroom were a surrogate for professional demands.

On the screen, the ersatz profession of journalism was often bathed in demo-cratic sentiment. "I don't like privileged people," Alan Ladd tells the big shots in his role as a reporter in *Chicago Deadline* (1949). Experts were disgraced by a desire to serve the few. It was service to all that made film heroes: the doctor or clergyman who would minister to outcasts, the lawyer who would take a poor man's case, or the journalist who would wake up Americans. Part outlaw, selfish or spoiled, the reporter could still save us. If only the journalist would keep free of temptation, if only the public listened.

A salute from reporter to the public was often a part of Hollywood's story of news. *Citizen Kane* was typical in its endorsement of democratic sentiment that had been betrayed by a publisher. The public turned on Kane and his papers when he strayed from truly representing the common man. In *Keeper of the Flame* (1941), Spencer Tracy assures his source that the reading public could absorb any shock. Katharine Hepburn, that source, has just shown him a list of newspaper editors who "felt that the public was a great stupid beast." But Tracy, as a reporter, trusts his readers:

> People are not children. Sometimes they act like children when you get 'em scared and confused. But down in their hearts they know and they're not afraid. They want the truth and they can take it.

Frank Capra's *Meet John Doe* (1941) said it simply: "The People! Try and lick that!" These were the sentiments of journalists in the film who had been ruthless cynics while working up the story of the everyman John Doe. According to the Warner Brothers script, "They exit, arm in arm, as the music swells—suggesting emergence from darkness and confusion to light and understanding."[27]

Most Hollywood films about news had it this way: the job of reporters was to be rogues who would guard the public; the role of the public was to be dupes just long enough for journalists to save them.

The most popular and honored picture about journalism of modern times, *All the President's Men* (1976), kept the faith that roguish reporters might restore a democracy that people in high places had ruined. Never before was the story line of a picture closer to real political change. The Washington *Post's* exposé of the Republican break-in at the Democratic headquarters at the Watergate had helped bring down the Nixon administration by the time the film came out. Carl Bernstein, played by Dustin Hoffman, and Bob Woodward, played by Robert Redford, are misfits who, like Hildy Johnson, come alive only as they can work on their big story. Though hardly the pirates who had taken command of the Hollywood newsroom of the 1930s, Hoffman and Redford will break rules, play tricks, and make mistakes. But no other profession, certainly not law enforcement, does better in meeting its responsibility to the public. The editors are godly and wise. The reporters triumph by listening to ordinary citizens who have been caught up in GOP dirty tricks. These secretaries and clerks carry the story as effectively as the high-placed and mysterious source called Deep Throat. The fear in the voices of Americans registers the sinister story that the reporters put together. Hoffman and Redford are hearing confessions with the patience of a psychologist or priest. (Rosalind Russell was the pioneer of this therapeutic manner in her version of Hildy Johnson in *His Girl Friday.*) In the end, you can't lick the people. A teletype pounds out the news that the Nixon administration has fallen.

Self-congratulatory and gruffly egalitarian as they were, Hollywood's journalism films could also be cruel, both to reporters and public. The California reporter in *I Cover the Waterfront* describes his most popular work as "a lot of cheap baloney dished up for the farmers who come out here to rot in the sunshine. Bunk! Fake! Drivel!" This was a reprise of Hildy Johnson's famous soliloquy on reporting in Chicago:

> Journalists! Peeking through keyholes! Running after fire engines like a lot of coach dogs! Waking people up in the middle of the night to ask them what they think of Mussolini. Stealing pictures off old ladies of their daughters that get raped in Oak Park. A lot of lousy, daffy buttinskis, swelling around with holes in their pants, borrowing nickels from office boys! And for what? So a million hired girls and motorman's wives'll know what's going on.[28]

Neither film shattered the romance of news, for the reporters recovered their breath, chased down big stories, and glowed when they made the front page. There was satisfaction in serving the farmers and hired girls, after all.

Hollywood, guided by ex-journalists, could play rougher. *Five Star Final* (1931), also at the Ur-level of Hollywood's newsroom, showed that self-respect was impossible on a gossipy tabloid and that the reading public could not be saved. Edward G. Robinson is a managing editor who does not worry about standing on a pedestal before readers, for "if I sat on a cigar box I'd be over ours." Reporter Boris Karloff follows his instructions and dresses as a clergyman to get the big story. But this scoop does not level society; it prompts the suicides of two blameless citizens. Robinson quits, throwing a telephone through *two* glass doors (a feat scaled back to a single window in *Meet John Doe*). He will not "sell papers to a gang of dirty illiterates." *Five Star Final* was based on the play by the editor of a New York tabloid who wrote, he said, to acknowledge his guilt.[29]

Billy Wilder pushed the amorality of reporter and reader to the limit in *Ace in the Hole* (1951). Wilder had chased after hot stories for papers in Vienna and Berlin during the 1920s, and in working on the screenplay he had the help of another ex-newsman, Lesser Samuels. They created a reporter who left an injured man in a cave for a week in order to draw out the string of good stories. Readers hang on the news of Leo Minosa's fate. The public gathers at the disaster site in order to buy souvenirs, ride the Ferris wheel, and hear the new song, "We're Coming, Leo."[30]

Hollywood has been giving up on readers ever since, especially when seasoned journalists have written the scripts. Fred Barron left the underground press to write *Between the Lines* (1977), an affectionate memoir of the counterculture that was made with the cooperation of leading alternative papers. Busy with their tangled lives, these reporters know nothing of their public except that "people don't care!" This is the kind of talk that Julie Christie hears from media consultants in *Power* (1986), a demolition of political handlers. Christie, the only print journalist in the story, hates the life enough to divorce the slickest consultant, but she cannot muster a defense of the public. This script was written by an award-winning reporter from Maine, begun on a Nieman Fellowship at Harvard. *Absence of Malice* (1981), one of the best-informed films ever made about the newsroom, is no more curious about readers. The screenplay was written by a Pulitzer Prize–winning journalist, Kurt Luedtke, in his first effort in this form after a fifteen-year career at top newspapers. His dialogue for the movie has the investigative reporter arguing with a businessman named Gallagher who has been cast under suspicion by her story:

> *Reporter:*   Look, Gallagher. If they clear you I'll write about that too.
> *Gallagher:*   What page? When you say somebody's guilty everybody believes you. See, you say he's innocent—nobody cares.
> *Reporter:*   It's not the paper's fault. It's people. People believe whatever they want to believe.

Ludetke's picture of bad sheep kept by careless press shepherds was drawn in richer detail in lectures that followed the success of the film. "The public knows whatever you choose to tell it, no more, no less," he told the American Newspaper Publishers Association. Ludetke dressed the publishers down because of their "arrogance." "The press is full of itself these days and, frequently, it is simply full of it," he said. The reporter quits the newsroom in the movie, and the screenwriter, figuratively, throws rocks at the bosses.[31]

Whether the reading public reached a political epiphany or was bamboozled when Hollywood was through with it, it was usually a faux public. To see what made it false, it is best to return to Bogart, who as managing editor in *Deadline U.S.A.* had many analytical gifts. This film begins with Bogart telling reporters how to make complex stories meaningful to readers. Translate economic statistics into personal budgets, he says; avoid a parade of bureaucratic names; help your readers to see how a tax plan will affect their lives. This is surely the only tough-guy picture to begin with sound advice on writing. There is more instruction in *Deadline U.S.A.* about discarding frivolous stories and making sure that citizens get the information they need. But readers are not simply taken seriously in the film; they are seen as people with a mind of their own and the ability to become full citizens, no matter where they start in America. Bogart's paper breaks the big story because its humblest readers trust it. The ace reporter and vital source are both taken out by organized crime; they cannot help the paper. The evidence Bogart needs is brought to him by a reader. The editor asks why she did not go to the police. With a heavy accent, this poor woman explains:

> I do not know police. I know newspaper. This newspaper. For thirty-one years I
> know this paper. I come to America. I wish to be good citizen. How to do this?
> From newspaper. It shows me how to read and write. . . . Your paper is not
> afraid, I am not afraid.

In 1990 Charles Champlin of the Los Angeles *Times* called this "as eloquent a
tribute as a metropolitan daily ever received." Champlin learned from Richard
Brooks, the screenwriter and director, what lay behind the scene:

> "That was my mother," Brooks told me. "My parents both learned to read and
> write English from the Philadelphia Bulletin. They both worked in factories and
> went to night school three nights a week, and read the Bulletin. And the Bulletin
> was the paper the movie was about."[32]

This brings into focus what the films about the press so conspicuously lack:
citizens who follow the news with a critical eye. The point is not that Hollywood failed to meet some quota of newspaper autodidacts or empowered
readers. The point is that in these films there were few people following the
press with a mind of their own. In most films, readers are ciphers. They do not
speak up or even show themselves.

Consider Hollywood's roasting of gossip sheets, a pious exercise that has
been going on for six decades. These are films about the retailers of scandal and
their victims, not readers hungry for this news. People who follow scandal are
no more than phantoms. The exception proves the rule. *Blessed Event* (1932)
opens with furious subscribers packed into the editor's office, waiting to tell
him what they think about the window into people's sex life his paper has just
opened. The editor will make time for only one reader, who explodes:

> Why, I used to be the only one in the house that looked at the morning paper!
> But since you've been running this filth about "blessed events," my wife and my
> two daughters and even my maid make a bee-line for that paper.

That is it for the public. People scrambling for information and reveling in
scandal are outside the frame Hollywood has built for the popular press. Nobody who is having *fun* with trashy news gets into these stories. Managing its
own fans, film has given little thought to the fans of another medium.

When we do see readers, they are gloriously depraved, as in the carnival of
readers in *Ace in the Hole*, or giddy with civic virtue (the Frank Capra version).
But what are they, really? In *Meet John Doe*, the line between depravity and
virtue is faint. The huge assembly of folks from the John Doe Clubs turns on
their hero when the fascist publisher sends newsboys into their ranks with the
extra, JOHN DOE A FAKE! MILLIONS VICTIMIZED! The plutocrat takes the
microphone away from John Doe and tells the people, "You can read all about
it in your newspapers there. . . . You look into your papers, ladies and gentlemen." That does it. The people assault John Doe with what they have read,
hurling the papers in his face, driving him out of the convention. Only when

the public has gone home, freed itself from the lying press, and begun to talk again about John Doe's ideas will citizens be ready for their saviour. On Christmas Eve John Doe is reborn in public esteem with the aid of the journalists who now see the light.[33]

The public melts away in *All the President's Men*. Hoffman and Redford may have the common touch, but the reporters are, so often, lone figures on the landscape. Workaholics, they hunker by themselves in rat's-nest rooms. Crowds disappear from the streets, parks, and buildings of the capital when these reporters venture forth. (By contrast, the President's multitude of admirers are the Greek chorus of the film, speaking up on the television sets that keep company with the lonely journalists.) There are few indications in this film that people will ever show up to take in the big story. In making up the front page, an editor jokes that an item about miraculous weather in the Philippines is the only story that everyone will read. "Nobody gives a shit" is the final verdict on Watergate by the managing editor. The only time the reporters make contact with a reader, and it is a very friendly reception, it is all a mistake and the reporters flee when they realize that this person cannot help them.

The Hollywood newsroom has been populated by reporters who keep their distance from readers. In fact and in legend, journalists have faced mobs, from the times of antislavery to the days of civil rights. While countless screen lawyers face down angry crowds, journalists have rarely been connected to bellowing readers. Briefly, we see rallies denouncing Charles Foster Kane as a reactionary and an octopus, but the publisher is in his sanctum of San Simeon. The castle in California is on a different scale than the apartments of Woodward and Bernstein, but these lonely workplaces all suggest a life cut off from the public. Alan Pakula, who directed *All the President's Men*, made the apotheosis of the reclusive journalist in *The Parallax View* (1974). Warren Beatty is the reporter at work in the deserted newsroom and lonely rented rooms. He does not look at his own paper, and he never meets a reader.

"Circulation" in the newspaper film is simply the hot blood and hormones that course through the reporter's body. The Walter Winchell–style columnist of *Sweet Smell of Success* (1957) sees his audience as nothing more than an extension of his own personality. The gossip reporter wants an innocent man he has quarreled with destroyed, for "that boy wiped his feet on the choice, the predilections of 60 million men and women in the greatest country in the world. . . . It wasn't me he criticized, it was my readers!" An obnoxious fellow, but the columnist makes the argument that was taken for granted in most Hollywood stories of the press: the reporter was the ideal citizen, and there was no need to bring the reading public into focus.

Modern newspaper movies, especially those shaped by real journalists, treat readers as unstable, even pathological elements in the story. *Absence of Malice* showed the Miami woman whose privacy had been violated gathering up the newspaper from her neighbors' front yards in a pathetic effort to hide the story. (It is typical of the genre that we learn nothing of people who *got* their paper.) *The Mean Season* (1985) brings the reader to life . . . as a serial killer. Kurt Russell is a young reporter for a Miami paper who is emotionally burnt out. Will he follow his girlfriend to renew community ties at a small paper in Colorado? He cannot because a series of murders is too big a story to miss. The killer calls him to praise his reporting and to see that he stays ahead of other journalists on the story. The lucky reporter also gets fan mail, for the first time. He is contemptuous of this correspondence and lets others read it to him. Russell takes the time to meet one reader who has a lead. This interview in a mobile home looks to be the same type of encounter with an eccentric citizen that gives texture to crime films. But the tip is a clever hoax, and Russell files a story that is wrong. This was no ordinary reader, but the killer himself. One nervous reader finally does come forward with a good tip for the police, but he seems to be almost as much a failure in life as the psychopath. *The Mean Season* was based on a novel by John Katzenbach, a reporter for the Miami *Herald*. Katzenbach was on the set to see that the story of news that got on the screen was true to life. As a reviewer noted, the film added to the impression that, in Florida at least, the ethics of the press wilted with the heat. More than the professionals, the public has broken down, and reading was equated with danger.[34]

It might be expected that films modeled after journalists' lives would give only a sketchy picture of readers. This audience is not very real to many reporters or editors. Their desks do not pile up with reader mail. Robert Darnton, now a historian of eighteenth-century France, has received more correspondence from readers in this field than he got in the 1960s when he was a reporter with stories on the front page of the New York *Times*. In the 1970s the sociologist Herb Gans was a fly on the wall of the leading newsweeklies and found journalists contemptuous of letters (save for the corrections of factual errors). Only recently has the newsroom had to bother with marketing surveys with their table of demographic categories and invitations to think about "Winter Affluents," waiting for news. Many news organizations have navigated the twentieth century with simple mental pictures of who they were writing for: a twelve-year-old girl. Sociologists have concluded that reporters and editors live by "audience lore," not by any coherent body of facts about their readers.[35]

These facts of life in the newsroom do not make Hollywood's determination to show news without its audience less remarkable. The inner life of their craft consumes the attention of most occupational groups. There is no reason for a storyteller to honor this narrow vision. Why not make the letters-to-the-editor page come alive, as well as the front page? As an *institution*, the press has been inundated with mail from readers. Hollywood got hold of the newsroom story at the very time that publications drew attention to reader opinions. The New

York *Times* gave letters a fixed place in the paper in 1931. *Time* came out with separate volumes of correspondence between 1934–37, the letters it could not fit into its extensive column for reader mail in the magazine. There are no reliable figures for the number of letters to the press over time, but no one in the industry has the impression that reader mail has fallen off. At the beginning of the 1970s, the New York *Times* was getting forty thousand letters to the editor every year. At *Time* magazine letters from readers doubled during Watergate. The newsweekly got eighty thousand letters to the editor as this story unfolded in 1973. In a fifteen-month period, *Time* editors got about thirty-five thousand pieces of mail on this one subject. *USA Today* was getting more than twenty thousand letters annually at the beginning of the 1990s. The *National Enquirer* gets a million letters a year and enjoys the distinction of having its own zip code. Hollywood has occasionally cast an eye on the lovelorn, writing to the press with their problems. But the citizen who wants to straighten out the editor, or other Americans, has played an exceedingly small role in the drama of news.[36]

Making a film about news in which the audience is asleep or deranged is like making a film about musicians in which the audience cannot hear. Only the convention is that this makes sense for films about news. Fans have an honored place in films about entertainers and athletes. It is a wonder that fans are an afterthought for films about the press. Screen lawyers appeal to juries who will get their moment in the film to deliberate; screen politicians must play scenes with voters; Hollywood's priests and evangelists have had followers who came to life. Journalists, alone, have found in Hollywood such splendid isolation from the people they addressed and claimed to serve.

4. Readers at the Gates

It is surprising to find that popular films about the press, over six decades, have had much to do with dust-ups about the status of journalism that began in the nineteenth century. It is more surprising that Hollywood's view of the reading public tracks what political philosophers and social scientists have been saying. In their view of the public, films about journalists have amplified the work of scholars.

Much of our political vocabulary, "electorate," "public," and "forum," for instance, consists of words that once meant visible things. These were groups of people or areas of ground that were easy to see in classical Athens or Rome. In the modern world, these terms can be meaningful only if media are doing their job. Most journalism is as an enterprise in forming imagined communities, ties among readers that are too weak to hold without constant reinforcement. A strong sense of nationhood can not be sustained without a press, and the media of early America were a daily promoter of nationalism. Partisan newspapers and magazines of this era made the citizen's duty clear. With their lists of names ("Ourselves" in the *Democratic Review*) and their mobilization of voters in rallies, the press assembled the Americans who had a role to play in politics and introduced them to one another. But in a vast urban nation where the right of political participation has become universal, it has become much harder to picture citizens in political life. Modern media must struggle to make the abstractions of a political community into something tangible. Even on the main street of Emporia, Kansas, a century ago, the "public" was becoming harder to grasp. Editor William Allen White was confounded by the rise of people who called themselves "populists" and also had to accommodate women into his picture of political life when they got the vote. In the twentieth century, journalists and social scientists have struggled to supply pictures of "the people" that are as concrete as those in earlier times.[37]

The vagaries of public opinion were already notorious among American social scientists at the beginning of the twentieth century. The "phantom public" was a term coined by Walter Lippmann, in the same books of the 1920s in which he told journalists that full professional standing would always be outside their grasp. Left to themselves, citizens were amorphous and confused, Lippmann argued. They were late-comers to the theater who took in the play only long enough to find a hero and a villain, and then were out the door. Without the aid of skilled political leaders and journalists, he believed, the public was ephemeral and impotent.[38]

The phrase "public opinion" became a synonym for polling data in Lippmann's day. The public was quantified in newspapers and magazines, as it was in scholarly work. George Gallup's research organization was founded on commissions for newspapers in the 1930s, and the tables of numbers they printed became the only clear picture a reader was likely to get of what the public wanted. Quantification was the way the press made the public real. The chart, that fire bell of typography, came into the news in the early twentieth century as a way to express public attitudes. Opinion now spiked up and fell, like a fever. Citizens could place themselves against the columns of a bar graph or on the slice of a pie chart. These visual abstractions have come to be taken for granted, though there was little precedent in the first two centuries of American journalism. Reducing the public to a chart may be the most arresting change made by the press of the twentieth century.[39]

Reporting public opinion in this way, even with proper statistical techniques and careful phrasing of questions, leads to many kinds of distortion. Surveys assign identities to citizens that they may regard as irrelevant (Democrat, Catholic, Generation X). Polling often teases opinions out of people who improvise to please the questioner. Political scientists have long known that most people on most issues have "non-attitudes," that is, unformed or contradictory feelings. The graphic display of polling data short-circuits the political process as it suggests that opinions are headed one way. The voice of the people, when polls are the listening device, is likely to be an echo as respondents give back what the polls tell them is the trend. Polls are poor devices to show a wide range of beliefs, and they cast citizens into rigid categories. Surveys usually ignore deliberative judgments, the views of citizens who have informed themselves on the issue and talked out their views. Thus polls show citizens placed on the spot, not their potential. This critique is associated with the left in modern America, arguably the loser in seeking public favor. It is well to remember, however, that many of these insights can be traced to conservatives at the beginning of the century who fought against anything resembling a plebescite.[40]

The press has followed social scientists in another problematic way of finding the public, the study of interest groups. Through work at the grass roots using direct mail, phone calls, and ads (with their handy coupons), interest groups can mobilize impressive audiences. Congress got twenty-two million letters in the early 1980s from citizens rallying to the cries of financial institutions about tax withholding on the individual investor. For many political scientists, organized interests are the full story of the public's role in governing. This is a powerful, but not a humble, outlook: "When the groups are adequately stated, everything is stated. When I say everything I mean everything." To be outside these groups, to be merely a member of the general public, was to have no influence at all. As with polling, the press is party to this simplification when it makes interest groups the narrative elements of coverage. If they are the only sources and their arguments are the story, unattached citizens seem irrelevant to the political process. This ignores roughly three-quarters of the American people: that majority at the end of the twentieth century who have not joined or contributed to groups with a political agenda. Seen this way, the public is in even worse shape than Lippmann thought. As most Americans hurry out of the theater, no one listens to them.[41]

In a review of the concept of the "public" in the social sciences (and in much of the press) it is difficult not to sound like a screenwriter. "The term has gone dead," a communications scholar concluded.[42]

But the press has not given up on the patient. While Hollywood and many scholars have found the public to be elusive, one-dimensional, and distracted, the press has made some progress in finding signs of life. Journalists of the late twentieth century have refined their methods of bringing the voices of ordinary people into the news. Letters-to-the-editor pages have flourished, as have regular features that answer reader questions. "Mood of America" pieces have grown into a genre in covering politics. On subjects such as the homeless, immigrant neighborhoods, black ghettoes, and the new urban landscape of AIDS patients and the mentally ill, reporters have matched the accomplishments of earlier journalists in telling stories of the underdog. The muckrakers of the first years of this century and the chroniclers of the Great Depression did not do a better job revealing the wide scope and rough texture of American life. The idea that journalism is capable of a "tough-minded civic transformation" is alive and well.[43]

If this were happening in a Frank Capra film, William Greider could write the dialogue for the scoffer, the apparently unassailable critic of democratic promise. In the pages of *Rolling Stone*, Grieder has observed how newspapers "run away from their own failure to communicate what matters to citizens." In 1992 Grieder was confident of this: "There is one experiment that newspaper editors are unwilling to undertake — to take responsibility for their own readers. That is, to speak frankly in their behalf, to educate them as citizens, to create a space for them in the political debate and draw them into it."[44]

Greider wants to be proven wrong, and he may be. This will not come from Capraesque heroes, but it might come from the driving forces of marketing and technology. The modern press is finding it in its own practical interest to transform a public that seems passive and distracted. Weak forms of citizenship make for weak customers. This is already recognized as a barrier to new information products. In the mid-1980s, when videotex services were being started by newspapers, Philip Meyer predicted that they would be difficult to operate at a profit so long as the public saw them as simply a tollgate that gave them faster access to news and so forth. Videotex, he wrote, "needs to establish itself as a presence in the community, to help the community define and improve itself, and even to create communities where none existed before." With the failure of the videotex service in the 1980s, publishers have many lessons; one is that new media forms are unlikely to make business sense unless they can build on a stronger feeling of community.[45]

"Welcome to the Electronic Neighborhood" was the way the Seattle *Times* greeted its readers on a new wave of information technology of the 1990s. This feature was an exchange about the Internet and other computer topics, fashioning a community for readers and winning them over to the old-fashioned medium of a newspaper. Electronic neighborhoods may be, literally, neighborhoods, when newspapers give the public its news on-line. The Los Angeles *Times* put a button on its service labeled "Your Town." Subscribers get all local news, keyed to their zip code. Journalists have begun to supply clusters of computer users with the scores in their local sports leagues, notes on the zoning fight down their block, even the explanations for the siren that woke up people on their street. This is the sort of news that disappeared from metropolitan papers long ago when cities expanded and the press ran short of space and imagination. On-line, newspapers can get back in the business of covering everybody's neighborhood. This is a promising way to make more people care again about the daily paper.[46]

The business logic of community building earned wide attention in 1990 when the CEO and board chairman of Knight-Ridder Inc. said that "community connectedness" was the key to the future of his twenty-six newspapers. James K. Batten said this in the annual William Allen White lecture that honors the small-town editor. Batten came to Kansas with his research department's figures to show that the citizen's link to the community was the distinguishing characteristic of his best customer for news. There is, indeed, an impressive body of research that shows that caring about the community creates newspaper readers.[47]

It is that term, community, that seems key. If one looks beyond the categories offered by pollsters and interest group theorists, if one sees through that gullible public that Hollywood put on the screen, there are notions of community in American life that the press can mobilize. Newspapers have begun to create political institutions that may function like the meeting places of the early republic, where neighbors and strangers came together to get the news.

In 1990 this happened right in William Allen White's backyard, in Wichita, Kansas. Editors swore off the "horse-race" polling in the governor's race and sought to look beyond the issues the candidates thought would be decisive. The Wichita *Eagle* did polling and lengthy interviewing instead to build a picture of what citizens thought was important. The newspaper framed the story as a question of how their state would be governed, not who was ahead and why. Carrying this approach through other political contests in Kansas, the paper has built ongoing forums and recovered readers for political journalism. (Kansas is America's experimental farm in raising new relationships between public and press. CityLine, the leading audiotex service, comes from the Sunflower State.)[48]

In North Carolina, the Charlotte *Observer* brought the same campaign for a "citizens agenda" to its coverage in the 1992 elections. The paper formed a five-hundred-member advisory committee and hosted meetings on the issues. Readers shaped campaign coverage as their views and questions became part of every story. This has happened in other medium-sized cities in the South and West as well as in Minneapolis and Detroit. News organizations are creating new forms of journalism that enable citizens to test their sense of community and set the agenda for professionals in the newsroom. These approaches are built on the notion that buried in citizens is the potential for activity, not simply disdain for politics.[49]

Nothing should be clearer to the readers of this book than that the history of newspapers and magazines does not point simply in this direction of civic highmindedness. Americans have wanted many, many things from the news. To sustain friendship and to get the upper hand with the people they know. To reach out to strangers and also to scoff and punish. To dream about a paradise of goods and to find models of selflessness. To cling to their community and also to be transported to far-away places. To transform the self into the alluring body or mind of the celebrity. Even to raise the very best hogs. After three hundred years, the press knows how to increase the scope and the appeal of these choices. As an enterprise to generate temptations, there is nothing better than print. But news that cannot sustain a sense of community, including civic responsibility, will be a poor business in the long run. Journalism loses its authority if it can only reach wafer-thin segments of the country. The press will not be a good place to sell either goods or ideas if it cannot take more risks to supply news for all.

ACKNOWLEDGMENTS

AND FURTHER

READINGS

I am grateful to Jeffrey Brooks, Clay Felker, Peter Fritzsche, Tom Goldstein, Sally Griffith, David Hollinger, Larry Jinks, Richard John Jr., Carol H. Leonard, Sheldon Meyer, and Ron Zboray for comments on large sections of this book. Robert Darnton, Richard Kaplan, William J. Leonhirth, Rita Roberts, and Eugene Smolensky were kind enough to offer suggestions on chapters in their special interests. India Cooper has been a patient, helpful copy editor, and Peter Leonard has saved me from computer blunders. I have enjoyed the support of the Graduate School of Journalism, the Committee on Research, and a Humanities Research Fellowship at the University of California, Berkeley.

Notes cannot give the full picture of my debts to others. Here I wish to acknowledge works that have played a more general role in determining my approach. I hope that this will help readers to answer their own questions about the course of American journalism.

1. Journalists and Popular Culture

Loren Ghiglione, *The American Journalist: Paradox of the Press* (Washington, D.C., 1990) is a comprehensive and intelligent presentation. The sixty-page section "The Press: Its Power and Its Enemies," *American Heritage* 33 (Oct.–Nov. 1982), is also a good source on the iconography of news gathering. Howard Good, *Acquainted with the Night: The Image of Journalists in American Fiction, 1890–1930* (Metuchen, N.J., 1986) and the same author's *Outcasts: The Image of Journalists in Contemporary Film* (Metuchen, N.J., 1989) are useful surveys. "Culture and Communications," in Warren Susman, *Culture as History* (New York, 1984), is a model essay on how film illuminates the rise of other new media. There is a vast literature on the passage from daily journalism to Hollywood; Doug Fetherling, *The Five Lives of Ben Hecht* (Toronto, 1977) is particularly helpful. The influence of the market forces in the popular press is treated with subtlety by Christopher P. Wilson, "The Rhetoric of Consumption: Mass Market Magazines and the Demise of the Gentle Reader, 1880–1920," in *The Culture of Consumption: Critical Essays in American History, 1880–1980* (New York, 1983).

Carl Fleischhauer and Beverly W. Brannan, eds., *Documenting America, 1935–1943* (Berkeley, 1988) provides a full description of the Farm Security Administration collection and interpretive essays by Lawrence W. Levine and Alan Trachtenberg. For a bibliography of work on political culture and popular journalism see Thomas C. Leonard, *The Power of the Press: The Birth of American Political Reporting* (New York, 1986).

My work has been influenced by new scholarship on the active role of audiences in shaping the meaning of texts: Janice A. Radway, *Reading the Romance: Women, Patriarchy, and Popular Literature* (Chapel Hill, 1984), John Fiske, *Understanding Popular Culture* (Boston, 1989), and "Popularity and the Politics of Information," in Peter Dahlgren and Colin Sparks, eds., *Journalism and Popular Culture* (London, 1992).

2. The Reading Public

The special issue of *American Quarterly* 40 (March 1988), "Reading America," ed. Cathy N. Davidson, is a good place to begin. Dennis P. Rusche, "An Empire of Reason: A Study of the Writings of Noah Webster" (Ph.D. diss., Univ. of Iowa, 1975), has a valuable discussion of orality in the early republic. For more recent scholarship see Ronald J. Zboray, *A Fictive People: Antebellum Economic Development and the American Reading Public* (New York, 1993); Richard D. Brown, *Knowledge Is Power: The Diffusion of Information in Early America, 1700–1865* (New York, 1989); William J. Gilmore, *"Reading Becomes a Necessity of Life": Material and Cultural Life in Rural New England, 1780–1835* (Knoxville, 1989); Carl F. Kaestle *et al.*, *Literacy in the United States: Readers and Reading Since 1880* (New Haven, 1991).

Kevin G. Barnhurst, *Seeing the Newspaper* (New York, 1994) is a path-breaking exploration of the social significance of typography. Barnhurst's bibliography spans the history of printing. For new scholarship on printing in the formation of American culture see Charles E. Clark, *The Public Prints: The Newspaper in Anglo-American Culture, 1665–1740* (New York, 1994) and Michael Warner, *The Letters of the Republic: Publication and the Public Sphere in Eighteenth-Century America* (Cambridge, Mass., 1990).

Two works by Leo Bogart are indispensable: *Press and Public: Who Reads What, When, Where, and Why in American Newspapers*, 2nd ed. (Hillsdale, N.J., 1989) and *Preserving the Press: How Daily Newspapers Mobilized to Keep Their Readers* (New York, 1991). See also Joe Schwartz and Thomas Exter, "The News from Here," *American Demographics* 13 (June 1991): 50. John J. Pauly, "Interesting the Public: A Brief History of the Newsreading Movement," *Communication* 12 (1991): 285–97, surveys the twentieth-century campaigns to teach youth to read the news.

Scholarship on other cultures helps to throw American print culture in a clearer light: Mitchell Stephens, *A History of News, from the Drum to the Satellite* (New York, 1988); Roger Chartier, *The Cultural Uses of Print in Early Modern France* (Princeton, 1987); Jeffrey Brooks, *When Russia Learned to Read: Literacy and Popular Literature, 1861–*

1917 (Princeton, 1985); Jeremy Popkin, ed., *Media & Revolution* (Lexington, Ky., 1995). I had the benefit of Peter Fritzsche, *"Berlin*, Berlin: Narrative Forms and Metropolitan Encounters Around 1900," prior to its publication by Harvard University Press.

3. The Business of News

John J. McCusker, *How Much Is That in Real Money? A Historical Price Index for Use as a Deflator of Money Values in the Economy of the United States* (Worcester, Mass., 1992) is the basis for my price comparisons. Historians have just begun to give weight to marketing in their study of the production of consumer goods; see the introduction to Richard S. Tedlow and Geoffrey Jones, eds., *The Rise and Fall of Mass Marketing* (London, 1992) and Carol Smith and Carolyn Stewart Dyer, "Taking Stock, Placing Orders: A Historiographic Essay on the Business History of the Newspaper," *Journalism Monographs*, no. 132 (Columbia, S.C., 1992). Ben H. Bagdikian, *The Media Monopoly*, 3rd ed. (Boston, 1990) is a powerful synthesis. More recently this topic has been addressed by C. Edwin Baker, *Advertising and a Democratic Press* (Princeton, 1994) and Gerald J. Baldasty, *The Commercialization of News in the Nineteenth Century* (Madison, Wisc., 1992). Nan Robertson, *The Girls in the Balcony: Women, Men, and the New York Times* (New York, 1992) provides a perspective on the business that has been neglected.

4. News and Community Life

James W. Carey, "The Press and the Public Discourse," *Kettering Review* (Winter 1992), 9–22, points to many of the directions I have travelled. John Nerone, *Violence Against the Press: Policing the Public Sphere in U.S. History* (New York, 1994) expands this subject beyond the traditional boundaries of constitutional law. On the philosophical roots and social prospects of communitarian journalism see Clifford G. Christians, John P. Ferré, and P. Mark Fackler, *Good News: Social Ethics and the Press* (New York, 1993). William Greider, *Who Will Tell the People: The Betrayal of American Democracy* (New York, 1992) examines the failure of the press to advance citizenship in the 1980s with a look back at newspapers that were more attuned to ordinary Americans. The prolific work by Jay Rosen has lead efforts to connect journalism with community; see the issue he edited on the theme "The Recovery of the Public World," *Communication* 12 (1991), also Jay Rosen and Davis Merritt Jr., *Public Journalism: Theory and Practice* (1994), Occasional Paper of the Kettering Foundation. Robert E. Park, *The Immigrant Press and Its Control* (New York, 1922) remains indispensable.

5. New Media

W. Russell Neuman, *The Future of the Mass Audience* (New York, 1991) looks beyond print but includes popular newspapers and magazines. George Gilder, "Digital Dark Horse-Newspapers," *Whole Earth Review*, 22 June 1994, p. 23 argues that print journalists (not broadcasters) play a strong hand in the new information age. Roger Fidler's work with the Knight-Ridder newspaper company is a good way to enter the futurology of the industry: "What Are We So Afraid Of?" *Washington Journalism Review* 14 (Oct. 1992): 22 and "'Mediamorphosis' Heralds the Digital Newspaper," *Intermedia* 20 (Nov. 1992): 42–43. For the counter winds of skepticism see Howard Kurtz, *Media Circus: The*

Trouble with America's Newspapers (New York, 1993); Jon Katz, "Online or Not, News-papers Suck," *Wired* 2.09 (1994). Menahem Blondheim, *News over the Wires: The Telegraph and the Flow of Public Information in America, 1844–1897* (Cambridge, Mass., 1994) covers the first revolution in media that inspired confident predictions that the newspaper was doomed.

NOTES

I do not know if some Victorians were right in thinking that unbound meant unworthy, but I am sure that unbound publications are an affliction on bibliographers. The publication facts of old newspapers and magazines may be indecipherable, either in the original or in the microfilm record that is the only practical source. Modern databanks usually omit all but the first page number of an article, if they give that. Sorting out editions would fill these notes to no purpose. An article may have one title on the cover, another in the table of contents, and another on the page where it appears. Many newspapers and magazines have modified their own titles to keep up with their times. I have ignored such variations and given the information that seems best designed to lead the reader to the source.

I have taken one liberty with texts. READING HEADLINES SET THIS WAY IS AN UNNECESSARY BURDEN. I HAVE ADJUSTED FONTS FOR THE SAKE OF CLARITY.

Introduction

1. Samuel Miller, *A Brief Retrospect of the Eighteenth Century*, 2 vols. (New York, 1803), II, 253. George Wilson Pierson, *Tocqueville and Beaumont in America* (New York: 1938), p. 244. Francois Marie du Lac, *Travels Through the Two Louisianas* . . . (London, 1807), p. 29. Thomas Hamilton, *Men and*

Manners in America, 2 vols. (Edinburgh, 1833), II, 73–74. Alexander Mackay, *The Western World, or Travels in the United States in 1846–47*, 3 vols. (London, 1850), III, 242. James Thompson, *Congressional Globe*, 31st Cong., 2nd Sess. (19 Dec. 1850), p. 85. Edward Dicey, *Six Months in the Federal States*, 2 vols. (London, 1863), I, 43.

2. J. Cutler Andrews, *Pittsburgh's Post-Gazette* (Boston, 1936), p. 13. John Bradbury, *Travels in the Interior of America . . .* (1819), in Reuben Gold Thwaites, ed., *Early Western Travels, 1748–1846*, 32 vols. (Cleveland, 1904–07), V, 89.

3. William David Sloan, James G. Stovall, and James D. Startt, *The Media in America: A History*, 2nd ed. (Scottsdale, 1993).

4. Quoted by Stanley M. Elkins, *Slavery: A Problem in American Institutional and Intellectual Life* (New York, 1963), p. 63. See also Lawrence W. Levine, *Black Culture and Black Consciousness: Afro-American Folk Thought from Slavery to Freedom* (New York, 1977), pp. 29–30, 43–53. See Stanley Fish, *Is There a Text in This Class? The Authority of Interpretive Communities* (Cambridge, Mass., 1980) on this approach toward literary texts. The most successful study of such an American community is Janice A. Radway, *Reading the Romance: Women, Patriarchy, and Popular Literature* (Chapel Hill, 1984). See also Shirley Brice Heath, *Ways with Words: Language, Life, and Work in Communities and Classrooms* (Cambridge, Eng., 1983) on the active role of news readers in the southeastern United States in selecting news and negotiating its meaning.

Chapter I

1. Robert M. Weir, "The Role of the Newspaper Press in the Southern Colonies on the Eve of the Revolution: An Interpretation," in Bernard Bailyn and John B. Hench, eds., *The Press & the American Revolution* (Worcester, 1980), p. 100. Eric Foner, *Tom Paine and Revolutionary America* (New York, 1979), p. 139. Weir is careful not to press too far with a two-step flow of information model. See also Everett Rogers, "Mass Media and Interpersonal Communication," in Ithiel de Sola Pool and Wilbur Schramm, eds., *Handbook of Communication* (Chicago, 1973), pp. 290–310, and Lloyd R. Bostian, "The Two-Step Flow Theory: Cross–Cultural Implications," *Journalism Quarterly* 47 (1970): 109–17. David Macrae, *Americans at Home: Pen-and-Ink Sketches of American Men, Manners, and Institutions*, 2 vols. (Edinburgh, 1870), II, 369.

2. Allan Pred, *Urban Growth and the Circulation of Information: The United States System of Cities, 1790–1840* (Cambridge, Mass., 1973), Table 2.1. William J. Gilmore, *"Reading Becomes a Necessity of Life": Material and Cultural Life in Rural New England, 1780–1835* (Knoxville, 1989), p. 194. On greater New York, see Alfred McClung Lee, *The Daily Newspaper in America: The Evolution of a Social Instrument* (New York, 1947), pp. 730–31. By 1850 there was a copy of a daily paper in circulation for one citizen in five.

3. Cathy N. Davidson, *Revolution and the Word: The Rise of the Novel in America* (New York, 1986), pp. 9, 69–70. Thomas Snell, *A Sermon Delivered by Rev. Dr. Snell, June 27th, 1848, Being the 50th Anniversary of His Ordination . . .* (West Brookfield, Mass., 1848), pp. 25–26. Joseph T. Buckingham, *Personal Memoirs and Recollections of Editorial Life*, 2 vols. (Boston, 1852), I, 26–27. S. G. Goodrich, *Recollections of a Lifetime*, 2 vols. (New York, 1857), I, 60–61. Mary Hubbard to Esther Beecher, Jan. 1806, in Charles Beecher, ed., *Autobiography, Correspondence, Etc., of Lyman Beecher, D.D.*, 2 vols. (New York, 1864–65), I, 140. Robert Penn Warren, *John Greenleaf Whittier's Poetry* (Minneapolis, 1971), pp. 167, 186. See also Beadsley, "Reminiscences," in Louis

C. Jones, ed., *Growing Up in the Cooper Country* (Syracuse, 1965), p. 66; Sterling T. Dow, *Maine Postal History and Postmarks* (Portland, Maine, 1943), p. 23. Jack Larkin, *The Reshaping of Everyday Life, 1790–1840* (New York, 1988), p. 36.

   4. Julian P. Boyd, ed., *The Papers of Thomas Jefferson* (Princeton, 1950), II, 207–8. Prospectus by James Cowan, 3 June 1789, reproduced in Dickson J. Preston, *Newspapers of Maryland's Eastern Shore* (Queenstown and Centreville, Md., 1986), p. 11. Caroline H. Gilman, *Recollections of a Southern Matron* (1838; 2nd ed., New York, 1852), p. 98. *Southern Quarterly Review* 1 (1842): 9.

   5. Pred, *Urban Growth and the Circulation of Information*, Table 2.1.

   6. John Sella Martin in John W. Blassingame, ed., *Slave Testimony: Two Centuries of Letters, Speeches, Interviews, and Autobiographies* (Baton Rouge, 1977), pp. 709, 711. Harriet Beecher Stowe, *Oldtown Folks*, ed. Henry F. May (Cambridge, Mass., 1966) [1869], pp. 253, 283. Goodrich, *Recollections*, I, 21–22, 107, 272–73.

   7. David Weir Conroy, "The Culture and Politics of Drink in Colonial and Revolutionary Massachusetts, 1681–1790" (Ph.D. diss., University of Connecticut, 1987), p. 3. Richard P. Gildrie, "Taverns and Popular Culture in Essex County, Massachusetts, 1678–1686," *Essex Institute Historical Collections* 124 (1988): 163. Carl and Jessica Bridenbaugh, *Rebels and Gentlemen: Philadelphia in the Age of Franklin* (New York, 1962), pp. 3, 21. Oliver W. Holmes and Peter Rohrbach, *Stagecoach East: Stagecoach Days in the East from the Colonial Period to the Civil War* (Washington, D.C., 1983), p. 143.

   8. W. J. Rorabaugh, *The Alcoholic Republic: An American Tradition* (New York, 1979), pp. 8, 16. Mark Edward Lender and James Kirby Martin, *Drinking in America: A History*, rev. ed. (New York, 1987), pp. 205–6. W. Harrison Bayles, *Old Taverns of New York* (New York, 1915), pp. 117–18, 278. In Boston *News-Letter*, 15 Feb. 1770, reproduced in Samuel Adams Drake, *Old Boston Taverns and Tavern Clubs* (Boston, 1917), facing p. 64. New York *Gazette and the Weekly Mercury*, 8 April 1776, p. 4. Kym S. Rice, *Early American Taverns: For the Entertainment of Friends and Strangers* (Chicago, 1983), p. 79. See also Carl Bridenbaugh, *Cities in Revolt: Urban Life in America, 1743–1776* (New York, 1955), p. 389. Mary Kupiec Cayton, "Print and the Construction of Social Identity in the Ohio Valley, 1786–1805," paper delivered for the Annual Meeting of the Organization of American Historians Convention, Anaheim, Calif., 15–18 April 1993, pp. 38–39. Delaware (Ohio) *Patron and Franklin Chronicle*, 31 Oct. 1821. *National Intelligencer*, 21 March 1822 (ad for Alexandria Coffee House). [William N. Blane], *An Excursion Through the United States and Canada During the Years 1822–23* (London, 1824), p. 84. C. D. Arfwedson, *The United States and Canada, in 1832, 1833, and 1834*, 2 vols. (London, 1834), II, 129. John Frederick Fitzgerald DeRos, *Personal Narrative of Travels in the United States and Canada in 1826* (London, 1827), p. 99.

   9. Fortescue Cuming, *Sketches of a Tour to the Western Country* (1810), in Reuben Gold Thwaites, ed., *Early Western Travels, 1748–1846*, 32 vols. (Cleveland, 1904–07), IV, 188. Paton Yoder, *Taverns and Travelers: Inns of the Early Midwest* (Bloomington, 1969), p. 93. DeRos, *Personal Narrative*, p. 99. Clarence S. Brigham, *Journals and Journeymen* (Philadelphia, 1950), pp. 108–9. Henry Bradshaw Fearon, *Sketches of America: A Narrative of a Journey of Five Thousand Miles* (London, 1818), p. 36. Jefferson Williamson, *The American Hotel: An Anecdotal History* (New York, 1930), pp. 16–17. Larry E. Sullivan, "The Reading Habits of the Nineteenth-Century Baltimore Bourgeoisie: A Cross-Cultural Analysis," *Journal of Library History* 16 (1981): 227–40.

   10. *Gentleman's Progress: The Itinerarium of Dr. Alexander Hamilton*, ed. Carl Bridenbaugh (Chapel Hill, 1948), p. 125. Milo M. Naeve, *John Lewis Krimmel: An Artist in*

Federal America (Newark, Del., 1987), p. 74. Tobias G. Smollett, *The Adventures of Peregrine Pickle*, ed. James L. Clifford (New York, 1983), p. 8. See also Conroy, "The Culture and Politics of Drink in Colonial and Revolutionary Massachusetts," pp. 219–20.

11. Freneau quoted in Vernon Louis Parrington, *Main Currents in American Thought*, 3 vols. (New York, 1954), I, 383. Alice Morse Earle, *Stage-Coach and Tavern Days* (New York, 1900), pp. 91–92. J. Winston Coleman, *Stage-Coach Days in the Bluegrass: Being an Account of Stage-Coach Travel and Tavern Days in Lexington and Central Kentucky 1800–1900* (Louisville, 1936), p. 57. Hugh Henry Brackenridge, *Modern Chivalry*, part 2, 1804–05, ed. Claude M. Newlin (New York, 1937), p. 380. Sarah Anna Emery, *Reminiscences of a Nonagenarian* (Newburyport, Mass., 1879), p. 250. Stowe, *Oldtown Folks*, p. 283.

12. *The Journal of Nicholas Cresswell, 1774–1777* (New York, 1924), pp. 45–46. Conroy, "The Culture and Politics of Drink in Colonial and Revolutionary Massachusetts," pp. 251–69. John Lambert, *Travels Through Canada, and the United States of North America in the Years 1806, 1807, & 1808*, 2 vols. (London, 1816), II, 35. Bayles, *Old Taverns of New York*, pp. 284–85. James Rivington's *Royal Gazette* no. 153, 24 Jan. 1778, printed an undated letter describing the tavern. Peter Clark, *The English Alehouse: A Social History, 1200–1830* (New York, 1983), p. 314, notes England's problems with the combination of political newspapers and drinking.

13. Peter John Thompson, "A Social History of Philadelphia's Taverns, 1683–1800" (Ph.D. diss., University of Pennsylvania, 1989), p. 19 and chap. 6, esp. pp. 447 and 511. Emery, *Reminiscences of a Nonagenarian*, p. 281. William Strickland, *Journal of a Tour in the United States of America, 1794–1795*, ed. J. E. Strickland (New York, 1971), p. 121. Frederick Marryat, *A Diary in America, with Remarks on its Institutions*, ed. Sydney Jackman (New York, 1962), pp. 141–43.

14. S. A. Ferrall [Simon Ansley O'Ferrall], *A Ramble of Six Thousand Miles Through the United States of America* (London, 1832), pp. 295–99, quoted p. 298. [Blane], *An Excursion Through the United States and Canada*, pp. 18–19. Henry Banks, *The Vindication and Reply of Henry Banks . . .* (Lexington, Ky., 1820), p. 26.

15. Thompson, "A Social History of Philadelphia's Taverns." E. T. Coke, *A Subaltern's Furlough: Descriptive of Scenes in Various Parts of the United States . . .* (London, 1833), p. 25.

16. Frances Trollope, *Domestic Manners of the Americans*, ed. Donald Smalley (New York, 1949) [1832], p. 103. Sean Wilentz, *Chants Democratic: New York City & the Rise of the American Working Class, 1788–1850* (New York, 1984), pp. 54–55.

17. Henry Bradshaw Fearon, *Sketches of America: A Narrative of a Journey of Five Thousand Miles Through the Eastern and Western States of America* (London, 1818), pp. 251–52. Francesco Arese, *A Trip to the Prairies in the Interior of North America*, trans. and ed. Andrew Evans (New York, 1934), p. 47. On Baltimore see Coke, *A Subaltern's Furlough*, p. 79.

18. See also Eastman Johnson's *Evening Newspaper* (1863) and the painting attributed to Enoch Wood Perry, *The True American* (circulated as a chromolithograph under title *The Bummers* in 1875), *American Paintings in the Metropolitan Museum of Art*, ed. Kathleen Luhrs, 3 vols. (New York, 1985), II, 346–48.

19. Isaac Holmes, *An Account of the United States of America* (London, 1823), p. 342. Francis Lieber, *The Stranger in America* (Philadelphia, 1835), p. 42. Aleksandr B. Lakier, *A Russian Looks at America . . .* (Chicago, 1979), p. 60. [Isaac Candler], *A Summary View of America . . .* (London, 1824), pp. 56–57. David Macrae, *The*

Americans at Home: Pen-and-Ink Sketches of American Men, Manners, and Institutions, 2 vols. (Edinburgh, 1870), II, 143. Karen Halttunen, *Confidence Men and Painted Women: A Study of Middle-Class Culture in America, 1830–1870* (New Haven, 1982) is a brilliant analysis of the social significance of genteel standards, but she did not explore the meaning of boorishness to the boors.

20. Timothy Dwight, *Travels in New England and New York,* ed. Barbara Miller Solomon, 4 vols. (Cambridge, Mass, 1969), IV, 3.

21. Gildrie, "Taverns and Popular Culture in Essex County, Massachusetts, 1678–1686," pp. 173–78. On the general phenomenon of social dominance through the dramatization of leisure see Erving Goffman, *The Presentation of Self in Everyday Life* (New York, 1959), pp. 101, 110–11. Rhys Isaac's valuable essay "Ethnographic Method in History: An Action Approach" has been reprinted in *Material Life in America, 1600–1860,* ed. Robert Blair St. George (Boston, 1988).

22. Oliver W. Holmes, "Levi Pease: The Father of New England Stage-Coaching," *Journal of Economic and Business History* 3 (1931): 260–61. Wesley Everett Rich, *The History of the United States Post Office to the Year 1829* (Cambridge, Mass., 1924), p. 98. Arthur Hecht, "Pennsylvania Postal History of the Eighteenth Century," *Pennsylvania History* 30 (1963): 434–35. Walter Lowrie and Walter S. Franklin, eds., *American State Papers: Documents, Legislative and Executive, of the Congress of the United States . . . : Post Office Department* (Washington, D.C., 1834), VII, 44. Eli Bowen, *The United States Post-Office Guide* (New York, 1851), p. 14. Holmes and Rohrbach, *Stagecoach East,* p. 68. Richard R. John Jr., "Private Mail Delivery in the United States During the Nineteenth Century: A Sketch," *Business and Economic History* 15 (1986): 135–47, and "Taking Sabbatarianism Seriously: The Postal System, the Sabbath, and the Transformation of American Political Culture," *Journal of the Early Republic* 10 (1990): 527–29.

23. Richard R. John Jr., *Spreading the News: The American Postal System from Franklin to Morse* (Cambridge, Mass., 1995), chap. 4. C. M. Sedgwick, "The Post Office," *Graham's Magazine* 23 (1843): 65.

24. These account books are cited in chap. 4, n. 29. Sedgwick, "The Post Office," p. 67. Trollope, *Domestic Manners of the Americans,* p. 305. James Oliver Robertson and Janet C. Robertson, *All Our Yesterdays: A Century of Family Life in an American Small Town* (New York, 1993), pp. 164–65. Alvin F. Harlow, *Old Post Bags* (New York and London, 1928), p. 330. Richard B. Kielbowicz, *News in the Mail: The Press, Post Office, and Public Information, 1700–1860s* (New York, 1989), pp. 3, 43–44, 106–7. Paul M. Angle, *The Lincoln Reader* (New Brunswick, 1947), p. 58. Benjamin P. Thomas, *Lincoln's New Salem* (New York, 1954), p. 98. Bowen, *The United States Post Office Guide,* p. 42. *Congressional Globe* (Appendix), 31st Cong., 2nd Sess. (19 Feb. 1851), p. 268. S. N. D. North, *History and Present Condition of the Newspaper and Periodical Press of the United States* (Washington, D.C., 1884), p. 150. For examples of congressmen as subscription agents see Elisha Whittlesey to Joseph Gales and William W. Seaton, 21 March 1831, in Gales and Seaton Papers, Library of Congress; *Congressional Globe,* 31st Cong., 2nd Sess. (19 Dec. 1850), p. 93; *The Correspondence of James K. Polk,* ed. Herbert Weaver, *et al.,* 8 vols. to date (Nashville, 1969–), I, 586; *The Papers of Willie Pearson Mangum,* ed. Henry T. Shanks, 5 vols. (Raleigh, 1950–56), II, 139, IV, 163–64; John S. Millson to John C. Rives, 12 July 1860, Virginia State Library and Archives, Richmond.

25. Donald H. Stewart, *The Opposition Press in the Federalist Period* (Albany, 1969), p. 464. Carl E. Prince, "The Federalist Party and Creation of a Court Press, 1789–1801," *Journalism Quarterly* 53 (1976): 239. Kielbowicz, *News in the Mail,* p. 43. House

of Representatives, 23rd Cong., 2nd Sess. (1835), Report No. 103, p. 212. Philip Kinsley, *The Chicago Tribune: Its First Hundred Years*, 3 vols. (New York, 1943), I, 154. George Britt, *Forty Years—Forty Millions: The Career of Frank A. Munsey* (New York, 1935), p. 71. The complaints lived on to the Civil War: Thomas Harrison Baker, *The Memphis Commercial Appeal: The History of a Southern Newspaper* (Baton Rouge, 1971), p. 50; Margaret Ross, *Arkansas Gazette: The Early Years, 1819–1866* (Little Rock, 1969), p. 323. Dorothy G. Fowler, *Unmailable: Congress and the Post Office* (Athens, Ga., 1977), p. 37.

26. Correspondence between William Gunnison and Postmaster Thomas Finley, 29–30 Sept. 1843, in Gunnison's papers located in Applications for Appointments as Customs Service Officers (1882), Record Group 56, General Records of the Department of the Treasury, National Archives, Washington, D.C. John, "Managing the Mails," p. 373.

27. Bowen, *The United States Post Office Guide*, p. 42. See also the comment of Sen. John Milton Niles, a former journalist and Postmaster General, in *Appendix to the Congressional Globe*, 29th Cong., 1st Sess., p. 985. Augustus Maverick, *Henry J. Raymond and the New York Press* (Hartford, 1870), p. 362.

28. North, *History and Present Condition of the Newspaper and Periodical Press*, p. 140, reprints Ritchie's circular letter to postmasters. John, *Spreading the News*, chap. 4.

29. Frances Wright D'Arusmont, *Views of Society and Manners in America*, ed. Paul R. Baker (Cambridge, Mass., 1963), pp. 120–21. Sandor Boloni Farkas, *Journey in North America, 1831*, ed. Arpad Kadarkay (Santa Barbara, 1978), p. 165. Andy Van Meter, *Always My Friend: A History of the State Journal-Register and Springfield* (Springfield, Ill., 1981), p. 84. James Silk Buckingham, *The Slave States of America*, 2 vols. (London, 1842), II, 352–53. Coke, *A Subaltern's Furlough*, p. 257. Lowrie and Franklin, eds., *American State Papers*, VII, 17. Wayne E. Fuller, *The American Mail, Enlarger of the Common Life* (Chicago, 1972), pp. 40, 47, 49. Hecht, "Pennsylvania Postal History of the Eighteenth Century," pp. 423–24. Holmes and Rohrbach, *Stagecoach East*, chap. 10. *Gales & Seaton's Register of Debates*, 22nd Cong., 1st Sess. (9 May 1832), p. 909; *Register of Debates*, 28th Cong., 2nd Sess. (18 Jan. 1845), p. 212. "The Hanover Subscription List for Newspapers," 14 March 1806, Item #806214 in the Dartmouth College Library. Jones, *Growing Up in the Cooper Country*, p. 67. George P. Rowell & Co., *Centennial Newspaper Exhibition,1876* (New York, 1876), p. 188.

30. Other gatherings for the news: *Post Office, San Francisco, California. A Faithful Representation of the Crowds Daily Applying at the Office for Letters and Newspapers*, c. 1850 in Gloria Gilda Deak, *Picturing America, 1497–1899* . . . (Princeton, 1988), p. 595; Bayard Taylor, *Eldorado* (New York, 1850), chap. 20; unidentified illustration of the Atlanta post office, 1879, in Carl H. Scheele, *Neither Snow, Nor Rain* . . . *the Story of United States Mails* (Washington, D.C., 1970), p. 65; Edward R. Foreman, ed., *Centennial History of Rochester, New York*, 4 vols. (Rochester, 1933), III, 61. In upstate New York of the late nineteenth century the clerk in one post office was obliged to read the news aloud from six daily papers to the locals: Millard Van Marter Atwood, *The Country Newspaper* (Chicago, 1923), p. 32. Rural Free Delivery at the turn of the century broke these habits of dependence, as one congressman noted in celebrating its success: *Congressional Record* (1916), 64th Cong., 1st Sess., p. 1383.

31. Art, of course, is not a sure guide to social reality. Roger Chartier has pointed out that genre artists in France celebrated a communal reading of books by peasants that reflected urban romanticism more than social habits in the countryside: *The Cultural Uses of Print in Early Modern France* (Princeton, 1987), pp. 218–28. American art of the

early nineteenth century seems more trustworthy about news reading in the post office, tavern, and home because of the rarity of what Chartier calls "private reading" in all types of illustration. There are very few depictions of an individual *alone* with a newspaper in American iconography before 1850. Elizabeth Johns, *American Genre Painting: The Politics of Everyday Life* (New Haven, 1991) persuasively covers the ordering of behavior in this art.

32. For a description of Kentuckians gathered around the best readers of newspapers in the 1780s see William Nelson, *Notes Toward a History of the American Newspaper* (New York, 1918), p. 132.

33. *The Hugh Finlay Journal*, pp. 41, 43, 67. Holmes, "Levi Pease," p. 251. On the "politics of the coachman" in determining rural reading see Lambert, *Travels Through Canada, and the United States of North America*, II, 499. See also Karl Bernhard, Duke of Saxe–Weimar Eisenach, *Travels Through North America During the Years 1825 and 1826* (Philadelphia, 1828), p. 55; Frederick Follett, *History of the Press in Western New-York* (New York, 1920), pp. 5–6; Rich, *The History of the United States Post Office*, pp. 98–99, 143–44; Milton W. Hamilton, *The Country Printer, New York State, 1785– 1830* (Port Washington, N.Y., 1964), p. 218; and Kielbowicz, "The Press, Post Office, and Flow of the News in the Early Republic," *Journal of the Early Republic* 3 (1983): 255–80, esp. 267.

34. Guillaume de Bertier de Sauvigny, "The American Press and the Fall of Napoleon in 1814," *American Philosophical Society Proceedings* 98 (1954): 363–64. In upstate New York, Eber D. Howe followed the rise of "that great human butcher" by listening to his father read the newspapers aloud to the family: *Autobiography and Recollections of a Pioneer Printer* (Painesville, Ohio, 1878), p. 3.

35. [William M. Baker], "Inside. A Chronicle of Secession," part 10, *Harper's Weekly*, 17 March 1866, p. 165. See also the 13th installment, 7 April 1866, pp. 213–14. "When printing became abundant," Richard D. Brown has said, "people were free to exercise privately their individual preferences for public information. As a result the measure of indoctrination, influence, and communal cohesion that accompanied face-to-face diffusion of information vanished." Richard D. Brown, *Knowledge Is Power: The Diffusion of Information in Early America, 1700–1865* (New York, 1989), p. 279. Brown draws this conclusion with qualifications. More are in order. For more evidence of the coercive uses of newspapers in Austin during the sectional crisis see Marilyn M. Sibley, *Lone Stars and State Gazettes: Texas Newspapers Before the Civil War* (College Station, 1983), p. 277. Similarly, crowds in Newark, New Jersey, supplied their own "reading" of the news from Fort Sumter which was to dismiss the first oral and even printed reports: see Alan A. Siegel, *For the Glory of the Union: Myth, Reality, and the Media in the Civil War* (Cranbury, N.J., 1984), pp. 22–23. See also Hubert Howe Bancroft, *Works of Hubert Howe Bancroft*, 39 vols. (San Francisco, 1882–90), XXV, 528.

36. Lambert, *Travels Through Canada, and the United States*, II, 498–500. Julian U. Niemcewicz, *Under Their Vine and Fig Tree: Travels Through America in 1797–1799, 1805 . . .* , ed. Metchie J. E. Budka (Elizabeth, N.J., [1965]), p. 111. John Palmer, *Journal of Travels in the United States of North America . . .* (London, 1818), p. 200.

37. Jürgen Habermas, *The Structural Transformation of the Public Sphere: An Inquiry into a Category of Bourgeois Society* (Cambridge, Mass., 1989), chap. 4. On the expansion of formal political debate in the press see Thomas C. Leonard, *The Power of the Press: The Birth of American Political Reporting* (New York, 1986), chap. 3.

38. Alexander Mackay, *The Western World, or Travels in the United States in 1846– 47*, 3 vols. (London, 1850), III, 242. For a striking example of hiving (and credit for the

term) see Robert A. Gross, "The Machine-Readable Transcendentalists: Cultural History on the Computer," *American Quarterly* 41 (1989): 501–21.

39. Laurel Thatcher Ulrich, "Housewife and Gadder: Themes of Self-Sufficiency and Community in Eighteenth-Century New England," in Carol Groneman and Mary Beth Norton, eds., *"To Toil the Livelong Day": America's Women at Work, 1780–1980* (Ithaca, 1987). Jackson Turner Main, *The Social Structure of Revolutionary America* (Princeton, 1965), pp. 41–47. Issue of 5 Jan. 1852 quoted in Archer H. Shaw, *The Plain Dealer: One Hundred Years in Cleveland* (New York, 1942), p. 60.

40. Stowe, *Oldtown Folks*, pp. 526–28. For instances of a master's gift of reading having the desired effect see Edward Miles Riley, ed., *The Journal of John Harrower, an Indentured Servant in the Colony of Virginia, 1773–1776* (Williamsburg, 1963), p. 56, and *Journal & Letters of Philip Vickers Fithian, 1773–1774: A Plantation Tutor of the Old Dominion*, ed. Hunter Dickinson Farish (Williamsburg, 1957), pp. 40, 131.

41. Hinton Rowan Helper, *The Impending Crisis of the South: How to Meet It*, ed. George M. Fredrickson (Cambridge, Mass., 1968), p. lvi. Thomas L. Webber, *Deep Like the Rivers: Education in the Slave Quarter Community, 1831–1865* (New York, 1978), p. 229. A slaveholder acknowledged that his servants had "free perusal" of papers arriving in his home and worried about "unpleasant circumstances" as abolitionist newspapers arrived in the mail: John Leeds Kerr to William Lloyd Garrison, *Liberator*, 16 Sept. 1842, p. 145.

42. Stephen Allen, "The Memoirs of Stephen Allen (1765–1852)," ed. John C. Travis, typescript, New-York Historical Society.

43. *American Farmer* 1 (1819): 265.

44. Of conventional family scenes see G. Hollingsworth, *The Hollingsworth Family* (c. 1840); Francis William Edmonds, *The Bashful Cousin* (1842); John L. Magee, *Reading of an Official Dispatch (Mexican War News)* (c. 1849); John B. Whittaker, *The Lesson* (1871); Edward L. Henry, *The Parlor on Brooklyn Heights of Mr. and Mrs. John Bullard* (1872). Complete citations and additional discussion can be found in the author's "News at the Hearth: A Drama of Reading in Nineteenth-Century America," *Proceedings of the American Antiquarian Society* 102, part 2 (1993): 379–401. For testimony that supports the genre scenes of news reading see Frank W. Scott, "Newspapers, 1775–1860," in William P. Trent *et al.*, eds., *Cambridge History of American Literature*, 3 vols. (New York, 1933), II, 248. *Boston Weekly Magazine* of 1839 did advertise itself with an illustration of a woman reading to a man: see Jane C. Nylander, *Our Own Snug Fireside: Images of the New England Home, 1760–1860* (New York, 1993), p. 112.

45. Gwendolyn Wright, *Building the Dream: A Social History of Housing in America* (New York, 1981), pp. 15, 77–78, 88–89. Sally Ann McMurry, *Families and Farmhouses in Nineteenth-Century America* (New York, 1988), chap. 5. Kathryn Kish Sklar, *Catharine Beecher: A Study in American Domesticity* (New Haven, 1973), p. 166. Nancy F. Cott, *The Bonds of Womanhood: "Woman's Sphere" in New England, 1780–1835* (New Haven, 1977), pp. 57, 63–67. See Walter Buehr, *Home Sweet Home in the Nineteenth Century* (New York, 1965), pp. 87–94. The influence of furniture design on female deportment has been noted by Katherine C. Grier, *Culture & Comfort: People, Parlors, and Upholstery, 1850–1930* (Amherst, 1988), pp. 110–11, 206, and Harvey Green, with the assistance of Mary-Ellen Perry, *The Light of the Home: An Intimate View of the Lives of Women in Victorian America* (New York, 1983), pp. 97–98.

46. Grier, *Culture & Comfort*, esp. pp. 19, 25–26, 39, 44, 53, 66.

47. [William M. Baker], "Inside. A Chronicle of Secession," part 3, *Harper's Weekly*, 27 Jan. 1866, p. 54. For another wife's reaction see 20 Jan. 1866, p. 37. Baker's preface

contains his claims as a social documentarian: 27 Jan. 1866, p. 36. American newspapers boasted of special features for women before mid-century, but long after this time many editors saw themselves supplying texts that women would follow from male lips. "A paper when completed should be one that the editor would be willing to read to his wife, his mother, his sister, or his daughter," a Connecticut paper advised in 1847, calling for a standard that papers were notorious for not living up to. Richard D. Birdsall, *Berkshire County: A Cultural History* (New Haven, 1959), pp. 205–6.

48. Gilman, *Recollections of a Southern Matron*, p. 297. William A. Alcott, *The Young Husband, or Duties of Man in the Marriage Relation* (Boston, 1839) devoted a chapter to the male's heavy responsibility of selecting news for his family.

49. Jane Grey Swisshelm, *Half a Century* (Chicago, 1880), p. 94. Oral transmission of the newspaper is suggested by women's choice of words in their letters and diaries at mid-century, e.g., "heard bad news in the paper": see Marilyn Ferris Motz, *True Sisterhood: Michigan Women and their Kin, 1820–1920* (Albany, 1983), pp. 72–73. [Anon.], "Every-Day Life of Woman," *Ladies' Repository* 11 (1851): 365–66, in *America's Families: A Documentary History*, Donald M. Scott and Bernard Wishy, eds. (New York, 1982), pp. 265–66. Edward W. Bok, *The Americanization of Edward Bok* (New York, 1921), p. 104. Brown, *Knowledge Is Power*, chap. 7, is the broadest study of women's diaries and correspondence to show the impact of print. For other evidence of women reading the news before 1870 see Merrill D. Peterson, *The Jefferson Image in the American Mind* (New York, 1962), p. 38; *A Girl's Life Eighty Years Ago: Selections from the Letters of Eliza Southgate Bowne* (New York, 1887), p. 166; Wilma King, ed., *A Northern Woman in the Plantation South: Letters of Trypehna Blanche Holder Fox, 1856–1876* (Columbia, S.C., 1993), pp. 10, 38–39; Rheta Childe Dorr, *A Woman of Fifty* (New York, 1924), pp. 92–93. Florence Finch Kelly, *Flowing Stream: The Story of Fifty-Six Years in American Newspaper Life* (New York, 1939), pp. 69, 477.

50. [Daniel K. Whitaker], "The Newspaper and Periodical Press," *Southern Quarterly Review* 1 (1842): 8–9. Gilmore, *"Reading Becomes a Necessity of Life,"* p. 221, notes a recognition of women's interest in the newspaper after 1815 in the Upper Connecticut Valley. There is no question, however, that women were addressed in new ways at mid-century. See Birdsall, *Berkshire County*, pp. 200–201, on special attention to items for women in the 1840s. Albert L. Demaree, *The American Agricultural Press, 1819–1860* (New York, 1941), chap. 7. See the targeting of women in Thomas Harrison Baker, *The Memphis Commercial Appeal: The History of a Southern Newspaper* (Baton Rouge, 1971), p. 45, and Lloyd Wendt, *Chicago Tribune: The Rise of a Great American Newspaper* (Chicago, 1979), p. 32. The New York *Daily Times*, 14 Oct. 1852, noted that women were as likely as men to read newspapers (in contrast with England).

51. Linda K. Kerber, *Women of the Republic: Intellect and Ideology in Revolutionary America* (Chapel Hill, 1980), pp. 235–64. Steven M. Stowe, *Intimacy and Power in the Old South: Ritual in the Lives of the Planters* (Baltimore, 1987), pp. 117–18. Cathy N. Davidson, *Revolution and the Word: The Rise of the Novel in America* (New York, 1986), p. 114. Sklar, *Catharine Beecher*, pp. 113, 134–35. Mary P. Ryan, *The Empire of the Mother: American Writing About Domesticity, 1830–1860* (New York, 1982), esp. pp. 45, 56. Ryan's *Cradle of the Middle Class: The Family in Oneida County, New York, 1790–1865* (Cambridge, Eng., 1981), p. 175, and Motz, *True Sisterhood*, pp. 5, 53–81, have excellent discussions of women's control of family correspondence.

52. *Kentucke Gazette*, 20 Oct. 1787, reprinted in *Kentucky Press* 8 (1937): 2–3. John D. Stevens, *Sensationalism and the New York Press* (New York, 1991), pp. 21, 37. *Peterson's Ladies' National Magazine*: on the promotion of weekly papers from Phila-

delphia with the assurance that they contained news see 28 (1853): 99; *ibid.* 29 (1856): 95; the "Editor's Table" or "Publisher's Corner" of most issues reprinted praise of the magazine in local weeklies, addressed to the newspapers' women readers. *Demorest's Illustrated Monthly Magazine* (June 1870) also lured female readers with subscription discounts on leading political papers. Ishbel Ross, *Ladies of the Press: The Story of Women in Journalism by an Insider* (New York, 1936), p. 14, helped to implant the notion that "housewives did not read the papers before 1870 and . . . the modern woman who reads her paper from the front page to the back does not inherit this taste from her grandmother."

53. Caleb Atwater, *Remarks Made on a Tour to Prairie du Chien* . . . (Columbus, Ohio, 1831), pp. 23, 259–60. See also *Liberator*, Nov. 1856, pp. 181–82.

54. *Harper's Weekly*, 12 Aug. 1865. Julia McNair Wright, *The Complete Home: An Encyclopedia of Domestic Life and Affairs* (Philadelphia, 1879), p. 481. *Gems of Deportment and Hints of Etiquette* (Chicago, 1881), p. 118. See also Maud C. Cooke, *Manual of Etiquette or Social Form: Manners and Customs of Correct Society* (Cincinnati, 1896), p. 168; Frank Luther Mott, *A History of American Magazines*, 5 vols. (Cambridge, Mass., 1966–68), II, 47.

55. See, for instance, Frank Smith, *Joining the Literacy Club* (Portsmouth, N.H., 1988). Kevin G. Barnhurst and John C. Nerone, "Design Trends in U.S. Front Pages, 1889–1985," *Journalism Quarterly* 68 (1991): 796–804.

56. Benedict Anderson, *Imagined Communities: Reflections on the Origin and Spread of Nationalism*, rev. ed. (London, 1991), chap. 2, pp. 35–36 quoted.

57. Katherine Verdery, "Whither 'Nation' and 'Nationalism'?" *Daedalus* 122 (Summer 1993): 41.

58. The essay is conveniently available in Allen W. Read, "Noah Webster's Project in 1801 for a History of American Newspapers," *Journalism Quarterly* 11 (1934): 258–59. Donald L. Shaw and Shannon E. Martin, "The Function of Mass Media Agenda Setting," *Journalism Quarterly* 69 (1992): 902–20.

59. Ronald P. Formisano, "Deferential-Participant Politics: The Early Republic's Political Culture, 1789–1840," *American Political Science Review* 68 (1974): 473–87.

Chapter 2

1. Walter D. Kamphoefner, Wolfgang Helbich, and Ulrike Sommer, eds., *News from the Land of Freedom* (Ithaca, 1991), p. 23. Renate Kieswetter, "German-American Labor Press: The *Vorbote* and Chicago *Arbeiter-Zeitung*," in Hartmut Keil, ed., *German Worker's Culture in the United States, 1850 to 1920* (Washington, D.C., 1988), p. 138. Robert E. Park, *The Immigrant Press and Its Control* (New York, 1922), esp. p. 79.

2. Day book of William H. Lewis, 1864–75, in New-York Historical Society. Virginia Ingraham Burr, ed., *The Secret Eye: The Journal of Ella Gertrude Clanton Thomas, 1848–1889* (Chapel Hill, 1990), p. 361, see also pp. 396–97.

3. William J. Gilmore, *"Reading Becomes a Necessity of Life": Material and Cultural Life in Rural New England, 1780–1835* (Knoxville, 1989), p. 175. Frank W. Scott, *Newspapers and Periodicals of Illinois, 1814–1879* (Springfield, Ill., 1910), p. xi; vol. 6 of *Collections of the Illinois State Historical Library*, 34 vols. (Springfield, Ill., 1903–59). William Nelson, *Notes Toward a History of the American Newspaper* (New York, 1918), p. 166. *The Commercial Appeal, 1840–1865* (Memphis, n.d.), p. 4. William Dean How-

ells, "The Country Printer," in *Impressions and Experiences* (New York, 1896), p. 19. The shortage of cash in the countryside does not explain reader delinquency: see Milton W. Hamilton, *The Country Printer, New York State, 1785–1830* (Port Washington, N.Y., 1964), pp. 65–66, and S. B. McCracken, "The Press of Michigan—A Fifty-Year View," Michigan State Historical Society, *Michigan Pioneer Historical Collections* 18 (1891): 388.

4. Isaiah Thomas, *The History of Printing in America*, ed. Marcus A. McCorison (New York, 1970), p. 491. Philadelphia *Gazette*, 4 Oct. 1739. Charles L. Cutler, *Connecticut's Revolutionary Press* (Chester, Conn., 1975), pp. 43–44.

5. Frank Luther Mott, *A History of American Magazines*, 5 vols. (Cambridge, Mass., 1966–68), II, 11–12. William R. Hogan and Edwin A. Davis, *William Johnson's Natchez: The Ante-Bellum Diary of a Free Negro* (Baton Rouge, 1951), p. 437. Jeffrey L. Pasley, "The Indiscreet Zeal of John Norvell: Newspaper Publishing and Politics in the Early American Republic," paper delivered at the Organization of American Historians Annual Meeting, 14 April 1994, p. 18. John Tyler to John R. Thompson, 14 Aug. 1849, Alderman Library, University of Virginia. Joseph Leonard King Jr., *Dr. George William Bagby: A Study of Virginian Literature, 1850–1880* (New York, 1927), pp. 86–87. Edward L. Tucker, "A Rash and Perilous Enterprise," *Virginia Cavalcade* 21 (1971): 20. Press comments on deadbeats were bound at the end of vol. 20 of the *Southern Literary Messenger*. *Liberator*, 7 Jan. 1853, p. 3. Albert L. Demaree, *The American Agricultural Press, 1819–1860* (New York, 1941), p. 118.

6. Howells, *Impressions and Experiences*, p. 18. Alice D. Schreyer, ed., "Mark Twain and 'The Old-Fashioned Printer,'" *Printing History* 3 (1981): 35. Publishers' figures and my estimates from Demaree, *The American Agricultural Press*, pp. 118, 376–85. Richard Bardolph, *Agricultural Literature and the Early Illinois Farmer* (Urbana, 1948), p.168, finds that in 1855 the *Prairie Farmer* was owed more than it earned and that non-payment by subscribers threatened the life of nearly every agricultural paper in the state before 1870.

7. [James Hall], "New Year Address," *Port Folio* 2 (1822): 168–71. Osman C. Hooper, *History of Ohio Journalism, 1793–1933* (Columbus, 1933), pp. 21–22, 52–53. Andy Van Meter, *Always My Friend: A History of the State Journal-Register and Springfield* (Springfield, Ill., 1981), pp. 104, 108. Randolph C. Randall, *James Hall: Spokesman of the New West* ([Columbus], 1964), pp. 96, 296 n. 60. McCracken, "The Press of Michigan," p. 388. I. A. Nichols, *Forty Years of Rural Journalism in Iowa* (Fort Dodge, Iowa, 1938), p. 51.

8. *Southern Quarterly Review* 9 (1846): 523–24. Ross, *Arkansas Gazette*, pp. 33, 277, 366. Wm. S. Ransom to Willie P. Mangum, 8 Feb. 1832, in Henry T. Shanks, ed., *The Papers of Willie Pearson Mangum*, 5 vols. (Raleigh, 1950–56), I, 475. Donald E. Reynolds, *Editors Make War: Southern Newspapers in the Secession Crisis* (Nashville, 1970), pp. 7–8. Robert Neal Elliott, *The Raleigh Register, 1799–1863* (Chapel Hill, 1955), p. 101. Ritchie quoted in New Orleans *Picayune*, 11 Feb. 1838 and 10 Dec. 1842. Edwin A. Miles, "The Mississippi Press in the Jackson Era, 1824–1841," *Journal of Mississippi History* 19 (1957): 7.

9. Monte Burr McLaws, *Spokesman for the Kingdom: Early Mormon Journalism and the Deseret News, 1830–1898* (Provo, 1977), pp. 32, 37–38. Publishers' figures and my estimates using Wesley Norton, *Religious Newspapers in the Old Northwest to 1861: A History, Bibliography, and Record of Opinion* (Athens, Ohio, 1977), pp. 16–18, 163, 171, 173.

10. Marilyn M. Sibley, *Lone Stars and State Gazettes: Texas Newspapers Before the*

Civil War (College Station, 1983), p. 226. James Silk Buckingham, *The Slave States of America*, 2 vols. (London, [1842]), II, 118–19. Henry Smith Stroupe, *The Religious Press in the South Atlantic States, 1802–1865* (Durham, 1956), pp. 11, 65, 88. Norton, *Religious Newspapers in the Old Northwest*, p. 18. *Religious Telescope*, 2 Jan. 1856.

11. "Delinquents to the Western Star and Watchman of the Prairies," account book in the Chicago Historical Society.

12. Allan Nevins, *The Evening Post: A Century of Journalism* (New York, 1922), p. 93, and *History of the State of New York*, ed. Alexander C. Flick, 10 vols. (New York, 1937), IX, 275. David P. Forsyth, *The Business Press in America, 1750–1865* (Philadelphia, 1964), p. 316. Pasley, "The Indiscreet Zeal of John Norvell," p. 18. Joseph T. Buckingham, *Personal Memoirs and Recollections of Editorial Life*, 2 vols. (Boston, 1852), II, 104. B. H. Green to Melzar Gardner, 17 Feb. 1842, Melzar Gardner Papers, Special Collections Library, Duke University, Durham, N. C., and Mott, *American Magazines*, I, 687. S. W. Jackman, "Tribulations of an Editor: Benjamin Silliman and the Early Days of the American Journal of Science and the Arts," *New England Quarterly* 52 (1979): 101. Wilbur Solomon Jr. to Robert L. Livingston, 23 May 1823, in Livingston Papers, New-York Historical Society.

13. "Letters of William Duane," *Proceedings of the Massachusetts Historical Society*, 2nd ser., 20 (1906–07): 263, 316, 392. Francis Wharton, *State Trials of the United States* (Philadelphia, 1849), p. 390. *Niles' Register*, 7 May 1831, p. 167. Gretchen Garst Ewing, "Duff Green: Independent Editor of a Party Press," *Journalism Quarterly* 54 (1977): 737. Frank Luther Mott, *American Journalism: A History, 1690–1960* (New York, 1962), pp. 159, 202.

14. William H. Hale, *Horace Greeley: Voice of the People* (New York, 1950), pp. 40–41. John Calhoun Papers, Chicago *Democrat* Subscription Book (1836) in Chicago Historical Society has 75 paid in full, 165 subscribers with money owed. *Evening Star* Subscription Book (1833–40), *passim*, New-York Historical Society, and Gappelberg, "M. M. Noah and the Evening Star," pp. 66–68. Rabun Lee Brantley, *Georgia Journalism of the Civil War Period* (Nashville, 1929), p. 10. Frederick G. Fassett, *Newspapers in the District of Maine* (Orono, Maine, 1932), p. 119. Julian E. Walsh, *To Print the News and Raise Hell! A Biography of Wilbur F. Storey* (Chapel Hill, 1968), p. 20. Fred F. Endres, "'We Want Money and Must Have It': Profile of an Ohio Weekly, 1841–1847," *Journalism History* 7 (1980): 69. Barbara L. Cloud, *The Business of Newspapers on the Western Frontier* (Reno, 1992), pp. 45–46.

15. *American Newspaper Reporter* 6 (2 Sept. 1872): 862. "I want money! and money I must have — and money I will have, (if I can get it)," sang the editor of the Providence *Impartial Observer* toward the end of its brief life in 1801: *Printers and Printing in Providence, 1762–1907* (Providence, 1907), p. 19. See also Everett W. Kindig, "'I Am in Purgatory Now': Journalist Hooper Warren Survives the Illinois Frontier," *Illinois Historical Journal* 79 (1986): 185–96.

16. *Penny Magazine* 10 (1841): 243; *American Farmer* 4 (1822): 99, noted the contrast; see also Buckingham, *Travels in the Slave States*, I, 130. Forsyth, *The Business Press in America*, p. 316.

17. Worthington (Ohio) *Western Intelligencer*, 5 May 1813; Zanesville (Ohio) *Express*, 5 Dec. 1816; Delaware (Ohio) *Patron and Franklin Chronicle*, 31 Oct. 1821 (quoted); Portsmouth (Ohio) *Western Times*, 2 Aug. 1828 (quoted); Fayette (Mo.) *Western Monitor*, 24 March 1830; Warren (Ohio) *Western Reserve Chronicle*, 9 April 1844; Athens (Ohio) *Messenger*, 25 Oct. 1850; Lebanon (Ohio) *Western Star*, 21 July 1854 (quoted).

18. William H. Lyon, *The Pioneer Editor in Missouri, 1808–1860* (Columbia, Mo., 1965), pp. 88–89, 94–95. I have used Lyon's version of the "Laws," which were often rephrased by local editors: Eddyville (Iowa) *Free Press*, 12 Jan. 1855; Fairfield (Iowa) *Ledger*, 1 Feb. 1855; *Western Star* (Lebanon, Ohio), 21 July 1854. Cloud, *The Business of Newspapers on the Western Frontier*, pp. 47–48. The post office repeatedly noted this canard, but it died hard; see *Bookseller, Newsdealer, and Stationer* 1 (15 March 1895): 597 and *Newspaper Maker* 1 (9 May 1895): 7.

19. Hooper, *History of Ohio Journalism*, p. 47. Hamilton, *The Country Printer*, p. 235.

20. "Newspaper Collecting," reprinted from an unidentified South Carolina paper in Memphis *Appeal*, 26 Jan. 1852. "I never will pay for it," a subscriber told the editor of the Alton (Ill.) *Observer* in 1837, "and the only wish I have upon the subject is, that you, your press and agent, were all in hell." Quoted in Merton L. Dillon, *Elijah P. Lovejoy: Abolitionist Editor* (Urbana, 1961), p. 105.

21. Clarence S. Brigham, *Journals and Journeymen: A Contribution to the History of Early American Newspapers* (Philadelphia, 1950), pp. 23–24. Alexis de Tocqueville, *Democracy in America*, 2 vols. (New York, 1956), I, 239. A. L. Lorenz, "'Out of Sorts and Out of Cash': Problems of Publishing in Wisconsin Territory, 1833–1848," *Journalism History* 3 (Summer 1976): 36. Frances Trollope, *Domestic Manners of the Americans*, ed. Donald Smalley (New York, 1949) [1832], pp. 306–7. Paul E. Rock, *Making People Pay* (London and Boston, 1973), pp. 2, 102. Eric Berne, *Games People Play: The Psychology of Human Relationships* (New York, 1964), pp. 82–84. Peter J. Coleman, *Debtors and Creditors in America: Insolvency, Imprisonment for Debt, and Bankruptcy, 1607–1900* (Madison, 1974). On "culpable neglect" by patients see George Rosen, *Fees and Fee Bills: Some Economic Aspects of Medical Practice in Nineteenth-Century America* (Baltimore, 1946), pp. 34–35. T. H. Breen, *Tobacco Culture: The Mentality of the Great Tidewater Planters on the Eve of Revolution* (Princeton, 1985) shows the importance of debt in political mobilization.

22. John Gill Shorter to Benjamin Yancey, 5 July 1839, in Benjamin Yancey Papers, Southern Historical Collection, University of North Carolina, Chapel Hill.

23. Donald T. Hawkins, "Customized Information: 'No, I don't want 'all the news that's fit to print,'" *Online* 14 (Sept. 1990): 117. Don Stanley, "Captain Hookup," Sacramento *Bee*, 6 Jan. 1993, p. SC1; Terry Carter, "TV Pirates Plying the Airwaves," *National Law Journal*, 12 Oct. 1987, p. 1; Robert A. Hamilton, "Cable TV Operators Unite to Fight Theft of Their Services," New York *Times*, 28 Sept. 1986, sec. 11CN, p. 10 (quoted); Michael Dorfsman, "Connecticut Opinion," New York *Times*, 18 Nov. 1984, sec. 11CN, p. 38; John Witt, "Amnesty for Cable TV Thieves?" United Press International, 13 Nov. 1984; Jonathan Greenberg, "Video Pirates," *Forbes*, 7 Dec. 1981, p. 96. William J. Thorn with Mary Pat Pfeil, *Newspaper Circulation: Marketing the News* (New York, 1987), p. 40.

24. Elaine Goldberg, manager of marketing operations, Chicago Tribune Co., quoted in "Database Marketing Is Key to Future," *Newspaper Financial Executive Journal* 47 (Jul.–Aug. 1993): 10. The poem is reprinted in Warren E. Stickle, "State and Press in New Jersey During the American Revolution," part 2, *New Jersey History* 86 (1968): 240. Howells, *Impressions and Experiences*, p. 33. *Literary Subaltern* (July 1829) quoted in the supplement to the Providence (R.I.) *Journal*, *A Hundred Years of the Providence Journal* (23 July 1929), pp. 6–7. Pasley, "The Indiscreet Zeal of John Norvell," p. 21. Culver H. Smith, *The Press, Politics, and Patronage: The American Government's Use of Newspapers, 1789–1875* (Athens, Ga., 1977), pp. 96–99; quoted p. 98 and p. 297 n. 45.

25. Greeley letter of 1853 reprinted in Frank E. Comparato, *Chronicles of Genius and Folly: R. Hoe & Company and the Printing Press as a Service to Democracy* (Culver City, Calif., 1979), p. 98. *Memphis Commercial Appeal*, p. 54, Memphis *Appeal*, 19 Jan. 1859; Nashville *Union & American*, 19 Jan. 1859 and 15 May 1859; George S. Merriam, *The Life and Times of Samuel Bowles*, 2 vols. (New York, 1885), I, 68; *Newspaper Maker* 1 (13 June 1895): 5. The age of the paying customer was heralded in interviews with publishers: [Charles Austin Bates], *American Journalism from the Practical Side* (New York, 1897), pp. 64, 147, 179, and *Circulation Manager* 1 (July 1902): 10, 20; *ibid.* (May 1903): 3.

26. Nathan Elliot, *Proposals for Publishing at Catskill, New York, a Weekly Paper, Entitled the American Eagle* (Catskill, 1806); prospectus of the *New York Gazetteer and Northern Intelligencer* in Joel Munsell, *The Typographical Miscellany* (New York, 1850), pp. 224–25; and for the *Eastern Herald and Gazette of Maine* and the *Oriental Trumpet* in Fassett, *History of the Newspapers in the District of Maine*, pp. 42–43; also for the Bridgeton (N.J.) *Observer* in Edward R. Barnsley, *Presses and Printers of Newtown Before 1868* (Doylestown, Pa., 1938), p. 32. Lyon, *The Pioneer Editor in Missouri*, pp. 33–35. Blair and Lee Family Papers, Princeton University, Box 35, Folders 9–10, hold a number of subscription papers.

27. Lynn Marshall, "The Early Career of Amos Kendall: The Making of a Jacksonian," (Ph.D. diss., University of California, Berkeley, 1962), p. 424. *Niles' Register* 49 (19 Sept. 1835): 43. Richard B. Kielbowicz, *News in the Mail: The Press, Post Office, and Public Information, 1700–1860s* (New York, 1989), p. 70.

28. *Democratic Review* 27 (1850): 285–88, 381–84, 477–80; *ibid.* 28 (1851): 93–96, 189–92, 382–84.

29. Elisha Whittlesey to Joseph Gales and William W. Seaton, 21 March 1831, in Gales and Seaton Papers, Library of Congress. *The Papers of Willie Pearson Mangum*, ed. Henry T. Shanks, 5 vols. (Raleigh, 1950–56), II, 139, IV, 163–64. Hamilton, *The Country Printer*, pp. 230–31. Kielbowicz, *News in the Mail*, p. 105. Lyon, *The Pioneer Editor in Missouri*, p. 90. Estal E. Sparling, "The Jefferson Inquirer," *Missouri Historical Review* 32 (1938): 161. Ross, *Arkansas Gazette*, p. 266. Randall, *James Hall*, p. 96.

30. Philip Kinsley, *The Chicago Tribune: Its First Hundred Years*, 3 vols. (New York, 1943), I, 154–55, 162, 164, II, 25, 54–55, 70–71. George Britt, *Forty Years—Forty Millions: The Career of Frank A. Munsey* (New York, 1935), p. 71.

31. *New Yorker* 55 (15 Oct. 1979): 39. Leo Bogart, *Preserving the Press: How Daily Newspapers Mobilized to Keep Their Readers* (New York, 1991), pp. 140–41.

32. Merton L. Dillon, *Elijah P. Lovejoy: Abolitionist Editor* (Urbana, 1961), pp. 99–100. *Liberator*, 22 Jan. 1847, p. 15. Dorothy Sterling, *Ahead of Her Time: Abby Kelley and the Politics of Anti-Slavery* (New York, 1991), pp. 2, 215. Ronald J. Zboray, *A Fictive People: Antebellum Economic Development and the American Reading Public* (New York, 1993), p. 120.

33. Kieswetter, "German-American Labor Press," p. 144. John Graham, ed., *"Yours for the Revolution": The Appeal to Reason, 1895–1922* (Lincoln, Neb., 1990), pp. 17–18, 42. James R. Green, "The 'Salesmen-Soldiers' of the 'Appeal' Army: A Profile of Rank-and-File Socialist Agitators," in Bruce M. Stave, ed., *Socialism and the Cities* (Port Washington, N.Y., 1975), pp. 13–40.

34. G. D. Crain Jr., *Teacher of Business: The Publishing Philosophy of James H. McGraw* (Chicago, 1944), pp. 26, 86.

35. Howells, *Impressions and Experiences*, p. 21. *Pennsylvania Freeman*, 22 March

1838, p. 3; *Advocate of Freedom*, 22 Oct. 1840, p. 108. *Liberator*, 28 Nov. 1856, p. 189. "Who Does the Reading?" *American Newspaper Reporter* 6 (1 Jan. 1872): 5.

36. Nelson, *Notes Toward a History of the American Newspaper*, p. 166. *Western Monitor* (Fayette, Mo.), 24 March 1830. Montgomery *Advertiser*, 29 Aug. 1860, photostat in Grover C. Hall Papers, Folder 6, Alabama Department of Archives and History, Montgomery. Memphis *Daily Appeal*, 22 Sept. 1855. Chicago *Tribune*, 8 July 1876, p. 1, and 24 July 1876, p. 1.

37. *Madisonian*, 25 July 1840. Kielbowicz, *News in the Mail*, p. 101. For an example of neighbors signing up for the *Tribune* see *Pennsylvania Freeman*, 16 June 1853, p. 93. John M. Harrison, *The Blade of Toledo: The First 150 Years* (Toledo, 1985), p. 102. Thomas Harrison Baker, *The Memphis Commercial Appeal: The History of a Southern Newspaper* (Baton Rouge, 1971), pp. 48–49. William Petersen, *Pageant of the Press: A Survey of 125 Years of Iowa Journalism, 1836–1961* (Iowa City, 1962), pp. vi–vii. On clubs in the trade press see the first issues of *American Rail-Road Journal*, 2 Jan. 1831 [*sic*; 1832], p. 1, and *Plumber and Sanitary Engineer*, Dec. 1877, p. 1.

38. Nashville Postmaster Account Book, 1833–34 (#3181), Southern Historical Collection, University of North Carolina Library, Chapel Hill. Clyde Hull Cantrell, "The Reading Habits of Ante-Bellum Southerners," (Ph.D. diss., University of Illinois, 1960), p. 163. James Oliver Robertson and Janet C. Robertson, *All Our Yesterdays: A Century of Family Life in an American Small Town* (New York, 1993), p. 273.

39. *Peterson's* 29 (1856): 175. *Liberator*, 14 April 1837, p. 64. The readers were in Cambridge, New York, a town of about two thousand, nearly a hundred miles from Brandon.

40. See *Pennsylvania Freeman*, 14 Feb. 1839, p. 1, and 19 Feb. 1846, p. 1; *American Anti-Slavery Standard*, 22 May 1858, p. 4. W. B. Colver to E. W. Scripps, 10 Dec. 1910, p. 6, in E. W. Scripps Papers, Series 1.2, Ohio University.

41. *Peterson's* 30 (1856): 340. Mary Ellen Waller-Zuckerman, "The Business Side of Media Development: Popular Women's Magazines in the Late Nineteenth Century," *Essays in Economic and Business History* 7 (1989): 44–45.

42. Nelson, *Notes Toward a History of American Newspapers*, p. 394. Modest offers of free subscriptions to club organizers: Petersen, *Pageant of the Press*, pp. vi–vii; Lyon, *The Pioneer Editor in Missouri*, p. 91. For an art print offer of 1854 see Ross, *Arkansas Gazette*, p. 305. *Emery's Journal of Agriculture* 1 (1858): 232. Richard Bardolph, *Agricultural Literature and the Early Illinois Farmer* (Urbana, 1948), p. 167. Harrison, *The Blade of Toledo*, p. 102. Cloud, *The Business of Newspapers on the Western Frontier*, p. 39. John R. G. Hassard, *The Fast Printing Machine* (New York, 1978) has the *Tribune* offer on a flyleaf. On Ochs see the 100th anniversary issue of *Editor & Publisher* 117 (31 March 1984): 39. Lyons, *Newspaper Story*, p. 103.

43. Jason Rogers, *Newspaper Building* (New York, 1918), pp. 78–79 (c. 1893). Alfred McClung Lee, *The Daily Newspaper in America: The Evolution of a Social Instrument* (New York, 1947), p. 283.

44. *Demorest's Illustrated Monthly*, Dec. 1868; March 1869; Jan. 1871, quoted.

45. Elinor Rice Hays, *Morning Star: A Biography of Lucy Stone, 1818–1893* (New York, 1961), p. 219.

46. *Scientific American* 21 (1869): 395; *ibid.* 22 (1870), 129; Michael Borut, "The *Scientific American* in Nineteenth-Century America" (Ph.D. diss., New York University, 1977), pp. 70, 217–18. Britt, *Forty Years — Forty Millions*, has found an exceptional cash reward scheme run by Frank Munsey in the 1890s, but his success was tied to the gaudy premiums of publishers in Augusta, Maine, where he learned the business: see ad

facing p. 39, 43–45, 69. *Circulation Management* 4 (Jan. 1938): 17; *ibid*. 3 (July 1937): 10. Richard Loyer, "Specialized Subscription Sales," in S. Arthur Dembner and William E. Massee, eds., *Modern Circulation Methods* (New York, 1968), p. 88.

47. *Godey's Lady's Book* 14 (1837): 48. "Why We Give Premiums," *Demorest's Illustrated Monthly*, Dec. 1868. For the persistence of fraud on rural readers see *Circulation Management* 1 (Nov. 1902): 3.

48. Susan Strasser, *Satisfaction Guaranteed: The Making of the American Mass Market* (New York, 1989), pp. 147, 180 (quoted), 186.

49. *Frank Leslie's Illustrated Newspaper*, 25 Oct. 1856, p. 310. Fort Dodge (Iowa) *Sentinel*, 6 May 1859. Demaree, *The American Agricultural Press*, p. 122. *Michigan Farmer* 11 (1853): 367 offered fifty dollars, about nine hundred in current buying power. Jim Allee Hart, *A History of the St. Louis Globe-Democrat* (Columbia, Mo., 1961), p. 36. *Emery's Journal of Agriculture* 1 (1858): 24. *Circulation Manager* 1 (Dec. 1902): 6 and (April 1903): 4. William R. Scott, *Scientific Circulation Management* (New York, 1915), pp. 184–85.

50. Nichols, *Forty Years of Rural Journalism in Iowa*, pp. 80–83. *Circulation Manager* 1 (Jan. 1903): 11.

51. *Circulation Manager* 1 (Jan. 1903): 11, (Feb. 1903): 14, and (March 1903): 7. Lee, *The Daily Newspaper in America*, p. 283. Lyons, *Newspaper Story*, pp. 101–2, 153. The prizes did find their way into working-class homes: see Katharine Anthony, *Mothers Who Must Earn*, (New York, 1914), p. 142.

52. *Newspaper Maker* 4 (12 Nov. 1896): 3; *ibid*. 5 (29 April 1897): 8, (5 Aug. 1897): 4. Pulitzer's rivals dismissed his early success in New York as "a gift enterprise," and historians have passed over these contests, noting the substantial features of the *World* that won readers. Neither approach does Pulitzer justice. Jason Rogers, a discerning contemporary, pointed out that "when he was playing to an audience large enough to suit his purposes with the guessing contest and semi-lottery stage business, he . . . gradually withdrew the cheap stage lightning and clown side-show performances and was able to hold a large proportion of this previous audience by another kind of show, the publication of a newspaper." *Newspaper Maker* 4 (26 Nov. 1896): 3. Don C. Seitz, *Joseph Pulitzer: His Life & Letters* (New York, 1924), pp. 172–73.

53. Montgomery *Advertiser*, 27 Sept. 1953. "Ledger of Post Office Accounts," Calhoun, Missouri, 1851–53, in James A. Tutt Papers and "Accounts of Henderson Post Office" in William W. Reavis Papers, Special Collections, Duke University, Durham, N.C. I made a random sample of 24 names from the 234 indexed by the postmaster. Women made up only 6 to 10 percent of the lists in this two-year period. Many women, of course, received periodicals under the name of the head of household. I used all the women receiving news under their own name in the last quarter of 1857 and chose the same number of males at random from that list of 121 names. The Missouri county had about four thousand residents; the North Carolina county had about seventeen hundred. Kielbowicz, *News in the Mail*, p. 113, has used these records for a different purpose. Postal records are imperfect measures of reading, for they do not track the publications that came postage free. But the stops and starts that postmasters struggled to keep up with in their ledgers speak clearly of a public casting about for information (and perhaps also, better premiums).

54. Thomas Low Nichols, *Forty Years of American Life*, 2 vols. (London, 1864), I, 325. Richard Watson Gilder, "The Newspaper, the Magazine, and the Public," *Outlook* 61 (1899): 318–19. *Circulation Manager* 1 (April 1903): 6. Jno. L. Foley, "Long Term Subscriptions," *Circulation Manager* 1 (Aug. 1902): 7. Julius Chambers in Melville

Philips, ed., *The Making of a Newspaper* (New York, 1893), p. 46. E. W. Scripps to W. H. Porterfield, 10 April 1905, and to E. H. Wells, 26 July 1905, Series 1.2, Box 5, Folders 5 and 8; circular letter from W. W. Thornton, 21 July 1905, in E. W. Scripps Papers, Ohio University, Athens. I am grateful to Gerald Baldasty for sharing copies of these documents.

55. Julius Chambers in Melville Philips, ed., *The Making of a Newspaper* (New York, 1893), p. 46. Mott, *A History of American Magazines*, I, 581, 593, II, 454–60, III, 327. Winkler, "Influence of Godey's Lady's Book," p. 4. O. F. Byxbee, *Establishing a Newspaper* (Chicago, 1901), p. 78. Thorn with Pfeil, *Newspaper Circulation*, p. 117. Leo Bogart, *Press and Public: Who Reads What, When, Where, and Why in American Newspapers*, 2nd ed. (Hillsdale, N.J., 1989), p. 65.

56. *Circulation Manager* 1 (July 1902) and (Oct. 1902) for premium ads; more elaborate knickknacks were announced in April 1903, "yours until the last penny is paid." On San Francisco see *ibid.* (Jan. 1903): 3.

57. Diane McFarlin, "Young People Don't See Themselves as Part of the Newspaper Reading 'Club,'" *Bulletin of the American Society of Newspaper Editors*, March 1994, pp. 5–7. Frank Smith, *Joining the Literacy Club* (Portsmouth, N.H., 1988).

Chapter 3

1. *Register of Debates*, 22nd Cong., 1st Sess. (4 May 1832), pp. 885–86, 888, and (9 May 1832), p. 910. Richard D. Birdsall, *Berkshire County: A Cultural History* (New Haven, 1959), pp. 207–8 (1846). For an earlier and more extreme alarm see Milton W. Hamilton, *The Country Printer: New York State, 1785–1830* (Port Washington, N.Y., 1964), pp. 234–35, 237. William H. Lyon, *The Pioneer Editor in Missouri, 1808–1860* (Columbia, Mo., 1965) p. 121. Grundy, "Postage on Newspapers" (19 May 1832), no. 120 in *American State Papers* (Washington, D.C., 1834), VII, 347–48. For the full context of this debate see Richard R. John Jr., *Spreading the News: The American Postal System from Franklin to Morse* (Cambridge, Mass., 1995).

2. *Congressional Globe*, 31st Cong., 2nd Sess. (18 Dec. 1850), pp. 72, 74.

3. W. Sherman Savage, *The Controversy over the Distribution of Abolition Literature, 1830–1860* (Washington, D.C., 1938), pp. 13, 92. Leonard L. Richards, *"Gentlemen of Property and Standing": Anti-Abolition Mobs in Jacksonian America* (New York, 1970). During July 1835, the month that ended with the Charleston disturbance, 175,000 publications were sent out, 20,000 of these through the mail to the South. Figures such as these have not always impressed historians: see, for example, John Nerone, *Violence Against the Press: Policing the Public Sphere in U.S. History* (New York, 1994), pp. 88–90. Calm appraisals that the print campaign "was more smoke than fire" (p. 89) miss the point that many antebellum Americans believed that they were trapped and doomed in a new political forum.

4. Savage, *The Controversy over the Distribution of Abolition Literature*, pp. 99–100. Alfred Huger to Amos Kendall, 29 July 1835 and 5 Aug. 1835, in the Richmond *Enquirer*, 25 Aug. 1835. "Postmaster Huger and the Incendiary Publications," ed. Frank Otto Gatell, *South Carolina Historical Magazine* 64 (1963): 193–201.

5. *The Trial of Reuben Crandall, M. D., charged with publishing seditious libels* . . . (New York, 1836), p. 58. Massillon *Gazette*, 5 Sept. 1835, in *Niles' Register* 49 (3 Oct. 1835): 80. On the opening of the slavery debate by the white South see William W. Freehling, *Prelude to Civil War: The Nullification Controversy in South Carolina, 1816–*

1836 (New York, 1968), pp. 327 ff., and Joe Williams, "Window on Freedom: South Carolina's Response to British West Indian Slave Emancipation, 1833–1834," *South Carolina Historical Magazine* 85 (1984): 135–44, esp. 141. Alison Goodyear Freehling, *Drift Toward Dissolution: The Virginia Slavery Debate of 1831–1832* (Baton Rouge, 1982) shows that the newspaper debate over slavery in this state was not confined to a brief period of time or a special region.

6. Janet Duitsman Cornelius, *"When I Can Read My Title Clear": Literacy, Slavery, and Religion in the Antebellum South* (Columbia, S.C., 1991), pp. 8–10.

7. Joseph C. Lovejoy and Owen Lovejoy, eds., *Memoir of the Rev. Elijah P. Lovejoy* (New York, 1838), pp. 141–42. "Address of the Anti-Slavery Society," in *Niles' Register* 49 (12 Sept. 1835): 28–29.

8. Freehling, *Drift Toward Dissolution*, pp. 196–201. Larry E. Tise, *Proslavery: A History of the Defense of Slavery in America, 1701–1840* (Athens, Ga., 1987), pp. 310–11. One of these early Southern columns against slavery was preserved in the Weld-Grimké household: Staunton (Va.) *Spectator*, 25 Nov. 1831, in Weld-Grimké Papers, William L. Clements Library, University of Michigan, Ann Arbor (hereafter, Weld-Grimké Papers).

9. Alfred Huger to Amos Kendall, 29 July 1835 and 5 Aug. 1835, in the Richmond *Enquirer*, 25 Aug. 1835. There was precedent for the mobbing of a post office to seize a hated newspaper: Frank Cassell, "The Great Baltimore Riot of 1812," *Maryland Historical Magazine* 70 (1975): 258.

10. *Niles' Register* 48 (29 Aug. 1835): 454–56; *ibid.* 49 (5 Sept. 1835): 9; *ibid.* (10 Oct. 1835), 90.

11. *Niles' Register* 48 (29 Aug. 1835): 454; *ibid.* 49 (5 Sept. 1835): 9–11, (12 Sept. 1835): 28, (3 Oct. 1835): 73.

12. Richards, *"Gentlemen of Property and Standing,"* pp. 14, 69, 91–92, 95–99, 101, 110, 113. *Niles' Register* 49 (3 Oct. 1835): 78, (31 Oct. 1835): 145.

13. John B. Pickard, ed., *Letters of John Greenleaf Whittier*, 3 vols. (Cambridge, Mass., 1975), I, 306. Richards, *"Gentlemen of Property and Standing,"* p. 128. Nerone, *Violence Against the Press*, p. 93, found that between a fifth and a sixth of 134 incidents were directed against the press. It is difficult to know, of course, whether actions against lecturers and others were set up by the spread of print.

14. *Niles' Register* 48 (22 Aug. 1835): 438; *ibid.* 49 (10 Oct. 1835): 89–90. Richards, *"Gentlemen of Property and Standing,"* pp. 27–29, 58, 115–17, 121–23.

15. *Niles' Register* 48 (22 Aug. 1835): 438. "The Fruits of Amalgamation" (1839), issued by John Childs, is reproduced in David Grimsted, ed., *Notions of the Americans, 1820–1860* (New York, 1970), p. 104.

16. *Memoir of the Rev. Elijah P. Lovejoy*, p. 220. Richard M. Rollins, *The Long Journey of Noah Webster* (Philadelphia, 1980), pp. 32–33, 127. See also Cynthia S. Jordan, "'Old Words' in 'New Circumstances': Language and Leadership in Post-Revolutionary America," *American Quarterly* 40 (1988): 491–513.

17. Clipping on Portland meeting from the *National Intelligencer*, 26 Aug. 1835, in Weld-Grimké Papers. *Niles' Register* 48 (29 Aug. 1835): 455–56.

18. Massillon *Gazette*, 5 Sept. 1835, in *Niles' Register* 49 (3 Oct 1835): 79–80, see also 72, 75.

19. [Calvin Colton], *Abolition a Sedition* (Philadelphia, 1839; 1973 reprint), pp. 31, 43–44, 104, 186, confirms Richards's picture of an elite scared of a new way of distributing political information. John C. Nerone, *The Culture of the Press in the Early Republic—Cincinnati, 1793–1848* (New York, 1989), pp. 264–274, qualifies Richards's

argument but emphasizes this town's fear that an antislavery paper would destroy Cincinnati's reputation. Robert P. Forbes, "Setting the Imps to Work: The Politics of Anti-Abolitionism and the Election of 1836" shows the role of national political strategists in the outbreak of demonstrations.

20. No scholar has estimated that more than 10 percent of slaves could read this material; see Cornelius,*"When I Can Read My Title Clear,"* pp. 8–10. *The Trial of Reuben Crandall,* pp. 58–62. *Niles' Register* 49 (5 Sept. 1835): 11. Clipping on Albany meeting from the *National Intelligencer,* 12 Sept. 1835, in Weld-Grimké Papers. Richards, *"Gentlemen of Property and Standing,"* p. 57.

21. Richards, *"Gentlemen of Property and Standing"* has the Tyler speech, pp. 56–58. Richard B. Kielbowicz, *News in the Mail: The Press, Post Office, and Public Information, 1700–1860s* (New York, 1989), p. 66 on the Virginia petitioners. *Niles' Register* 49 (12 Sept. 1835): 20–21, (3 Oct. 1835): 74, 77. Richmond *Enquirer* quoted in *Emancipator,* Oct. 1835. Richard Yeadon, *The Amenability of Northern Incendiaries . . .* (Charleston, 1853) [1835], p. 17. Cassius M. Clay, the antislavery editor from Kentucky, held up his own new press as the perfect expression of a free labor system that the South could not match. See the selection from *The True American,* 10 June 1844, in Grimsted, ed., *Notions of the Americans,* p. 295.

22. David Paul Nord, "Systematic Benevolence: Religious Publishing and the Marketplace in Early Nineteenth-Century America," in Leonard I. Sweet, ed., *Communications and Change in American Religious History* (Grand Rapids, Mich., 1993). Cincinnatus (William Plumer ?), *Freedom's defence, or, A candid examination of Mr. Calhoun's report on the freedom of the press made to the Senate of the United States, Feb. 4, 1836* (Worcester, 1836), p. 22.

23. *Manufactures of the United States in 1860 . . . the Eighth Census* (Washington, D.C., 1865), p. cxlii. Hinton Rowan Helper, *The Impending Crisis of the South: How to Meet It,* ed. George M. Fredrickson (Cambridge, Mass., 1968) [1857], pp. 390–92. Ottis Clark Skipper, *J. D. B. DeBow: Magazinist of the Old South* (Athens, Ga., 1958), pp. 24–25, 50, 61–63, 83–84, 87–88, 125.

24. The *Emancipator* (Oct. 1835) praised Green for republishing more antislavery material than Southern mobs had burned and warned him that he might be lynched by his friends. William S. Pretzer, "'The British, Duff Green, the Rats, and the Devil': Custom, Capitalism, and the Conflict in the Washington Printing Trade, 1834–36," *Labor History* 27 (1985–86): 5–30, esp. 13–15. Fletcher M. Green, "Duff Green, Militant Journalist of the Old School," *American Historical Review* 52 (1947): 256–58. The *Southern Press* (1850–52) was another failed effort to build a counter-weight to leading Northern papers.

25. "Report from the Select Committee on the Circulation of Incendiary Publications," 4 Feb. 1836, *The Papers of John C. Calhoun,* ed. Robert L. Meriwether, 21 vols. (Columbia, S.C., 1959–1993), XIII, 65–66. The Postmaster General's report to the President for 1835 drew an analogy between the abolitionist press and subversive papers sent to the laboring population of another country. Each was a just cause of war, he said. See report of 19 Dec. 1835, pp. 277–78. For another expression of fear of the corrupting power of print in both North and South see [William J. Hobby], *Remarks upon Slavery, Occasioned by Attempts Made to Circulate Improper Publications in the Southern States* [Charleston, 1835], p. 23, reprinted in *A Defense of Southern Slavery and Other Pamphlets* (New York, 1969).

26. *Niles' Weekly Register* 49 (5 Sept. 1835): 10–13. Clipping on Cooperstown meeting from *National Intelligencer,* 2 Oct. 1835, in Weld-Grimké Papers. *Niles' Weekly*

Register 48 (22 Aug. 1835): 446, (29 Aug. 1835): 455. Russel B. Nye, *Fettered Freedom: Civil Liberties and the Slavery Controversy, 1830–1860* (East Lansing, 1964), p. 77n.

27. *Letters of Theodore Dwight Weld, Angelina Grimké Weld, and Sarah Grimké, 1822–1844*, ed. Gilbert H. Barnes and Dwight L. Dumond, 2 vols. (Gloucester, Mass., 1965), II, 717.

28. Katharine Du Pre Lumpkin, *The Emancipation of Angelina Grimké* (Chapel Hill, 1974), p. 171. Benjamin P. Thomas, *Theodore Dwight Weld* (New Brunswick, 1950), p. 169. We do not know to what extent the two women may have led this project. We should not assume that Weld was the guiding force simply because he followed the convention of accepting credit on the title page for collaborative work with females. The feminist press of both the nineteenth and twentieth centuries has had a habit of excerpting and subverting press comment: see Linda Steiner, "Oppositional Decoding as an Act of Resistance," in Robert K. Avery and David Eason, eds., *Critical Perspectives on Media and Society* (New York, 1991), pp. 329–45.

29. Thomas M. Owen, "An Alabama Protest Against Abolition in 1835," *Gulf States Historical Magazine* 2 (July 1903): 26–34. *American Slavery as It Is: Testimony of a Thousand Witnesses* (New York, 1839), p. 172. The next item exposed a distinguished leader of the Charleston mob, Robert Y. Hayne, as a divider of slave families.

30. *American Slavery as It Is*, p. 175. Donald E. Reynolds, *Editors Make War: Southern Newspapers in the Secession Crisis* (Nashville, 1970), pp. 4–5. Ronald J. Zboray, *A Fictive People: Antebellum Economic Development and the American Reading Public* (New York, 1993), p. 122. Harriet Beecher Stowe, *A Key to Uncle Tom's Cabin . . .* (Boston, 1853), p. 21. *Emancipator*, 27 June 1839 and 11 July 1839, reprinted in Richard O. Curry and Joanna Dunlap Cowden, eds., *Slavery in America: Theodore Weld's American Slavery as It Is* (Itasca, Ill., 1972), pp. 243–44.

31. In April and May 1839, the *Emancipator* printed excerpts from the Weld-Grimké newspaper collection. This magazine took orders for antislavery window blinds, 13 June 1839, and commended a pilgrimage to the newspaper archive on 20 Feb. 1840. Frederick Douglass, *Narrative of the Life of Frederick Douglass, an American Slave, Written by Himself*, ed. Benjamin Quarles (Cambridge, Mass., 1988) [1845], pp. 13–14. Louise H. Johnson, "The Source of the Chapter on Slavery in Dickens's *American Notes*," *American Literature* 14 (1942–43): 427–30. Thomas, *Theodore Weld*, p. 223. Stowe, "The Story of Uncle Tom's Cabin," *Old South Leaflets*, General Series, 4 (Boston, [1897]), no. 82, p. 6, is her direct testimony that she read the Weld-Grimké pamphlet when she was writing the novel. See also Gilbert H. Barnes, *The Antislavery Impulse, 1830–1844* (New York, 1964), p. 231n. Stowe's intellectual debt to the pamphlet was large, but Barnes is incorrect in saying that *The Key to Uncle Tom's Cabin* was "composed largely" of the Weld-Grimké work. Stowe made her own investigation of newspapers in the slave states.

32. Stowe, *A Key to Uncle Tom's Cabin*; see pp. 21, 109–10 for the Weld-Grimké clippings. Stowe's scrapbook emphasized the callous listings of blacks for sale (items that *American Slavery as It Is* had passed over). In a survey of two South Carolina papers over a single week of 1852 she found eighteen invitations to split up slave families. Even before this work, there was culling of the Southern press to vindicate *Uncle Tom's Cabin*, e.g., *Pennsylvania Freeman*, 25 Sept. 1852, pp. 153–54. This would continue, e.g., *The New "Reign of Terror" in the Slaveholding States, for 1859–1860* (New York, 1860).

33. *Emancipator*, 10 Sept. 1840, cited in Thomas, *Theodore Weld*, p. 172. *Southern Literary Messenger* 9 (1843): 62. The anti-abolitionist press made no specific charges of inaccuracy. The most likely explanation is that they found none. In preparing an

abridged edition of *American Slavery as It Is*, the editors checked a random sample of about 30 percent of the Weld-Grimké documentation. They found no errors. See Curry and Cowden, eds., *Slavery in America*, p. ix. Nehemiah Adams, *A South-Side View of Slavery* (Boston, 1860) [1854], pp. 71–73; at p. 52 and p. 120, Adams showed that clippings from the Northern press might be used to underscore Southern arguments.

34. Adams, *A South-Side View of Slavery*, pp. 94–96, reprints but does not identify this exchange in a Southern paper. A Citizen of Georgia, *Remarks upon Slavery, Occasioned by Attempts Made to Circulate Improper Publications in the Southern States* [1835], in *A Defense of Southern Slavery and Other Pamphlets* (New York, 1969), pp. 18–19, 24. Philip Kinsley, *The Chicago Tribune: Its First Hundred Years*, 3 vols. (New York, 1943), I, 158. Southern publishers produced two thick volumes of the most celebrated proslavery writings before the war came. The contributors did not use the Northern press to their advantage: *The Pro-Slavery Argument* . . . (Charleston, 1852) [1968 reprint] and E. N. Elliott, ed., *Cotton is King, and Pro-Slavery Arguments* . . . (Augusta, 1860) [1969 reprint]. George M. Fredrickson, *The Black Image in the White Mind: The Debate on Afro-American Character and Destiny, 1817–1914* (Middletown, 1987) points out that abolitionists had a difficult time explaining the troubles of the free black communities (pp. 35–39). The South did little to probe this weakness. For the exceptional Southern paper that did cull the Northern press for items that discredited that society see William L. Barney, *The Secessionist Impulse: Alabama and Mississippi in 1860* (Princeton, 1974), p. 163.

35. Bellinger's speech in *Emancipator*, Nov. 1835. Simms's pamphlet of 1838 reprinted in *The Proslavery Argument* (1852), quoted, pp. 175–76; see also p. 174 for James H. Hammond's insistence that he had not written with publication in view. Tise, *Proslavery*, p. 262. Henry F. James, *Abolitionism Unveiled* (Cincinnati, 1856), a novel answering *Uncle Tom's Cabin*, told readers not to expect a key to document his charges against the North (p. 250).

36. William M. Moss, "Vindicator of Southern Intellect and Institutions: The *Southern Quarterly Review*," *Southern Literary Journal* 13 (1980): 77, 84–85. Drew Gilpin Faust, *A Sacred Circle: The Dilemma of the Intellectual in the Old South, 1840–1860* (Baltimore, 1977), pp. 90–95, 109, 112, 117. Skipper, *J. D. B. DeBow*, pp. 125, 131. Barney, *The Secessionist Impulse*, p. 47.

37. Ronald T. Takaki, *A Pro-Slavery Crusade: The Agitation to Reopen the African Slave Trade* (New York, 1971), chap. 7.

38. See Takaki, *A Pro-Slavery Crusade*, pp. 160 ff., esp. p. 198.

39. *The Pro-Slavery Argument* (1852), pp. 2–3, 174–76, 293, 489. Elliott, the editor of *Cotton is King* (1860), noted that there was no special effort to find a market and that the work was not stereotyped to make future editions easy: pp. xii, 26. Use of abolitionist journalists as foils in debate was a common tactic for George Fitzhugh: see *Cannibals All! or, Slaves Without Masters*, ed. C. Vann Woodward (Cambridge, Mass., 1960), pp. 9, 92–95, 257–59; p. 192 quoted. His calls for a bolder Southern press with a broader readership are in *Sociology for the South; or, The Failure of Free Society* (Richmond, 1854), pp. 146, 290.

40. The embargo on news is documented in the *Liberator*, 19 Dec. 1856, p. 203; 25 Sept. 1857, p. 156; 27 Nov. 1857, p. 189; 11 May 1860, p. 73. See also *The "Reign of Terror" in the Slaveholding States*, esp. pp. 10, 100, 116, 119, 143.

41. August Meier and Elliott Rudwick, "The Boycott Movement Against Jim Crow Streetcars in the South, 1900–1906," *Journal of American History* 55 (1969): 756–75. The most widely circulated magazine of the late nineteenth and early twentieth centu-

ries published only one article on blacks in a half century: Salme H. Steinberg, "Reformer in the Marketplace: Edward W. Bok and the Ladies' Home Journal, 1889–1919" (Ph.D. diss., Johns Hopkins University, 1971), p. 134. *Editor & Publisher* 86 (31 Oct. 1953). Ann Waldron, *Hodding Carter: The Reconstruction of a Racist* (Chapel Hill, 1993) tells the story of Carter's growing boldness on this issue.

42. Loudon Wainwright, *The Great American Magazine: An Inside History of Life* (New York, 1986), p. 174. James L. Baughman, *Henry R. Luce and the Rise of the American News Media* (Boston, 1987), p. 165. A. J. van Zuilen, *The Life Cycle of Magazines* (Uithoorn, Netherlands, 1977). Shirley Tucker, *Mississippi from Within* (New York, 1965) used embarrassing clips taken from five thousand issues of papers in that state and was the closest counterpart to *American Slavery as It Is*.

43. On peaceful harassment see Anthony Lewis, *Make No Law: The Sullivan Case and the First Amendment* (New York, 1991), pp. 34–45. CBS kept its crew out of Alabama during 1962–63 out of fear of being served papers in a libel suit over a story it had broadcast on the abridgment of voting rights: Robert Schakne, Panel 1, *Covering the South: A National Symposium on the Media and the Civil Rights Movement* (videotape), 3–5 April 1987. When the Northern media used Southern authors and sources, these locals were menaced: see, for example, William Peters, *The Southern Temper* (Garden City, N.Y., 1959), pp. 26–28; "Segregation," part 4, *Life*, 24 Sept. 1956; Robert T. Elson, *The World of Time Inc.* (New York, 1973), p. 407.

44. Fred Powledge, *Free at Last? The Civil Rights Movement and the People Who Made It* (Boston, 1991), pp. 515–16, and *Covering the South*, Panels 1–2. Bob Warner, "The Southern Story," *Editor & Publisher* 94 (10 June 1961): 76, (17 June 1961): 55. Michael Dorman, *We Shall Overcome* (New York, 1964), p. 54. What follows is based on the records I have found of fifty-two assaults, 1956–65, involving thirty photographers and broadcasters, eight Time-Life staffers, and six black journalists.

45. Bob Considine quoted in Philip Schuyler, "Panelists Agree: Journalistic Code Violated at Little Rock," *Editor & Publisher* 90 (2 Nov. 1957): 66. Claude Sitton in Howell Raines, *My Soul Is Rested: Movement Days in the Deep South Remembered* (New York, 1977), p. 380.

46. Atlanta *Constitution*, 24 Sept. 1957. *Editor & Publisher* 95 (6 Oct. 1962): 11. Charles Dunagin, Karl Fleming, John Lewis, and Charles Quinn, *Covering the South*, Panel 2. At the time, Grover C. Hall of the Montgomery *Advertiser* saw the attack as Lewis was later to describe it: *Editor & Publisher* 94 (10 June 1961): 13. Taylor Branch, *Parting the Waters: America in the King Years* (New York, 1988), pp. 444–45, 559.

47. Benjamin Fine in "The Mob and the Newsmen," *Bulletin of the American Society of Newspaper Editors* (*BASNE*), Nov. 1957, p. 2. "Newsmen Attacked as Police Look On," *Editor & Publisher* 96 (27 Feb. 1965): 15. On the alliance between mob and police in Birmingham see Powledge, *Free at Last?* pp. 273–74.

48. Washington *Post*, 20 Oct. 1962, p. 9; Wallace Westfeldt, "The Mob and the Newsmen," *BASNE*, Nov. 1957, p. 5; Stephen J. Whitfield, *A Death in the Delta: The Story of Emmett Till* (New York, 1988), pp. 117–18. Osborn Elliott, *The World of Oz* (New York, 1980), p. 72. Powledge, *Free at Last?* p. 516. Peters, *The Southern Temper*, p. 151. James Graham Cook, *The Segregationists* (New York, 1962), pp. 266–67. Richard Lentz, *Symbols, the News Magazines, and Martin Luther King* (Baton Rouge, 1990).

49. Thomas Davis, Benjamin Fine, Walter Lister Jr., Bert Collier, Robert S. Ball, Herbert F. Corn, and Wallace Westfeldt, "The Mob and the Newsmen," *BASNE*, Nov. 1957, pp. 1–5, quoted p. 2.

50. Washington *Post*, 24 Sept. 1957, p. A10; New York *Times*, 24 Sept. 1957, pp. 18–

19. Don Shoemaker, *BASNE*, Oct. 1957, p. 1. New York *Times*, 21 May 1961, p. 78. At the University of Georgia, a KKK newspaper spread through the mob a short time before reporters came under attack; see Atlanta *Constitution*, 12 Jan. 1961, p. 1, and New York *Times*, 11 Jan. 1961, p. 1.

51. Dorman, *We Shall Overcome*, p. 58. Richard Valeriani in Raines, *My Soul Is Rested*, p. 371. Bob Warner, "Camera is a Red Flag to Mob," *Editor & Publisher* 94 (10 June 1961): 13. Daisy Bates, *The Long Shadow of Little Rock: A Memoir* (New York, 1962), p. 92.

52. *Time* 70 (7 Oct. 1957): 24–25; Elizabeth Huckaby, *Crisis at Central High, Little Rock, 1957–58* (Baton Rouge, 1980) reproduces the photo of white schoolgirls from the *Arkansas Gazette*; on the other photo Gov. Faubus used, see *Life*, 7 Oct. 1957, p. 43. *Eyes on the Prize* part 1 has a film clip of the Governor holding up the picture of the bleeding agitator, C. E. Blake. Haynes Johnson, *Dusk at the Mountain* (New York, 1963), pp. 132–33. Richard Sanders, *Covering the South*, Panel 5. Nelson Benton in Raines, *My Soul Is Rested*, pp. 385–86.

53. W. Fitzhugh Brundage, *Lynching in the New South: Georgia and Virginia, 1880–1930* (Urbana, 1993) shows that secrecy played a role but that, in its most popular form, lynching called for a "visible, explicit, public act of participation" (p. 40). Howard Smead, *Blood Justice: The Lynching of Mack Charles Parker* (New York, 1986), p. 77. Warner, "Camera is a Red Flag to Mob," p. 13. "Newsmen's Attackers Are Fined," *Editor & Publisher* 96 (13 March 1965): 10.

54. Erik Barnouw, *The Image Empire: A History of Broadcasting in the United States*, vol. 3 (New York, 1970), p. 65. Frank Luther Mott, *American Journalism: A History, 1690–1960* (New York, 1962), pp. 682–83. Branch, *Parting the Waters*, p. 323. J. Fred MacDonald, *Black and White TV: African Americans in Television Since 1948*, 2nd ed. (Chicago, 1992), pp. 49–54.

55. *Covering the South*, Panel 1.

56. *Life*, for instance, showed (11 Oct. 1954) that a Russian propaganda film concocted press accounts of black protest to show that capitalism was unjust. Richard Lentz and Pamela A. Brown, "'The Business of Great Nations': International Coverage, Foreign Public Opinion, and the Modern American Civil Rights Movement," paper read at the Western Journalism Historians Conference, University of California, Berkeley, 28–29 Feb. 1992, pp. 4–7, 10. Branch, *Parting the Waters*, pp. 184, 425–26. Memphis *Commercial Appeal*, 22 May 1961, as quoted in Hugh Davis Graham, *Crisis in Print: Desegregation and the Press in Tennessee* ([Nashville], 1967), p. 211. Horror at the national and world audience for pictures of local strife is sharply expressed in the Florida Legislative Investigative Committee report of 1965, reprinted in David Garrow, ed., *St. Augustine, Florida, 1963–1964: Mass Protest and Racial Violence* (Brooklyn, 1989), pp. 190–91.

57. John Lewis in *Covering the South*, Panel 3. Papers of the Congress of Racial Equality, Swarthmore College. "The Albany Story," broadside in Martin Luther King Jr. Papers, King Center Library and Archives, Atlanta, Ser. I, Box 1, Folder 27. See also Branch, *Parting the Waters*, illustration 29 and pp. 288–89.

58. On the iconography of lynching: Ida B. Wells, *A Red Record* (Chicago, [1894]), pp. 55–56. Walter White, *Rope and Faggot: A Biography of Judge Lynch* (New York, 1969) [1929], p. 27. Arthur F. Raper, *The Tragedy of Lynching* (Chapel Hill, 1933), p. 420. James R. McGovern, *Anatomy of a Lynching: The Killing of Claude Neal* (Baton Rouge, 1982), pp. 84–85, 96. McGovern, noting the dramatic drop in the number of lynchings, argues that in the mid-thirties "the new national community created by the

media now provided an effective inhibitor" (p. 142). A 1935 postcard of a Mississippi lynching, suitable for sending a message, is in the Josiah William Bailey Papers (Box 326), Special Collections Library, Duke University, Durham, N.C.

59. [Albert C. (Buck) Persons], *Sex and Civil Rights: The True Selma Story* (Birmingham, 1965), pp. 16–19, 28. William Bradford Huie, "Los Angeles & Hayneville — A Connecting Thread," New York *Herald Tribune*, 22 Aug. 1965, p. 14. Theodore H. White, *In Search of History: A Personal Adventure* (New York, 1978), p. 507; see also Edward Bliss Jr., *Now the News: The Story of Broadcast Journalism* (New York, 1991), p. 321. Nelson Benton in Raines, *My Soul Is Rested*, p. 386.

60. Bob Warner, "Reporting Racial Strife in the South," *Editor & Publisher* 94 (10 June 1961): 76. Bob Warner, "Omens in Alabama," *ibid.* (17 June 1961): 55 (quoted). Bob Warner, "Violence & the News," *ibid.* (24 June 1961): 15. Waldron, *Hodding Carter*, pp. 243–47.

61. The African American reporter Ted Poston has a memoir of Hall in Paul L. Fisher and Ralph L. Lowenstein, eds., *Race and the News Media* (New York, 1967), 65–66. David J. Garrow, *The Walking City: The Montgomery Bus Boycott, 1955–1956* (New York, 1989), p. 234. Bob Warner, "Omens in Alabama," p. 14.

62. Montgomery *Advertiser*, 29 March 1956, p. 4, 13 April 1956, p. 4, and 14 April 1956, p. 4.

63. "Tell It Not in Gath," *Time* 67 (23 April 1956): 62–63. Robert W. Brown, "Sage of Goat Hill," *BASNE*, Nov. 1956, pp. 5–6. *Christian Science Monitor*, 10 April 1956, p. 7. Daniel Webster Hollis, *An Alabama Newspaper Tradition: Grover C. Hall and the Hall Family* (University, Ala., 1983), pp. 107–8. Graham, *Crisis in Print*, pp. 302–3. Capital Citizens Council, *The Little Rock School Board's Plans for Your Child* [1961], in author's possession. Harry S. Ashmore, *An Epitaph for Dixie* (New York, 1958), p. 158. Numan V. Bartley, *The Rise of Massive Resistance: Race and Politics in the South During the 1950s* (Baton Rouge, 1969) finds this series "was very likely the most successful of all deliberative southern efforts to influence northern opinion" (p. 179).

64. Grover C. Hall Papers, Alabama Department of Archives and History, Montgomery, Folders 2 and 9, document an award for reporting on black sports and praise for attention to an NAACP event in early 1954. Three years after King left Montgomery, a friend sent him a clipping of Hall's uncomplimentary views: Charles S. Conley to MLK, in Martin Luther King Jr. Papers, King Center Library and Archives, Atlanta, Ser. I, Box 1, Folder 21. Martin Luther King Jr., *Stride Toward Freedom: The Montgomery Story* (New York, 1958), pp. 49, 85, 176. John Lewis, *Covering the South*, Panel 3. Jo Ann Gibson Robinson, *The Montgomery Bus Boycott and the Women Who Started It . . .* , ed. David J. Garrow (Knoxville, 1987), pp. 81–82, 106. Brown, "Sage of Goat Hill," p. 5.

65. Wayne Greenhaw, *Watch Out for George Wallace* (Englewood Cliffs, 1976), pp. 116–17. Ray Jenkins, "Wallace Beats the Press," *Nieman Reports* 24 (1970): 6. Grover C. Hall Jr., "Faust at Tuscaloosa," *Masthead* 15 (1963): 12–16.

66. George C. Wallace, *Stand Up for America* (Garden City, N.J., 1976), pp. 22–23. Bill Jones, *The Wallace Story* (Northport, Ala., 1966), pp. 149, 201, 432. [Jack House], *George Wallace Tells It Like It Is* (Selma, 1969), pp. 77–79. Jenkins, "Wallace Beats the Press," pp. 3–8.

67. Marshall Frady, *Wallace* (New York, 1968), pp. 25, 169. Jenkins, "Wallace Beats the Press," p. 4. E. Culpepper Clark, *The Schoolhouse Door: Segregation's Last Stand at the University of Alabama* (New York, 1993), pp. 201, 215.

68. Jones, *Wallace Story* is a compendium on the hypocrisy theme from the stump:

pp. 9, 109, 126, 146, 182, 201, 252. This was seconded by the Montgomery *Advertiser* (p. 86) during Wallace's first appearance before a panel of journalists on a network, "Meet the Press" in 1963. Wallace brought Hall along for this interview.

69. Civil rights scholars have rarely employed social science models to explain the role of media in changing attitudes. David J. Garrow, *Protest at Selma: Martin Luther King, Jr., and the Voting Rights Act of 1965* (New Haven, 1978) is an exception, drawing on the theories of E. E. Schattschneider. Todd Gitlin, *The Whole World Is Watching: Mass Media in the Making & Unmaking of the New Left* (Berkeley, 1980) is the most ambitious and successful attempt to fit theories to the practice of journalism in modern protests, but this book does not take up the first decade of civil rights coverage in the national media. William A. Gamson and Gadi Wolfsfeld, "Movements and Media as Interacting Systems," *Annals of the American Academy of Political and Social Science* 258 (1993): 114–25, revived interest in "scope enlargement" and the "struggle over meaning," but these theories are untested in American racial discourse. There are superb narrative and institutional histories of the civil rights struggle, but the press has been gone over lightly. "We are on unploughed ground," Jack Nelson said in welcome to his fellow correspondents of this era to the conference *Covering the South* in 1987. The same can be said today.

Chapter 4

1. Frank Luther Mott, *A History of American Magazines*, 5 vols. (Cambridge, Mass., 1966–68), I, 341–2, IV, 11.

2. David Paul Nord, "Religious Reading and Readers in Antebellum America," paper delivered at the Annual Meeting of the Society for Historians of the Early American Republic, July 1993, p. 13. E. L. Godkin, "Newspapers Here and Abroad," *North American Review* 150 (1897): 203. B. B. Herbert, ed., *The First Decennium of the National Editorial Association of the United States* (Chicago, 1896), pp. 535–36. John B. Opdycke, *News, Ads, and Sales* (New York, 1914), pp. 76–77.

3. Julia McNair Wright, *Practical Life; or, Ways and Means for Developing Character and Resources* (Philadelphia, 1882), pp. 214–19, 218–19 quoted.

4. On reading at the edge of settlement see William Nelson, *Notes Toward a History of the American Newspaper* (New York, 1918), p. 132; Robert Penn Warren, ed., *John Greenleaf Whittier's Poetry* (Minneapolis,1971), pp. 185–86; Ella Sterling Cummins [Mighels], *The Story of the Files: A Review of California Writers and Literature* (San Francisco, 1893), p. 79; [William M. Baker], "Inside. A Chronicle of Secession," part 6, in *Harper's Weekly*, 3 Feb. 1866, p. 70, and part 20, 26 May 1866, p. 326. Whitelaw Reid, *American and English Studies*, 2 vols. (New York, 1913), II, 290–91.

5. Philip Van Doren Stern, ed., *The Annotated Walden* (New York, 1970), p. 188. *The Works of Henry David Thoreau: Walden*, ed. J. Lyndon Shanley (Princeton, 1971), p. 94. An experiment along this line had been tried. On July 17, 1843, the *Illinois Statesman* said, "Our paper is small, and if our readers will for the present just have the goodness to imagine a certain due proportion of fires, tornadoes, murders, thefts, robberies and bully fights, from week to week, it will do just as well, for we can assure them they actually take place."

6. *The Journal of Henry D. Thoreau*, ed. Bradford Torrey and Francis H. Allen, 14 vols. bound as 2 (New York, 1962), II, 45 (quoted), 102, 179, 181, 182, III, 208, V, 87

(quoted); "Slavery in Massachusetts," in *The Writings of Henry David Thoreau*, 11 vols., Riverside ed. (Boston, 1884–94), X, 184.

7. Stern, ed., *The Annotated Walden*, pp. 13, 86, 157–58, 179, 297, 299. *Journal*, VI, 121 (quoted). Henry D. Thoreau, *The Maine Woods*, ed. Joseph J. Moldenhauer (Princeton, 1972), p. 17.

8. Walter Harding, *The Days of Henry Thoreau* (New York, 1965), pp. 70, 117, 152. Steven Fink, *Prophet in the Marketplace: Thoreau's Development as a Professional Writer* (Princeton, 1992), pp. 78, 139, 147, 201.

9. Molly Lefebure, *Cumberland Heritage* (London, 1970), p. 91. E. W. Emerson and W. E. Forbes, eds., *The Journals of Ralph Waldo Emerson*, 10 vols. (Boston, 1909–14) VI, 496. Harding, *The Days of Henry Thoreau*, pp. 56–57, 157–59. Martha C. Brown, "Henry David Thoreau and the Best Pencils in America," *American History Illustrated* 15 (1980): 31–34. Henry Petroski, *The Pencil: A History of Design and Circumstance* (New York, 1990), chap. 9.

10. Oliver P. Hubbard, "Two Centuries of the Black Lead Pencil," *New Englander and Yale Review*, n.s. 18 (1891): 151–59. "Pencil" to describe prose seems not to have figured in the title of a book by a British author during Thoreau's lifetime. American authors did make the pencil a metaphor for their writing, e.g., Eliza Leslie, *Pencil Sketches* (Philadelphia, 1833–37) and Park Benjamin, "Pencilled Passages," *Southern Literary Messenger* 5 (1839): 356ff., 379ff.

11. Stern, ed., *The Annotated Walden*, pp. 32–33. Adele Millicent Smith, *Printing and Writing Materials: Their Evolution* (Philadelphia, 1904), pp. 107–12; Harding, *The Days of Henry Thoreau*, pp. 16–17, 56–57, 261–63.

12. Samuel D. Warren and Louis D. Brandeis, "The Right to Privacy," *Harvard Law Review* 4 (1890): 195, 197. Frank E. Comparato, *Chronicles of Genius and Folly: R. Hoe & Company and the Printing Press as a Service to Democracy* (Culver City, Calif., 1979), p. 527. Don R. Pember, *Privacy and the Press: The Law, the Mass Media, and the First Amendment* (Seattle, 1972), p. 39. Louis M. Lyons, *Newspaper Story: One Hundred Years of the Boston Globe* (Cambridge, Mass., 1971), pp. 16, 26–27.

13. Walter Harding and Carl Bode, eds., *The Correspondence of Henry David Thoreau* (New York, 1958), p. 611. Scholars differ on the dates of the Brown-Thoreau meetings; in what follows I have relied on Harding, *The Days of Henry Thoreau*.

14. The Boston *Advertiser* used one of the first wire reports and said that Brown was in a "dying state" in an October 19 edition. F. B. Sanborn, *The Personality of Emerson* (Boston, 1903), pp. 87–88.

15. Thoreau gave warning about his use of dates in the *Journal*, IX, 306. For a discussion of his method see Perry Miller, *Consciousness in Concord* (Boston, 1958), pp. 19–27. *The Writings of Henry D. Thoreau, Journal*, vol. 1, 1837–44, John C. Broderick, ed. (Princeton, 1981), 599. *Journal*, XII, 435. "A Plea for Captain John Brown," *The Writings of Henry David Thoreau*, Riverside ed., X, 207, 212. *Journal*, XII, 401, 405–7, 412, 424, 434–36, 439.

16. Harding, *The Days of Henry Thoreau*, p. 416.

17. Rumors about antislavery violence were rejected in the Concord circle. F. B. Sanborn, the Concord schoolmaster who had taken Brown into Thoreau's home, was quick to accept the leader's word that justice had been served. James C. Malin, *John Brown and the Legend of Fifty-Six* (Philadelphia, 1942), pp. 230, 349. Michael Meyer, "Thoreau's Rescue of John Brown from History," in *Studies in the American Renaissance, 1980* (Boston, 1980), pp. 301–16. John Edward Byrne, "The News from Harper's Ferry: The Press as Lens and Prism for John Brown's Raid" (Ph.D. diss., George

Washington University, 1987), pp. 245–46, 270. *Writings of Henry D. Thoreau, Journal,* vol. I, Broderick, ed., 594. Emerson, *Journals,* IX, 82 (the editors have mistakenly called this February rather than March 1857). The Concord circle read each other's journals, and it is likely that Thoreau had seen this passage.

18. *Journal,* XIII, 6 (repeated in "The Last Days of John Brown"). This speech was written and published in July 1860. Brown's love for blacks was often public, but the embrace of a black mother and child could not have happened at the execution site. The false report appeared in the New York *Tribune* of 5 Dec. 1859, the same day Thoreau dated his journal entry. On the elaboration of the myth see Benjamin Quarles, *Allies for Freedom: Blacks and John Brown* (New York, 1974), pp. 120–24. There are many suspects and no conclusive evidence to establish who wrote the false report: see Byrne, "The News from Harper's Ferry," pp. 315–20, and Paul Finkelman, "Manufacturing Martyrdom: The Antislavery Response to the John Brown Raid," paper read at the American Historical Association Convention in Washington, D.C., Dec. 1987.

19. HDT to Parker Pillsbury, 10 April 1861, in Harding and Bode, eds., *The Correspondence of Henry David Thoreau,* p. 611.

20. *Writings of Henry David Thoreau,* Riverside ed., X, 210, 215–16. Thoreau meant to sink the widely reprinted editorial in the New York *Tribune* of 19 Oct. 1859, the source of these quotations.

21. *Writings of Henry David Thoreau,* Riverside ed., X, 228.

22. Alfred Frankenstein, *After the Hunt: William Harnett and Other American Still Life Painters, 1870–1900* (Berkeley, 1969), pp. 163–87.

23. John Clyde Oswald, *Benjamin Franklin in Oil and Bronze* (New York, 1926). See the Thomas portraits by Ethan Allen Greenwood (1818). James Rivington, perhaps the most hated loyalist in New York, did pose with the newspaper. Not surprisingly, patriots did not pick up the habit. On the cover of James N. Green, *Mathew Carey: Publisher and Patriot* (Philadelphia, 1985) there is an engraving from 1786 showing the journalist with the Irish newspaper that forced him to leave the British Isles. On Rivington see John Hill Morgan, *Early American Painters* (New York, 1921), pp. 60–61.

24. Frankenstein, *After the Hunt,* p. 55.

25. Harnett's typical subject matter has been called a bachelor's nook, and he favored objects associated with men, as in his paintings of currency. But his gender code was strongest for news. When Harnett pictured books or musical instruments, for example, there is often no indication of the owner's sex.

26. Frankenstein, *After the Hunt,* nos. 21a, 21b, 77, and 117.

27. Barbara S. Groseclose, "Vanity and the Artist: Some Still-Life Paintings by William Michael Harnett," *American Art Journal* 19 (1987): 51–59, and Chad Mandeles, "William Michael Harnett's *The Old Cupboard Door* and the Tradition of *Vanitas,*" *ibid.* 18 (1986): 51–62. See also *William M. Harnett,* ed. Doreen Bolger, Marc Simpson, and John Wilmerding (New York, 1992).

28. Michelle Perrot, ed., *A History of Private Life, Vol. 4: From the Fires of Revolution to the Great War,* trans. Arthur Goldhammer, gen. eds. Phillippe Aries and Georges Duby (Cambridge, Mass., 1990), pp. 346, 356, and in general "At Home." Thomas C. Leonard, "News at the Hearth: A Drama of Reading in Nineteenth-Century America," *Proceedings of the American Antiquarian Society* 102, part 2 (1993): 379–401, has an Appendix on the art.

29. The range was 29 to 52 percent. See Frank J. Heinl, "Newspapers and Periodicals in the Lincoln-Douglas Country, 1831–1832," *Journal of the Illinois State Historical Society* 23 (1930–31): 371–438. Elmer E. Barker, "What Crown Pointers Were Reading

One Hundred Years Ago," *New York History* 31 (1950): 31–40. "Account of News-papers and Magazines Sold in Westford, New York, 1849–51," from the Library, New York State Historical Association, Cooperstown, N.Y. This is a typescript from an account book and diary of George Skinner and appears to be post office transactions. Electa F. Jones, *Stockbridge, Past and Present* (Springfield, Mass., 1854), pp. 234–35. Helen R. Watson, "A Journalistic Medley: Newspapers and Periodicals in a Small North Carolina Community, 1859–1860," *North Carolina Historical Review* 60 (1983): 457–85.

30. *Democratic Review* 27 (1850): 285–88, 381–84, 477–80; *ibid.* 28 (1851): 93–96, 189–92, 382–84. This is the magazine's published sample of about 60 percent of its circulation. The method of collection undercounted the out-of-the-way subscribers.

31. *Appeal to Reason*, 7 Feb. 1903.

32. Similarly, Richard Wright, *12 Million Black Voices* (New York, 1941), p. 65, used a Russell Lee photo, "Tenants' Children Reading." For additional examples of the decorative display of news on the walls see LC-USF-342-8276A and LC-USZ62-40994 by Walker Evans.

33. Everett N. Dick, *The Sod-House Frontier, 1854–1890* . . . (Lincoln, Neb., 1954), p. 59.

34. Arthur F. Raper, *Preface to Peasantry: A Tale of Two Black Belt Counties* (Chapel Hill, 1971) [1936], p. 63, and Rupert B. Vance, *How the Other Half Is Housed: A Pictorial Record of Sub-Minimum Farm Housing in the South* (Chapel Hill, 1936), unpaged. Tom E. Terrill and Jerrold Hirsch, eds., *Such as Us: Southern Voices of the Thirties* (Chapel Hill, 1978), p. 79. George W. McDaniel, *Hearth & Home: Preserving a People's Culture* (Philadelphia, 1982), p. 15.

35. Russell Lee, LC-USF 34-31995-D, LC-USF 34-319-D, and LC-UCF 31682-D. Decorating fireplaces not in use has a long tradition: see William H. Gerdts and Russell Burke, *American Still-Life Painting* (New York, 1971), p. 20. McDaniel, *Hearth & Home*, p. 142. *These Are Our Lives, as Told by the People and Written by Members of the Federal Writers' Project of the Works Progress Administration in North Carolina, Tennessee, and Georgia* (Chapel Hill, 1939), p. 357. Terrill and Hirsch, *Such as Us*, p. 87.

36. Newbell Niles Puckett, *Folk Beliefs of the Southern Negro* (Montclair, N.J., 1968) [1926], p. 148. Raper, *Preface to Peasantry*, p. 63.

37. Arthur F. Raper, *Tenants of the Almighty* (New York, 1943), plate 34. Advertising was proudly displayed over the mantel of other homes visited by FSA photographers. See, for example, Marion Post Walcott, LC-USF 34-54654-D.

38. Erskine Caldwell and Margaret Bourke-White, *You Have Seen Their Faces* (New York, 1937), pp. 55, 85 (unpaged). Margaret Bourke-White, *Portrait of Myself* (New York, 1963), pp. 127–28. Here Bourke-White reproduces the photograph of a black boy framed by ads and misidentifies these as newspaper pages. The pages most prominent are from *Collier's*, 18 Oct., 11 Nov., and 5 Dec. 1936. For rooms insulated with signs and flattened cardboard boxes see *Marion Post Wolcott, FSA Photographs* (Carmel, Calif., 1983), plate 4. *Circulation Management* 3 (Sept. 1937): 9; *ibid.* 4 (Dec. 1938): 8. Raper, *Preface to Peasantry*, p. 67.

In memoirs from the South of this era, subjects have often given the impression of a passive role in getting the news—as words handed down to illiterates by an elite. See Jane Maguire, *On Shares: Ed Brown's Story* (New York, 1975), p. 15. The interviewers in the 1930s found some households without media or dependent on neighbors to learn the news: John L. Robinson, *Living Hard: Southern Americans in the Great Depression* (Washington, D.C., 1981) pp. 30, 135. But many poor whites and poor blacks claimed to have a regular supply of newspapers and magazines either as subscribers (see *Living Hard*, pp. 55, 105, 120, 157) or as borrowers (*Living Hard*, pp. 52, 136; *These Are Our Lives*, pp. 221, 334, 356–57). Harry Harrison Kroll in his autobiographical *I Was a Share-Cropper* (Indianapolis, 1937) describes a family driven by poverty to desperate measures—but well supplied with periodicals (pp. 84, 155).

39. Kirk Varnedoe and Adam Gopnik, *High and Low: Modern Art and Popular Culture* (New York, 1990).

40. The photos from Florida and Arkansas were taken in the summer of 1936. Bourke-White made the Louisiana photo in the spring of 1937. In all cases, the magazines were from October through February. This of course is when an agricultural family would have the most time for the job.

41. Margaret Jarman Hagood, *Mothers of the South: Portraiture of the White Tenant Farm Woman* (Chapel Hill, 1939), p. 98.

42. Rupert B. Vance, *Human Factors in Cotton Culture* (Chapel Hill, 1929), pp. 240, 259. Nat L. Hardy, a journalist, noted the absence of pictures in these tenants' homes before World War I: see *"Yours for the Revolution": The Appeal to Reason, 1895–1922*, ed. John Graham (Lincoln, 1990), p. 157.

43. Works Progress Administration, *These Are Our Lives*, p. 357.

44. William Randolph Hearst to George Hearst, 1887?, in Phoebe Hearst Collection, Box 63, Bancroft Library, University of California, Berkeley. Robert E. Park, *The Immigrant Press and Its Control* (New York, 1922), pp. 73–74. Advertising Research Foundation, *The Continuing Study of Newspaper Reading*, no. 1 (1939–40), Summary, 5. Other studies, later in the century, found comparable interest in ads: see Leo Bogart, *Press and Public: Who Reads What, When, Where, and Why in American Newspapers*, 2nd ed. (Hillsdale, N.J., 1989), pp. 49–50, and *The Magazine Handbook, 1992–93* (no. 64 of Magazine Publishers of America Research Newsletters), pp. 14, 18. Frank Denton and Howard Kurtz, *Reinventing the Newspaper* (New York, 1993), p. 21.

45. *These Are Our Lives*, p. 158. Harry Crews, *A Childhood: The Biography of a Place* (New York, 1978), p. 54. The attraction of readers to ads has not drawn the attention of many historians, but see Roxanne Marie Zimmer, "The Urban Daily Press: Baltimore, 1797–1816" (Ph.D. diss., University of Iowa, 1982), pp. 341–42. *Circulation Manager* 1 (Dec. 1902): 11.

46. Camilo J. Vergara, New York *Times*, 14 June 1987, sec. 11, p. 28.

47. The single exception to this pruning of anti-New Deal pages is a cartoon from the *Post* on the wall in the Arkansas home showing a bail of cotton battered by government planning (26 Oct. 1935, p. 23). For a picture of radical and reactionary forces at work in this state see Stephen F. Strausberg, "The Effectiveness of the New Deal in Arkansas," in *The Depression in the Southwest* (Port Washington, N.Y., 1980).

48. Green, *In the Light of the Home*, pp. 95–96. The file of Bourke-White photos shot while working on *You Have Seen Their Faces* is at the George Arents Research Library, Syracuse University. The only part of the *Collier's* story missing from the wall is page 61, which had to be sacrificed in order to paste up page 62. None of Bourke-White's photos in this Louisiana house reveal the most colorful spread in this issue of *Collier's*, an ad for General Motors, "Who Serves Progress Serves America." This showed blacks working cotton in the eighteenth century under white bosses and, as evidence of progress, white workers in a modern factory.

49. Charles E. Martin, *Hollybush: Folk Building and Social Change in an Appalachian Community* (Knoxville, 1984), pp. 28–31.

50. As the illustration on p. 107 suggests, the decoration of walls may often have been

an extension of a sorority of quilters. On the tradition of this activity see John Mack Faragher, *Women and Men on the Overland Trail* (New Haven, 1979), pp. 56, 126–27.

51. The most comprehensive survey is Victor H. Mair, *Painting and Performance: Chinese Picture Recitation and Its Indian Genesis* (Honolulu, 1988). The title notwithstanding, this has a substantial discussion of continental Europe.

52. George C. Wallace, *Stand Up for America* (Garden City, N.J., 1976), p. 23. On the social function of news pages and clips in a southern community see Shirley Brice Heath, *Ways with Words: Language, Life, and Work in Communities and Classrooms* (Cambridge, Eng., 1983), pp. 196, 220–21.

53. Walter Lippmann, *Public Opinion* (New York, 1922) and *The Phantom Public* (New York, 1925). W. Russell Neuman, *The Future of the Mass Audience* (New York, 1991), pp. 80–85. Michel de Certeau, *The Practice of Everyday Life* (Berkeley, 1984), p. 172.

54. Edward Bellamy, "With the Eyes Shut," in *The Blindman's World and Other Stories* (Boston, 1898), pp. 335–65, reprinted in Neil Harris, ed., *The Land of Contrasts, 1880–1901* (New York, 1970), p. 51 quoted.

Chapter 5

1. Richard D. Brown, *Knowledge Is Power: The Diffusion of Information in Early America, 1700–1865* (New York, 1989), pp. 38, 104. *The Papers of Josiah Bartlett*, ed. Frank C. Mevers (Hanover, N.H., 1979), pp. 98, 102, 188, 213, 228, 253, 266, 267, 274, 332, 354, 427.

2. Seth Ames, ed., *Works of Fisher Ames*, 2 vols. (Boston, 1854), I, 329, 373. Clay to Jonathan Russell, 19 April 1823, in James F. Hopkins, ed., *The Papers of Henry Clay* (Lexington, 1959–), III, 409. Hazel Dicken-Garcia, *To Western Woods: The Breckinridge Family Moves to Kentucky in 1793* (Rutherford, N.J., 1991), p. 35. James Oliver Robertson and Janet C. Robertson, *All Our Yesterdays: A Century of Family Life in an American Small Town* (New York, 1993), p. 87.

3. Lillian B. Miller, ed., *Selected Papers of Charles Willson Peale and his Family*, 3 vols. (New Haven, 1983–91), II, part 1, p. 308.

4. David Outlaw to Emily Outlaw, 10 May 1850, David Outlaw Papers, Southern Historical Collection, University of North Carolina, Chapel Hill (hereafter, SHC-UNC). "The Country Post Office," *Musical World*, 22 Oct. 1859, pp. 5–6. I owe this reference to Richard John. *A Girl's Life Eighty Years Ago: Selections from the Letters of Eliza Southgate Bowne* (New York, 1887), p. 166. Barbara L. Cloud, *The Business of Newspapers on the Western Frontier* (Reno, 1992), pp. 36–37.

5. This issue and the press are reproduced in J. Cecil Alter, *Early Utah Journalism* (Salt Lake City, 1938), pp. 12, 281.

6. *The Papers of Josiah Bartlett*, p. 274. Cloud, *The Business of Newspapers on the Western Frontier*, pp. 36–37.

7. Richard B. Kielbowicz, *News in the Mail: The Press, Post Office, and Public Information, 1700–1860s* (New York, 1989), pp. 85–86, 91, 105, 113. C. A. Wickliffe letter of 10 Nov. 1842 as printed in unidentified newspaper in Scrapbook of Circulars, Notices, Instructions . . . , Item #27 of Records of the Office of the Postmaster General, National Archives. Alvin F. Harlow, *Old Post Bags* (New York, 1928), p. 325. Barnabas Bates, *A Brief Statement of the Exertions of the Friends of Cheap Postage . . .* (New York, 1848), p. xviii.

8. Burwell J. Corban Books (#3496), I, 31–32, 40–42 in SHC-UNC. For more detail on this accounting see Kielbowicz, *News in the Mail*, pp. 112–13.

9. *Congressional Globe*, 31st Cong., 2nd. Sess., p. 141. *A Gentleman of Much Promise: The Diary of Isaac Mickle*, ed. Philip English Mackey, 2 vols. (Philadelphia, 1977), I, 157. Brown, *Knowledge Is Power*, pp. 218–44. David F. Halaas, *Boom Town Newspapers: Journalism on the Rocky Mountain Mining Frontier, 1859–1881* (Albuquerque, 1981), p. 103. Oliver Knight, "The Owyhee Avalanche: The Frontier Newspaper as a Catalyst in Social Change," *Pacific Northwest Quarterly* 58 (1967): 78.

10. Christopher Clark and Donald M. Scott, "The Diary of an Apprentice Cabinet-maker: Edward Jenner Carpenter's 'Journal' 1844–45," *Proceedings of the American Antiquarian Society* 98, part 2 (1988): 303–94; quoted, 368–69. See also Thomas Dublin, ed., *Farm to Factory: Women's Letters, 1830–1860* (New York, 1981), pp. 101, 105.

11. *Lucy Breckinridge of Grove Hill: The Journal of a Virginia Girl, 1862–1864*, ed. Mary D. Robertson (Kent, Ohio, 1979), pp. 111, 116, 122, 125.

12. Dublin, *Farm to Factory*, pp. 140–45 (quoted) and other exchanges pp. 111, 157, 159–60. Judy Nolte Lensink, *"A Secret to be Burried": The Diary and Life of Emily Hawley Gillespie, 1858–1888* (Iowa City, 1989), pp. 58, 211.

13. Lensink, *"A Secret to be Burried,"* p. 162, 211. Jabez Whiting to Zabina Eastman, 9 June 1874, in Zabina Eastman Papers, Chicago Historical Society. Wilma King, ed., *A Northern Woman in the Plantation South: Letters of Trypehna Blanche Holder Fox, 1856–1876* (Columbia, S.C., 1993), pp. 10, 38–39. N. E. Bursoco (?) to Benjamin Yancey, 15 May 1840, Benjamin Yancey Papers, SHC-UNC. Philip B. Holmes to Melzar Gardner, 25 Jan. 1841, in Melzar Gardner Papers, Special Collections Library, Duke University, Durham, N.C. Marsha L. Vanderford, "The *Woman's Column*, 1888–1904: Extending the Suffrage Community," in Martha M. Solomon, ed., *A Voice of Their Own: The Woman Suffrage Press, 1840–1910* (Tuscaloosa, 1991), p. 132. Carpenter subscribed to a temperance paper and may have shared it through the mails.

14. *"Yours for the Revolution": The Appeal to Reason, 1895–1922*, ed. John Graham (Lincoln, Neb., 1990), pp. 206, 208–9.

15. *Lowell Letter-Writer* (1845) quoted in Ronald J. Zboray, *A Fictive People: Antebellum Economic Development and the American Reading Public* (New York, 1993), pp. 120–21. Dublin, *Farm to Factory*, p. 128.

16. *Fourth Estate*, 2 Feb. 1895, p. 2. *Newspaper Maker* 4 (12 Nov. 1896): 5, (3 Dec. 1896), 2. Alfred McClung Lee, *The Daily Newspaper in America* (New York, 1947), p. 731. Extensive fraud in recycling, based on clipping coupons, is still with us. See Barbara Demick, "Coupon-Clipping Big, and So Is the Fraud," Chicago *Tribune*, 25 March 1990, p. 14D.

17. Michael Garry, "Gift Subs: The Present That Pays and Pays," *Folio* 19 (April 1990): 102. Dan Thomas, "New Mexico Magazine Reaches Outside State with Some of Its Mail Subscription Efforts," *DM News*, 15 March 1987, p. 10. Leo Bogart, *Press and Public: Who Reads What, When, Where, and Why in American Newspapers*, 2nd. ed. (Hillsdale, N.J., 1989), p. 242.

18. *Ebony*, Aug. 1992, p. 136. Patricia Nealon, "Domestic Abuse Poses Challenge," Boston *Globe*, 24 Sept. 1989, p. 1.

19. *Massachusetts Spy*, 14 Aug. 1783. Louis T. Griffith and John E. Talmadge, *Georgia Journalism, 1763–1950* (Athens, Ga., 1951), p. 19. Alter, *Early Utah Journalism*, pp. 12, 281. Brown, *Knowledge Is Power*, pp. 184, 273.

20. Samuel Eliot Morison, ed., "William Manning's The Key of Liberty," *William*

and Mary Quarterly 13 (1956): 211–13, and Michael Merrill and Sean Wilentz, *The Key of Liberty: The Life and Democratic Writings of William Manning, "A Laborer,"* 1747–1814 (Cambridge, Mass., 1993), p. 51. J. A. Leo Lemay, *Men of Letters in Colonial Maryland* (Knoxville, 1972), p. 233.

21. Albert L. Demaree, *The American Agricultural Press, 1819–1860* (New York, 1941), p. 35. *Peterson's Ladies' National Magazine 30* (1856): 414. William J. Gilmore, *Reading Becomes a Necessity of Life: Material and Cultural Life in Rural New England, 1780–1835* (Knoxville, 1989), pp. 407–8. Arthur John, *The Best Years of the Century: Richard Watson Gilder, Scribner's Monthly, and the Century Magazine, 1870–1909* (Urbana, Ill., 1981), p. 99. *Scribner's Magazine* 15 (1894) ad bound with Jan. and Feb. issues at Doe Library, University of California, Berkeley.

22. *Fourth Estate*, 12 May 1895.

23. Harbottle Dorr Papers, Massachusetts Historical Society, Boston; for a full description see Bernard Bailyn, "The Indexes and Commentaries of Harbottle Dorr," *Proceedings of the Massachusetts Historical Society* 85 (1973): 21–35. William Gunnison's papers located in Applications for Appointments as Customs Service Officers (1882), Record Group 56, General Records of the Department of the Treasury, National Archives, Washington, D.C. Thomas C. Leonard, *The Power of the Press: The Birth of American Political Reporting* (New York, 1986), pp. 88–90. Oliver Wendell Holmes Jr. Papers (microfilm: University Press of America, 1985), Reel 61. Merle Thorpe, ed., *The Coming Newspaper* (New York, 1915), pp. 144–45.

24. Jason Niles Papers, SHC-UNC. All manner of amateur productions with newsprint from this era survive in libraries, much of it the work of years of collecting. The University of California, Berkeley, for example, has more than a hundred scrapbooks with news saved before 1900.

25. *Newspaper Maker*, 28 Oct. 1898, p. 7. Elbert Hubbard, *A Little Journey to Hemstreet's Press Clipping Bureau* (East Aurora, N.Y., 1916), p. 17. Jerome K. Wilcox, *Directory of Press Clipping Bureaus* (Chicago, 1932).

26. *Newspaper Maker* 12 (3 Jan. 1901): 14. Chicago *Tribune*, 5 Nov. 1912, p. 11. "Our Native Industries," *Life* 102 (Dec. 1935): 17–19. Rebecca Aikman, "An Unlikely Gold Mine: Newspaper Clippings," *Business Week*, 4 March 1985: p. 114.

27. G. Bernard Shaw, *My Expensive Scrap Book* (East Aurora, N.Y., 1916), pp. 5, 7. Hubbard, *A Little Journey to Hemstreet's*, pp. 4–6. Neil Harris, "John Philip Sousa and the Culture of Reassurance," pp. 11–40 in Jon Newsom, ed., *Perspectives on John Philip Sousa* (Washington, D.C., 1983).

28. *Advertising Experience*, June 1899, p. 6. Earnest Elmo Calkins and Ralph Holden, *Modern Advertising* (New York, 1916) [1905], pp. 266–69. *Selling Forces* (Philadelphia, 1913), pp. 98–99. Because advertising matter was often discarded when periodicals were bound for libraries, it is extremely difficult to chart the growth of the coupon. Early specimens that required the reader to mutilate editorial material: ads for National Manufacturing Co. in *Frank Leslie's Weekly* 76–77 (1893); *Literary Digest* 11 (1895): 94, 124; *ibid.* 18 (1899): 412.

29. Harold J. Rudolph, *Four Million Inquiries from Magazine Advertising* (New York, 1936), pp. ix, 61. Leo Bogart finding in Philip S. Cook, Douglas Gomery, and Lawrence W. Lichty, eds., *The Future of News: Television—Newspapers—Wire Services—Newsweeklies* (Washington, D.C., 1992), p. 95. In the mid-1990s, American companies issued roughly 300 billion coupons, triple the figure circulated a decade earlier. Newspapers carried about three-quarters of these. See William Serrin, "The Couponing of America," *New York Times*, 13 Aug. 1980, p. C1; Philip H. Dougherty, "Redemption

of Coupons," New York *Times*, 13 July 1988, p. D21; "Couponers Clip Print Media Use," *Presstime* 14 (Nov. 1992): 42.

30. *Peterson's* 33 (1858): 176.

31. James Kelley Papers, Chicago Historical Society, Folder 2, has both specimens. David Paul Nord, "Reading the Newspaper: Strategies and Politics of Reader Response, Chicago, 1912–1917," *Journal of Communication* (forthcoming).

32. Taylor Branch, *Parting the Waters: America in the King Years, 1954–63* (New York, 1988), illustration 29 and pp. 288–89. Dale Russakoff, "Fears Linger over a Grand Canyon Dam," Washington *Post*, 24 July 1983, p. A15; coupon page for Fish Forever, New York *Times*, 2 June 1994, p. A5. David R. Brower, *Work in Progress* (Salt Lake City, 1991), p. 101. Jeffrey M. Berry, *The Interest Group Society*, 2nd ed. (Glenview, Ill., 1989), p. 107. Joyce Wadler, "N.Y. Governor's Race Proving a Paradise for Coupon Clippers," Washington *Post*, 19 Feb. 1982. "No Sacred Cows," *Common Cause*, April–June 1992.

33. Linda Steiner, "Oppositional Decoding as an Act of Resistance," in Robert K. Avery and David Eason, eds., *Critical Perspectives on Media and Society* (New York, 1991), pp. 329–45. Athelia Knight, "S&L Fury Engulfs Congress; Letter Writers Demand 'Villains' Be Punished," Washington *Post*, 26 Oct. 1990, p. A25. "Up and Up . . . ," *U.S. News & World Report*, 10 March 1975, p. 16. Robin Toner, "Back at Grass Roots, Congressman Is All Ears," New York *Times*, 18 Aug. 1989, p. 1A. *USA Today* ad in *New York* 23 (7 May 1990): 13. Frank Denton and Howard Kurtz, *Reinventing the Newspaper* (New York, 1993), p. 45.

34. Herbert O'Keef Papers, SHC-UNC, clipping of 5 May 1964. Jacqueline Trescott, "The New Insensitivity . . . ," Washington *Post*, 2 June 1981, p. B1. Emmanuel Modu, "Taking Care of Business," *Essence*, March 1992, p. 103. W. Phillips Davison, "Mass Media, Civic Organizations, and Street Gossip: How Communication Affects the Quality of Life in an Urban Neighborhood," Working Paper of the Gannett Center for Media Studies, no date (c. 1986), pp. 4, 18–19. Dolores Kong, "City Tries to Stem Youth Violence," Boston *Globe*, 25 Feb. 1990, p. 23. On the sophisticated media strategies of gangs, across racial lines, see Martín Sánchez Jankowski, *Islands in the Street: Gangs and American Urban Society* (Berkeley, 1991), pp. 302–8.

35. Junda Woo, "Lawyers May Use Newspaper Clippings to Tout Themselves," *Wall Street Journal*, 23 March 1992, p. B8. Howard Kurtz, "Bill Clinton's Press for Success," Washington *Post*, 28 March 1992, p. C1, and "When Democrats Throw Down the Gauntlet, It's Often 'Read My Clips,'" *ibid.*, 5 Feb. 1992, p. A14.

36. R. W. G. Vail, *The Ulster County Gazette and Its Illegitimate Offspring* (New York, 1951), pp. 5, 21. Joseph Gavit, *A List of American Newspaper Reprints* (New York, 1931), p. 10. What follows draws on Gavit's pamphlet and the Library of Congress circulars.

37. W. T. Coggeshall, *The Newspaper Record . . .* (Philadelphia, 1856), pp. 131–32.

38. Edmund Burke Huey, *The Psychology and Pedagogy of Reading* (New York, 1908), pp. 20–30, 411 (quoted).

39. Donald R. Murphy, *What Farmers Read and Like* (Ames, 1962), pp. 77–78.

40. Publication Research Service, "Comments Regarding Editorial Content of Memphis Commercial Appeal for Aug. 10, 1939," pp. 9, 11–12, issued with Advertising Research Foundation, *The Continuing Study of Newspaper Reading*, no. 1 (1939–40). The "Comments" brochures issued with the other fifteen studies in this volume have comparable data.

41. *Continuing Study of Newspaper Reading*, no. 1, Summary, 10, 19, 28. Bogart, *Press*

and Public, pp. 157, 279–80. The myth that women, once upon a time, only read women's pages lives on, even among researchers who should know better: Ruth Clark, "More Changing Needs for the Ever-Changing Reader," *Bulletin of the American Society of Newspaper Editors,* May-June 1982, p. 15.

42. Alfred Politz Research, *A Study of the Accumulative Audience of Life* (New York, 1950), pp. 106, 108, and *A Study of Four Media: Their Accumulative and Repeat Audiences* (New York, 1953), p. 145. Martin Mayer, *Madison Avenue, U.S.A.* (New York, 1958), p. 190. Leo Bogart, *Preserving the Press: How Daily Newspapers Mobilized to Keep their Readers* (New York, 1991), p. 133. Hugh S. Hardy, ed., *The Politz Papers: Science and Truth in Marketing Research* (Chicago, 1990), pp. 3–4, 193. *Life's Continuing Study of Magazine Audiences,* 1938, no. 1, pp. 9–10. Alfred Politz Research, *Characteristics of Readers and Non-Readers of the New York Mirror* (New York, 1951), p. 139.

43. Leo Bogart, "How Do People Read Newspapers?" *Media/Scope* (1961). Bogart, *Press and Public,* pp. 280–82.

44. Poynter Institute, *Eyes on the News* (St. Petersburg, Fla., 1991).

45. *Eyes on the News,* pp. 40–41. Walter Bender quoted in Laurent Belsie, "Publishing Without Paper or Ink," *Christian Science Monitor,* 26 March 1992, p. 12. By interviewing readers, Doris A. Graber concluded that 18 percent of the stories in an average daily were read in full: *Processing the News: How People Tame the Information Tide* (New York, 1984).

46. Counting picture spreads as stories, Politz demonstrated that the average reader of *Life* had looked at 69 percent of its editorial contents. When this researcher studied the *Saturday Evening Post,* with its longer texts, he dodged this question. Politz, *A Study of the Accumulative Audience of Life,* p. 110. Magazine Publishers Association, *Magazine Handbook,* 1992–93, p. 32. Erik Larson, *The Naked Consumer: How Our Private Lives Become Public Commodities* (New York, 1992), p. 195.

47. I found 116 scenes of people with newspapers by reading through the captions of the roughly seventy-seven thousand photographs in the FSA collection. Many of the captions mention a paper or magazine, but I also checked settings such as living rooms. On examination, 103 photographs pictured active readers (not simply people with reading material at hand). Only 36 scenes showed readers alone. Of the 67 readers in groups, 42 seemed conscious of sharing a text as they read, and 25 were reading the same publication together. For example: Esther Bubley, LC-USW 3-38320-E; John Collier, LC-USW 3-19019-E; Marjory Collins, LC-USW 3-22101-E; Jack Delano, LC-USF 34-46264-D and LC-USW 3-69D; Russell Lee, LC-USF 33-11130-Mi; Arthur Rothstein, LC-USF 34-RA 5655-E and LC-USW 3-6332-D; John Vachon, LC-USF 34-64199-D.

48. "Fewer Consumers Read Newspapers Cover-to-Cover . . . ," *Presstime* 13 (July 1991): 51. Denton and Kurtz, *Reinventing the Newspaper,* p. 18. David Weaver, "On Using Newspaper Readership Research," *Newspaper Research Journal* 2 (1981): 15–21.

49. New York *Times,* 21 Oct. 1989, p. 16.

50. David Paul Nord, "Teleology and News: The Religious Roots of American Journalism, 1630–1730," *Journal of American History* 77 (1990): 9–38. Benjamin Franklin, "Apology for Printers" (1731), *The Papers of Benjamin Franklin,* ed. Leonard W. Labaree *et al.,* 30 vols. (New Haven, 1959–93), I, 194–99. Kevin G. Barnhurst and John C. Nerone, "Design Trends in U.S. Front Pages, 1889–1985," *Journalism Quarterly* 68 (1991): 803. Janet E. Steele, *The Sun Shines for All: Journalism and Ideology in the Life of*

Charles A. Dana (Syracuse, 1993), pp. 82–83. Alice D. Schreyer, ed., "Mark Twain and 'The Old-Fashioned Printer,'" *Printing History* 3 (1981): 36.

51. Joseph Goulden, *The Curtis Caper* (New York, 1965), p. 19. *The Autobiography of Lincoln Steffens*, 2 vols. (New York, 1958) [1931], II, 393. Christopher P. Wilson, "The Rhetoric of Consumption: Mass Market Magazines and the Demise of the Gentle Reader, 1880–1920," in *The Culture of Consumption: Critical Essays in American History, 1880–1980* (New York, 1983).

52. *Farm Journal* 86 (March 1962): 20–21, (Aug. 1962): 16–17. *Folio* 21 (1 Sept. 1992): 64; *Graphic Arts Monthly*, Jan. 1993; Scott Donaton, "The Personal Touch," *Advertising Age* 52 (6 Oct. 1991): 22.

53. In emulating mass mailers, *Time* earned their scorn. The junk mail issue was greeted as "a self-serving attack on a competing advertising medium and an insult to their own customers who have subscribed to the magazine by mail" by Stan Rapp, "Look Who's Bad-Mouthing Junk Mail Now," *Direct Marketing Magazine* 53 (Jan. 1991): 77. *Time*'s hog is in *Agency* 1 (Spring 1994): 7. The magazine used similar copy with a view of the Capitol Hill, no livestock, in the mainstream press: New York *Times*, 31 May 1994, p. C8.

54. Karen Berman, "Targeted Approach: Database Marketing and Selective Binding," *Folio* 22 (Nov. 1993): 58. Jerry Calabrese, "Customized Editorial: Pros and Cons," *Folio* 16 (Sept. 1987): 115. Chuck Appleby, "Binding Arbitration," *Information Week*, 20 Dec. 1993, p. 32.

55. Ruth Clark, "Researcher Ruth Clark Is Talking to Our Readers," *Bulletin of the American Society of Newspaper Editors*, Nov. 1978, p. 8; Ruth Clark, *Changing Needs of Changing Readers: A Qualitative Study of the New Social Contract Between Newspaper Editors and Readers* (Reston, Va., 1979); Judith G. Clabes, "The Great Readership Battle," *BASNE*, May-June 1979, p. 13; Robert J. Cochnar, "Implementing the Findings of 'Changing Needs . . . ,'" *ibid.*, Dec 1979–Jan. 1980, p. 3 (quoted). Bogart, *Preserving the Press*, pp. 131–43.

It remains a mystery just how many of the roughly 120 people in the twelve focus groups voiced the ideas that Clark presents, since she says that only "basic trends found in several, if not all, of the groups, were chosen for inclusion in this report" (p. 9). *Changing Needs* was issued with proper warnings from ASNE officials that this was "highly experimental and its findings quite preliminary" (pp. 2, 6). Clark listed the limitations of focus groups in the next-to-the-last section, after the substantive discussion of what readers "want." In publicizing the findings, the tenuous basis of the Clark report was overlooked.

56. Philip Meyer, *The Newspaper Survival Book: An Editor's Guide to Marketing Research* (Bloomington, 1985), p. 95. Carl Sessions Stepp, "When Readers Design the News," *Washington Journalism Review* 13 (April 1991): 20–24. Howard Kurtz, *Media Circus: The Trouble with America's Newspapers* (New York, 1993), p. 339. At the Newspaper Association of America convention in San Francisco in April 1994, Kristin McGrath, president of Minnesota Opinion Research Inc., presented the conclusions from focus groups conducted for the American Society of Newspaper Editors. No one on the panel, no one in the packed hall, raised a question about her warrant for proposals that "we need to 'make over' some of the basics of our craft" ("Remarks on 1993–94 Potential Readers Research," p. 2). Her remarks, as delivered and in their published form, provided no evidence beyond impressionistic statements. "When people ask me to describe a typical potential," Dr. McGrath told the ASNE convention in April,

NOTES TO PAGES 142–144

"there's a woman in Concord, N.H., who keeps coming to mind." The discovery of this Yankee with "the kind of poise, and understated attractiveness that I kind of associate with traditional New England" was big enough news to be set off in a pink box. As with Ruth Clark, editors again swallowed: Jean Davidson, "A Matter of Time," Chicago *Tribune*, 6 May 1994.

57. Michael Hoyt, "The Wichita Experiment," *Columbia Journalism Review* 31 (July-Aug. 1992): 43–47, quoted p. 43. Edward D. Miller, "The Charlotte Project Helping Citizens Take Back Democracy," *Poynter Papers*, no. 4 (1994). David Shaw, "Some Papers Seek Readers' Guidance in Shaping Coverage," Los Angeles *Times*, 1 April 1993, p. 18. Larson, *The Naked Consumer*, p. 15. Sam Zagoria, "An Improving Image," Washington *Post*, 30 May 1984, p. A18. Clark's second report was heralded in her "More Changing Needs for the Ever-Changing Reader," *BASNE*, May–June 1982, pp. 14–15, and released by ASNE in 1984 as "Relating to Readers in the '80s." Earl W. Foell, "What Do Readers Want? Mystery of the Missing Me Generation," *Christian Science Monitor*, 21 May 1984, p. 3.

58. Susan Miller, "America's Dailies and the Drive to Capture Lost Readers," *Gannett Center Journal* 1 (Spring 1987): 64 (this finding was at variance with research cited in this issue, p. 49). Howard Schneider, managing editor of *Newsday* in New York, learned from focus groups that women did not want more women's features: "Squaring with the Reader," *Kettering Review*, Winter 1992, p. 41. Douglas E. Kneeland, "Years of Research Led to Tribune's 'Mini-Newspaper' for Women," Chicago *Tribune*, 17 June 1991, p. 13. See also Maria Braden, "Women: Special Again," *Washington Journalism Review* 13 (June 1991): 30–32. *Prototypes for the Future: How Readers Look at Newspapers, Future of Newspapers Report* [available through ASNE Foundation, Washington, D.C.] April 1990, pp. 81–83, reports the wide swings in reader reaction. In direct mail, where reader response is the only objective, the post-publication research favored by newspapers is rare. Direct mail enterprises experiment all the time and test new copy against a control group in the midst of campaigns. They do not spend money on focus groups or surveys. This is another example of how dailies have lagged their competition in marketing savvy.

59. Conrad C. Fink, *Strategic Newspaper Management* (Carbondale, Ill., 1988), p. 123. Haynes Johnson, "Death in the Afternoon: Commentary on Changing Tastes," Washington *Post*, 8 Sept. 1981, p. A2. *Prototypes for the Future*, p. 29.

60. Meyer, *The Newspaper Survival Book*, pp. 157–61.

61. William H. Jones, "Publishers View 'Tailored Newspaper,'" Washington *Post*, 7 May 1978. "Newspapers in the Year 2000 Envisioned," *Editor & Publisher* 123 (23 June 1990): 28. Bob Dorf, "Tossing the Newspaper from a Bike on the Information Superhighway," *Ideas* (Institute of Newspaper Marketing Association) 7 (Feb.–March 1994): 15–16. The *Wall Street Journal* launched its Personal Journal in 1995.

62. Tom Sims, "Knight-Ridder's Wichita Experiment," *Presstime* 15 (Sept. 1993): S11. Gail DeGeorge, "Knight-Ridder's Knight in Electronic Armor?" *Business Week*, 18 Nov. 1991, p. 100. Kenneth Allen quoted in Laurent Belsie, "Publishing Without Paper or Ink," *Christian Science Monitor*, 26 March 1992, p. 12. Wallys W. Conhaim, "Comtex Provides Searching Alternative . . . ," *Information Today* 9 (May 1992): 56. John Markoff, "A Media Pioneer's Quest: Portable Electronic Newspapers," New York *Times*, 28 June 1992, sec. 3, p. 11. John Markoff, "Silicon Valley Concerns Offer Specialized News," New York *Times*, 21 July 1994, p. C4. *The Dawn of the Information Robots*, sales brochure from Farcast Inc. (1994). Michael Conniff, "In Search of the Personal Newspaper," *Editor & Publisher* 126 (6 March 1993): 15TC. William Glaber-

son, "In San Jose, Knight-Ridder Tests a Newspaper Frontier," New York *Times*, 7 Feb. 1994, p. C1. Michael A. Silver, "Keys to the Highway," *Presstime* 16 (May 1994): S10-S11. Ira Teinowitz, "Farm Magazines Yielding Promise for Interactivity," *Advertising Age* 65 (2 May 1994): 48.

63. *Facts About Newspapers* (Reston, Va., 1994), p. 26. *Newspapers in the Year 2000: A Report from the Associated Press Managing Editors Association*, 1989, p. 5. Alex S. Jones, "Papers Finding New Ways to Make Faxes a Business," New York *Times*, 6 July 1992, p. D6. Kurtz, *Media Circus*, pp. 366–67. Michael Welch, "Pressing On: Record Results Are Not Enough for Star Tribune Publisher," *Corporate Report Minnesota* 23 (Dec. 1992): 30. Michael A. Lev, "Personal Ads Helping Singles Fill in Blanks," Chicago *Tribune*, 1 July 1992, p. 1. William Glaberson, "Newspapers Redefining Themselves," New York *Times*, 26 April 1993, p. C1. Doug Underwood, "Reinventing the Media: The Newspapers' Identity Crisis," *Columbia Journalism Review* 31 (March–April 1992): 24. Thomas Palmer, "Newspapers Expand Services. . . ," Boston *Globe*, 15 April 1991, p. 11. Cook, Gomery, and Lichty, eds., *The Future of News*, p. 113. Jack D. Lail, "Newspapers On-Line: Electronic Delivery Is Hot . . . Again," *Quill* 82 (Jan. 1994): 39. Micro Voice Applications Inc. of Minneapolis, promotional material of 1993. "Voice Information Can Open Doors to Businesses," *Newspaper Financial Executive Journal* 47 (Jul.–Aug. 1993): 9.

64. Brite Voice Systems ad for PinPoint, May 1993. "The Latest Online!" (ad), Chicago *Tribune*, 23 April 1993. Lorne Manly, "New York's Online Service Grows," *Folio* 22 (15 May 1993): 18. Deidre Carmody, "For Magazines, a Multimedia Wonderland," New York *Times*, 11 Oct. 1993, p. C1. John Markoff, "The View from Cyberspace: The Revolution Will Be Digitized," New York *Times*, 29 May 1994, p. E7. Philip Elmer-Dewitt, "Beyond Shovelware," *Folio* 23 (15 Oct. 1994): 54–55. Brian Hammerstein, "Interview: A Look Inside Time Online," *Digital Media* 3 (16 May 1994): 10.

65. "Paper's Editors Able to Scan a Vast Range of News Sources . . . ," *Business Wire*, 19 Sept. 1986. John Markoff, "17 Companies in Electronic News Venture," New York *Times*, 7 May 1993, p. C1. Christy Fisher, "Newspapers of Future . . . ," *Advertising Age* 63 (5 Oct. 1992): S1.

66. Scott Donaton, "The Personal Touch," *Advertising Age* 62 (6 Oct. 1991): 22. "Squaring with the Reader," *Kettering Review*, Winter 1992, p. 50. Ray Cave, "Musings of a Newsmagazine Editor," *Gannett Center Journal* 1 (Spring 1987): 84. Stepp, "When Readers Design the News," pp. 20–24. Eugene Patterson, "Spectrum: Editors in Evolution," *Washington Journalism Review* 1 (April-May 1978): 78; M. L. Stein, "Managing Editors Hear Newsroom Study Results," *Editor & Publisher* 115 (13 Nov. 1982): 13; Dan Fost, "Newspapers Enter the Age of Information," *American Demographics* 12 (Sept. 1990): 14; Edward Wasserman, "Cotton-Candy News Leads to Society Decay," *Connecticut Law Tribune*, 7 Oct. 1991, p. 21. Taking the pledge to give readers what they ask for (especially in focus groups) is commonplace: Anne M. Russell, "Know Thy Reader," *Focus* 20 (15 May 1993): 6 (quoted); John Jordan, "Gannett's New Executive Editor Plans to Expand Local Coverage," *Westchester County Business Journal*, 1 Feb. 1993, p. 6. Michael Fancher, "The Metamorphosis of the Newspaper Editor," *Gannett Center Journal* 1 (1987): 74 (quoted). John Evans of Murdoch's News Corp. quoted in Josh Hyatt, "Future Subscribers," Boston *Globe*, 3 Sept. 1993, sec. 1, p. 71.

67. *Folio* 22 (April 1993): 83. If editors only laughed at this ad, they did indeed miss an opportunity. That year, World Pork Expo, which calls itself "the world's largest pork-specific event," drew seventy thousand people to Cowles's home state: "World

Pork Expo . . . ," *PR Newswire*, 1 June 1994. "Mass Customization: It's How to Compete Now," *Inside R&D* 22 (10 Feb. 1993): 3. B. Joseph Pine II, *Mass Customization: The New Frontier in Business Competition* (Boston, 1993). "Schermer Outlines How Newspapers Can Be Reinvented," *Presstime* 13 (June 1991): 30.

Chapter 6

1. *The Papers of Thomas Jefferson*, ed. Julian P. Boyd *et al.*, 25 vols. (Princeton, 1950–92), II, 49. Mary Kupiec Cayton, "The Making of an American Prophet: Emerson, His Audiences, and the Rise of the Culture Industry in Nineteenth-Century America," *American Historical Review* 92 (1987): 597–602. Lawrence W. Levine, *Highbrow/Lowbrow: The Emergence of Cultural Hierarchy in America* (Cambridge, Mass., 1988). Claire Badaracco, "Marketing Language Products 1900–05: The Case of *Agricultural Advertising*," *Essays in Economic and Business History*, ed. Edwin J. Perkins, VIII (1990), 133.

2. *Gales & Seaton's Register of Debates in Congress*, 22nd Cong., 1st Sess. (3 May 1832–4 May 1832), pp. 876–99. Donald H. Stewart, *The Opposition Press of the Federalist Period* (Albany, 1969), pp. 460–63. Richard R. John Jr., *Spreading the News: The American Postal System from Franklin to Morse* (Cambridge, Mass., 1995), chap. 6. Richard B. Kielbowicz, *News in the Mail: The Press, Post Office, and Public Information, 1700–1860s* (New York, 1989), pp. 35–37. "Free Newspaper Postage," *Fourth Estate*, 13 Dec. 1894.

3. New York *Herald*, 6 May 1835, reprinted in James Melvin Lee, *History of American Journalism* (Garden City, 1923), p. 195. Thomas L. Brasher, *Whitman as Editor of the Brooklyn Daily Eagle* (Detroit, 1970), frontispiece. Augustus Maverick, *Henry J. Raymond and the New York Press* (Hartford, 1870), pp. 94, 96, 102.

4. George Juergens, *Joseph Pulitzer and the New York World* (Princeton, 1966), p. 16; see the front page of 10 May 1885. Florence Finch Kelly, *Flowing Stream: The Story of Fifty-Six Years in American Newspaper Life* (New York, 1939), p. 476. Addison Archer [Charles. A. Bates], *American Journalism from the Practical Side* (New York, 1897), pp. 28, 228–29. C. D. Warner, *Harper's* 97 (1897): 971. Jason Rogers in *Circulation Manager* 1 (Feb. 1903): 2. O. F. Byxbee, *Establishing a Newspaper* (Chicago, 1901), p. 25.

5. Oliver Knight, ed., *I Protest: Selected Disquisitions of E. W. Scripps* (Madison, Wisc., 1966), pp. 73, 78, 225–28, 269–70, 318. This is a constant in his correspondence: see, for example, to William D. Wasson, 23 Jan. 1904, Letter Book, Series 2 in E. W. Scripps Papers, Series 1.2, Ohio University, Athens.

6. Arthur Pond, *The Only Thing Worth Finding: The Life and Legacies of George Gough Booth* (Detroit, 1964), p. 162, has this undated correspondence, c. 1896.

7. Marilyn McAdams Sibley, *Lone Stars and State Gazettes: Texas Newspapers Before the Civil War* (College Station, 1983), p. 9. S. H. Parker, "Printing and Journalism," *American Newspaper Reporter* 6 (1 July 1872): 655. Horace G. Davis Jr., "Newspapers of Pensacola, 1821–1900," *Florida Historical Quarterly* 37 (1958–59): 422. Betty Carolyn Congleton, "The Louisville Journal: Its Origins and Early Years," *Register of the Kentucky Historical Society* 62 (1964): 94–95. *Public Ledger Building* . . . (Philadelphia, 1868), p. 11. George P. Rowell & Co., *Centennial Newspaper Exhibition, 1876* (New York, 1876), p. 184.

8. John Philip Sousa, *Marching Along: Recollections of Men, Women, and Music*

(Boston, 1928), pp. 115–17. Charles H. Dennis, *Victor Lawson: His Time and His Work* (Chicago, 1935), p. 96. For pictures of New York crowds reading the news on buildings see Harry W. Baehr, *The New York Tribune Since the Civil War* (New York, 1936), facing p. 226, and James F. O'Donnell, *100 Years of Making Communications History: The Story of the Hearst Corporation* (n.p., 1987), p. 18. Garrett D. Byrnes and Charles Spilman, *The Providence Journal: 150 Years* (Providence, 1980), pp. 95–101. Detroit *Free Press*, 12 Oct. 1876, p. 1. I owe this reference to Richard Kaplan. Chicago *Tribune*, 5 Nov. 1912, p. 1, and 6 Nov. 1912, p. 11. Pond, *The Only Thing Worth Finding*, p. 154.

9. Whitelaw Reid, *American and English Studies*, 2 vols. (New York, 1913), II, 265. Michael Borut, "The *Scientific American* in Nineteenth-Century America" (Ph.D. diss., New York University, 1977), pp. 67–69. Julian S. Rammelkamp, *Pulitzer's Post-Dispatch, 1878–1883* (Princeton, 1967), p. 202, n. 153. *Journalist* 1 (29 March 1884): 7. Ted Curtis Smythe, "The Advertisers' War to Verify Newspaper Circulation, 1870–1914," *American Journalism* 3 (1986): 167–80, see esp. p. 171. [C. A. Bates], *American Journalism*, p. 361. *Newspaper Maker*, 9 June 1898, p. 4.

10. George P. Rowell, *Forty Years an Advertising Agent, 1865–1905* (New York, 1906), p. 161.

11. *Ibid.*, pp. 266, 411–12. *Newspaper Maker*, 24 Sept. 1896, p. 5.

12. Loren Ghiglione, *The American Journalist: Paradox of the Press* (Washington, D.C., 1990), p. 118; Lloyd Wendt, *Chicago Tribune: The Rise of a Great American Newspaper* (Chicago, 1979), pp. 282, 334. James E. Cebula, *James M. Cox: Journalist and Politician* (New York, 1985), pp. 22–27. Janet E. Steele, *The Sun Shines for All: Journalism and Ideology in the Life of Charles A. Dana* (Syracuse, 1993), pp. 96–99. *Centennial Newspaper Exhibition*, pp. 221, 263. Frank E. Comparato, *Chronicles of Genius and Folly: R. Hoe & Company and the Printing Press as a Service to Democracy* (Culver City, Calif., 1979), p. 267.

13. James Weldon Johnson, *The Autobiography of an Ex-Colored Man* [1912] in *Three Negro Classics* (New York, 1965), pp. 432–33. *Along This Way: The Autobiography of James Weldon Johnson* (New York, 1967) [1933], pp. 60, 137.

14. Jane Addams, *Twenty Years at Hull House* (New York, 1961) [1910], p. 298. Royal L. Melendy, "The Saloon in Chicago, 1," *American Journal of Sociology* 6 (1900): 293. Perry R. Duis, *The Saloon: Public Drinking in Chicago and Boston, 1880–1920* (Urbana, Ill., 1983), pp. 120–21. Hamilton Holt, ed., *The Life Stories of Undistinguished Americans as Told by Themselves* (New York, 1906), p. 58. *Collier's* 47 (2 Sept. 1911): 22. See also Ernest Poole, "New Readers of the News," *American Magazine* 65 (1907–08): 4. Byrnes and Spilman, *The Providence Journal*, p. 100. Sousa, *Marching Along*, pp. 117–18, 200.

15. New Orleans *States-Item*, 8 Nov. 1885, quoted in John Wilds, *Afternoon Story: A Century of the New Orleans States-Item* (Baton Rouge, 1976), p. 177. *Newspaper Maker*, 12 July 1900, p. 1. [Elizabeth Oakes Smith], *The Newsboy* (New York, 1854), pp. 65–66. David E. Whisnant, "Selling the Gospel News; or, The Strange Career of Jimmy Brown the Newsboy," *Journal of Social History* 5 (1971–72): 276. Vincent DiGirolamo, "Crying the News: Children and the American Press, 1830–1880, with a Case Study of the Great Newsboy Strike of 1899" (Master's Essay, University of California, Santa Cruz, 1989). David Nasaw, *Children of the City, at Work and at Play* (Garden City, N.Y., 1985), pp. 149, 152, 164, 177. Roy Ashby, *Saving the Waifs: Reformers and Dependent Children, 1890–1917* (Philadelphia, 1984), chap. 4. Philip Davis, *Street-Land: Its Little People and Big Problems* (Boston, 1915), pp. 54–56, 217–18.

16. William Inglis, "Yuxtreee-yuxtor!" *Harper's Weekly* 57 (15 Feb. 1913): 7–8. George Burns, *The Third Time Around* (New York, 1980), p. 39. Nasaw, *Children of the City*, pp. 77–80, p. 80 quoted.

17. Pauline Kael, *The Citizen Kane Book* (New York, 1971), p. 350. New York *Times*, 31 May 1911, p. 10. Sara A. Brown, "Juvenile Street Work in Iowa," *American Child* 4 (1922): 134, 142. John Cooney, *The Annenbergs* (New York, 1982), pp. 31–35.

18. Ernest Poole, "Waifs of the Street," *McClure's* 21 (1903): 40. Nasaw, *Children of the City*, pp. 62–63, 86–87. Whisnant, "Selling the Gospel News," p. 272, notes that a Black Panther paper of 1969 celebrated Mao's rejection of capitalism, specifically condemning black capitalists . . . and on the next page lured African American children to sell the *Black Panther* and win a new bike.

19. Jan Cohn, "The Business Ethic for Boys: *The Saturday Evening Post* and the Post Boys," *Business History Review* 61 (1987): 185–215, quoted, 189, 191; see also her *Creating America: George Horace Lorimer and the Saturday Evening Post* (Pittsburgh, 1989), pp. 39–43.

20. Ronald J. Zboray, *A Fictive People: Antebellum Economic Development and the American Reading Public* (New York, 1993), pp. 32–33. *Covering a Continent: A Story of Newsstand Distribution and Sales* (New York, 1930), pp. 9, 48. Harry E. Keller, "Handling Newsstand Sales," *Circulation Management* 2 (1936): 18–19. Carl F. Kaestle *et al.*, *Literacy in the United States: Readers and Reading Since 1880* (New Haven, 1991), p. 164.

21. Patricia Frantz Kery, *Great Magazine Covers of the World* (New York, 1982), p. 25.

22. *Newspaper Maker*, 17 Sept. 1896, p. 4.

23. New York *World*, 10 May 1885. James M. Mosely, "Pointers on Newsstand Sales," *Circulation Management* 2 (1936): 14–15, 30–31. Phillips Wyman, *Magazine Circulation: An Outline of Methods and Meanings* (New York, 1936), p. 30. On shopkeepers see William Leach, "Strategists of Display and the Production of Desire," in Simon J. Bronner, ed., *Consuming Visions: Accumulation and Display of Goods in America, 1880–1920* (New York, 1989), p. 106 quoted.

24. *Bookseller, Newsdealer, and Stationer* 1 (1894): 121.

25. *Ibid.* 3 (1896): 544, 552. *Newspaper Maker*, 12 Nov. 1896, p. 5. Sue M'Namara, "Richest Newsboy in the Country," *American Magazine* 80 (Sept. 1915): 53–55.

26. *American News Trade Journal* 1 (Oct. 1919): 1, (Jan. 1920), 10, (March 1920), 8; *ibid.* 2 (June 1920): 5; *ibid.* 3 (March 1921): 5–6, (April 1921): 4 (quoted); *ibid.* 4 (Feb. 1922): 12; *ibid.* 14 (Jan. 1932): 10; *ibid.* 19 (Aug. 1937): 5.

27. Benjamin M. Compaine, *The Business of Consumer Magazines* (White Plains, 1982), pp. 24, 36.

28. S. J. Campbell, "Tips on Getting Effective Newsstand Display," *Circulation Management* 1 (1935): 13, 42. Mosely, "Pointers on Newsstand Sales," 15, 30. *Covering a Continent*, p. 31.

29. William J. Thorn with Mary Pat Pfeil, *Newspaper Circulation: Marketing the News* (New York, 1987), chap. 9, esp. p. 274. Deirdre Carmody, "Newsstands Dwindle, but Some Still Thrive," New York *Times*, 29 Oct. 1990, p. D8.

30. David C. Smith, "Wood Pulp and Newspapers, 1867–1900," *Business History Review* 38 (1964): 328–45. Reid, *American and English Studies*, II, 220–21.

31. James Creelman, "The Romance and Tragedy of Wood Engraving," *Pearson's Magazine* 17 (1907): 293. Neil Harris, "Iconography and Intellectual History: The

Half-Tone Effect," in John Higham and Paul K. Conkin, eds., *New Directions in American Intellectual History* (Baltimore, 1979). John Milton Cooper Jr., *Walter Hines Page: The Southerner as American, 1855–1918* (Chapel Hill, 1977), pp. 98–99.

32. *Journal*, 6 Nov. 1898, as cited in Roy Everett Littlefield III, *William Randolph Hearst: His Role in American Progressivism* (Lanham, Md., 1980), p. 29. William R. Scott, *Scientific Circulation Management for Newspapers* (New York, 1915) tried to persuade publishers that high circulation could be improvident (p. 62). Joseph Goulden, *The Curtis Caper* (New York, 1965), p. 32.

33. Joyce Milton, *The Yellow Kids: Foreign Correspondents in the Heyday of Yellow Journalism* (New York, 1989), pp. 32–44, 204, 294.

34. John, *The Best Years of the Century*, pp. 98–99. Daniel Pope, *The Making of Modern Advertising* (New York, 1983), p. 30. Alfred McClung Lee, *The Daily Newspaper in America: The Evolution of a Social Instrument* (New York, 1947), p. 171. John Bakeless, *Magazine Making* (New York, 1931), pp. 4–5. C. Edwin Baker, *Advertising and a Democratic Press* (Princeton, 1994) has a review of estimates of the share of revenues from advertising (p. 143 n. 2).

35. Knight, ed., *I Protest*, pp. 244. E. W. Scripps to L. T. Atwood, 17 Feb. 1903, E. W. Scripps to George Putnam, 28 April 1903, and E. W. Scripps to E. H. Wells, 28 Nov. 1903, in E. W. Scripps Papers, Series 1.2, Ohio University, Athens. Gerald J. Baldasty, "The Scripps Concern and Advertising: Strategies for Preserving Press Independence," paper delivered to Western Journalism Historians Conference, University of California, Berkeley, 28 Feb. 1992.

36. J. Lincoln Steffens, "The Business of a Newspaper," *Scribner's Magazine* 22 (1897): 447–67, quoted p. 465.

37. The seminal article was Wendell R. Smith, "Product Differentiation and Market Segmentation as Alternative Marketing Strategies," *Journal of Marketing* 21 (1956): 3–8. Richard S. Tedlow, *New and Improved: The Story of Mass Marketing in America* (New York, 1990).

38. Tedlow, *New and Improved*, p. 159.

39. *Advertising Experience*, June 1899, p. 6. James H. Bates and Lyman D. Morse, *Advertiser's Handy Guide for 1896* (New York, 1896), p. 636. I am grateful to Gerald Baldasty for these two references. *Newspaper Maker*, 21 May 1896, p. 4; *ibid.*, 28 May 1896, p. 4; *ibid.*, 4 June 1896, p. 4; *ibid.*, 15 Oct. 1896, p. 6. Reid, *American and English Studies*, II, 302, 306. Bakeless, *Magazine Making*, p. 247. Ronald E. Frank, William F. Massy, and Yoram Wind, *Market Segmentation* (Englewood Cliffs, 1972), p. 176.

40. Jean M. Converse, *Survey Research in the United States: Roots and Emergence, 1890–1960* (Berkeley, 1987), pp. 89–90, 445 n. 35. *Selling Forces* (Philadelphia, 1913), prepared by the advertising department at Curtis, insisted that the quality and quantity of the audience were compatible attractions of their magazines: see pp. 102, 212–21. *Life's Continuing Study of Magazine Audiences* (1938–), no. 1, p. 8. *Continuing Study of Newspaper Reading* (1939–). Silas Bent, *Ballyhoo: The Voice of the Press* (New York, 1927), pp. 203–4, is the testimony of an insider that dailies pursued quantity, not quality.

41. Alfred Politz Research, *The Readers of the Saturday Evening Post* (New York, 1957), pp. xxxix, 110, 139. Alfred Politz Research, *Characteristics of Readers and Non-Readers of the New York Mirror* (New York, 1951).

42. *A Free and Responsible Press* (Chicago, 1947), p. 52. Robert M. Hutchins Papers, University of Chicago, Commission on Freedom of the Press, Document #97, pp. 38–39, Box 10, Folder 1, and Document #120, p. 46, Box 10, Folder 5.

43. *Life's Continuing Study of Magazine Audiences*, no. 3, 1 Jan. 1940, p. 9. *Mike Looks*

Back: The Memoirs of Gardner Cowles, Founder of Look Magazine (New York, 1985), pp. 109–10 (Magazine Audience Group figures). Chris Welles, "Can Mass Magazines Survive?" *Columbia Journalism Review* 10 (July-Aug. 1971): 7. A. J. van Zuilen, *The Life Cycle of Magazines* (Uithoorn, Netherlands, 1977), p. 159. Hedley Donovan, *Right Places, Right Times* (New York, 1989), p. 274. Alfred Politz Research, *A Study of Four Media: Their Accumulative and Repeat Audiences* (New York, 1953), pp. 12, 116. James L. Baughman, *Henry R. Luce and the Rise of the American News Media* (Boston, 1987), p. 91.

44. Donovan, *Right Places, Right Times*, p. 265. Baughman, *Henry R. Luce*, p. 94. On the symbiosis between these magazines and Hollywood see *Mike Looks Back*, pp. 98–99, 153–55. Susan Strasser, *Satisfaction Guaranteed: The Making of the American Mass Market* (New York, 1989), chap. 1.

45. Gordon Grossman, "Direct-Mail Testing," reprints the mailings in S. Arthur Dembner and William E. Massee, eds., *Modern Circulation Methods* (New York, 1968), pp. 27–58, sec. 4-A quoted. Van Zuilen, *Life Cycle of Magazines*, pp. 88, 91, 101. Paul C. Smith, *Personal File* (New York, 1964), p. 439. Baughman, *Henry R. Luce*, p. 93; Welles, "Can Mass Magazines Survive?" p. 8. Otto Friedrich, *Decline and Fall* (New York, 1970), p. 65.

46. Friedrich, *Decline and Fall*, p. 22 and picture following p. 84. Smith, *Personal File*, p. 428.

47. Friedrich, *Decline and Fall*, pp. 390–93. Van Zuilen, *Life Cycle of Magazines*, p. 106.

48. Martin S. Ackerman, *The Curtis Affair* (Los Angeles, 1970), p. 15. New York *Times*, 22 April 1970, p. 75; 5 May 1970, p. 46; 13 May 1970, p. 84; 19 May 1970, p. 80. *Advertising Age* 42 (30 Aug. 1971): 159, (9 Aug. 1971): 45.

49. Friedrich, *Decline and Fall*, p. 371. *Advertising Age* 42 (9 Aug. 1971): 45.

50. Michael Schudson, *Advertising, the Uneasy Persuasion: Its Dubious Impact on American Society* (New York, 1984), p. 73.

51. Karyl Van in *Modern Circulation Methods*, p. 13. *Advertising Age* 42 (18 Jan. 1971): 6 (ad) and "American Magazine Conference," *ibid.* (26 Oct. 1992): 3. Welles, "Can Mass Magazines Survive?" p. 8. Van Zuilen, *Life Cycle of Magazines*, pp. 174–75. Subjective assignments of a value for "climate" also affected the formulae used in media buys at this time: see James F. Engel, Henry F. Fiorillo, and Murray A. Cayley, eds., *Market Segmentation: Concepts and Applications* (New York, 1972), p. 308.

52. "When Magazine Statistics Come Unstuck," *Business Week*, 27 Jan. 1975, p. 68. Van Zuilen, *Life Cycle of Magazines*, pp. 151, 164. Compaine, *Business of Consumer Magazines*, pp. 78–83, surveys the intellectual bankruptcy of the figures on readership. See also William H. Taft, *American Magazines for the 1980s* (New York, 1982), pp. 305–10. Publishers and advertising executives have gone further, calling the total readership figures "nonsense," "totally ludicrous," "a big farce" and "Sophisticated Wild Ass Guesses Not Easily Refuted." See Verne Gay, "Louis Schultz . . . ," *Mediaweek* 2 (7 Dec. 1992): S10; Scott Donaton, "MPA Hedges on Lintas Reader Study," *Advertising Age* 63 (16 Nov. 1992): 18; and James A. Autry, "Syndicated Research Is No Match for Rate Base," *Folio* 22 (1 May 1993): 60.

53. Richard Loyer, "Specialized Subscription Sales," in *Modern Circulation Methods*, pp. 74, 90.

54. Philip H. Dougherty, "McCall's Plans to Cut Rate Base to 5 Million," New York *Times*, 14 Oct. 1985, p. 9. Kevin Sghia, "Delivering More with Less . . . ," *Folio* 19 (April 1990): 29. See also Amy Alson, "Clip and Save: Trimming a Magazine's Rate

Base," *Marketing & Media Decisions* 23 (Feb. 1988): 25. Scott Donaton, "Quality Circulation is Goal for 1990," *Advertising Age* 62 (14 Oct. 1991): 40.

55. Albert Scardino, "Glimpsing a Day When No 2 Copies Will Be Alike," New York *Times*, 29 April 1989, p. C9.

56. Christine D. Urban, "10 Myths About Readers," *Bulletin of the American Society of Newspaper Editors* July–Aug. 1986, pp. 19–21. M. K. Guzda, "Lifestyle Segmentation," *Editor & Publisher* 117 (9 June 1984): 16–17, reported results after "whittling down the original methodology." Barbara E. Bryant, an officer of MOR and source for this article, had stressed that an interview must be at least forty-five minutes and that, even then, the results would be "a somewhat impressionistic kind of research." "Marketing Newspapers with Lifestyle Research," *American Demographics* 3 (Jan. 1981): 25.

57. Thorn with Pfeil, *Newspaper Circulation*, pp. 82–83.

58. William B. Blankenburg, "Newspaper Ownership and Control of Circulation to Increase Profits," *Journalism Quarterly* 59 (1982): 390–98. James D. Squires, *Read All About It! The Corporate Takeover of America's Newspapers* (New York, 1993), pp. 90–91. Conrad C. Fink, *Strategic Newspaper Management* (New York, 1988), p. 175. Ira Lacher, "The Register Regroups," *Columbia Journalism Review* 30 (May-June 1991): 16. William Glaberson, "The Los Angeles Times Steps Back from a 'Sky's the Limit' Approach," New York *Times*, 13 Dec. 1993, p. D6.

59. Ellis Cose, *The Press* (New York, 1989), p. 113. Thomas J. Holbein and Perry Williams, "Database Marketing: Newspaper Sales in a One-on-One Environment," pp. 18–19, International Newspaper Marketing Association, May 1991.

60. Deborah Walker and Jane Wilson, "The Battle for Waterloo," supplement to *Presstime* 13 (Sept. 1991). "A Reprise for Ned the Newsboy," *Presstime* 14 (July 1992): 37. Don E. Schultz, "Strategic Newspaper Marketing," International Newspaper Marketing Association (1993), p. 141. Burl Osborne's work for the Future of Advertising Readership Task Force, "Readers: How to Gain and Retain Them," in the late 1980s was a call for an inclusive circulation, but it went against the tide of this industry. See Fink, *Strategic Newspaper Management*, p. 130.

61. Marshall Fine, "Reducing Organizational Costs: How to Handle a Soft Economy," *Newspaper Financial Executive Journal* 43 (Jan. 1990): 5–7; Lee B. Templeton, "The Folly of Circulation Cutbacks," *News Inc.*, July-Aug. 1990, pp. 35–36. Otto A. Silha and Lee B. Templeton, "The Ugly Truth That Won't Go Away," *Newspaper Financial Executive Journal* 47 (March 1994): 13. See also George Garneau, "Cloudy Forecast for Newspapers Is Disputed," *Editor & Publisher* 126 (6 March 1993): 13.

62. James Truman remarks on the panel "Should Newspapers Be More Like Magazines?" at the Newspaper Association of America convention in San Francisco, 26 April 1994.

63. Glen L. Urban and Steven H. Star, *Advanced Marketing Strategy: Phenomena, Analysis, and Decisions* (Englewood Cliffs, 1991), 387–415, is a case study.

64. Among those who have passed the story on as fact: Richard Harwood, "Obsolete Theory of Newspapers," Washington *Post*, 5 Feb. 1993, p. A25; Martin Mayer, *Making News* (Garden City, N.Y., 1987), p. 204; Charles Kaiser and Nancy Stadtman, "The Daily News on the Brink," *Newsweek*, 25 Jan. 1982, p. 85. On Murdoch's principles and advertising see David Gelman with Betsy Carter and Lea Donosky, "How Murdoch Does It," *Newsweek*, 30 May 1977, p. 90. "Minutes from a Meeting at Mervyn's," *Presstime* 14 (Aug. 1992): 17, gives some corporate thinking within the Dayton-Hudson Corporation.

65. W. Russell Neuman, *The Future of the Mass Audience* (New York, 1991), pp. 117–18. Donald L. Shaw, "The Rise and Fall of American Mass Media: Roles of Technology and Leadership," *Roy W. Howard Public Lecture in Journalism*, no. 2, 4 April 1991.

Chapter 7

1. Carl F. Kaestle *et al.*, *Literacy in the United States: Readers and Reading Since 1880* (New Haven, 1991), pp. 164, 172, 188. In 1909, the year that the number of daily papers peaked, an industry survey found a 2.5 cents average single copy price; allowing for inflation, that is 36 cents in a 1990 dollar. The industry reported a 31 cents average single copy price in 1990. The predominant price (2 cents v. 25 cents) was also *higher*, in real terms, when newspapers were more popular. This is the best available data, but it should be noted that the early survey was of about a third of the dailies and the 1990 figure covered all dailies. See Alfred McClung Lee, *The Daily Newspaper in America: The Evolution of a Social Instrument* (New York, 1947), p. 272 and *Facts About Newspapers: A Statistical Summary of the Newspaper Business Published by the American Newspaper Publishers Association* (Washington, D.C., 1991), p. 22.

2. "Daily Circulation Falls Below 60 Million," *Presstime* 16 (June 1994): 25.

3. Leo Bogart, *Preserving the Press: How Daily Newspapers Mobilized to Keep Their Readers* (New York, 1991), p. 272.

4. John Bakeless, *Magazine Making* (New York, 1931), p. 235. Bogart, *Press and Public*, p. 63; Albert Scardino, "Magazines Raise Reliance on Circulation," New York *Times*, 8 May 1989, p. C9. Deirdre Carmody, "For Leading Magazines, a Newsstand Slump," New York *Times*, 6 Dec. 1993, p. C6. William J. Thorn with Mary Pat Pfeil, *Newspaper Circulation: Marketing the News* (New York, 1987), pp. 276–77.

5. Bogart, *Preserving the Press*, pp. 39, 70, 118, 272. Leo Bogart, *Press & Public: Who Reads What, When, Where, and Why in American Newspapers*, 2nd ed. (Hillsdale, N.J., 1989), pp. 6, 177.

6. Conrad C. Fink, *Strategic Newspaper Management* (New York, 1988), p. 182.

7. James N. Rosse, "The Evolution of One-Newspaper Cities," Stanford University, Department of Economics, Studies in Industry Economics, no. 95, prepared for the Federal Trade Commission, 14–15 Dec. 1978, p. 61. Profit comparisons are complicated by the range of sizes and lucrative side businesses of newspaper companies. But for consistent conclusions over several decades see Benjamin M. Compaine, *The Newspaper Industry in the 1980s: An Assessment of Economics and Technology* (White Plains, N.Y., 1980), pp. 13–15; Jonathan Kwitny, "The High Cost of High Profits," *Washington Journalism Review* 12 (June 1990): 19–29; Marty Tharp and Linda R. Stanley, "A Time Series Analysis of Newspaper Profitability by Circulation Size," *Journal of Media Economics* 5 (Spring 1992): 3–12; C. Edwin Baker, *Advertising and a Democratic Press* (Princeton, 1994), p. 20. Robert G. Picard *et al.*, eds. *Press Concentration and Monopoly: New Perspectives on Newspaper Ownership and Operation* (Norwood, N.J., 1988), p. 47.

8. Rebecca Ross Albers, "Investing in Content: Extra! Extra?" *Presstime* 16 (June 1994): 54–56. Morton Research, *Newspaper Newsletter*, 31 July 1994, p. 2. William B. Blankenburg and Robert L. Friend, "Effects of Cost and Revenue Strategies on Newspaper Circulation," *Journal of Media Economics* 7 (1994): 1–13. In the six large cities they survey, spending more money to gather news yielded more readers; in the short run, profits were hurt by quality. William Glaberson, "Departures at Paper Ignite Debate on Owners' Priorities," New York *Times*, 2 Feb. 1995, p. C1.

9. Edward Linsmier, "The '80s: Marketing/Promotion," *Presstime* 2 (Jan. 1980): 27. George Garneau, "Rethinking Newspapers," *Editor & Publisher* 121 (10 Dec. 1988): 16. Thorn with Pfeil, *Newspaper Circulation*, p. 124. "Schonfeld Tracks Ad Spending," *Advertising Age* 56 (15 July 1985): 39.

10. "Schonfeld Tracks Ad Spending," p. 39. Fink, *Strategic Newspaper Management* has no entry on contests in the index.

11. *Facts About Newspapers: A Statistical Summary of the Newspaper Business Published by the Newspaper Association of America* (Reston, Va., 1994). This is an annual supplement to the June issue of *Presstime*. The word "monopoly" is not used in this business survey. For a technical discussion of why the word fits the facts about newspapers see Picard *et al.*, eds., *Press Concentration*, pp. 14-17.

12. Leo Bogart, "Second Thoughts: The Prospects and a 'Modest Proposal' for Two-Paper Markets," *Presstime* 14 (Dec. 1992): 36.

13. Paul Frichtl, "Circulation Direct Marketing: New Twists on Proven Techniques," *Folio* 19 (Jan. 1990): 99. Stan Rapp and Thomas L. Collins, "The New Marketing: Sell and Socialize," New York *Times*, 20 Feb. 1994, sec. 3, p. 11.

14. Lynn Simross, "Consumers: No Sure Bet in Mail Sweepstakes," Los Angeles *Times*, 18 July 1990, p. E1. Linda Saslow, "It's Sweepstakes Time, and It's a Frenzy," New York *Times*, 20 Jan. 1991, p. 1. Randall Rothenberg, "Read This and Win $10 Million!!" New York *Times*, 31 Jan. 1989, p. C1. *Reader's Digest* has awarded almost fifty-seven million dollars to more than 1.7 million Americans. American Family Publishers gave out about thirty million dollars in prizes in the 1980s. The Publishers Clearing House has distributed more than forty million dollars in prizes to more than two million people. *Reader's Digest* and Publishers Clearing House, alone, had put checks in the hands of nearly four million subscribers by the beginning of the 1990s. MPA marketing surveys reported in Paula Span, "Sweep Dreams, America! Think You've Got a Shot at a Zillion Bucks?" Washington *Post*, 28 Jan. 1993, p. C1. Agencies are thought to account for 35 percent of new subscriptions: Debby Patz, "Citibank Expands Sub Program," *Folio* 23 (15 May 1994): 28.

15. James R. Rosenfield, "Sweeps Seen as an Artifact of Our Culture," *DM News*, 29 Jan. 1990, p. 18. John D. Klingel, "Open Me: The Art of the Envelope," *Folio* 12 (March 1983): 127. Rothenberg, "Read This and Win $10 Million!!" p. C1. Magazines have also created new forms of community with their "involvement devices." Three of the most successful publications of the late twentieth century, *National Geographic*, *Natural History*, and *Smithsonian*, have offered membership cards in scientific societies.

16. Thorn with Pfeil, *Newspaper Circulation*, p. 139. Fink, *Strategic Newspaper Management*, p. 267.

17. John Klingel, "Original Ways to Find New Subscribers," *Folio* 18 (Feb. 1989): 105. Stewart McBride, "Low-Slung, High-Sprung," *Christian Science Monitor*, 31 July 1980, p. B4. Vicki Torres, "Lowrider Car Show May Not Return," Los Angeles *Times*, 19 May 1992, p. B3. This may be another instance of the limited value of editing a paper on the basis of what readers say. "All our research and focus groups show that Hispanics want to read in their native language," according to the managing editor of the Miami *Herald's* Spanish-language supplement: Dan Fost, "Newspapers Enter the Age of Information," *American Demographics* 12 (Sept. 1990): 14.

18. Mark Sullivan, *The Education of an American* (New York, 1938), pp. 188-91. Hazel Dicken-Garcia, *Journalistic Standards in Nineteenth-Century America* (Madison, Wisc., 1989), pp. 188, 215-16. Gerald J. Baldasty, *The Commercialization of News in the Nineteenth Century* (Madison, Wisc., 1992), chap. 3.

19. Lawrence C. Soley and Robert L. Craig, "Advertising Pressures on Newspapers: A Survey," *Journal of Advertising* 21 (Dec 1992): 1. Doug Underwood, *When MBAs Rule the Newsroom: How Marketers and Managers Are Reshaping Today's Media* (New York, 1993), chap. 10. Ben H. Bagdikian, *The Media Monopoly*, 3rd ed. (Boston, 1990), pp. 37–45, 163–64. Baker, *Advertising and a Democratic Press*, chap. 2.

20. Martin Mayer, *Whatever Happened to Madison Avenue?: Advertising in the 90's* (Boston, 1991) finds professionals in the same mood as James D. Squires, *Read All About It!: The Corporate Takeover of America's Newspapers* (New York, 1993). Media criticism is associated with anti-commercialism, but it is also practiced by junk mailers: Ray Schultz, "Freedom to Pander," *DM News*, 3 Feb. 1992, p. 50.

21. John J. Curley, chief operations officer for Gannett Newspapers, in *Associated Press Managing Editors Conference: The Newspaper World After 2001*, 24 Oct. 1986, p. 19. "Clutter Complaints Rise," *Public Pulse* 7 (Sept. 1992): 4.

22. Gloria Steinem, "Sex, Lies, & Advertising," *Ms.*, July-Aug. 1990, pp. 18–28. Daniel J. Boorstin, *The Americans: The Democratic Experience* (New York, 1973), part 2.

23. Squires, *Read All About It!* pp. 72–73. John Brady, "The Erosion of Editorial Integrity," *Folio* 22 (1 Aug. 1993): 35. Tony Silber, "Time Inc.'s Church-and-State Metamorphosis," *Folio* 20 (1 Dec. 1991): 38. Eric Utne, "Tina's New Yorker," *Columbia Journalism Review* 31 (March–April 1993): 35. Ronald K. L. Collins, *Dictating Content: How Advertising Pressure Can Corrupt a Free Press* (Washington, D.C., 1992) is marvelously, but at times wrongheadedly, comprehensive: see, for example, p. 45.

24. David L. Protess and Maxwell McCombs, *Agenda Setting: Readings on Media, Public Opinion, and Policymaking* (Hillsdale, N.J., 1991).

25. Sophia Vitakis, "Teaming Up on the New AutoZone Section," *Customer Connection*, San Francisco Newspaper Agency Quarterly Newsletter, Sept. 1992. Analytical pieces on new car sales are an endangered species of newspaper reporting, in the San Francisco Bay area and beyond. See Trudy Liberman, "What Ever Happened to Consumer Reporting?" *Columbia Journalism Review* 33 (Sept. 1994): 34. Patricia A. Stout *et al.*, "Trends in Magazine Advertorial Use," *Journalism Quarterly* 66 (1989): 960–64. The American Society of Magazine Editors drew up new guidelines in the eighties and nineties to insist that promotional stories be better identified. Randall Rothenberg, "Messages from Sponsors Become Harder to Detect," New York *Times*, 19 Nov. 1989, sec. 4, p. 5. Jonathan Alter, "The Era of the Big Blur," *Newsweek*, 22 May 1989, p. 73.

26. Nan Robertson, *The Girls in the Balcony: Women, Men, and the New York Times* (New York, 1992), pp. 81–84. Steinem, "Sex, Lies, & Advertising," p. 24. Report from the Travel Task Force, National Council Meeting, distributed at the National Newspaper Association, San Francisco Convention, 17 July 1994, contains the correspondence on advertorial campaigns. *Advertising Shared Ideas* (a quarterly report from Scripps Howard Newspapers), July 1994, p. 3.

27. Howard Kurtz, *Media Circus: The Trouble with America's Newspapers* (New York, 1993), p. 341. Many papers have learned that doing serious reporting is an excellent way to gather readers: Gene Goltz, "Reviving a Romance with Readers Is the Biggest Challenge of Many Newspapers," *Presstime* 10 (Feb. 1988): 19–20; Edward Wasserman, "Cotton-Candy News Leads to Society Decay," *Connecticut Law Tribune*, 7 Oct. 1991, p. 21.

28. Wayne Markham, assistant managing editor of the *Herald*, cited in Elizabeth Lesly, "Realtors and Builders Demand Happy News—And Often Get It," *Washington Journalism Review* 13 (Nov. 1991): 23.

29. James H. Hollis, "New NAB Study . . . ," *Presstime* 13 (May 1991): 60. Dave

Jensen, "Journal/Sentinel Hatches New Papers to Boost Revenue, Widen Reader Base," *Business Journal–Milwaukee* 9 (18 Nov. 1991), sec. 2, p. 10.

30. "Print's New Priorities: the Experts' Views," *Marketing & Media Decisions* 20 (Sept. 1985): 44. Janet Meyers, "Retailers Press Papers for Targeted Buys," *Advertising Age* 61 (15 Jan. 1990): 6.

31. *Technology and the Future: A Guide for Editors, Future of Newspapers Report* (April 1989), p. 31. Available through ASNE Foundation, Washington, D. C.

32. Ads from April and May issues of *Folio*, 1993 and 1994. Jean Marie Angelo, "Finding Alternatives to Direct Mail . . . ," *Folio* 22 (15 Aug. 1993): 40, is its first annual survey of magazine marketing trends, reporting a range of nine to twelve cents per name and 3.9 percent of circulation revenues. Stone's biographer, D. D. Guttenplan, has seen the books of the *Weekly* and kindly shared this information in a letter to me of 3 Feb. 1994.

33. Lambeth Hochwald, "Tobacco Ads Still Smoking," *Folio* 22 (1 Jan. 1993): 17.

34. Larry Tye, "List-Makers Draw a Bead on Many," Boston *Globe*, 6 Sept. 1993, p. 1.

35. Karen Berman, "Database Marketing: A New Secret Weapon," *Folio* 22 (1 March 1993): 50. Anitra Brown, "Publishers Beef Up Database Efforts," *Folio* 22 (1 June 1993), 81. Scott Donaton, "Publishers Find Gold in Databases," *Advertising Age* 64 (7 June 1993): 27. Deborah L. Jacobs, "They've Got Your Name. You've Got Their Junk," New York *Times*, 13 March 1994, sec. 3, p. 5.

36. This strategy is proposed in broad terms in Paul Haker, "Newspapers & Database Marketing: Unleashing the Power" (1993), published by CompuServe Collier-Jackson, a supplier of marketing software, and Jim Rosenberg, "Target Marketing with Insight," *Editor & Publisher* 126 (19 June 1993): 34. Thomas J. Holbein and Perry Williams, "Database Marketing: Newspaper Sales in a One-on-One Environment," International Newspaper Marketing Association, May 1991, p. 18. Kim Ann Zimmermann, "Banks Zoom In on Customers," *United States Banker*, April 1991, p. 31. Tye, "List-Makers Draw a Bead on Many," p. 1.

37. Alex S. Jones, "Times Settles Legal Dispute with Independent Dealers," New York *Times*, 31 Oct. 1989, p. C19; Jack Kramer, "Special Report . . . Mailbox Bonanza," *Presstime* 13 (May 1991): 32. Kurt Foss, "Bits of Gold," *Presstime* 15 (July 1993): p. 72. Michael Conniff, "The Great American Database," *Editor & Publisher* 126 (18 Dec. 1993): 40.

38. Christy Fisher, "Databases Fill the Need in Targeted Counterattack," *Advertising Age* 64 (26 April 1993): S12. Shaun Higgins, "Newspapers of the '90s," *Direct Marketing Magazine* 54 (July 1991): 22. M. L. Stein, "Establishing a Database Marketing System," *Editor & Publisher* 126 (22 May 1993): 26. Higgins quoted in *ASTech from Vision to Realization: Services and Resources* (published by Applied Segmentation Technology, n.d.), p. 6.

39. Ann Marie Kerwin, "Making Database Marketing Work for Newspapers," *Editor & Publisher* 126 (10 July 1993): 19. Tony Case, "Fax, CD-Rom, On-Line Services and Newspapers," *ibid.* 127 (16 July 1994): 51. Bob Inhofe, "All This Sophistication in Cedar Rapids, Iowa?" reprint from *Optimum Delivery*® distributed by Decisionmark, the parent company of MediaStar, 1994.

40. I am grateful to Brian T. Dalziel for sales literature on this software and a demonstation at the Newspaper Association of America Marketing Conference, San Francisco, 19 July 1994.

41. Shaun O'L. Higgins, "Database Marketing Applications for Newspapers," International Newspaper Marketing Association (March 1993), p. 13.

42. Lou Levin-Cutler, "The Data Field of Dreams," *Ideas*, Jul.–Aug. 1993, p. 25. Michael Conniff, "Where Are We Going?" and John Puerner, "Tribune Invests in Database Marketing," *Editor & Publisher* 126 (6 March 1993): 10TC and 18TC. Underwood, *When MBAs Rule the Newsroom*, p. 110. Maryalice Hurst, "How Does Your Firm Handle Opt-Out?" *Cowles Report on Database Marketing* 3 (July 1994): 10. *Folio* 24 (15 Apr. 1995):9. Erik Larson, *The Naked Consumer: How Our Private Lives Become Public Commodities* (New York, 1992), pp. 12, 14. Holbein and Williams, "Database Marketing," p. 26. Shaun O'L. Higgins has expressed his concerns about privacy publicly (in "Database Marketing Applications for Newspapers," p. 10) and in a letter to this author of 8 Sept. 1993. To date, no press association has drawn up its own rules on this matter. "New Book Is 'How-To-Guide' for Database Marketing," *Business Wire*, 28 June 1994. Peter Winter quoted in Dorothy Giobbe, "Framework for the Cox Interactive Plan," *Editor & Publisher* 127 (11 June 1994): 34.

43. For a typical invocation of the railroads, see Bill Winter, "Another View on the 'New Journalism,'" *Editor & Publisher* 125 (4 April 1992): 7. Tom Ratkovich, "Sustainable Competitive Advantage," *ASTech On Line* 7 (Spring 1994): 1–2.

44. Glen L. Urban and Steven H. Star, *Advanced Marketing Strategy: Phenomena, Analysis, and Decisions* (Englewood Cliffs, 1991), p. 119.

45. Lorne Manly, "The Daily Dilemma," *Mediaweek*, 23 Sept. 1991, p. 24.

46. Bagdikian, *Media Monopoly*, pp. 128–29. Gilbert Cranberg and Vincent Rodriguez, "The Myth of the Minority Reader," *Columbia Journalism Review* 32 (Jan.-Feb. 1994): 42–43. Chrisine D. Urban, "10 Myths About Readers," *Bulletin of the American Society of Newspaper Editors*, July–Aug. 1986, p. 19. Maxwell McCombs, "Attitudes That Really Count for Newspaper Readership," pp. 5–6, International Newspaper Marketing Association (1985). Bill Kovach, "About the News: Of Literacy and Legs," *Newsday*, 14 March 1991, p. 70.

47. Jean Gaddy Wilson and Iris Igawa, "Readership," *Presstime* 13 (June 1991): 72. The immigrant figure lumps legals and illegals on the basis of Census Bureau and Immigration and Nationalization Service figures: see Ben J. Wattenberg, *The First Universal Nation: Leading Indicators and Ideas About the Surge of America in the 1990s* (New York, 1991), pp. 74, 392.

Chapter 8

1. *Autobiography of William Allen White*, ed. Sally Foreman Griffith (Lawrence, Kan., 1990), p. 143.

2. Samuel Haber, *The Quest for Authority and Honor in the American Professions, 1750–1900* (Chicago, 1991).

3. Douglas Birkhead, "The Power in the Image: Professionalism and the 'Communications Revolution,'" *American Journalism* 1 (Winter 1984): 1–14. The earliest attempt to equate journalists in America with a profession seems to be J. P. Brissot de Warville, *New Travels in the United States of America, 1788*, ed. Durand Echeverria (Cambridge, Mass., 1964), pp. 185–86.

4. Walter A. Steigleman, "Newspaper Confidence Laws—Their Extent and Provisions," *Journalism Quarterly* 20 (1943): 233. See also David Gordon, "The 1896 Mary-

land Shield Law: The American Roots of Evidentiary Privilege for Newsmen," *Journalism Monographs*, no. 22 (1972).

5. *The Gilded Age Letters of E. L. Godkin*, ed. William M. Armstrong (Albany, 1974), p. 371.

6. Hartley Davis, "Reporters of To-Day," *Everybody's Magazine* 14 (1906): 64. *Autobiography of William Allen White*, ed. Griffith, p. 329.

7. Stephen Vaughn, *Holding Fast the Inner Lines: Democracy, Nationalism, and the Committee on Public Information* (Chapel Hill, 1980).

8. John Hohenberg, *The Pulitzer Prizes* (New York, 1974), p. 11. Joseph Pulitzer, "The College of Journalism," *North American Review* 178 (1904): 657. Edwin L. Shuman, *Practical Journalism: A Complete Manual of the Best Newspaper Methods* (New York, 1903), p. 31. William M. Glenn, *The Sigma Delta Chi Story* (Coral Gables, Fla., 1949) pp. 34, 53, 55, 61, 76.

9. Nelson A. Crawford, *The Ethics of Journalism* (New York, 1924), pp. 25, 239. See also Casper S. Yost, *The Principles of Journalism* (New York, 1924).

10. Ray Stannard Baker, *American Chronicle: The Autobiography of Ray Stannard Baker* (New York, 1945) p. 113.

11. Julia Wilcox, "Journalism as a Profession," *Galaxy* 4 (1867): 798, 799. See also Ted C. Smythe, "The Reporter, 1880–1900: Their Working Conditions and the Influence on the News," *Journalism History* 7 (1980): 1–10. Daniel J. Leab, *A Union of Individuals: The Formation of the American Newspaper Guild, 1933–1936* (New York, 1970), pp. 4–5.

12. Leab, *A Union of Individuals*, p. 12. William H. Freeman, *The Press Club of Chicago: A History* (Chicago, 1894), pp. 14, 37, 143.

13. Theodore Dreiser, *A Book About Myself* (London, 1929), pp. 469–70.

14. Walter Lippmann, *Public Opinion* (New York, 1946) [1922], p. 272.

15. *Proceedings*, Eleventh Annual Convention, American Society of Newspaper Editors (Washington, D.C., 1933), p. 14. The annual volumes were bound under the title *Problems of Journalism*.

16. Steigleman, "Newspaper Confidence Laws," p. 234.

17. Leab, *A Union of Individuals*, pp. 54, 63 85, 125; *Proceedings*, ASNE (1934), pp. 84, 95.

18. Leab, *A Union of Individuals*, pp. 39–40, 282. A 1976 ruling of the National Labor Relations Board denied reporters the status of professionals. The label continues to bedevil the field; see, for example, "Suit Studies the Wages of Journalism," New York *Times*, 20 July 1986, sec. 1, p. H12.

19. Leo C. Rosten, *The Washington Correspondents* (New York, 1937), pp. 159, 163. Michael Kirkhorn, "This Curious Existence, Journalistic Identity in the Interwar Period," in Catherine L. Covert and John D. Stevens, eds., *Mass Media Between the Wars: Perceptions of Cultural Tension, 1918–1941* (Syracuse, 1984), pp. 127–39. Michael Schudson, *Discovering the News: A Social History of the American Newspaper* (New York, 1978), pp. 121–59.

20. A. M. Sperber, *Murrow: His Life and Times* (New York, 1986) and Ronald Steel, *Walter Lippmann and the American Century* (New York, 1981) give exhaustive accounts of these reputations.

21. Hamilton Holt, *Commercialism and Journalism* (Cambridge, Mass., 1909), pp. 36–37. Silent films fastened onto the newsroom. By 1922 a book about journalism needed to correct the "bunkum" about the craft spread through the silver screen: see

advertising copy pasted in Henry Justin Smith, *Deadlines* (Chicago, 1922) in the library of the Graduate School of Journalism, University of California, Berkeley.

22. Alex Barris, *Stop the Presses! The Newspaperman in American Films* (South Brunswick, N.J., 1976). Robert C. Toll, *The Entertainment Machine: American Show Business in the Twentieth Century* (New York, 1982), pp. 38, 40. Debra Gersh, "Stereotyping Journalists," *Editor & Publisher* 124 (5 Oct. 1991): 18.

23. Films about the theater were, of course, even more inbred. Joseph McBride, *Frank Capra: The Catastrophe of Success* (New York, 1992), pp. 221–23, 305, 681. Roy Peter Clark, "Mystery in Blue," St. Petersburg *Times*, 28 Jan. 1989, p. 4E, is the most extensive examination of Connolly in print.

24. Ben Hecht and Charles MacArthur, *The Front Page* (New York, 1928), pp. 133, 143. Marten Pew, "Shop Talk at Thirty," *Editor & Publisher* 61 (29 Sept. 1928): 36.

25. The screenplays were chunks of amber, preserving the names of reporters and their coups and pranks of a quarter century before. This is easily misunderstood as Americana. These films could not have been made without prompts from Europe. Hecht, MacArthur, and Herman Mankiewicz had been correspondents in central Europe after World War I. The nihilism of their plots, the noise and confusion, owed something to Dada in Vienna and Berlin, not simply to the dailies in Chicago and New York.

26. Ben Hecht, *A Child of the Century* (New York, 1954), p. 191. This was understatement compared to what the ex-journalist said on his television program: "We were outside the routines of greed and social pretense. . . . There wasn't one of us who in the first ten years of penal servitude under the city desk, wouldn't have refused an authentic pass to heaven." "Ben Hecht Show," 23 Sept. 1958, transcript in the Mike Wallace Papers, Box 8, Bentley Historical Library, University of Michigan, Ann Arbor.

27. Final script of *Meet John Doe*, screenplay by Robert Riskin, in the Fay Wray Collection, Archives of Performing Arts, University of Southern California. Tracy's measured defense of readers was echoed by William Holden in *The Turning Point* (1952).

28. Hecht and MacArthur, *The Front Page*, p. 40. I have quoted from the play text because each of the film versions in this period changed it slightly.

29. Erik Weitzenkorn, *Five Star Final*. This was remade as *Two Against the World* (1936), switching the medium to radio.

30. Maurice Zolotow, *Billy Wilder in Hollywood* (New York, 1977), pp. 26–29, 175. Newspaper films made without the assistance of people who knew journalism firsthand often are more respectful of the public and hopeful that the press can engage its audience on a more serious level. For instance, Fay and Michael Kanin's script for *Teacher's Pet* (1958) has dialogue on the fate of dailies in the 1950s that is particularly thoughtful.

31. Arthur Frederick, "From Reporter to Screenwriting Success," *United Press International*, 26 Jan. 1986 (interview with David Himmelstein). Kurt Luedtke, "An Ex-Newsman Hands Down His Indictment of the Press," *Bulletin of the American Society of Newspaper Editors*, May–June, 1982, p. 17. Kurt Luedtke, "What Good Is Free Speech If No One Listens?" Los Angeles *Times*, 7 Jan. 1987, sec. 2, p. 5.

32. Charles Champlin, "Critic at Large: A Veteran of Tough Times and Tough Films," Los Angeles *Times*, 23 Oct. 1990, p. F1. Movie-goers in New York would have thought of the demise of the *World*, Joseph Pulitzer's exemplary paper that succumbed to many of the forces that Bogart fought.

33. This is the ending of the final version for national release. The film's first audi-

ences did not see the reading public being brought back from depravity to virtue. One of the reasons Capra changed the ending was because early viewers wrote him letters, complaining that he had been too tough on the public. See McBride, *Frank Capra*, p. 436.

34. Terry Kelleher, "Sunburned Ethics," *Newsday*, 8 May 1988, p. 97. In the small Florida town of *A Flash of Green* (1985) every story prompted a psychological breakdown, a bribe, or a beating. Rarely has reading been more perilous.

35. Herbert J. Gans, *Deciding What's News: A Study of CBS Evening News, NBC Evening News, Newsweek, and Time* (New York, 1979), pp. 230–36. Robert Darnton, *The Kiss of Lamourette: Reflections in Cultural History* (New York, 1990), pp. 61–62, 73.

36. Kalman Seigel, *Talking Back to the New York Times: Letters to the Editor, 1851–1971* (New York, 1972), pp. 5–7. Gans, *Deciding What's News*, pp. 228, 354 n. 42. *Time* 126 (28 Nov. 1990): 22. Robin Derosa, "War Brings Increase in Letters to Editors," Gannett News Service, 4 Feb. 1991. *Call Northside 777* (1947) is the exception to the rule of dismissing reader response to a news story.

37. Walter Dean Burnham, *Critical Elections and the Mainsprings of American Politics* (New York, 1970), p. 73. Richard Jensen, *The Winning of the Midwest: Social and Political Conflict, 1888–1896* (Chicago and London, 1971), p. 13. John Hartley, *The Politics of Pictures: The Creation of the Public in the Age of Popular Media* (London and New York, 1992), p. 36 and chap. 5.

38. Paul F. Lazarsfeld, "Public Opinion and the Classical Tradition," *Public Opinion Quarterly* 21 (1957): 33–53.

39. Kevin G. Barnhurst, *Seeing the Newspaper* (New York, 1994), pp. 106–7. Warren I. Susman, *Culture as History: The Transformation of American Society in the Twentieth Century* (New York, 1984), pp. 263–68.

40. James S. Fishkin, *Democracy and Deliberation: New Directions for Democratic Reform* (New Haven, 1991), esp. pp. 1, 19, 23, 81–104. W. Russell Neuman, *The Paradox of Mass Politics* (Cambridge, Mass., 1986), p. 23. Anne Norton, *Republic of Signs: Liberal Theory and American Popular Culture* (Chicago, 1993), p. 39. On the heritage of conservative skepticism see Stow Persons, *American Minds: A History of Ideas* (Huntington, N.Y., 1975), chap. 21, esp. pp. 388, 401, and A. Lawrence Lowell, *Public Opinion and Popular Government* (New York, 1913).

41. Arthur Bentley quoted in the editor's essay in Mark P. Petracca, ed., *The Politics of Interests: Interest Groups Transformed* (Boulder, Colo., 1992), pp. 4, 7. Jeffrey M. Berry, *The Interest Group Society*, 2nd ed. (Glenview, Ill., 1989), chap. 5, p. 114 on letters.

42. James W. Carey, "The Press and the Public Discourse," *Kettering Review*, Winter 1992, p. 11.

43. Clifford G. Christians, John P. Ferré, and P. Mark Fackler, *Good News: Social Ethics and the Press* (New York, 1993), p. 91. This critique gives due attention to irresponsible practices but is noteworthy in finding a large foundation for the communitarian journalism the authors propose.

44. William Greider, *Who Will Tell the People: The Betrayal of American Democracy* (New York, 1992), p. 303.

45. Philip Meyer, *The Newspaper Survival Book: An Editor's Guide to Marketing Research* (Bloomington, 1985), p. 153.

46. "A Word of Welcome," Seattle *Times*, 17 April 1994, p. D6. "Cox and Prodigy Unveil Access Atlanta," Business Wire Inc., 10 March 1994.

47. The Batten speech has been published by the White Foundation and is also

excerpted in Jay Rosen, "Community Connectedness Passwords for Public Journalism," *Poynter Papers*, no. 3 (1993). Maxwell McCombs, "Newspapers and the Civic Culture," *Newspaper Research Journal* 4 (Summer 1983): 5–9. All of this issue explores this theme. Keith R. Stamm and Lisa Fortini-Cambell, "The Relationship of Community Ties to Newspaper Use," *Journalism Monographs*, Aug. 1983.

48. Michael Hoyt, "The Wichita Experiment," *Columbia Journalism Review* 31 (July-Aug. 1992): 43–47. Brite Voice Systems Inc. is headquartered in Wichita.

49. Jay Rosen, "Forming and Informing the Public," *Kettering Review*, Winter 1992, pp. 60–70. Edward D. Miller, "The Charlotte Project Helping Citizens Take Back Democracy," *Poynter Papers*, no. 4 (1994). For a skeptical view of this approach to election coverage see Susan Rasky, "Voice of the Voter," *California Journal* 25 (May 1994): 19.

INDEX

Figures in italics refer to illustrations.